CW01475540

RING OF FIRE

RING
OF
FIRE

A NEW HISTORY OF THE
WORLD AT WAR: 1914

ALEXANDRA CHURCHILL
AND NICOLAI EBERHOLST

PEGASUS BOOKS

NEW YORK LONDON

RING OF FIRE

Pegasus Books, Ltd.
148 West 37th Street, 13th Floor
New York, NY 10018

ISBN: 978-1-63936-927-0

10 9 8 7 6 5 4 3 2 1

Printed in the United States of America
Distributed by Simon & Schuster
www.pegasusbooks.com

For our friend Rob Thompson.
We miss you.

Do not ignore the human element! The little flags which you pin into large-scale maps, the little wooden blocks which you manoeuvre as you would chessmen, these are in reality men like you.

Arthur Corbett-Smith

Contents

Global map, 1914

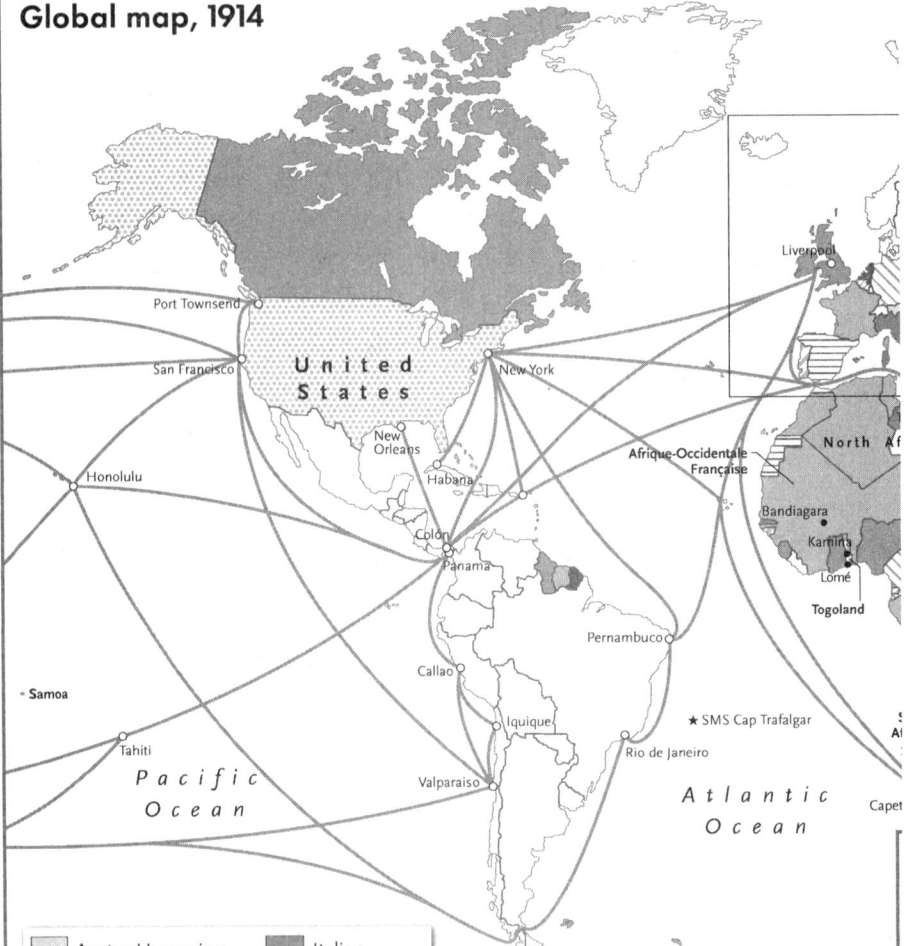

Port Townsend
San Francisco
United States
New Orleans
New York
Honolulu
Habana
Colón
Panama
Samoa
Callao
Tahiti
Iquique
Valparaiso
Rio de Janeiro
Pernambuco
Pacific Ocean
Atlantic Ocean

Liverpool
Afrique-Occidentale Française
North Af
Bandiagara
Kamina
Lomé
Togoland
★ SMS Cap Trafalgar
Capet

Legend:

- Austro-Hungarian
- Belgian
- British
- Dutch
- French
- German
- Italian
- Ottoman
- Portuguese
- Russian
- Spanish
- United States
- — Major steamship trade routes
- ★ Naval clashes

White areas are not part of any empire

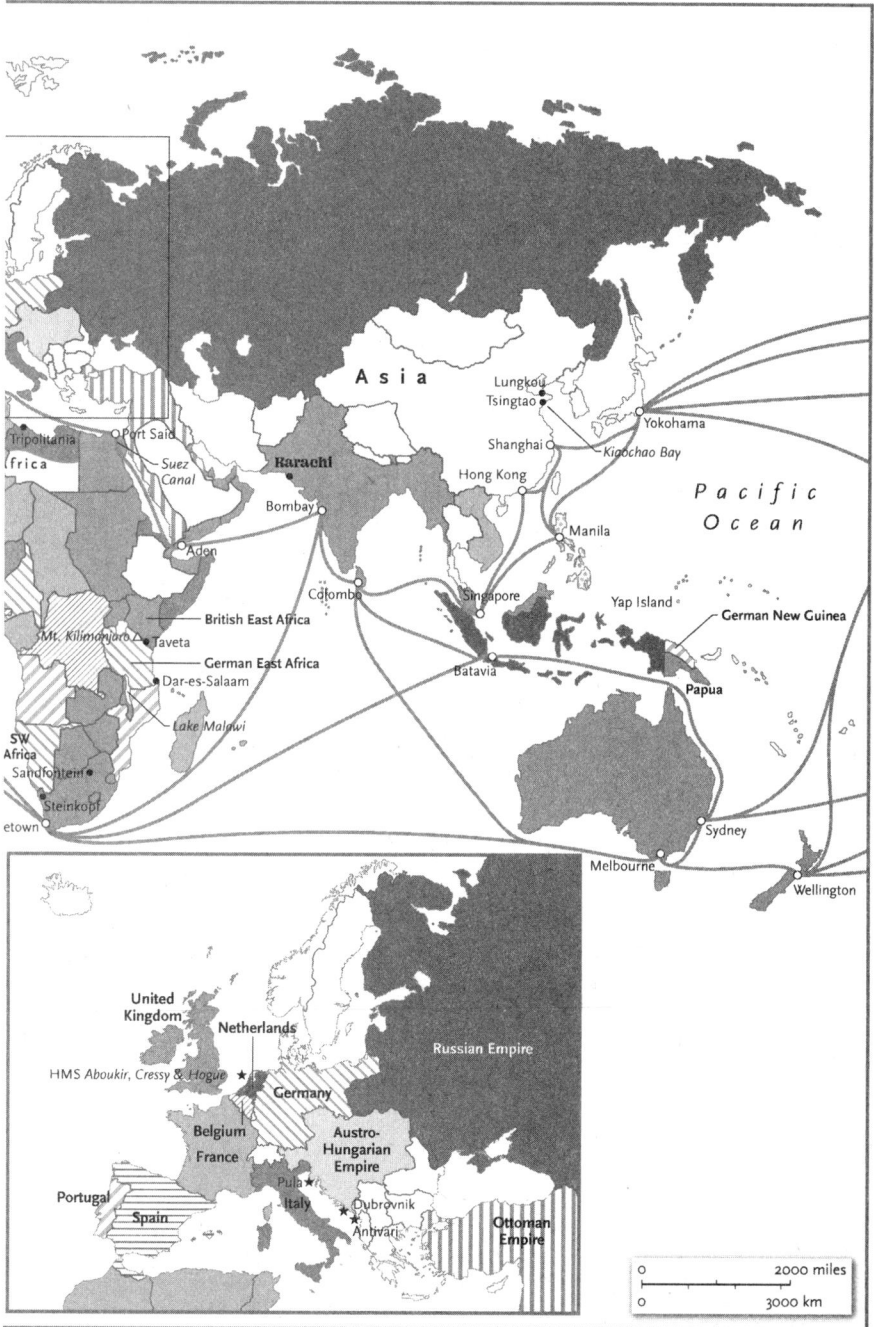

Asia

Lungkou
Tsingtao
Yokohama
Shanghai
Kiaochao Bay
Hong Kong
Manila

Pacific
Ocean

Tripolitania
O Port Said
Suez Canal
frica
Karachi
Bombay
Aden
Colombo
Singapore
Yap Island
German New Guinea
British East Africa
Mt. Kilimanjaro
Taveta
German East Africa
Dar-es-Salaam
Lake Malawi
Batavia
Papua

SW Africa
Sandfontein
Steinkopf
etown

Sydney
Melbourne
Wellington

United Kingdom
Netherlands
HMS Aboukir, Cressy & Hogue ★
Germany
Russian Empire
Belgium
France
Austro-Hungarian Empire
Portugal
Spain
Pula ★
Italy
Dubrovnik ★
Antivari ★
Ottoman Empire

0		2000 miles
0		3000 km

Opening phase
of the Schlieffen Plan

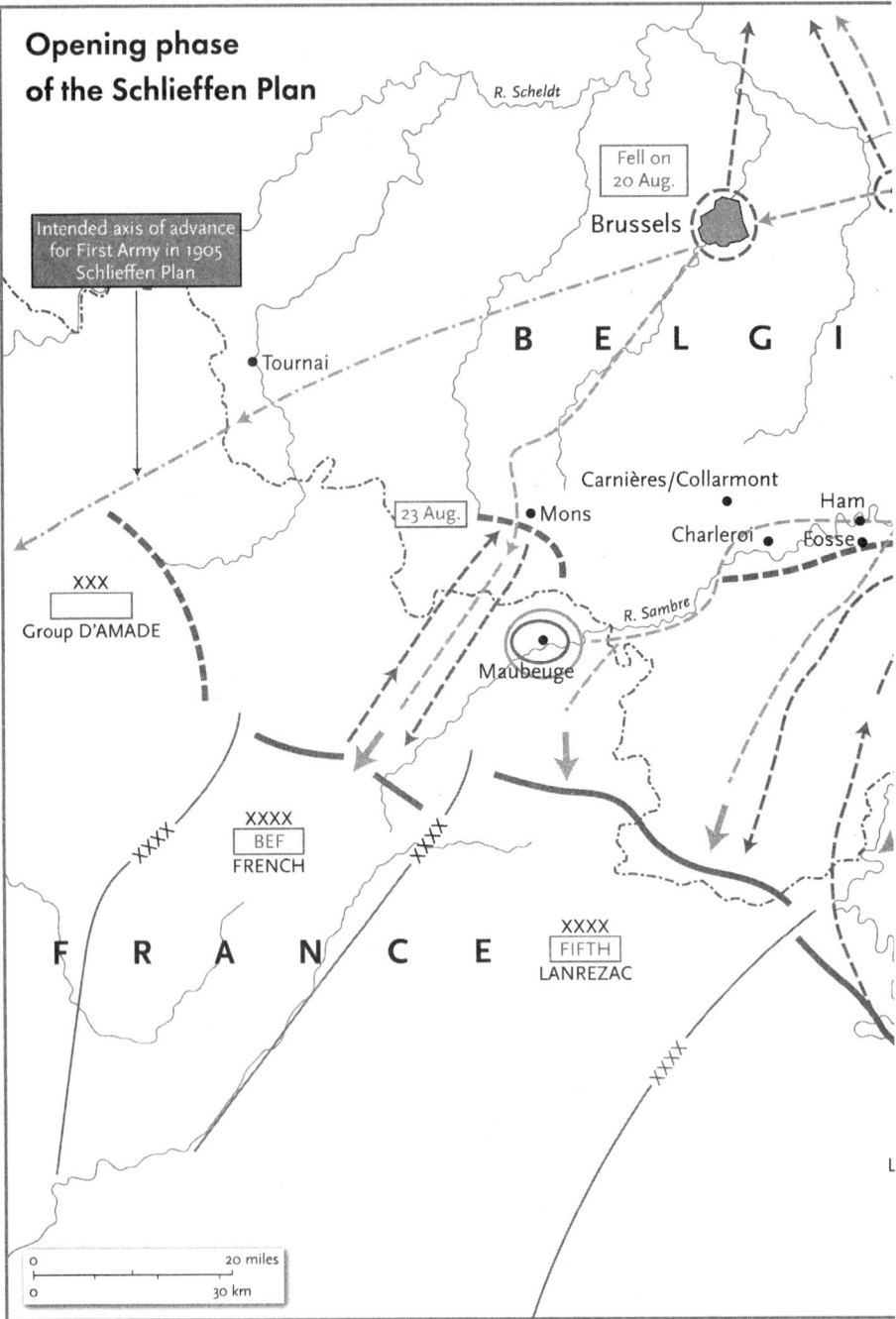

R. Scheldt

Fell on
20 Aug.

Brussels

Intended axis of advance
for First Army in 1905
Schlieffen Plan

B E L G I

● Tournai

Carnières/Collarmont
●

Ham

23 Aug.

● Mons

Charleroi
●

Fosse
●

```
  XXX
┌─────────┐
│         │
└─────────┘
```
Group D'AMADE

R. Sambre

Maubeuge

```
  XXXX
┌─────────┐
│  BEF    │
└─────────┘
FRENCH
```

XXXX

XXXX

F R A N C E

```
  XXXX
┌─────────┐
│  FIFTH  │
└─────────┘
LANREZAC
```

XXXX

0   20 miles
├─────────────────┤
0   30 km

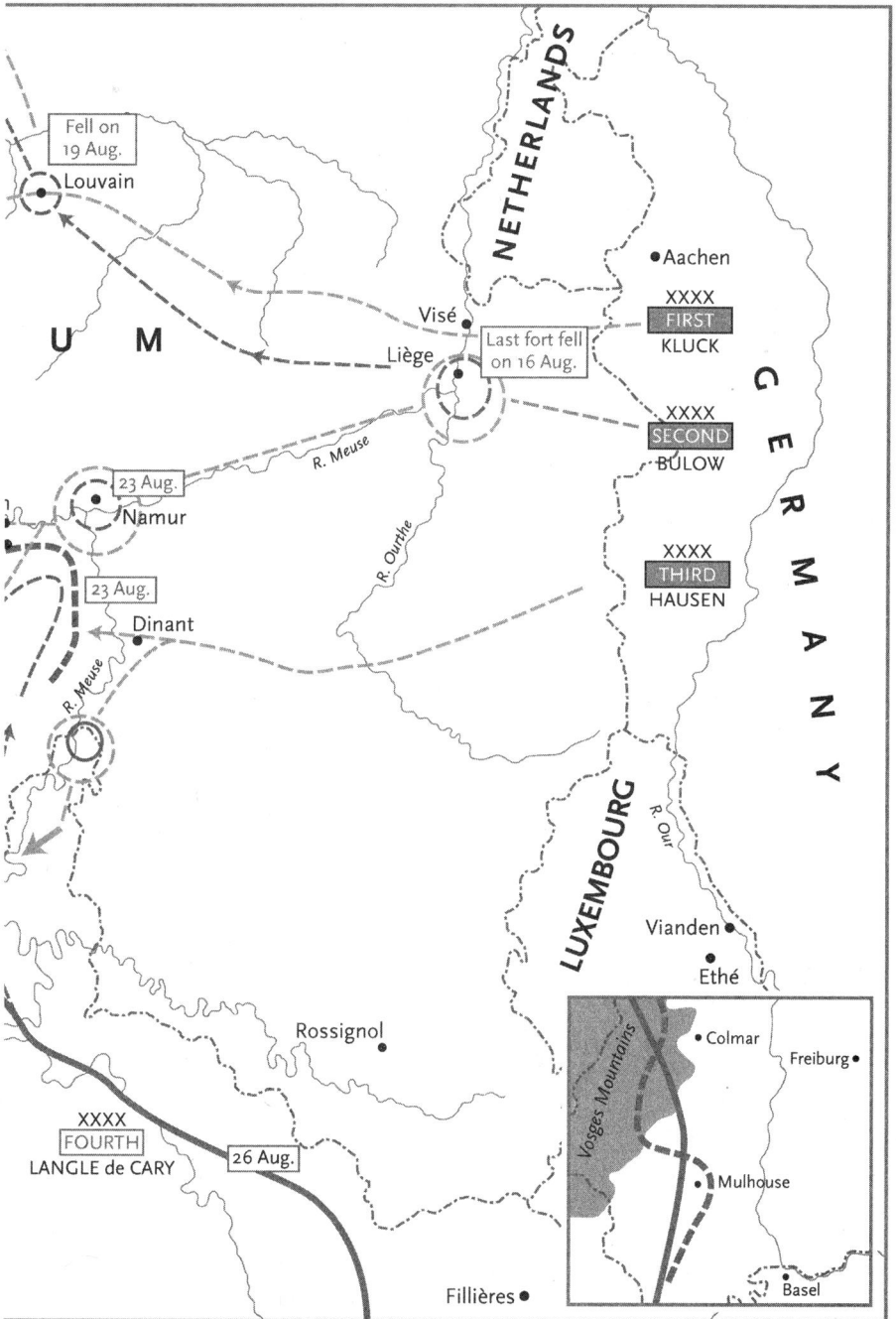

Fell on
19 Aug.
● Louvain

● Aachen

U   M

Visé ●

XXXX
FIRST
KLUCK

Liège ●

Last fort fell
on 16 Aug.

XXXX
SECOND
BÜLOW

R. Meuse

23 Aug.
● Namur

R. Ourthe

XXXX
THIRD
HAUSEN

23 Aug.
● Dinant

R. Meuse

NETHERLANDS

G
E
R
M
A
N
Y

LUXEMBOURG

R. Our

Vianden ●

● Ethé

● Rossignol

XXXX
FOURTH
LANGLE de CARY

26 Aug.

Fillières ●

Vosges Mountains

● Colmar

Freiburg ●

● Mulhouse

● Basel

The final stages of the German push towards Paris

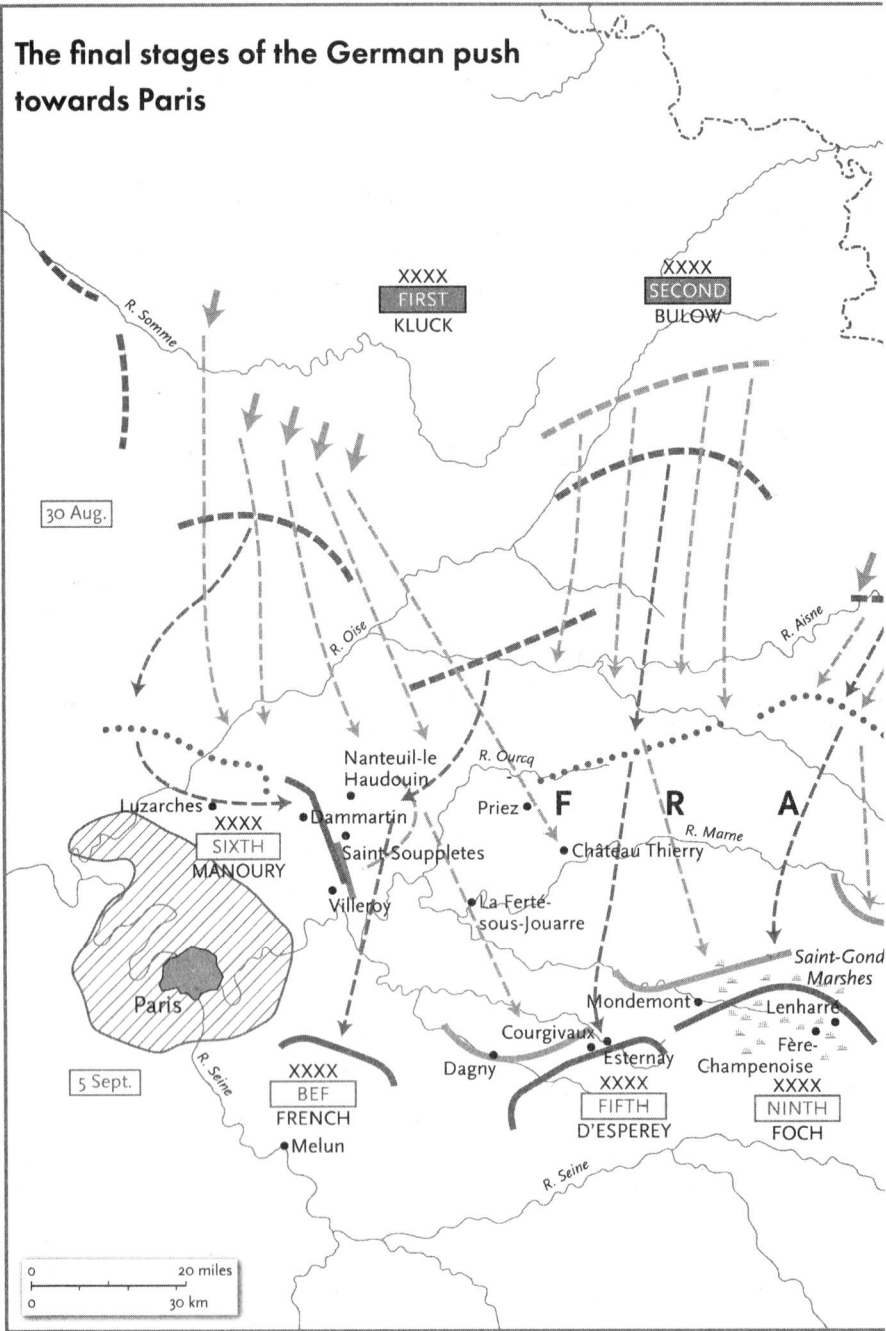

XXXX
FIRST
KLUCK

XXXX
SECOND
BÜLOW

R. Somme

30 Aug.

R. Oise

R. Aisne

R. Ourcq

Nanteuil-le Haudouin

Luzarches

Priez

F   R   A

XXXX
SIXTH
MANOURY

Dammartin

Château Thierry

R. Marne

Saint-Souppletes

Villeroy

La Ferté-sous-Jouarre

Saint-Gond Marshes

Paris

Mondemont

Lenharre

Courgivaux

Fère-Champenoise

5 Sept.

R. Seine

XXXX
BEF
FRENCH

Dagny

Esternay

XXXX
NINTH
FOCH

XXXX
FIFTH
D'ESPEREY

Melun

R. Seine

0   20 miles

0   30 km

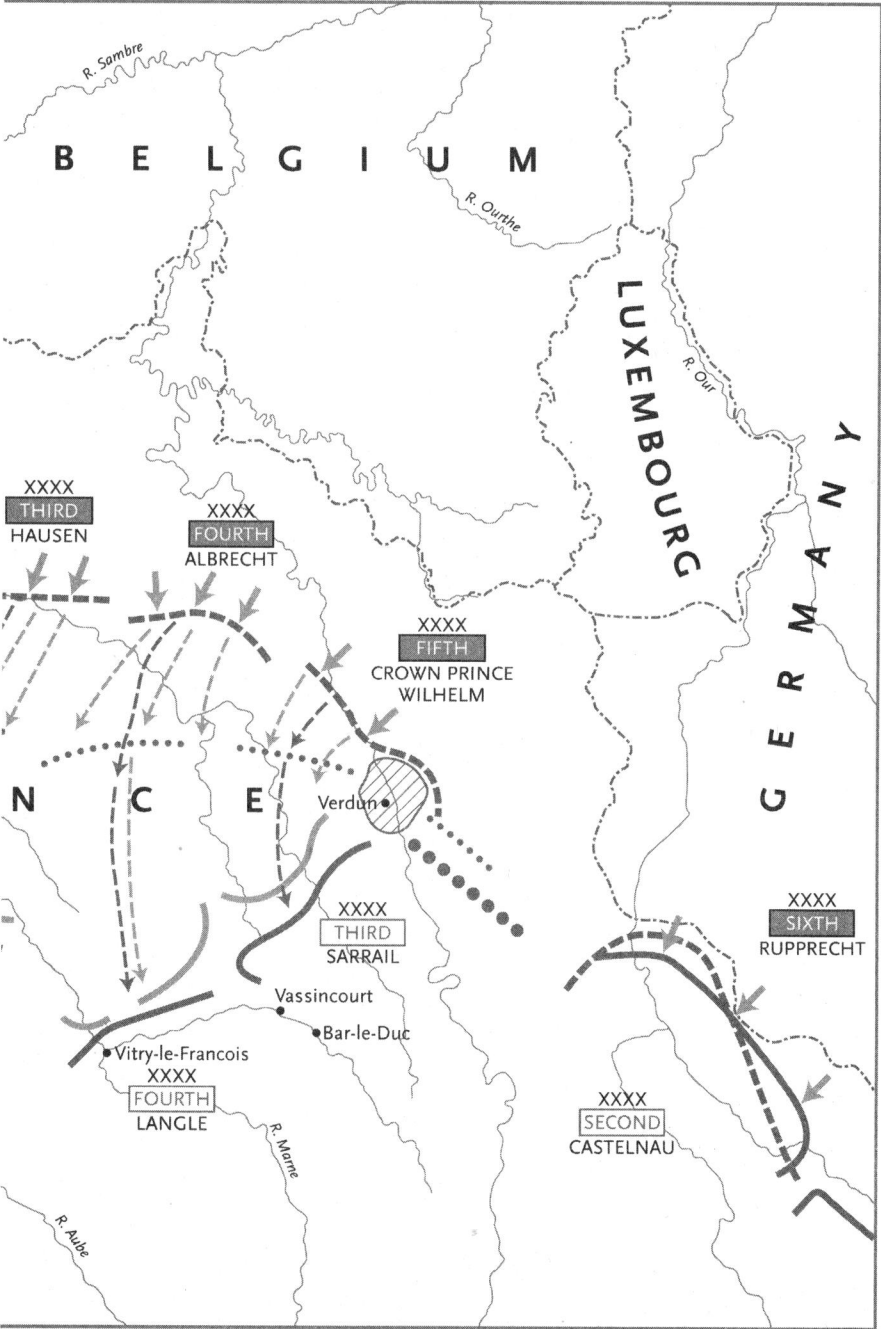

R. Sambre

BELGIUM

R. Ourthe

LUXEMBOURG

R. Our

GERMANY

XXXX
THIRD
HAUSEN

XXXX
FOURTH
ALBRECHT

XXXX
FIFTH
CROWN PRINCE
WILHELM

Verdun

N   C   E

XXXX
THIRD
SARRAIL

XXXX
SIXTH
RUPPRECHT

Vassincourt
Bar-le-Duc

Vitry-le-Francois

XXXX
FOURTH
LANGLE

R. Marne

XXXX
SECOND
CASTELNAU

R. Aube

Eastern Front

Königsberg •

Danzig •

XXXX
EIGHT
HINDENBURG

Allenstein •

Hohenstein •

G E R M A N Y

• Berlin

XXX
WOYRSCH

• Kalisz

• Łódź

A U S T R I A - H U N G A R Y

Kraków •

Carpathian

| 0 | 100 miles |
| 0 | 100 km |

Stałupönen
Gumbinnen
Goritten

XXXX
FIRST
RENNENKAMPF

XXXXX
NORTHWEST
ZHILINSKY

Bischofsburg
Masurian Lakes

XXXX

XXXX
SECOND
SAMSONOV

R U S S I A

Warsaw

XXXX
NINTH
LECHITSKY

XXXX
FORTH
SALZA

XXXX
FIFTH
PLEHVE

XXXXX
SOUTHWEST
IVANOV

Kraśnik
Polichna
Zamość
Telantyn
Wasylów
Tomaszów

XXXX
FIRST
DANKS

R. San

XXXX
FOURTH
AUFFENBERG
Rawa Ruska

XXXX
THIRD
RUZSKI

Przemyśl

Lemberg
Złoczów

XXXX
EIGHTH
BRUSILOV

XXXX
THIRD
BRUDERMANN

R. Gnila Lipa
R. Złota Lipa

KOVESS
GROUP

26 Sept.

M o u n t a i n s

1 Sept.

XXXX
SECOND
BOHM ERMOLLI

Balkans

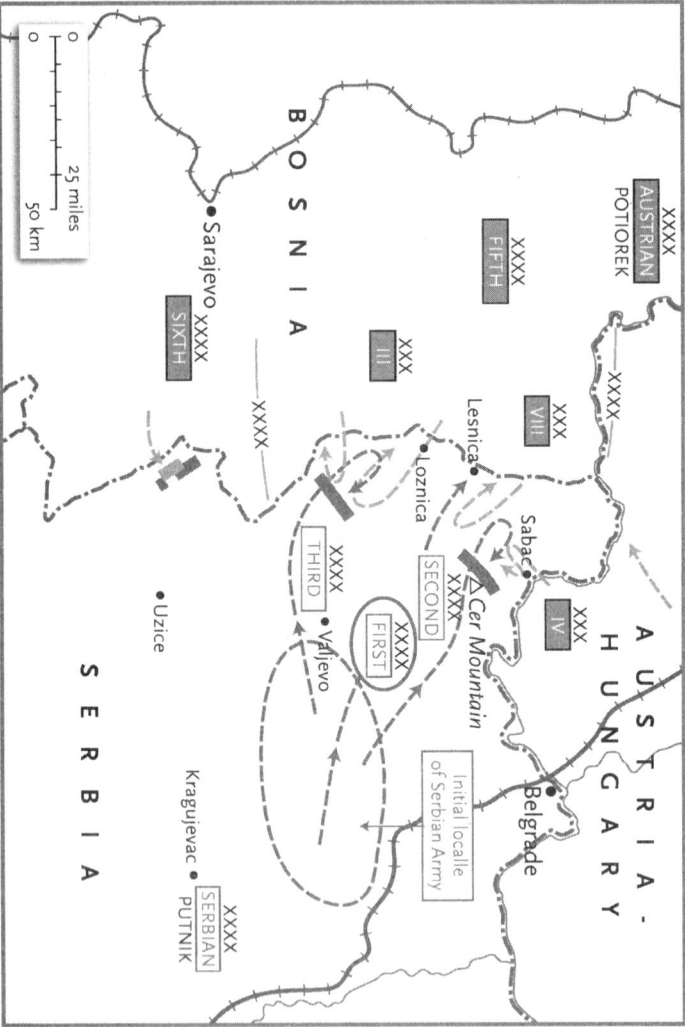

BOSNIA

AUSTRIAN
POTIOREK
XXXX

FIFTH
XXXX

SIXTH
XXXX

III
XXX

• Sarajevo

XXXX

VIII
XXX

• Lesnica

XXXX

• Loznica

Sabac •

IV
XXX

△ Cer Mountain

THIRD
XXXX

SECOND
XXXX

FIRST
XXXX

• Uzice

• Valjevo

AUSTRIA-
HUNGARY

• Belgrade

Initial locaIie
of Serbian Army

SERBIA

Kragujevac •

SERBIAN
PUTNIK
XXXX

0
25 miles

0
50 km

Introduction

The opening weeks of the First World War shaped everything that was to come in Europe and beyond. More than any other part of the conflict, the events of August and September 1914 ordained what would happen before peace was achieved in 1918. Even then, the grandiose plans for a swift decisive outcome executed in this period, their failure, and the far-reaching consequences of every combatant nation repeatedly trying to find a solution to the conundrum of modern, industrialized warfare would continue to have a knock-on effect for decades. There are even some historians who claim that the Second World War is the same conflict, with a break in between.

Millions of words have been expended on *why* the First World War began; chronicling alliances, old grudges and political machinations and turning points. In this book, we're sticking to a different theme, and that is *how*. How did these weeks appear to those experiencing them in myriad different ways? How well did people appreciate the sheer magnitude of the events sweeping them off their feet and altering their lives and the world in which they lived for good? How did they feel? *What did 1914 look like from the inside?* We've taken the outbreak of war and reconstructed it through the eyes of everyday men, women and children; not those stalking the corridors of power and setting events in motion.

Nobody anywhere on earth had one single response to the outbreak of war in 1914. Alan 'Tommy' Lascelles was destined to one day serve as Private Secretary to multiple British sovereigns, but on 31 July 1914, he was a twenty-seven-year-old traveller hurrying home from South America, confused, worried that it would be over before he returned. He said that it was 'like dropping 100 years through space, and waking up in another century'.[1]

We think about the First World War in absolutes. This country declared war on this day, this battle started and ended then. However, even at the beginning, though the hope until the very last was that it might all come to nothing and everyone might be able to stand down and go home, no nation simply went to war on one specific day. The reality of July and August 1914 was that countries were mobilized in stages, not on a whim. Britain was an exception, since to all intents and purposes the Royal Navy was at war for a week before war was formally declared on 4 August. Just like Europe's armies, naval men crept steadily towards readiness, just in case.

Along the south coast of England, sailors' plans for how to spend their leave – to gamble, joy-ride, feast on lobster or dance – crumbled. Some officers remembered seeing a vague reference to trouble in the Balkans, but eyebrows were barely raised. There was always trouble in the Balkans. The next day, notices were flashed on cinema screens ashore, recalling men to their ships. The navy was being sent to its war stations. Chutes dumped piles of coal on decks and men scrambled to get it into bunkers. Off Dover, a daunting line of warships exited the straits in procession, lit up by powerful searchlights sweeping the Channel. As they sailed north, men dug out ammunition, fused shells and manned the guns. They put warheads on the torpedoes. 'After this war was looked on as an odds-on chance.'[2]

The main strength of the Royal Navy made for the Orkney Islands in miserable weather; a steady drizzle and strong winds. Daylight on 1 August revealed countless ships ensconced in the vast, sheltered enclave of Scapa Flow. 'In the Fleet the general attitude was a longing for more news and annoyance at being so cut off from the world.'[3] Rumours filled the void. One elderly local had been telling sailors that: 'all the butchers from the Fleet had been landed the previous night, that they had slaughtered continuously at Kirkwall till 3.00 a.m. in order to get meat for the ships'.[4] At that point, exhausted by this frenzied savagery, the butchers had apparently passed out oblivious in puddles of blood. The storyteller solemnly claimed that he could not possibly guess how many animals had been done to death.

In ports around the world, the Royal Navy beached tables, chairs, chests of drawers. Days before Britain was officially at war, aboard HMS *Southampton* at Scapa, Stephen King-Hall was put in charge of stripping wood off the decks, since splinters flying through the air in battle could be catastrophic. 'I left the ship in charge of a miscellaneous assortment of cutters, whalers, and skiffs, which were to be… hauled up on the beach… I noted with amusement that one of the boats was the… craft, [on which] myself and fifteen others were supposed to seek safety in the case of the necessity of abandoning ship ever arising.'[5]

*

On 4 August, the day that Britain finally declared war, in Paris a memorable scene played out in the Chamber of Deputies. It was packed to capacity. Many of the representatives were reservists and took their seats in uniform. One witness watched Prime Minister René Viviani give a speech 'in which he placed upon Germany crushing responsibility for the catastrophe which has overtaken Europe'. He was constantly interrupted by shouts of *Vive la France*! He finished: 'We are without reproach. We shall be without fear!'

> [He] swept the whole Chamber off its feet. The vast [room] was a compact mass of cheering deputies, all waving aloft in their hands papers and handkerchiefs. From the tribunes of the public gallery shout after shout went up. At the foot of the presidential platform the grey-haired usher, with his 1870 war medals on his breast, was seated, overcome with emotion, the tears coursing down his cheeks.[6]

Why was the elderly usher crying? Was he moved to tears of joy, because he thought that Alsace and Lorraine were about to be avenged? Or was he terrified? Was it because he might now outlive his sons? Was he feeling all of those emotions at the same time?

*

A common image of those days in the summer of 1914 is one of enthusiasm, a universal 'spirit'; people waving flags and rushing forth in their eagerness to fling themselves at the enemy. That sentiment did indeed exist in some places. For several nights, large crowds took to the streets of Berlin. They sang *Deutschland, Deutschland über alles. Burgfrieden,* or 'fortress truce', was an old principle that called for a nationwide unity; and it was called for again now by the Kaiser.

If Germany had Burgfrieden, France found solidarity in the *Union sacrée.* This 'Sacred Union' pulled all political parties together in defence of the country. Far from Paris in Corsica, men sang *La Marseillaise.* Across the island, the tricolour flag was waved with the Union Flag and that of Russia. 'We did not hesitate to make the air ring out with numerous revolver shots,' wrote one witness. 'The spirit of the population is excellent.'[7]

In Brno, 130 miles south-east of Prague, Oscar Bittner was serving with an artillery regiment in the Austro-Hungarian army. 'The enthusiasm of the population was indescribable. An actual, unaffected enthusiasm from all walks of life and from all nationalities... It happened to me like many other soldiers and officers that you were suddenly lifted onto the shoulders of complete strangers and carried through the streets a long way with shouts of "*Hoch die Armee*". The jubilation was universal.'

But was it? In Germany, one publication commented on the composition of those patriotic crowds in Berlin: 'it wasn't poor workers whose poverty and agony, whose need and suffering, whose anger over the bloody mockery of their rights and interests has driven them to the streets; it was youth, dressed in the... latest fashion... students and sales clerks... and debonair types'.[8] As the week went on, in cities like Dortmund, those gathering were characterized as drunken louts with nothing better to do.

A huge crowd assembled outside the Winter Palace in St Petersburg. It was uniquely diverse, in that among some 250,000 people, the working class was heavily represented. 'All of Palace Square was filled to overflowing with people,' wrote a watching priest. 'Workers, members of the intelligentsia, women and children stood shoulder to shoulder. It seemed as if the whole population of St Petersburg had flocked there.'[9] When the tsar appeared, people spontaneously fell to their knees. 'The mood of the masses is most patriotic,' a young officer told his father. 'As I passed through a crowd, people leapt onto the footboards of my cab and kissed the shoulder straps of my uniform.'[10] All of this flew in the face of the German ambassador in St Petersburg, who had predicted a revolution as soon as war was declared.

Perhaps surprisingly, the biggest crowds of all assembled on the other side of the Atlantic in a country that was not even going to war. America was a nation of immigrants, many of whom felt ties to an old homeland. Up to 400,000 people fanned out from Times Square in New York. Crowds marched up and down Broadway. More groups gathered in Greenwich Village and on both the Upper and Lower East Sides. Two days later, the mayor was so fed up with the disruption that he put out an edict forbidding any more demonstrations.

The 'Spirit of 1914' frequently comprised an element of patriotic resolve. 'I experience cruel anguish,' wrote one Frenchman on his way to the front:

> I know what our adversaries are worth; their army is the most formidable military instrument the world has ever known; to get out of this mess... it will be necessary for us soldiers to fight with superhuman energy and courage... good news arrives from hour to hour: around Germany and Austria a ring of iron and fire is taking shape.[11]

In Berlin, Otto Braun had only just turned seventeen, and he tried to articulate his feelings to his father. 'Germany cannot perish... we have not yet fully realized ourselves. The Germany we carry in our hearts is not yet incorporated in concrete form… It seems stupid and contemptible to spare or preserve oneself… I want to fight for the preservation of the German spirit and for its fulfilment. Who and what could hold me back from this?'[12]

The most obvious manifestation of enthusiasm was in the shape of men racing to enlist. In most countries those left to come forward of their own accord were not generally deemed suitable for service. In Freiburg, boys as young as fourteen poured out of secondary schools to try to get into the German army. At the other end of the scale, August Würth, a seventy-four-year-old veteran of the Franco-Prussian War, wanted to serve again. One hundred criminals were even pardoned from the local jail so that they might redeem themselves in uniform.

In Belgium, as many as 20,000 additional men came forward. In Mechelen, men in their forties and boys of sixteen waited in long lines. Meanwhile, Russia was carrying out the first general mobilization of reserve armed forces in her history. On the one hand, the authorities expected the surge they saw in young men at the upper end of society trying to obtain exemptions from military service. On the other hand, what they did not expect was the enthusiasm from thousands of others who had not been summoned. They were largely made up of ethnicities like Tatar Muslims who were exempt from conscription, or the lower tier of the militia, or even those who had an existing deferral that they now wanted to ignore. The government had no contingency for dealing with these volunteers, and it was not until war actually broke out that they managed to set up the infrastructure to process them.

The famous phenomena that saw men queue for hours at a time in their thousands was a short-lived British experience for one reason. Britain did not employ conscription, so had not already mobilized her potential manpower. As a result civilians raced to volunteer in August and September 1914. By October, numbers dwindled rapidly again, but for a few weeks, men and boys went to great lengths to enlist. Raymond Mann was fifteen years old and was swept along on a tide of patriotism:

On about the 4th August I went down to... Trafalgar Square and bought myself a driving licence... I went to North Kensington to try and join motorcycle despatch riders and further down the road to Talbot's Works, but couldn't get accepted. However, by some means, I found out that there was a unit of motor transport being formed at Kew Gardens and on 12th August I went in the gates, and up the drive, and joined the few people queuing outside a tent to join the army. I remember very well being asked my age. I said 18.[13]

*

So although the 'Spirit of 1914' did exist, considering this reaction in isolation is like looking at a work of art with your nose pressed against it. The whole picture was far more complex. Rushing to the colours did not necessarily mean that a man was filled with blind, unquestioning patriotism. Honour, duty and peer pressure all motivated men to go to war in 1914. Mikhail Lemke reasoned with himself that his call-up this time was a far cry from the Russo-Japanese War. He was fighting this time 'not because I rush into battle as a loyal subject of Nicholas... in contrast to 1904, I have no reason to consider this war exclusively the work of the Tsar and his associates'.[14] This war was international, a clash of empires and a fight for survival, not a land grab for the benefit of an autocrat. Russian officer Alexander Verkhovsky thought that he knew what everyone was really thinking. 'Twenty million people... have abandoned their homes and families, [for] death and suffering, without personally expecting any benefits... But if you ask each of these twenty million quietly, so that no one hears, whether he would like to return home and not go to war? Undoubtedly, nineteen million out of twenty will say with conviction: "Let's go home."'[15]

In deepest Asia, boredom was as much a motivator as defending Russia. Fifteen-year-old Laila Sharov lived in Manchuria. Her father was on the staff of the Chinese Eastern Railroad Company, which was controlled by the Russian government.

When war broke out, the Russian community in Harbin, some 40,000 people, erupted:

> The mood rose to a fever pitch... Nearly everyone was ready to [fight]. They were tired of the atmosphere they themselves had created... Tired of 'wine and women', the lavish spending of money and the continuous, meaningless gaiety. Everyone wanted a goal in life, a golden halo around his head. War and Russia were the answer, leading to new adventures and new excitement.[16]

In places like Australia, some immigrants saw war as a free passage back to Europe. In East Africa, of a large number of men interviewed in Nyasaland, modern Malawi, a few said that they went because it was the manly thing to do, but the overwhelming majority volunteered to fight for one thing: to escape crippling poverty. Armed service offered a massive windfall. 'I was there with them because I wanted money,' said Joseph Mandana.[17] Enlisting was an economic transaction. The promise of £5 payable to those left behind if he died was also tantalising. Men also coveted the uniform, free clothes and more. When Kazibule Dabi was asked why he chose to fight for Germany, he replied: 'They said that after the war they would build us brick houses with an iron roof and that we would live in our own country.'[18] Mbwana Mdoke summed it up from the village of Chindamba: 'People went in the way they go into the mines here. Nobody doesn't know that life in the mines is miserable, but people still go. It is money they want.'[19]

The same logic prevailed in North Africa. Mustafa Tabti was an Arab tribesman who had served the French as a teenager, motivated by the idea of adventure and the desire 'to play with gunpowder'.[20] Since then, he had spent twenty years scraping a living. He enlisted again in his mid-thirties because the French army could promise him food, a place to live and a regular income.

Some people did remain excited as the war began. They felt a sense of anticipation about what was to come. Across the globe, the clamour for news did not subside. In Morocco, where he was stationed with a French colonial unit, Senegalese soldier Bakary Diallo remarked that:

> Casablanca looks and feels different... Bugles sound everywhere... The Serjeant-major reads a despatch out loud. It's a bit long and we only grasp two things from it: 'Germany has declared war on France... And France calls on all her children.' Once we've understood... we get giddier and giddier. It's incredible how a sense of excitement takes hold of us, overwhelms us, lifts our souls aloft.[21]

*

There seemed to be no escaping the outbreak of war. Strangers chattered on the top decks of London's buses. In Buenos Aires, 'loudly with truly extraordinary interest... nothing else was discussed in theatres, on the streets, on public walks, and wherever a group of people formed'.[22] Even in Theiriat, a sleepy village high in the hills in the remote north-east of India, inhabitants were mesmerized by the war. 'Since that time', recalled one local, 'everyone, male or female, except small children, became very interested in getting news... It became the main subject of conversation in all gatherings.'[23]

It is also important to remember that someone waving a flag and cheering in early August might have felt very different a week later. After exuberance, for some came relief. 'The incomprehensible and yet long expected has really come,' wrote Walter von Rummel. 'At last! No matter what grave and even graver things may come, the last weeks, and especially the last days were unbearable. The leaden nightmare grew hourly more oppressing.'[24]

People were also confused. Every nation had blurred lines within it when it came to loyalties. A Pole might find himself called to serve Germany, Russia or Austria–Hungary. Was he loyal to one of those? Or to a free Poland? Twenty-one-year-old Stanislaw Kawczak was a student, but was carrying out his national service in Kraków, wearing an Austro-Hungarian uniform. Desperate for news, he went to the university:

> The billiards room was in an uproar. Everybody was arguing... We should take advantage of this unique moment, as another such occasion is not likely to happen. I trudged back to the barracks, pondering what to do. Should I desert? I could not reconcile myself to it somehow... while in the Austrian army I could merely expect hardship, compulsion, mistrust, if not hatred from the Germans.[25]

There were no appealing choices.

*

Once the war began, the nature of the crowds changed. In Glasgow, clerk Thomas Macmillan thought people looked rudderless. 'The street was abnormally busy: people of all ages were walking rather aimlessly about... while scattered here and there were groups, earnestly discussing the momentous news.'[26] On the Ramblas in Barcelona, too, people wandered about trying to make sense of events. In Nyasaland, churchman Petro Kilekwa was being subjected to a barrage of questions. He had preached to indigenous flocks about Christian love and charity. Now they wanted to know: 'Are the Germans Christians? Why have the Christians gone to war?'[27] On the other side of the continent, in what is now Mali, confusion was also rife. Baye Tabéma Tembély, a soldier, tried to explain events to his family: 'I know Europeans well and all the twists and turns of their words... I have the impression that before long the gunpowder will speak in France.'[28] Tembély showed more understanding than certain troops in Russia. There, General Alexei Brusilov asked some of his men why they thought they were at war. The answer was always that 'some [man] and his wife were killed by someone, and therefore the Austrians wanted to offend the Serbs... who the Serbs were, almost no one knew, what are Slavs, that was also dark, and why the Germans decided to fight because of Serbia, that was completely unknown'.[29]

If some people were baffled about what was happening, it passed others by completely. This was especially so among children, who had more immediate concerns than comprehending the indirect impact of a global conflict. In South Wales, when Bessie Davies heard her parents talking about the outbreak of war, she was ambivalent. A far-away war could not compare to what she had seen with her own eyes: a colliery explosion a few months before. 'Four hundred and thirty-nine men and boys lost their lives… for days and days they were bringing out the dead… [The war] didn't seem nothing to me to what the explosion was because I knew people that had been killed.'[30]

In West Africa, Amadou Hampâté Ba Amkoullel had fresh recollections of a famine that impacted the entire Niger Bend region. The memory of watching people tossed into mass graves far surpassed the outbreak of a war in Europe:

We saw two men… each dragging the body of a human by the feet. Now, if one is dead, the other is visibly still only dying. The two gravediggers, hardened, perhaps, by habit, laugh and speak loudly as if they were dragging… common tree branches. Arriving at the edge of the mass grave, they throw the two bodies there, then turn on their heels and leave.

But one of the bodies was still alive.

The dying person, in a last burst of his desire to live, lets out a hoarse moan… His fingers, convulsed, try in vain to hold on to something. His body twitches, liquid oozes from his mouth. Suddenly it stiffens like dry wood, then, a few seconds later, sags limply. His motionless, almost white eyes remain focused on the sky. The unfortunate man has just expired, already lying among the dead.[31]

Some people's response to the outbreak of war was selfish, as opposed to disinterested. Alan Lascelles was disgusted by this sentiment in South America:

Most of the Anglo–Argentines look on the whole thing solely from the point of view of their immediate business interests, much as if we had missed a train… One man was in a tearing fuss for fear he should miss a meeting… and a little rat sitting opposite me said he had just resigned his commission in the territorials, so he needn't go home. I told him without any justification I fear, that he would almost certainly be shot as a deserter if he didn't, which scared him considerably.[32]

Others reacted with complete disbelief. Many people clung to the idea that the war would be short, but did they actually believe it or was this a comfort in trying to process terrifying events? Some reasoned that war was so expensive, that nobody could keep it up for long on this scale. But at what point were people latching onto the idea of a short war to make themselves feel better? *It will all be over soon. It won't be as bad as we expected.*

When the reality of the war's probable length emerged, people sank into depression. Some men were mortified at the thought that they could have done more to maintain peace. When Walter Page, the US Ambassador to London, went to see his German counterpart, Prince Lichnowsky, he found his colleague distraught in his pyjamas. Page thought that the prince 'might literally go mad' and called this interview 'one of the most pathetic experiences of my life'.[33] When Page met with Edward Grey, Britain's foreign secretary, the British statesman sat and cried.

In the Paris suburbs, priest Felix Klein was plagued with dark thoughts and insomnia. 'I have felt myself incapable of settling down to any occupation… The writings I had on hand are abandoned; no more correspondence even… The night was worse than the day. I don't speak only of the [insomnia] that would not allow sleep lasting more than five minutes.' He thought the noise would drive him mad:

Train followed train with intervals of just a few minutes… heavy carts, motor-cars shook the ground. Over my head…

squadrons of aeroplanes hummed... It was truly like the sound of a flood, a flood at the height of a storm, but which, instead of waves to the distant sea, was rolling men, men, and still more men into the jaws of the guns.[34]

There were clear distinctions throughout the world based on class. For those living on the poverty line, giving up pay to loiter in the streets and sing songs was not an option, and being sent away to war and potential death was nothing to be excited about if your family could barely make ends meet. In a locomotive plant in Kharkov, 300 miles east of Kyiv, hundreds of workers gathered in the courtyard. Alexei Selyavkin noticed that 'they stood in silence with stern, gloomy faces, smoked, and occasionally exchanged remarks about the bitter fate of their loved ones being abandoned'.[35] Karel Tůma, a Czech miner in Bohemia said the same thing: 'People standing around, crying and wailing, while others are already going to the pub to drink in mourning.'[36]

People were also rightly terrified in 1914. War was a career for many men. They had trained for this eventuality, but it did not mean that they were not afraid. On HMS *Marlborough*, James Somerville panicked when Britain's ultimatum to Germany expired. 'I felt sure we should be attacked during the night. It's a bit trying to the nerves, expecting to be blown up at any moment but I don't think I showed it and I did my best to encourage my staff with many quips and jests.'[37] General Émile Fayolle was destined to win fame in this war, but as hostilities commenced, he, too, was scared. 'I'm afraid of being afraid, of being inferior to my task,' the Frenchman wrote.[38]

At the other end of the ranks, soldier Dominik Richert was twenty years old and serving in Mulhouse in the 'lost' province of Alsace when he heard that war had broken out. His comrades burst into a rendition of *Deutschland über alles*. Dominik did not join in. 'I did not feel like singing, because I thought straight away that the most likely thing that can happen to you in a war is that you will be shot dead. That was a really unpleasant prospect. In addition, I was worried about my relatives and my home, because they were near the border and therefore at risk of being destroyed.'[39] Frenchman André de Maricourt feared for his mother. '[She] has "guts", but... at 76 seeing the Germans a second time would be difficult.' She was preoccupied with invasion. 'To anticipate everything I look for hiding places. Obviously, you have to be ready... In any case, the clear role now is to try and instil in women a confidence that I would like to have.'[40] Concerns varied, but the world over, fear reigned. In the Netherlands, defensive strategies included flooding flat landscapes to hold back an invader. When people realized that if war broke out their homes and businesses would be inundated, they panicked, 'stacking furniture, taking down curtains, and storing food, hay, and fodder in their attics'.[41]

Karonga lies on the far north-western side of Lake Malawi, which means that in 1914 it sat in British Nyasaland and faced German East Africa. The lake is one of the largest in Africa, and whoever dominated it would have the upper hand in the region when war came. The locals articulated different reasons for their fear: 'We were afraid because we knew the whites would take us to war to fight for them,' said Vmande Kaombe.[42] An impending sense of Armageddon terrified more than one young person: 'I was very much terrified when the old people said that this war would wipe out all the human race; we would all perish,' recalled Diamond Chirwa.[43] Young Konsala Mwakisahi learnt of the war on seeing the British at district headquarters digging shelters. 'When we asked, they told us the Germans were coming. I don't remember clearly, but we were filled with fear of death and began to make preparations for escape to the hills.'[44] This flight was not an isolated occurrence. Many opted to run and hide from the white man's war. At the southern end of the lake, with long memories of slave traders and previous conflicts, people fled into the bush. They gradually returned, 'but for the better part of a week there was scarcely a soul about the place'.[45]

Across the world, fear and a lack of information led to rumours and then panic. The most common manifestation of this was spy fever. Germany was said to be overrun with Russian agents. Vigilantes prowled the country looking for them. In Munich, Ernst Toller witnessed a grim attack: 'Somebody had heard two women speaking French, and they were immediately surrounded and set upon. They protested that they were Germans, but it did not avail them in the least; with torn clothes, disheveled hair and bleeding faces they were taken off by the police.'[46] Berliners were convinced that Russians had poisoned the Muggel-See, which supplied part of the city's water. Based on similar nonsense, the people of Brussels were attempting to brew tea using rainwater. In France, Maggi incurred the wrath of a mob. Rumours spread first that the dairy company was backed by German money, then that it had sold milk poisoned by an enemy agent, killing 300 children in Boulogne. Felix Klein described the destruction of one of their shops in Paris:

Most of the raiders were women. There was some jesting, and some dry wit, but mostly it was serious business. The work was carried forward painstakingly and thoroughly. The iron screen... was torn off... and the window itself was smashed to bits... every bit of glass or crockery was shattered into fragments against the sidewalk and the pieces were ground into powder under the heels of the raiders. Account books... were torn sheet by sheet into the tiniest bits and strewn up and down the street... and all woodwork was smashed into kindling.[47]

One last, obvious emotion evident across the planet on the outbreak of war was anger. Ferdinando Martini, the Italian colonial minister, was enraged with the regimes involved:

These emperors in their proclamations and speeches always speak of God and invoke him. But do they believe in God? And if they believe it, how have they not refrained from throwing Europe... into the abyss of desolation and misfortune? And how can they think that God does not punish them for their bloody outrage, their boundless ambition?[48]

In Russia, a unique situation resulted in violence. People were distinctly unimpressed with the government's decision to ban the sale of alcohol. Not only that, but supplies were supposed to be destroyed. This was coming at precisely the time when most Russians felt a particular need to drink. In Naumiestis, 150 miles north-west of Vilna in Lithuania, the authorities seized boxes of vodka, took them out on the street and smashed them. 'Vodka like rainwater flowed on a pavement down to the Šešupė river', wrote one resident, 'as locals jumped to the alcohol rivulet with buckets, boxes, and empty bottles ignoring the gendarmes who tried to chase them away.' One hundred miles south-east at Suwałki, near the border with East Prussia, there were bizarre scenes the day after the ban came into effect, when the local police chief wanted everyone to take their supply up a hill to smash it. People sobbed. 'The peasants threw themselves down on the ground, lapped the vodka with their tongues, and when they could swallow no more they rolled over and over in it!'[49]

The alcohol ban came on top of mobilization, the departure of breadwinners, and a loss of freedoms and property associated with the war. Two thousand miles away from St Petersburg, where these laws were being made, in Siberia, there was significant unrest. Soldiers had to be called in. 'The mobs threw stones at them, one rifleman was wounded with bullets, as a result of which the troops opened fire... two were killed, two were seriously wounded,' read one account. The requisitioning of horses was halted. The worst incident of 1914 occurred in Barnaul, a city some 220 miles south of Tomsk, closer to Mongolia than it was to Europe and the main theatres of war. Rioters set fire to houses, shops and a warehouse that held alcohol, and more than a hundred men died in a string of tiny battles with the authorities.

All over the world, people had a sense of what was to come: hardship and loss. Joseph Ilyin, a Russian officer, was disgusted when he and his men received a telegram from a general celebrating the fact that Germany had declared war on Russia. 'I just can't understand, what is there to congratulate! Mass slaughter, hundreds of thousands of mutilated, ruined cities and villages!' Writer Zinaida Gippius, one of the major figures in Russia's symbolism movement, declared: 'Now Europe is a ring of fire... I look at these lines, written by my hand, as if I was out of my mind. *World War*!'[50] The American ambassador to London, Walter Page, had watched the terrifying spectre of war unfold in the English countryside:

I walked out in the night a while ago. The stars are bright, the night is silent. The country quiet... Millions of men are in camp and on warships. Will they all have to fight and many of them die, to untangle this network of treaties and alliances, and to blow off huge debts with gunpowder so that the world may start again?[51]

1

What is to Become of Us?

The outbreak of war caused millions of people to move from one place to another. By far the most regimented cause of the massive displacement witnessed in 1914 was the mobilization of armies and navies around the world. The largest number of men in history was being brought forward to participate in a war, and significantly, not primarily because they wanted to fight, but because they had been forced to.

The methods used to summon these men were diverse. In France, posters went up in Paris. At Besançon, close to the border with Switzerland, a gun was fired. 'A silent stupor invades the crowd,' wrote a local priest. 'Everyone stops nailed to the spot... A second cannon shot heightens the emotion; cries escape from the lips; women cry and hide their faces with their hands.'[1] In Belgium, policemen walked the streets with letters, while in Copenhagen, twenty-year-old factory worker Åge Houlby was woken up at midnight by his mother after a yellow notice was presented at the front door ordering him to report for duty immediately. In rural areas of Europe, the news often came by messenger, in a car, or on a horse.

In Turkey, where a large part of the population was illiterate, men walked through towns and villages rhythmically chanting the contents of mobilization orders, accompanied by musical instruments. Ismail Hakki Bey even composed *The Patriotic March* to accompany them. At the conclusion of the Muslim holy month of Ramadan, which occurred at the end of August

1914, the French used similar methods to start recruiting North Africans in large numbers. Drummers came into public spaces in smart, colourful uniforms, accompanied by the high-pitched sound of the *ghaita*, a double-reed horn. 'The serjeant-major brought the music to an end once it had achieved the desired effect,' Messali Hadj recalled. 'An Arab serjeant would take the floor and elaborate with great eloquence all of the benefits that volunteers would enjoy. His propositions were most attractive, particularly to those with empty stomachs.' Their parents, on the other hand, 'lived in anguish' at the prospect of losing their sons to foreign wars.[2]

Men were not the only ones on their way to war. Women mobilized on a scale never seen before. They took on more roles, in larger numbers, than in any other conflict before 1914. Nursing was a traditional role for women in wartime. In Baku, deep in the Caucasus, Khristina Semina told her husband Ivan that she wanted to be a nurse. He was mortified, thinking she would not stand up to the strain, but as soon as he left for the front, she trained anyway. On 8 August, in Silesia, Ilse von Richthofen spent her birthday making herself a nurse's uniform. 'More than anything, [she] wants to lend a hand wherever she goes,' wrote her mother.[3]

Across Europe, women from wealthy backgrounds put their homes at the disposal of the war effort too. In London, affluent Mayfair was full of aristocratic women turning rooms over for convalescent officers and men. In Warsaw, Polish women, particularly the intelligentsia, came forward in numbers. To prepare for the wounded arriving from the front, they received permission from the Russian government to organize nursing courses, and luxurious homes were dedicated to convalescent men.

Women also fought as combatants from the beginning of the First World War. Some of the world's first female doctors, scholars and scientists came from Russia. There was also a long appreciation in Russian culture of strong female figures, so it should not be surprising that here, of all places, women found a way to the front. Some of these young women disguised themselves as men, others assumed a sort of neutral gender, while others made no attempt to hide their sex. Some were from military families – Colonel Tomilovsky had more than one daughter procure a uniform to go and fight in 1914. One of them distinguished herself near Augustów in the opening weeks of the war. Working-class women also found ways to enlist. Sixteen-year-old Alexandra Shirakova was working in a tailor's shop in Moscow when the war broke out. She used shop materials to make herself clothes, cut off all of her hair and passed herself off as a teenage boy. She changed her name to Sasha, joined a unit going to the front and was soon under heavy fire. Further south, Cossack women could be especially keen to serve. In September, eighteen-year-old Tatiana Kaldinkhina convinced the military commander of Astrakhan, on the Caspian Sea, to send her to the front. She had lived alongside German immigrants, and using her language skills won numerous medals carrying out reconnaissance missions.[4]

*

Mobilization did not mean fighting. It meant getting an army ready to fight if need be, and to that end, more countries underwent the process of preparing to fight than those generally described in 1914. They did not have a choice. From Bangkok, the government of Siam proclaimed neutrality as early as 6 August, but could not avoid sending men to defend Phuket from potential enemies or to southern provinces to protect German miners. In Switzerland, in just five days, almost 240,000 men were under arms, more than double the force of the one that Britain was sending to France. The Dutch mobilization plan was also highly detailed. Railways were seized immediately. By 4 August, more than 177,000 men had been moved, along with 6,600 horses and almost 500 vehicles.

In Italy, as early as 6 August reservists were blocked from leaving the country. In Turkey, mobilization began on 2 August and was described as 'a wholesale looting of the civilian population'. A brutal new edict demanding that men of all races and backgrounds come forward fell on a country that had recently gone through similar turmoil during the Balkan Wars, with terrible results. At the British embassy, junior diplomat Charles Lister was sympathetic. 'The soldiers, called up for the fourth time within three years, cannot be fed, armed, or clothed. They openly state they will desert at the first opportunity.' Unsurprisingly, those that did report for duty often presented a diverse but miserable display of the Ottoman empire's manpower. On a scale never attempted before, more than a million men went into uniform:

> Arabs, bootless and shoeless, dressed in their most gaily coloured garments, with long linen bags (containing the required five days' rations) thrown over their shoulders, shambling in their gait and bewildered in their manner, touched shoulders with equally dispirited Bedouin, suddenly snatched from the desert. A motley [collection] of Turks, Circassians, Greeks, Kurds, Armenians, and Jews, showing signs of having been summarily taken from their farms and shops, constantly jostled one another.[5]

In 1914, many men of service age from around the world found themselves in an absurd situation. Having emigrated, they were summoned back to the homelands they had chosen to leave behind to serve in the military. Austria–Hungary expected some 200,000 men in the United States to return to Europe. Germans in Georgia, Tennessee, Alabama, the Carolinas and Florida were all ordered to report to Atlanta for transport back to Germany. There were similar drives to assemble reservists all over South America: in Argentina, Brazil, Chile and Paraguay. By no means did all of these men want to comply. In New Orleans, plenty of Frenchmen refused. The French consul-general was outraged. He protested that such men were not only traitors and cowards, 'but are so void of honour that they should be denied the right of citizenship in the United States or other foreign countries'.[6] He called for the French societies of New Orleans to throw them out. Nobody listened.

In reality, no government had the infrastructure, the money, or the time to focus on enforcing these orders in 1914. For example, not only were emigrants born in Italy expected to return, but also so were second and third generation Italians, the children and grandchildren of these emigrants, who might never have set foot in Italy. The Italian government threatened those who did not comply, but was not always helped by other countries. Australia seemed willing to use police to force Italians to return for mobilization, but the largest group of Italians living outside their homeland were in America, and in August 1914, Secretary of State William Jennings Bryan announced that the US would not force any man born abroad to go 'home' and fight. In all, of the men expected to return to Italy, perhaps only about one in four actually did. As many as 800,000 Italians in America potentially ignored their summons.

Those who complied had complicated reasons. One young Italian had emigrated to Belgium with his father prior to the war. In September 1914 he received a telegram from Italy with details of his mobilization. He hoped to obtain a medical certificate in Belgium that would lead to his rejection for military service, meaning that he could stay in Brussels. His father ruined his plan: 'Papa absolutely wants to leave... and therefore I must accompany him in spite of myself... A son's duty compels me to follow Papa in such sad circumstances. So I leave but with sad premonitions.'[7]

*

One thing that staggered people all over Europe on the outbreak of war was the extent of the planning that had gone into preparing for mobilization. Britain's rail network comprised some 23,000 miles of track. On 4 August 1914, 130 companies were effectively taken over by the government. At Aldershot, near London, from 5 August officers were being handed dossiers that revealed the plan for their departure. For instance: 'Train No. 463 Y will arrive at Siding B at 12.35 a.m., 10th August. You will complete loading by 3.40 a.m.'[8] Troop trains bound for Southampton would soon be arriving on the coast every twelve minutes. Given 60 hours to send 350 trains to Southampton packed with troops, the London and South Western Railway did it in 45.

Each country was faced with its own unique challenges, but broadly speaking, mobilized men on the continent were digging trenches and manning forts. They were also chopping down trees, commandeering strategically placed houses and razing buildings to the ground. There was a buzz about proceedings, fuelled by nerves. In Italy, a mad rush was on to find enough uniforms, while governments were stockpiling munitions, food and equipment for their armies. The Russian navy was chomping at the bit, too. Constantine Benckendorff had joined the *Poltava*, which was moored on the Neva at St Petersburg, now renamed Petrograd because it sounded less German. The navy had been humiliated a decade previously by its Japanese counterpart, but things had changed:

> Stricter discipline, more formality in dress and harsher and more frequent punishment for petty crimes, were the outward manifestations of that state of affairs; even movement on deck had taken on a sort of goose-steppy... appearance. This, however, did not in any degree affect the keenness of all ranks to get to grips with the enemy... Both on the material side, and in training, great things had been achieved since the disasters in the Pacific, and this made all the younger men, both officers and ratings, only dimly conscious of any change, and rather proud of the sense of efficiency the new régime gave them.[9]

In Casablanca, tirailleur Bakary Diallo and his comrades also felt anticipation building. These African troops served France, and it quickly transpired that they would be shipped off to war. 'We're given uniforms made of thick dark material, the sleeves and collars edged with narrow yellow braid... The battalion marches to the harbour where we'll board our ships.' He felt a pang of sadness that instead of sailing for West Africa as planned, to see their families for the first time in years, they were rumoured to be going to Europe. He felt embarrassed. 'I felt even worse hearing my brothers in arms say the name "France" over and over so passionately, like lovers coming to the rescue of a damsel in distress while I seemed to be the only one whose thoughts strayed from France back to Senegal.'[10]

For every excited man, there were many more who were miserable about the hand that fate had dealt them. Edward Spears spent decades in the British army and served in both world wars:

> I have never met a conscripted soldier who did not long for his release, who did not find the call of duty an almost intolerable waste of the best years of his life, rendered bearable only by the sense of accomplishing a noble and necessary duty. On the contrary, anti-militarism is born in a barrack-room and gains vigour and strength by strenuous exercise on the square, while pack drill gives added bitterness to its spleen.[11]

For half a century, Danes in Schleswig-Holstein had found themselves living under German rule. In 1914, this meant they were conscripted into the Kaiser's army. For men like Hans Petersen, the word '*Mobil*', was devastating. 'It was as if I'd witnessed something horrible. The word had a repulsive, ominous ring to it like sharp, piercing steel and iron.'[12] Some men simply did not turn up as commanded, choosing to become fugitives instead. In Paris, many '"brave" petty bourgeois... took flight... Of all the French networks, that of Orleans, which connects Paris to the south-west, was the most crowded with these "cowards"'.[13] Others did report for duty, then thought better of it. In Poland, in a district 70 miles north-west of Warsaw, of 2,000 men who initially reported at one depot, 10 per cent then disappeared.

Some felt duped into serving. In Corsica, the locals were fearful of Italy joining the war on the side of the Central Powers. The military governor on the island permitted anyone who came forward to volunteer; whether they be woefully underage and lacking any parental consent, or elderly and infirm. Their expectation had been that they would be simply protecting their own homes, so men flooded forward, but then these recruits were summoned to mainland France. The 373e Régiment d'Infanterie arrived at the front in September looking extremely conspicuous: 'greying beards and hair, sometimes white, old faces tanned by the sun'.[14] Back in Corsica there were loud protests. Some of these men had left behind families of eight, even ten children.

*

Throughout the world, men prepared to depart for war. At Louvain in Belgium, a medieval university town some 18 miles east of Brussels, a few soldiers were manning a guard post at dawn on 5 August:

> With the first streaks of light we heard the rhythmic tramp of feet on the Malines road; soon singing became audible, and came nearer: we recognized the melody and the words of 'The Lion of Flanders'. Then, in the grey morning light, the head of the column appeared on the sunken road which enters the city... The soldiers passed with a joyful and proud air, in spite of the fatigue of the march, covered with dust and dripping with perspiration, but in perfect order, without stragglers.[15]

The population came out in force to cheer them on their way. 'They were overwhelmed with attention... Factory girls left their work to bring the soldiers their simple lunches, university professors kept open house and handed round armfuls of bottled beer.'[16] The 'torrent of hospitality' was so generous that the authorities had to ask the townspeople to stop. South of the border with France, with the 276e Régiment d'Infanterie, Victor Boudon watched their train pull slowly into the station:

> In a few moments, from the first to the last car, our train is decorated, adorned with flags and flowers... Huge inscriptions... 'Pleasure Train for Berlin', 'Death to Guillaume and

the Boches!', 'Long Live France and its allies!' Caricatures, little flattering to our enemies, cover the train from one end to the other, while the front of the locomotive is adorned with a superb decoration with allied colours.[17]

Across Europe, plenty of conscripts dealt with their grim prospects by getting drunk. Georg Pöllmann embarked for war with the Austro-Hungarian army from Salzburg. 'When we arrived at the train station, we were given beer... Many a poor comrade probably drank down the pain.' In Normandy, 750 miles to the west, it seemed like the whole population turned out to bid goodbye to the 129th RI on 8 August. What they witnessed, according to twenty-four-year-old philosophy student Etienne Tanty, was drunk and disorderly:

> The weather was sweltering... at 5.45 p.m., when the company was assembled, it was a spectacle which would have been comical, but which was not. It was just lamentable. Two-thirds no longer knew where they were, they lost everything, they turned everything upside down, they could no longer stand up, they showed up half-equipped, screaming.[18]

The overwhelming, gut-wrenching thread running through recollections of mobilization was the anguish of separation. Cossacks were a people well versed in sending their men to war. 'For centuries my people have been... a military nation,' wrote Marina Yurlova. 'Though not professional soldiers, they were in constant training and ready for any emergency... Cossacks, both men and women, have been brought up to believe that... when war is declared that their duty to country, religion, and Tsar becomes something not to be questioned.'[19]

None of this meant that departures were easy. Marina and her fellow villagers walked 3 miles to the station to see the men off. 'Fatigue and desperation and the choking dust made some of the women clutch at the men on horseback.' As the procession moved along, the men sang:

Hey, woman!
Your husband is a Cossack,
And die he surely must.
For country, for religion, for our father Tsar.
The time has come,
The time has come.
Die we must,
Die we must.
Hey! Cossacks, away! Away.[20]

Scenes were even more pathetic when the men leaving were so clearly unsuited to the active service that they might have to face. In Antwerp, Jozef Muls watched 'all those elderly men in their often no longer appropriate military uniforms saying goodbye'. Meanwhile, in Copenhagen Agnes Bremer had been walking about in a state of shock for several days:

At the Storm Bridge, I saw conscripted young people in boats being sailed out to their barracks. They waved at us, and it seemed completely incomprehensible to me... what was the point of sending young people, who were about to start life, to war? Why didn't they send the old people, who had already had their time?[21]

Several Danes departing with the German army had their misery compounded by the fact that this did not feel like their fight. Karl Klemmesen had to bid goodbye to his wife and three-day-old daughter. 'I don't know how I managed to say goodbye to them both,' he later recalled. 'The thoughts were: will you see them again, or will you be a cripple, when you [do?] And what was going to happen to them.'[22]

In Prague, Karel Tůma witnessed the assembling of a regiment in Wenceslas Square: 'I see women crying, while the soldiers are carrying children in their arms. In my mind I'm thinking: children, maybe your dad is carrying you for the last time.'[23] Some 20 miles away, thirteen-year-old Zdeňka Konopáskova's father was a stationmaster at Kladno. She watched local men depart to join the Austro-Hungarian army. 'Already… all the roads in the area, converging on the station, spewed a flood of recruits. With their typical, black suitcases, with frightened children in their arms, they filled the station platform… It is as if they are accompanying the living to the grave.' With her mother and father, Zdeňka watched as isolated episodes of sadness combined to create a wider scene of human tragedy:

> Here the old parents are saying goodbye to their only son. The father firmly shakes his hand and admonishes: 'Watch out for yourself and write often!' The mother, with tears, crosses and kisses him, begging the virgin Mary, so that she will protect her only child, she secretly slips a talisman of some kind into his pocket… There, a woman with three children. She lifts up one after the other and puts them in the arms of her husband, so that he can kiss them for the last time. The children, silent and frightened, widen their gullible eyes filled with tears, hard for them to understand what a tragic moment this is for them, they see only how the mother throws herself crying onto the chest of the father, who then disappears inside the carriage filled with the noisy mass of the conscripts. Maybe he'll disappear forever.[24]

Similar, heartbreaking scenes were playing out in rural Russia. 'My God, how many tears were spilt when we had to go,' wrote Ivan Kuchernigo:

> My five-year-old daughter sat in my arms and, pressing against me, said 'Daddy, why are you going? Why are you leaving us? Who's going to earn money and get bread for us?' Her little arms clasped me about the neck and tightly, tightly hugged me. I heard the beating of her little heart, and heard her lips begin to kiss my neck. I couldn't answer her questions, and couldn't hold back my own tears, and just answered, 'I'll be home soon, baby.'[25]

*

For the British Expeditionary Force, mobilization was complicated by the need to get some 80,000 men across the English Channel. In the years leading up to 1914, the army and the Royal Navy had worked out in minute detail how they would land this force. Instead of heading for the Belgian ports, or Calais, they would be making a longer, less obvious journey to the French harbours at Havre, Boulogne or even Rouen. At Avonmouth, in the south-west of England, most of the heavy transport was being embarked:

> Outside the dock gates, by all the approach roads into the little town, there were streaming in hundreds upon hundreds of great motor lorries... The organisation of it!... You picture a vividly green lorry of a big whisky distillery up north, axle to axle with the scarlet of a Brixton firm with its blatant advertisement of somebody's corsets. 'Can't you imagine Tommy's comments when he finds a Johnnie Walker van bringing up his ammunition in the wilds of Belgium,' was the general remark, 'but I suppose they'll give them a coat of paint first.' They didn't, as a matter of fact; at least not for several months.[26]

It was 'a period of extreme psychological tension' for Winston Churchill as First Lord of the Admiralty as the BEF prepared to cross the Channel.[27] The navy had envisaged every worst-case scenario: an attempted German invasion or a naval raid on the transports. There were to be no convoys. Instead, vessels were to sail in no more than pairs, as and when they were ready to leave. The navy kept a cautious distance. The system of cover was based on closing both ends of the Channel against raids. The only failsafe for the troops crossing to the continent was the Life Saving Patrol, small craft cobbled together and pressed into service, waiting to fish men out of the water if the enemy managed to slip into the Channel. On 12 August, the main bulk of the BEF began embarking, and would continue to do so for nearly a week. Accordingly, the Grand Fleet sailed out into the North Sea to guard against the sudden emergence of the German High Seas Fleet.

Some 250 ships had to be requisitioned to carry the BEF, and the quality varied greatly. A man might find himself on an ocean liner built for comfort, or a tramp steamer that leaked. The *Seahound,* an Irish cattle boat, was filthy and still smeared with animal faeces. Those that could brave the cold stayed out on deck rather than sleep down below during the crossing. Army Service Corps officer Herbert Stewart was also uninspired when he passed through the dock gates at Southampton on the morning of 11 August, came along the wharf and found a tramp steamer dubbed the *Seven Seas.* 'There were no crowds, all goodbyes had been said outside the dock gates, and the dingy little steamer, our crowded condition on her decks, and our very meagre field kits, brought home to us the great errand on which we were bound.'[28] There was silence when the engine-bell clanged and the men felt the first throb of the engines. The cheer sending them on their way was muted, limited to the embarkation staff and dockworkers.

Intelligence Officer George Fletcher was luckier, and painted a rather more romantic picture of his departure on board a small ocean liner. 'You can well imagine the sailing of our transport… on a perfect summer evening down Southampton water was a thing that can never be forgotten.' His elder brother was an officer in the Royal Navy and George had consummate faith in its protective powers. 'We knew that we were safe in the hands of the navy after the lights of England had disappeared.' Herbert Stewart felt a similar sentiment when his transport passed a single destroyer about its business:

As she drew abreast the sailors whipped off their caps and cheered; the soldiers on *Seven Seas* swarmed up the rigging and returned their cries; then the ship cheerfully disappeared over the horizon with a wave from the commander. Her advent, however, gave us a feeling of security, and we felt that though the British navy was out of sight yet our safety had been considered and provided for.[29]

Far away, on *Canopus*, Captain Heathcoat Grant was nervous. 'We were in constant expectation of an attack… One misty morning it was confidently reported that three enemy cruisers were standing directly for us, and their appearance was sufficient to warrant all hands being at their action stations, until the doubtful craft were satisfactorily made out to be three of our own destroyers.'[30] Meanwhile, on *Agamemnon*, Midshipman Denham was bored of going back and forth. 'To cover against what? No one could explain. There was no sign of the enemy.'[31]

The last significant day saw thirty-four vessels make the crossing. In a week, little had occurred to panic the authorities. The tiny size of the BEF compared to the French and German contingents, which numbered in the millions, meant that the enemy's attitude was let them come. Some 80,000 men hardly threatened to derail German war plans. The Imperial German Navy, the *Kaiserliche Marine*, aware that it was outgunned by its British counterpart, knew exactly what would happen if they tried to disrupt the transportation. It was not worth the risk. 'We could only interfere with it at the price of a decisive battle with the English fleet,' wrote Admiral Reinhard Scheer.[32]

*

Throughout the world, some people found themselves in the wrong place at the wrong time as war was declared. In the Grand Hotel in Paris, a note was posted at the counter: 'Germans and Austrians are kindly requested to leave the hotel without delay.'[33] The displaced persons who were arguably the easiest to deal with were tourists. They had homes to go to, and they wanted to return. They had just had the misfortune to find themselves abroad when the world caught fire. The problem was, though, that many of these tourists did not have the means or the connections to find their way home under the circumstances. In Germany, there was suddenly no post, while telegrams had to be sent exclusively in German, and were liable for censorship. Letters of credit and traveller's cheques were no longer valid.

The obvious port of call for any citizen in distress was an embassy, and across Europe these were suddenly inundated. This was, after all, the height of the tourist season. Myron Herrick was the American ambassador in Paris. Most of those arriving at his door did not have passports, because people did not usually need them in 1914. Herrick and his staff had to design forms, print them up and issue them to people who were able to prove, somehow, that they were American citizens. Eric Fisher Wood was in Paris and immediately volunteered at the embassy. He watched as men and women blustered and made demands:

> Most of them… announced to no one in particular that it was their right to see 'their Ambassador' in person. They demanded information! They needed money!… What was 'the government' going to do about sending them home? Was Paris safe? Would there be immediate attacks by Zeppelins? Could they deposit their jewels in the Embassy vaults? Were passports necessary? WHY were passports necessary? They asked the same questions over and over, and never listened to the answers.[34]

In Berlin, the American ambassador James Gerard was undergoing a similar ordeal. He was buying steerage tickets in bulk, 200 or 300 at a time, and they were resold by his female volunteers, even given away to those with no funds. Typically, not everyone was grateful for the help that they received:

> One morning an American woman spoke to me and said she would consent to go home on one of [our] ships provided she was given a state-room with a bath and Walker-Gordon milk for her children, while another woman of German extraction used to sit for hours in a corner of the ball-room, occasionally exclaiming aloud, with much feeling, 'O God, will them ships never come?'[35]

One woman went on a hunger strike because she did not want to travel steerage. They sat her in a rocking chair in the lunch room and she abandoned her protest within a few hours. The most ludicrous demand belonged to the woman who wanted a written guarantee that their ship would not be sunk by a submarine. They made out a certificate to keep her quiet.

Aside from tourists, who were merely having to change their plans, across the world people who had emigrated at some point in their lives now found themselves unwelcome or unsafe. Italy was still officially an ally of Germany and Austria–Hungary, so thousands of Italian workers in France were given twenty-four hours to leave. As a result, neighbouring Switzerland experienced a massive influx of Italian refugees. By 10 August, the southern canton of Ticino alone had recorded an incredible 188,000 people moving towards the Italian peninsula. Spaniards who worked as labourers in France also saw their livelihoods implode. They poured south over the border in their thousands, to the extent that Spanish towns and local councils put them up in shelters and tried to reintegrate them back into their towns of origin.

Germans in Belgium ran for the Netherlands. By 3 August, the Dutch border town of Roosendaal was experiencing an invasion of its own as endless carts rolled into town. 'For a week, droves of German citizens cross the border,' wrote a local. 'They are loaded with suitcases, chests, baskets and makeshift bags… Among them are Jews of German nationality who have lived in Antwerp for years. I hear one ask a police officer in half-Flemish, half-German: "Can we stay here for the time being? We have at least four weeks' worth of money with us." The decent man says he has lived in Antwerp for thirty years and has now been forcibly driven home.'[36]

As soon as Japan declared war against Germany, all Japanese people were imprisoned in the latter, supposedly for their own safety. Eventually it was arranged to get them out via Switzerland. Even members of a Siamese legation were treated badly. The explanation? They looked so like the Japanese to their European hosts that it was a case of mistaken identity. Regardless, 'for a long time [they] did not dare move about freely in Berlin or even leave their houses'.[37] For some, the forced migration and upheaval was too much: 'Mrs Anna-Catherine Schneider,' reported *Le Petit Journal*, 'born May 29, 1858, in… Germany and residing *Rue Grange-aux Belles*, committed suicide this morning at four o'clock.'[38] The fifty-six-year-old had thrown herself from her fifth-floor bedroom window. Anna had been told that she was to be sent away from her home in Paris to a detention camp.

Some of the repatriation journeys endured were torrid. Copenhagen was full of Russians hoping to return home. Some 1,400 of them on one train suffered a particularly miserable adventure. 'Many dragged all their earthly possessions along in suitcases or bundles. It was a sad sight to see the distraught masses. Old people with white hair, who dragged themselves along, dead tired. Crowds of women with fear painted on their faces, babbling children, who didn't understand a word of it all.'[39] They described having been given twelve hours to get out of the country before they would be imprisoned.

Travelling in the same direction, a Danish woman visiting family in East Prussia experienced the rough treatment foreigners in Germany were subjected to first hand, when her train to Berlin was stopped by a platoon of soldiers looking for Russians. 'The windows were opened and the curtains drawn. We were all then ordered to stand up and stand with our backs to the windows. At every door stood an officer, and on every side outside and inside there were soldiers pointing loaded guns at us. "Whoever turns around will be shot."'[40]

Few people, however, could have told a story like that of Anna Gibbs. A German emigrant, when she stepped off *Campania* in New York in November 1914, she was dressed all in black and accompanied by her daughter. Her cousin had come to meet her, and on seeing her clothes he only had one question. *Where were her other two children?* At this point, Anna burst into tears, pointed at little Martha, and cried: 'She is all I have.'[41]

Born in East Prussia, Anna returned to Europe with her three children in summer 1914 to see her sister, who lived in the Russian border town of Wirballen. On the outbreak of war, Anna panicked. 'The people were all leaving town before the German soldiers should come, as they were afraid of the Uhlans.' Anna claimed that she set off on 2 August, with the intention of a three-day walk to Vilna, where she had friends and where she could escape the Russo-German frontier, where skirmishes were already breaking out. Unfortunately, she got lost. 'I found that we were right in the midst of the Russian soldiers, and that I had walked in the wrong direction.'[42] The soldiers jumped up, grabbed the children and ushered them all to safety.

'I spent the night... with my children looking up at the stars,' claimed Anna. She had noticed that her son was running a slight fever the day before. 'In the night he became worse, owing to the noise of the guns and the exposure, and died in my arms at dawn.'[43] Curtis Gibb died aged seven on what would become the Eastern Front.

When the fighting ceased, Anna picked up her son's body, and with four-year-old Anna and three-year-old Martha clinging to her skirts, she went to find her sister:

The place seemed deserted so I walked on until I came to an undertaker's shop which I entered and called out to see. If anyone was there. No reply came. So I found a coffin, laid out my boy in it and carried it on my shoulder to the house of my brother-in-law. They had all gone too so I dug a grave in the soft soil in the garden and put the coffin into it. I had no strength to do more and the children were crying for food.[44]

Anna did not feel like going anywhere for the next few days, then she tried once again to walk to Vilna. Aided by rides on passing farmers' carts, she made it in three days, but her namesake daughter did not. Little Anna died of a combination of exposure and hunger. Her mother buried her in a little cemetery at Vilna: 'By this time I had become inured to hardship and sorrow. I did not care for my own life, but I was determined to bring my youngest child, Martha, back to her father.'[45] From Vilna she travelled to Petrograd by train. There she applied for an American passport to get her home. In Finland, she was lucky enough to meet an older American woman who lent her some money and they crossed the Atlantic together. Finally, at Gothenburg, an American government official bought her passage to New York via England. The description of her journey is supported at every turn by official documents.

*

Perhaps the most distasteful journeys were inflicted on people who had spent their lives in a country, only to be labelled outcasts in 1914. Elsa Cahen was living a comfortable life in a leafy Paris suburb. She had a British father and Irish mother, and had been raised in Paris before marrying an Austrian. She considered all of these countries 'home'.

Rumour immediately had it that they would be forced to leave Paris. 'Since dawn I have been packing, the garden is full of boxes, paper and disorder. Our neighbours... will take charge of some boxes in which I have put our silver and valuables... But we must smuggle the things in the evening over the walls which separate our gardens, so that the neighbours may not see.'[46] On 5 August Elsa learnt their fate. 'We are to be transported, evacuated, exposed, whichever you like, to... Normandy... Only hand luggage is allowed.'[47] The family left their home less than a week after the declaration of war. 'The half empty cups on the table, the teapot still warm... shall we ever return? We got up early to get away before our friends came to go with us. We were ashamed, laden as we were with boxes, baskets, knapsacks, and bags. We looked like unhappy emigrants.'[48]

A large crowd was loaded into cattle trucks like animals and from then on their dignity continued to ebb. 'We were counted like a flock of sheep.'[49] They were not allowed out at halts. 'After several hours, the doors were opened, and we could get out and a hurrying crowd flung itself, women to right, men to left.' Crammed into the cattle trucks, these undesirables were terrified:

> It became dark, we had no lights, and the children were very tired. I sat on the ground. They all three crept to me, laid their heads in my lap and fell asleep in spite of the dreadful wrenching and vibration of the springless wagon. It was remarkable how cold it became. I could just about recognize still the silhouette of grandpapa's poor head which nodded mightily in his sleep... it is hard at this age to pass through all this. In my corner of the floor I felt utterly miserable. I covered the children as well as I could. Through the narrow windows the telegraph posts rushed past in the shadow of the night. What was to become of us?[50]

The French government had rapidly opened a dozen detention camps, and the Cahen family arrived at one 40 miles south of Caen. Men and women were separated on the platform by soldiers. Housed in a convent, the conditions were cramped, but Elsa emphasized that at the beginning, they were 'treated with the greatest consideration and kindness'. Elsa took to sitting out in the garden to avoid the stuffiness of the long dormitory housing women and their howling children. It almost felt like 'a kind of forced summer holiday, which was not so very unpleasant'. But then the first wounded soldiers arrived in the town and people looked at them differently, 'became bitter... and we felt no longer safe when we went out'. Living in a room with twenty strangers wore thin quickly:

> I wash myself either in darkness, or very early when nobody is awake. A horrible two-year-old called Felix sleeps near me, he has not been properly trained and must be consistently attended to, and the windows always closed. I get up at night and open one, very quietly, just as quietly soon after, my anxious stuffy neighbour gets up and closes it, that goes on till one or other of us gets so tired that she falls asleep.

On 4 September they were told to pack again. 'Where to? No answer.' The locals cursed and abused them, and they once again climbed into cattle wagons. 'To our horror... the railwaymen had used them as a WC.' Now they were told they were being sent 500 miles south to the Pyrenees. Elsa did not sleep. 'There are a good many in our wagon... We were all crowded together like sheep... All my fellow travellers were still asleep, dirty and pale on the ground.' Locals en route took them for Belgian refugees and Elsa and her fellow passengers were not about to correct them when they were given food. After a second night in their cattle wagon, they were turned out of the train after passing Lourdes.

> We are tired, hungry, dirty and hot, and let ourselves be led to the market house dumb and passive... We mothers with children have been brought to a gymnasium... We got nothing to eat, our baggage was held back... For fear of fire no light was allowed, so that it was quite dark when we got some straw and spread it out on the floor. In the darkness the women quarrelled, the hungry children howled. One could not move without touching somebody, it was pandemonium. Added to that came a thunderstorm... Many cried out in terror, and the thunder rolled and growled.

A final 10-mile journey in hay carts and the group reached Garaison, 65 miles south-west of Toulouse, where they were to live at another convent. That evening, Elsa reached one of her lowest points:

> No preparation had been made for us... towards evening, it was announced straw has arrived... like wild beasts, the 'ladies' flung themselves upon the great heaps and tore and scratched and fought with each other, it was hateful. The soldiers had to insist on order. I satisfied myself with making a bundle of what others in their haste had lost... It was really a fight for existence.

The plight of Elsa and immigrants all over the world was a war of its own kind. A fight for survival, a fight for dignity, all based on where they happened to have been born and where they lived. There was also the terrifying question of what they might eventually return home to. In mid-September Elsa's sister sent bedding, towels and winter clothes, but warned that that would be the last time she would be allowed into their home to retrieve things. The house had been seized by the government, along with everything Elsa's family had in the bank.[51]

2

The German Locomotive

Luxembourg and Belgium

Tiny Luxembourg would fit into Belgium more than ten times, and so, unsurprisingly, on the outbreak of war nobody expected the Grand Duchy to mount any opposition to a massive, neighbouring army. Paul Eyschen had been the prime minister since 1888. He was experienced enough to know that nobody coveted his territory as a possession. Instead, his neighbours were concerned with the Luxembourg Gap, the most obvious route between Germany and France, and unfortunately for Eyschen, that meant that at least one of them was about to try to march through his country.

The attitude of most Luxembourgers towards Prussia meant that people anticipated trouble from that direction. However, in August 1914, the Germans arrived so quickly that the population was stunned. They thought that mobilization, concentration and then a march would buy time for their government to negotiate. 'While they were thus turning the matter over in their minds, there came the thunder-clap.' English writer Francis Gribble was staying in the picturesque town of Vianden, right on Luxembourg's German frontier. He watched the border closed at the nearby village of Roth. 'The first serious symptom was the glittering helmet of a very fat gendarme, whom we saw toiling laboriously up the hill towards us... [He] gravely got off his bicycle and, with equal gravity, fastened a steel chain across the road... between him and us. That was the formal closing of the frontier.'[1]

In military terms, the Grand Duchy commanded no respect from the German war planners. Without any declaration of war, troops crossed the frontier in the early hours of 2 August. At 9.00 a.m. a locomotive pulled into Trois Vierges station in north Luxembourg pulling nine wagons laden with rails and a company of German engineers, who began jumping down onto the platform as if they owned the place. Their officer marched up to the stationmaster and demanded the surrender of the telegraph apparatus. Whereupon, apparently, the stationmaster picked up the biggest movable part he could lift and dramatically threw it at him. He missed completely, but this, if true, was the sum total of any violent act at this point by a Luxembourger. The invasion was over as soon as it had begun.

At first, Luxembourg was assured that it was all a mistake and over-exuberance on some unnamed officer's part, but meanwhile, German guards had begun taking up positions on bridges. 'Patrols criss-crossed the road in all directions; sentries were placed in the post office buildings.'[2] As soon as Eyschen heard that the bridges on the Moselle and the Sure rivers were barred, he demanded that both France and Germany respect the Grand Duchy's neutrality. Neither answered him. They did not need to: Luxembourg only had some 300 soldiers to its name, 'employed mostly in the postal service, the railways and foundries or growing wheat, wine and roses'.[3] Ordinarily they formed a palace guard and a band, and the invaders dealt with them mainly by locking them in their barracks. '[They] could no more withstand the Prussian army than a kitten could hold a staircase against a pack of hounds. Why bother to be ceremonious with such a helpless crew?'[4]

There were inevitably Luxembourgers who were pro-German, or at least not anti-German. Children, for one, were impressed by the sight of soldiers, and 'gathered round them in an admiring ring'. The border town of Vianden had two fiercely pro-German citizens, and they were not popular. One retired tanner proudly hung a German flag outside his house and lent the invaders his car. A wily old woman kept the peace when she convinced him to take the flag down on the basis that he might get bombed if the

Allies thought it was a headquarters, but it was soon out again. Then there was the chemist. He was regarded as an oddity, and would pontificate about politics to his customers along the lines of: 'I have no objection whatever to the inclusion of Luxembourg in the German Empire on the same terms as, say, the Grand Duchy of Baden. We already have all the disadvantages of belonging to Germany, and we may as well have the advantages also.' His argument was not appreciated by the vast majority of his neighbours.[5]

As for the German troops themselves, most of them bore little animosity to the Luxembourgers. Some of them admitted freely that they had no idea what they were doing in the country and that they wanted to go home. Passing Saxons were seen weeping on the shoulders of a large, matronly woman at Vianden. 'Nothing could have been less like an arrogant procession of bloodthirsty barbarians, marching through raping and plundering to the overthrow of civilization.'[6] According to Gribble, the Saxons in question were by no means the only ones who wanted no part of this war. Yet war was upon them all. As traumatic as this all was, Luxembourgers put up no resistance. The loss of their freedom was bloodless. For the people of Belgium however, who were about to try to stand their ground rather than see their territory violated, the German invasion was going to be a brutal experience.

*

Belgium presented a bigger stumbling block than Luxembourg, both in terms of its standing as a nation and its ability to put up some kind of resistance. The German representative in Brussels put an ultimatum in the hands of the Belgian foreign minister on 2 August. It was an unsubtle attempt at bullying a smaller nation. The document not only outlined why German troops had no choice but to march across the border, but claimed they must do so before any other foreign army could. It then proceeded to demand something referred to as 'benevolent neutrality'. In other words, Belgium must stand aside and let Germany use the country as a thoroughfare to invade France, before France invaded Germany. This would not be neutral behaviour by any stretch of the imagination. If, however, Belgians so much as fired a shot, or did anything else to halt this German procession, they would be deemed enemy combatants and would be dealt with accordingly. The benevolence was only supposed to occur in one direction. An emphatic response went back to Berlin in a matter of hours, declining to accept such terms. Belgium's neutrality was not a preference, it was a long-standing promise, guaranteed by Great Britain, France, Prussia, Russia and Austria, and it was on this basis that, when Germany invaded, Belgium appealed to the other powers for aid.

In the meantime, Belgians watched the shared border with a growing feeling of dread, and with good reason. Belgium had been guilty of a certain laziness when it came to military affairs. With their paper guarantee that they would be kept out of any war, why spend vast amounts of money on training and equipping an army when five massive powers were backing her not to get involved? They had a written assurance that war was impossible. Except now it apparently was very possible indeed. Belgium could never hope to match Germany militarily, but the army was in a much worse state than it could have been. As well as a shortage of men, there was a complete lack of heavy artillery. Reforms in 1913 had acknowledged these issues, but guns, detonators and fuses were still only on order when the German ultimatum was delivered, and the orders for material were actually mainly with German firms. The Belgian army boasted just 102 machine-guns. So, when the Kaiser's men crossed the border, the Belgians were deficient in men, material, adequate training and experience. The only thing the army had going for it was sheer defiance and an unrealistic belief in the ranks that their determination to protect their homeland would prevail.

*

Strategy is planning how a war is waged. Tactics are how you physically put that plan into action. In terms of the former, in August 1914, seven German armies were going west. Only one was initially sent to protect the East Prussian border with Russia.

Germany's worst-case scenario was fighting a prolonged war on two fronts at once, and officers had spent much time prior to 1914 working on how they might avoid this in a future war. Their ideas had developed, but were still named after their original architect, Count Alfred von Schlieffen. The plan was based on the belief that Russia would be slow to mobilize, and so they settled on the idea of attacking her ally, France, first. Sweeping through Belgium in an arc, they would come crashing down on Paris. Finishing up in the west quickly, they could then turn all of their strength to face the tsar's vast manpower.

Earlier in 1914, General Helmut von Moltke, supreme commander of the German armies, had declared that in the event of war, he wanted to crush the French in six weeks. Success was going to hinge on speed. Seven armies formed an overwhelming force, but that created its own issues. The Germans had no practical experience of operating on such a massive scale. Moving such vast numbers of men, feeding them, equipping them and putting them into battle had never been done before. It was all theory. The flow of troops and supplies required was staggering, and delays might be potentially catastrophic to operations.

Railways were utterly vital to the war plans of all combatants in August 1914. Germany possessed almost 30,000 locomotives, which ran on some 40,000 miles of track and pulled almost seven million wagons. Plans to utilize this infrastructure in the event of a war had been painstakingly organized. An army corps required 141 trains pulling 6,010 wagons, 170 carriages for officers, 965 for the men, 2,960 horse wagons and 1,915 more for equipment. In August 1914, there were some dozen corps heading for Belgium alone.

As soon as the war began, little Aachen, the last town before the border with Belgium, was transformed into a military hub. The local population was amazed. 'For weeks the regiments moved through here like a rolling wave on the sea, without beginning, without end,' wrote one woman. 'Soldiers, horses, ammunition columns, supply trains... artillery, engineers and then hundreds of vehicles... One could not believe it... Everything had been thought of... this ocean of people followed an invisible lead, calm, serious, teeth clenched.'[7] 'All roads were filled,' added one conscript. 'Regiment after regiment. In front of us, behind us, at the sides, everywhere the long, long columns thronged incessantly towards the Belgian frontier.'[8]

Rejecting Germany's ultimatum, Belgium took matters a step further and decided to make a stand against invasion. The Belgian army vastly outnumbered the British contingent in August 1914. Excepting those garrisoning fortresses, on paper it numbered just short of 120,000 men. As for what to do with them, King Albert, placed in command by the constitution, favoured caution. He wanted to make a stand along a strategic position on the River Meuse. However, he knew that the strength of the German force they would face would inevitably prevail, and so his plan was to subsequently retreat to the fortress city of Antwerp to wait for Allied intervention, having done all he could to delay an invasion force but stopping short of exposing his army to complete annihilation. Such determination was unexpected. On 4 August Germany's representative in Brussels, Herr von Strum, appeared to be baffled by Belgium's determination to defend her borders. 'These poor stupid Belgians!' he declared to his American counterpart. 'Why don't they get out of the way? It will be like laying a baby on the track before a German locomotive!'[9]

Belgians understood exactly how important railways were to the German war plans. Belgium possessed the densest railway network in the world, among it those key lines connected to Aachen that would make it possible for the invading army to carry men, horses and supplies. The German war plan was only viable if the army had unfettered access to the dense network of tracks running back and forth across the shared border with Belgium and south into France. Invading armies need constant reinforcements, food for men and horses, and ammunition. The German army had a number of engineer units specifically geared to tend to these railways, comprising some 26,000 men. Twelve dedicated trains were ready to deploy, loaded with sleepers, miles of track, pre-constructed bridges and everything needed to repair sabotage. Having been cast in the role of plucky underdog, it became a certainty that when the German ultimatum was rejected, Belgium would attempt to delay the enemy by attacking its own transport network. The ultimatum had even warned against this exact type of subterfuge, because it was such an obvious move.

As early as 31 July the Belgians began turning a destructive eye towards the railways, but although this sabotage had been part of army doctrine since 1895, rather than a tactical plan to be executed in the event of war, it was a vague concept. Then railway directors were summoned to meet military engineers, and on the night of 3 August they were ordered to start destroying their livelihoods. Tunnels and bridges were prime targets. According to German reports, bolts holding the rails in place on the sleepers were removed, the heads of screws were sawn off and replaced to make them look normal, and signs were removed to cause confusion. Far more dramatically, lines were obstructed by deliberately wrecking locomotives. A section of rail, often inconveniently located deep inside a tunnel, would be removed. The engines, sometimes a dozen, were then run into those tunnels at full speed, their crews jumping clear at the last moment, before their precious charges came to grief and blocked the line. Most of these locomotives were usually employed to pull heavy freight trains. At the crucial Verviers-Est near the border, two 48-ton monsters were toppled over in the tunnel. The results were not always as destructive as hoped, but addressing the damage took precious time that the invaders could ill afford to waste.

For the men who drove and shovelled fuel into these beasts, and agonized over their timetables as they coaxed them back and forth daily, what they were being asked to do was hateful. Arthur Pasquier begged for a reprieve for his locomotive, *Cuckoo*. 'The poor little machine spits flames through its chimney, so much does it want to give life force to the wagons it sends. And what reward?' Pasquier could not bear to watch it intentionally smashed. 'My love of machines strikes me to the heart: we are going to kill the only locomotive in which I have ever travelled.

I intercede for it... "Colonel, don't you think we might still need it?"[10] Whatever he said worked. *Cuckoo* was saved from being launched into oblivion.

Beginning on 4 August, along Belgium's roads, German infantry was followed by cyclists and automobiles, driven with one hand while nervous chauffeurs brandished revolvers with the other. By 10.00 a.m. on that day, the German columns had passed around enough felled trees and makeshift barricades to realize that this was not going to be a case of a simple route march. The ordinary soldiers carrying out the invasion were still none the wiser about what they were doing. The men of one engineer battalion were clueless when they were hauled out of bed by an officer and propelled across the border: 'He told us we were at war with Belgium,' wrote an ordinary sapper who published an anonymous book in 1917, talking about the beginning of the war. 'That we should acquit ourselves as brave soldiers, earn iron crosses, and do honour to our German name.' That was simple enough. Then the speech got rather convoluted:

> The lives and property of civilians are under the protection of international law, but you soldiers must not forget that it is your duty to defend your lives... for the protection of your Fatherland, and to sell them as dearly as possible. We want to prevent useless shedding of blood as far as the civilians are concerned, but I want to remind you that a too great considerateness borders on cowardice, and cowardice in face of the enemy is punished very severely.[11]

Baffled by what exactly all of that conflicting sentiment meant in practice, the men were instructed to give three cheers as they crossed the frontier. It began to dawn on them all that this was not like training. Somewhere out there in the unknown, strangers wanted them dead.

*

The small Belgian town of Visé, situated on the Meuse, attracted all manner of Belgian, German and Dutch holidaymakers. In August 1914, however, the town had the misfortune to sit directly in the path of the invader. In fact, it was imperative for the Germans that they should seize it and get across the river at this point. On 1 August, the Belgian 12e Regiment de Ligne began arriving to defend the town. In command, Major Charles Collyns was under no illusion as to the importance of his task. His unit was still mid-mobilization when his orders came, and so he sprinted to the barracks, pulled together the 400 men he found, and boarded a train.

At Visé, Collyns's force was spread thin, but his men were keen. Much of 3 August was spent blocking roads, but most importantly, planting explosives on the bridges crossing the Meuse. They needed to delay the German army from crossing the river for as long as possible, but when the order to blow the bridges came, despite a lot of noise, the crossing at Visé was still comfortably passable. Watching civilians had the audacity to snigger at their failure, and Collyns made himself feel better by shouting at them. He then telephoned through to his superiors in the city of Liège 10 miles away with an urgent request for more explosives. 'The wait was endless… Finally, here were some cars… This time, the explosion was formidable.'[12] Huge blocks of stone were propelled nearly 700 feet through the air. The central part of the bridge shuddered and then collapsed into the Meuse.

The following day, the Germans were attempting to get around Liège both to the south and the north. They hoped to encircle the city, and on the latter route sat Visé. Collyns had no idea what to do next. The explosions had ruptured all communications. The bridges were down. Should he return to Liège for the next job? Or defend the river crossing? None of the couriers he sent to ask for orders returned. 'Too bad, my decision is made: I am there, I stay there.'[13] At dawn on 4 August, Collyns was placing men in the houses along the west bank of the river. Supported by the guns at nearby Fort Pontisse, the 12th Regiment settled down to wait and see what would happen next. The vanguard of the German invasion, cavalry, reached Visé at lunchtime:

> My soldiers, anxious, their hearts beating, their finger on the trigger, follow them with their eyes. 'Wait,' I said, 'wait, let them approach.' When I saw them at the first part of the bridge, I yelled 'Fire!'... The gunfight crackles. Frightened, the horses cower, struggle; riders roll in the river; others, turning back, throw themselves into the following ranks, jostle them and, in a frantic race, escape through the fields of clover and oats. What a stampede! At this moment, an intense fire started from the houses on the [east] bank, near the bridge. It was the Germans who, without our knowledge, occupied these buildings.[14]

Things at Visé took a more serious turn with the arrival of enemy artillery. Collyns's men did not even have a machine-gun. He continued to encourage them, but their situation inevitably deteriorated in the face of overwhelming odds. By early evening, part of his hugely outnumbered battalion was pinned down by artillery fire and retreat looked to be the only option. Their left flank had caved in and they risked being cut off. The retirement was carried out in good order, protected by rearguards. Disgusted as they were to lose the town, the men of the 12th departed the scene singing 'The Lion of Flanders'. They were not beaten yet.

*

For many of those fighting in the early days of the war, it was their first time under fire. The anonymous German sapper attempted to sum up the conflicting emotions 'swimming' through his mind when he heard bullets fly for the first time.[15] He remembered being determined to convince everyone around him that he was not afraid, though he doubted that he succeeded. The knowledge that he might die at any moment caused events to become muddled; time slowed down and then sped up. He found that he tried to reason with himself about his chances. First he tried to convince himself that by the time he reached the fight, he would not be needed. Then he reminded himself that statistically, most wounds were apt to be mere flesh wounds. He actually found that rationalizing helped, however nonsensical the things he told himself. The very act of keeping his mind busy distracted him from the danger he was in.

Then he witnessed two men die in front of him. Any resolve that he had built up, any distractions that had calmed him now evaporated in the face of dead comrades. 'I was seized by a terrible horror... I had completely lost command over myself and was absolutely incapable to think or act.'[16] Once he began shooting, though, there were no more thoughts. His training kicked in. He was in a semi-conscious state where all of his senses were heightened and his movements became mechanical. It was almost like an out-of-body experience, a feeling of weightlessness: 'I was seized by an irrepressible excitement, took hold of my gun, and began to fire away blindly... Suddenly I found myself content with myself and my surroundings, and when a little later the whole line was commanded, "March, march!" I ran forward demented like the others.'[17]

So far as the Belgian population was concerned, their reactions to the invasion ranged from impressed, to bemused, stunned or enraged. Serjeant Haars was part of a German patrol sent towards Argenteau. 'The only thing that was striking was that the people in the villages stood curiously and shaking their heads along the roads and made fun of us, as if no one took the war seriously.' Others were more wary. 'At a farm we observed people cutting down a tree. They ran away in fright and hid in the houses as we approached.'[18] There were protests, too. 'In Dalhem we were received by a large crowd, who with shouts expressed their anger at the march in. It didn't worry us.'[19]

Far from finding Belgium a cowed nation, the Germans were discovering that their enemy was not behaving in the way they anticipated. Once it became clear that Belgium was not going to grant their armies free passage through her territory, the Germans believed that they would need to closely follow their opponents in short bursts, always preventing the Belgians from occupying a new position and putting up adequate defences. But they found that the defenders had no intention of establishing themselves in fixed positions. As soon as the Germans found them, they skilfully disengaged and moved off again. Cleverly, they were delaying the advance without exposing themselves to pitched battles against a superior foe. They improvised – utilizing buildings, slinging up barricades, using the terrain to their advantage – and it meant that there was no opportunity for the Germans to stop, regroup and then continue. Instead, they stumbled on, always chasing a foe who then evaporated out of their grasp. The invasion of Belgium, for the ordinary German soldier, was a disorientating venture, punctuated with moments of heightened confusion and fear as they found themselves pursuing a spectral enemy:

> We had to walk. [This] was… felt by us to be a great injustice. And though our scolding and anger did not help us in the least, it turned our thoughts from the heaviness of the 'monkey' (knapsack) which rested like a leaden weight on our backs. The heat was oppressive, the perspiration issued from every pore; the new and hard leather straps, the new stiff uniforms rubbed against many parts of the body and made them sore, especially round the waist.[20]

*

The city of Liège, 60 miles south-east of Brussels, was the gateway to the rest of Belgium, and the Schlieffen Plan hinged on securing its railway infrastructure. The Belgians understood its strategic importance, and a dozen forts had been built around the city. Typically, they comprised tunnels and draughty chambers buried underground, covered with thick layers of concrete and surrounded by a deep ditch. The whole lot was hidden by earth and grass, but the forts bristled with cupolas, exposed just enough for the soldiers to stick their guns above ground level. They boasted heating, ventilation, even indoor showers. When they were built, by the standard of the day, they were the very height of modernity.

The problem was, that day was no later than 1892, when the last of them was completed. Despite its integral role in the country's defence, the fortress ring at Liège was another example of military neglect in Belgium prior to 1914. Everything about the forts had been surpassed technologically, and the Germans were not anticipating much opposition. 'Once our troops are in town,' reasoned Moltke, 'I don't believe the forts will dare to bombard the city and they will probably capitulate.'[21] Taking Liège was entrusted to General Otto von Emmich, a veteran of the Franco-Prussian War. He faced General Gérard Leman, a sixty-three-year-old native of Liège, for whom the complete defence of his own city in the face of an unbeatable enemy was a daunting prospect.

The first damage to Belgian land and Belgian property in the war was caused by the Belgians themselves. Leman ordered his men to begin clearing the landscape for artillery and a field of fire 2,000 feet deep was flattened around each of the forts for observation. Woods and hedges were removed. Homes were also knocked down, 'to the great dismay of their inhabitants'. Understandably so, for people watched as everything they had ever worked for was set on fire. At Boncelles 'the villagers had a quarter of an hour to leave their homes. The order caused a panic. The poor people hastily gathered a few articles and left the condemned village, wheeling the old folk and children in wheelbarrows. They let the cattle loose and drove them away, but many beasts perished in the flames.'[22] By 5 August any surviving walls had been blown up and the village ceased to exist.

Meanwhile, inside Liège itself, the inhabitants were amused by watching livestock being driven into their city. They had all been plucked from the outlying towns and villages that were likely to fall first to the German invader, so that not only would the urban population remain fed, but the enemy was also denied a generous food supply. Paul Hamelius was a professor of English literature at Liège University and was struck by the bizarre din:

The poor cows had suffered... they were frightened at the noise and traffic about them, they had been... irregularly milked, and they kept bellowing plaintively day and night in the meadows and open grounds in which they had been fenced. Many caught fevers, lay down, and died... Through all the human anguish and pain the bellowing of the cattle sounded like the voice of universal suffering in the clutches of a pitiless fate.[23]

All those waiting in the city could do was hope that the ring of forts surrounding them would hold out. They could hear battle raging day and night. Hamelius lay in bed trying to rationalize it all in his head. 'First the boom of distant guns, Fort Boncelles firing... nothing new in that. Then the crackle of musketry... Two pitches, the deeper probably infantry rifles, the higher carbines of the cavalry... All at once, cannon-shot near my house, the window-panes shaking. They must have put a battery on the hill behind the garden.'[24]

Despite the buoyancy of the Belgian troops, soldiers began to retire through Liège as early as 5 August:

Suddenly a number of Belgian cannon drove up the road... Behind the artillery rode a body of lancers... away they went over the hill... Their knapsacks were getting too heavy for them and were dropped on the road side... The road was lined with arms, sacks and military accoutrements which had been abandoned... These were promptly picked up and removed by the city scavengers.[25]

That night, Liège became the first European city to suffer bombardment from above when an airship drifted menacingly into view. The Zeppelins' capability for destruction might have been relatively benign by future standards, but to the people of 1914 they were terrifying. *Z.VI* was 500 feet long. She carried a crew of a dozen men and could travel at almost 40 miles per hour. That night, as she approached through a storm, she carried eight artillery shells. In the early hours of the morning, she floated above the lights of Liège. It was all over in fifteen minutes. A few locals were killed, but no widespread panic ensued, despite what German propaganda later claimed.

*

As well as garrisoning the forts themselves, the Belgian army had the unenviable task of manning more than 30 miles of open ground between them. This unhappy lot fell mainly on 3rd Division. On the night of 5 August, the German plan was to attack the gaps between the eastern forts and rupture the defences connecting them. Columns of men were primed to sneak forward in the early hours and measures had been taken to minimize the confusion in the dark. They had been issued with a white armband so that they might identify comrades and were allocated passwords to exchange. In order to prevent friendly fire, they were to march with their rifles unloaded, relying on bayonets only. Having surrounded Liège, Emmich's men were then to emerge at dawn and race in to preserve vital structures like tunnels, train stations and bridges before they could be sabotaged.

This plan proved to be overambitious. Some columns were running late, and communications had broken down. Those preparing to attack had been marching all day in the height of summer, and were exhausted as storms broke out and darkened the landscape. Generals were anticipating meeting about 6,000 hastily assembled Belgians strung out thinly to cover all of the intervals between the forts. They found the defence much stronger than that, and better prepared than they had hoped. Resistance turned out to be fierce. At Fort Boncelles the order to fire was given and the guns roared to life. Searchlights swung into action. Soldiers manning the parapets aimed down at the Germans rushing towards the shallow trenches below, their rifles flashing as they picked them off. Machine-guns cut through the attacking ranks. The defenders had at least had a day or two to take in their surroundings in daylight. In contrast, the Germans were utterly disorientated. Some of them turned and ran. Fighting with Infanterie Regiment Nr.25 (IR 25) near Fort Barchon, twenty-year-old Second Lieutenant Friedrich-Wilhelm Krüger was confused:

I lay down behind the stump of a tree... Nothing could be discerned... One thing was certain: the enemy was shooting well. One in two men collapsed, dead or injured... very close to me, I could hear the cries: 'I'm in pain!'; 'Help!'; 'Some water!'; 'Mummy!'... 50 yards to my right were two machine-guns... I wanted to support them... I only realized later that they were Belgian machine-guns... One can imagine how dark it was so that I couldn't perceive friend and foe.[26]

As for the Belgians, their first experience of battle was proving terrifying. However many shadowy figures they cut down, more kept coming. At Fort Barchon, the troops plugging the gaps on either side gradually grew more and more demoralized as grey hordes advanced towards them. 'The whole country around, illuminated by dazzling searchlights, quaked as if shaken by a seismic convulsion.' Germans clambered over the dead and dying bodies of their comrades coming towards them 'like the waves of a stormy sea'.[27]

One of the fiercest battles took place between Forts Fléron and Evegnée. To Second Lieutenant Becke of IR 27, the night attack had a strange beauty to it, the flashes of rifle muzzles combining with a bright glow coming from Fléron's guns. They set out soon after midnight. Becke and his comrades found it hard to make their way through the built-up environment and around purposely placed obstructions while trying to stay in any kind of meaningful formation. Nervous men had begun loading their rifles. In the confusion, they opened fire and shot their comrades.

Under a thin veil of drizzle, the battlefield, full of inexperienced troops, descended into chaos. German officers leading the columns became casualties. As for the men, on both sides many of them had been clerks and farmers and students just days ago. They were all exhausted after rushing into action, had little if any idea of where they were, and strangers were bent on killing them. The Belgians were by no means enjoying themselves either. They found that for all their fierce resistance, ammunition was short and nerves began fraying in the face of overwhelming numbers.

Our cartridges are giving out and our rifles are burning our hands... The end is approaching. Eighty yards away we see the flash of German rifles... I fire. I crouch down to reload; a ball goes through my shako at the same moment. I have only fifteen cartridges left. My shots get slower and slower... everyone firing at longer intervals, taking careful aim. The Germans keep on advancing. They have got to within eight or ten yards of us.[28]

German soldiers began surging down the road to Liège, singing, accompanied by trumpets. They found, however, more men determined to mount a resistance in front of them for as long as possible. Four miles away from where Friedrich-Wilhelm Krüger was fighting, his father was in command of IR 27. A catastrophe occurred when a number of staff officers came under sudden artillery fire. The brigade commander Friedrich von Wussow became the first German general to fall in the Great War. Colonel Krüger was also killed by a shell. Emmich's deputy chief of staff, forty-nine-year-old General Erich Ludendorff, was a ruthless man who would stop at nothing to get results. He survived this barrage and was about to make a name for himself. He recalled a confused fight in the darkness. 'I will never forget the very distinct sound of bullets sinking into the human body. We made a few leaps towards the invisible enemy, whose fire was becoming more intense. In the dark, it was not easy to orient ourselves. But, without a doubt, we had taken the wrong way.'[29] He promptly took charge and managed to get matters back on track. Against the odds, the Germans began to advance, and Feldartillerie Regiment Nr.4 turned Howitzers onto the next village in their path. Belgian rifle bullets were pouring towards them, but Captain Friedrich Rübesamen was proud of his work:

In the morning twilight, [we] soon spotted two enemy guns... A shell that passed just above them sent the crews fleeing into the surrounding houses for cover. Shots were raining down from every house, infantry rifles and hunting rifles were being fired at the troops from everywhere... The screams of the defenders clearly indicated the good effect.[30]

By 8.00 a.m. the light was still bad. 'Our advance and the fighting had happened so quickly and with such excitement', wrote Rübesamen, 'that our thoughts had become so confused that many of us now didn't know whether it was morning or evening.[31] And yet, despite the chaos of the German advance, Liège lay sprawled in front of Ludendorff and his men.

Rumours about what was happening in the surrounding countryside flew through the city. Instructions had by now been issued by the local authorities. Circulars from the burgomaster appeared in residents' letterboxes, advising submission if the enemy entered their streets. They were starting to fear the worst. By the morning of 7 August, Ludendorff had realized that the Belgian forces had left Liège without even blowing the bridges across the River Meuse to hinder the German pursuit. At first light, the occupying force entered the city, whereupon he walked up to the Citadel and politely knocked on the door.

*

Away from Liège, the gargantuan task that the Schlieffen Plan had placed on the shoulders of the German army was already apparent. Traffic jams were an immediate issue when units got across the border. The cavalry failed to encircle Liège to the south as planned because they were held up by plodding infantry and a baggage train. These delays meant that the Belgian troops from the gaps between the forts at Liège managed to get away. The River Gette was some 30 miles back from the Meuse and the next logical place to stop and try and mount a defence, but the inexperience of King Albert's army was telling. The retirement was largely disorganized. Desertion was rife. Somewhere between the fall of Liège and reaching the new line, potentially thousands of men wandered off. Others, exhausted, abandoned their equipment, including their rifles, meaning that they were of little use as fighting troops when they did turn up. By mid-August, more than a third of the Belgian army's initial strength had to be chalked off. Meanwhile, the German army was feeling its way westward, sending cavalry out to scout the ground leading up to the Gette. It was a fraught time for the Belgians. The heat was oppressive, made all the more uncomfortable by their thick, dark uniforms. Deprived of proper intelligence, men lived in a perpetual state of anxiety, wondering when they would be attacked.

They were, however, about to receive a huge boost to morale. A significant clash occurred at the village of Haelen, on the left of the Belgian line. It was a particularly vulnerable point held by the army's single cavalry division, including cyclist units. The latter were troublesome enough that the Germans were about to nickname them 'The Black Devils'.

On 12 August, the Germans made a concerted effort to get across the Gette and break the Belgian line outside Haelen. Few could have anticipated just how badly the day would pan out for the German cavalry. While the Belgian commander, Léon de Witte, had his men dismount to fight, German cavalry officers were often snobbish about such a modern concept. Stubbornness is one thing, but it still need not have led to launching numerous suicidal, Napoleonic-style charges at the enemy. Arthur Brühe described what it was like participating in one of them:

> The lance was held level in the right fist; reins held loosely in the left hand. The wild chase began... Many hundreds of hooves trampled the land... The terrain in front had not even been reconnoitred... We horsemen did not know the situation. Nobody had explained it to us. All we knew at Haelen was we had to ride very fast because the Belgian artillery fire was increasing. A hailstorm of steel came raining down on us.[32]

Some of the Belgian positions were not ideal. One group of cyclists were sitting ducks, deployed in the middle of an open field with Germans advancing from Haelen in front of them and their own lancers shooting from behind. In charge, Major Siron was unimpressed. 'My right flank is adjacent to nothing. I'm going to have myself butchered here. I should be covered and my right should be reconnoitred. I see nobody.'[33]

Again, the German cavalry charged. It was an intimidating sight. They bore lances and screamed as they approached in a cloud of dust. German horses were not in optimum condition; slowed down by the oppressive heat and by a lack of oats. Colonel Herman Baltia, the cavalry's chief of staff, was moved by the plight of these animals: 'The moment is tragic, a number of horses wandering at random, mad with terror and pain, red with blood, galloping wildly... panic spreads among them and, at one moment, an immense herd descends in the plain, in the middle of rifle shots and bursts of shrapnel.'[34] The repeated failure of the German charges had a palpable effect. In the square at Haelen, wounded cavalrymen gathered. Nearby, others were putting down horses that could not be saved. General Graf von Schimmelmann sat down on a bench glumly. When an adjutant rode up, bringing the order for his brigade to mount another attack, he responded, 'I do not have a brigade anymore.'[35]

In the afternoon, Belgian infantry arrived. To get to the battle, they had traversed nearly 15 miles in sweltering heat: 'Under the burning midday sun, [they] advanced relentlessly; the dust blinded the men, stuck to the sweat of their faces; a burning thirst parched their throats; the bag and the rifle weighed terribly heavy on the shoulders.'[36] The first men thrown into the fray were met with machine-guns hidden in houses, but on they pressed, and as evening arrived, the Germans began to falter.

The sun sank below the horizon. 'Gradually, the battlefield becomes mute, a veil of darkness, mourning and terror covers this land where so many young men who only yesterday smiled at life, sleep their last sleep, or groan in pain, abandoned.'[37] The ground was littered with the silver helmets of the fallen horsemen that would give the battle its nickname, and the German military machine was learning all the time that the Belgians were no pushovers.

3

The Light Skins' War

Not everything about the opening weeks of the First World War revolved around Europe. Fighting immediately broke out across the world, and everyone assumed that this would be the case. The first British shot of the war is said to have been discharged by a Black man, weeks removed and thousands of miles from what would become the Western Front. War would inflict its misery on people of all ethnicities. Europeans controlled territory throughout the globe, and with perhaps the exception of Belgium, no imperial nation went into the First World War without wanting to gain more. Imperial interests and ambitions were arguably the biggest motivation to go to war.

Without more than two million imperial troops, Britain could not have participated in a global war. France, too, had 90,000 colonial subjects from North and West Africa, Madagascar and Indochina under arms in 1914. Belgium employed indigenous troops in their thousands, with the Congolese *Force Publique* matching the size of the Belgian army in Europe. Even with its comparatively tiny empire, Germany would employ 14,000 Black troops in East Africa alone.

Britain was unique in that it held sway over white dominions. Whether or not they had a choice in going to war is blurred. Britain had substantial control over foreign policy, and dominion defence was tied to her, dependent on her, even. Realistically, the dominions were going to war and really only had control over the extent of what they were prepared to offer in terms of men and material. None of them baulked at the prospect in the end. 'The dominions are as jealous of each other as cats,' remarked one civil servant.[1] Fighting for prominence, Canada pledged 25,000 men. Australia promised 20,000, which they surpassed without compelling anyone to serve. Many Australians still felt a connection to Britain, and from the other side of the world they voiced this loyalty loudly. New Zealand offered 8,000 men for the war effort. People responded with enthusiasm, and even the Maori offered their fighting services, though there were exceptions. Members of the Waikato and Taranaki tribes did not. Burnt by the wars against Britain in the 1860s, they wanted no part of this new conflict. Of the remainder, however, an estimated 1 per cent of all Maori men would die on active service once the authorities withdrew objections to sending them to face white armies. Even tiny Newfoundland, with a population of about 250,000, offered men. The first 106 departed for naval service at the beginning of September. On land, Newfoundland had no more than a few cadet corps, but after a public meeting the dominion pledged to raise 500 more men to serve in the British army. They reached their target within days.

The situation in the Union of South Africa was slightly more complicated. Having only had dominion status since 1910, Prime Minister Louis Botha, an enemy of Britain during the Second Boer War, believed that the only way to unify white South Africa – those of British origin and Afrikaners of German or Dutch heritage – was by working with the British empire. By 1914, he had not achieved this unity, and resentment simmered. Despite this tension, and despite the fact that the Union Defence Force was only just beginning to evolve, Botha committed his country to Britain's war and himself to convincing Afrikaners to fight on the side of their recent enemy.

*

Unlike Britain's dominions, which had some control over their involvement in the war, colonies and protectorates did not. Regardless, the declarations of loyalty continued. Whether or not they should be accepted at face value, however, is a different matter. India was a unique case. The provinces ruled by Britain supplied 85 per cent of the huge number of Indian troops – more than 1 million – who fought in the war. About 120,000 more came from some 560 states ruled by rich princes with titles like maharajah, khan or nizam. The last 100,000 came from a combination of stateless Islamic Pashtun tribesmen, Gurkhas and Afghans ruled by the emir of Kabul.

The viceroy of India unsurprisingly declared that the Raj was ready to support Britain. Some of the princely states were not allowed to provide soldiers, so they offered money, or even ships to transport troops. The maharaja of Gwalior donated 40 motor ambulances, 4,000 horses, thousands of pounds in donations, and combined with the begum of Bhopal to fund a hospital ship.

But fighting a war is a service, and minorities expected something in return. Notables in the Indian National Congress backed the war effort because this might be a glowing opportunity for India. Fighting alongside white troops in Europe, showing loyalty, what might the reward be? Perhaps even dominion status? 'Whatever intrigues Germany may stir up in Turkey,' wrote Bhupendra Nath Bose, president of the Congress, 'Muslim and Hindu in India are alike united in their unswerving devotion and loyalty to the Empire in this crisis.'[2] A forty-four-year-old Mahatma Gandhi stepped ashore in Britain in August 1914, and declared that, 'It was thought desirable by many of us that... those Indians who are residing in the United Kingdom and who can at all do so, should place themselves unconditionally at the disposal of the authorities.' Once again, there was a caveat. India wanted something in return, 'to share the responsibilities of membership of this great Empire, if we could share its privileges'.[3]

Princely and political support is one thing, the support of the people is another. There were undeniable public demonstrations of loyalty in India. People gathered in cities, just as they did in Europe. However, in Calcutta, Robert Palmer, a subaltern in the Hampshire Regiment could not quite work out what indigenous opinion was:

There are hardly any outward indications of what Indians think about the war. But I'm told that they are very much excited, and on the whole keen for us to win. Even the extreme Nationalists are said to take the view that 'it has taken us 100 years to teach the English how to govern us and we can't afford the time to begin again on the Germans'.[4]

In the Punjab, one song revealed that economic considerations were important:

Get enlisted, the recruits who stand out there,
Here you get broken slippers, there you'll get full boots, get
    enlisted,
Here you get torn rags, there you'll get suits, get enlisted,
Here you get dry bread, there you'll get biscuits, get enlisted,
Here you'll have to struggle, there you'll get salutes, get
    enlisted.[5]

Among the soldiers themselves, a British officer recorded his Pashtun troops' response when he asked what they expected from fighting with the Germans. 'The men are very keen,' he wrote, 'though the chief desire is to be allowed to keep any German rifles they capture.' He thought they might have been somewhat conditioned to bloodshed owing to feuds at home, 'but they have never had to lie in the open under shell fire', he mused. 'Still, I think they will do it well. They are fatalists absolutely. Man can only die once, they say, and war is a worthy place to die.'[6]

However, there is evidence of dissent against the war in India, too. 'Oh men in arms why are you supporting my oppressors?' was a line that appeared in one poem that was published in 1914.[7]

Just as not everyone has the same views on race now, neither did people all respond and interact identically with different ethnicities in 1914. It is important to remember that indigenous soldiers were being exposed to new places, new people and new cultures. For example, not every tribe in West Africa was familiar with or liked every other. Bakary Diallo, however, found himself warming to the camaraderie growing between them:

> I'm with the Wolof who joined up a short time before we did, and even though we don't speak the same language, we manage to make ourselves understood. Some of the men speak Fula and like me, they think the Fula and the Wolof are brothers. I enjoy being with them. The ones who can speak my language also begin to teach me theirs. This interests me greatly and I'm a good student.[8]

In Eritrea, Italy boasted twenty-six companies of *askari*, local troops, and a few more indigenous troops in Somalia. Yemenis also volunteered, and recruitment in North Africa had begun in 1912. Italians had set out to forge an empire considering themselves an enlightened power, benevolent and progressive compared to other European nations. Reality differed. During the invasion of what would become Libya just before the First World War, 'soldiers and civilians alike were referred to by Italian troops as animals or as beasts, snakes to be killed or flies to be crushed'.[9] In newspapers, Arabs were described as less than human. In 1914, a military review had to refute the belief that Black soldiers felt no pain.

Even by the standards of 1914, Germany's reputation regarding her attitudes to non-whites was uncomfortable. Military forces in one of her African colonies murdered at least 60,000 Black men, women and children in a three-year purge that had only ended in 1907. Germany would employ Black troops in Africa, but they had no vast reservoir of men overseas. Their empire was simply too small. Their attitudes towards non-white soldiers would mellow somewhat once Turkey joined the war on the side of the Central Powers, but never to the extent that they would condone Black troops fighting in Europe. As the war began, the German press were brutal about the use of French colonial and Indian troops. They portrayed them as racial inferiors who should not set foot on European soil. Sociologist

Max Weber described these non-white troops as 'an army of n– – – – –s, Gurkhas and all the barbarians of the world'.[10] Bavarian artist Karl Götz even produced bronze medallions portraying Indian troops arriving in France as elephant handlers with a travelling circus.

There were certain racial tropes that were visible across several combatant nations, often driven by fear of what people did not know, did not understand or could not predict. In Jamaica, the authorities were arguably more afraid of an indigenous uprising than they were about the threat posed to the island by Germany. Some South Africans had similar fears. There was a concern that any disturbance to the status quo threatened to bring the whole imperial house of cards tumbling down. While the whites were looking the other way, and exiting the country in droves to fight their war, *what might the natives get up to?*

It was a legitimate concern in some cases. Russia was so awful to her Jewish subjects that Jews both in and outside her empire framed the First World War as a holy war to wipe the tsar's anti-Semitic regime off the map. One fear was that once Black men were allowed to fight whites in Europe, the floodgates would open. These men would be trained, armed, and everywhere. A common attitude was also the way in which white people regarded themselves in a parental light over Blacks, Arabs and every other minority. 'They are big children,' said one French cavalry major as his regiment passed some North African troops in the opening weeks of the war in the west. 'They are gentle, resigned, but courageous and devoted until death.' This infantile portrayal was not necessarily presented in a negative light. The officer he was talking to interpreted it very differently:

What ideas can, at this time, haunt the brains of these uprooted people, torn from their tribe... to learn of the deadliest, most savage struggle that has ever existed... You are now and forever our great friends, true Frenchmen!... The Moroccan soldiers will... reap the greatest reward, perhaps tomorrow, because, as I have just known them, they will fall by the dozen, by the hundreds... side by side with their white brothers in arms, and if they shed their blood on the land of France, without regret... they will also offer, to the country of Africa which saw them born, the immortal glory of having helped Europe to save itself from Germanic domination.[11]

It was an odd mix of attitudes. In 1913, the governor-general of Australia, Thomas Denman, actually railed against the belittling of aboriginal peoples, while somehow still condoning it:

The fashion in these days... is to regard the aboriginal as something beneath our contempt. In fact one of our great scientists... has gone so far as to say that [they are] little better than the anthropoid ape. Those of us who know the aboriginal at all, believe this to be entirely false. They are, it may be said, a child race, and they are often very trouble-some children. Still they have the keen observation of children and can be taught and influenced.[12]

To this end, there was a sentiment on the outbreak of war that imperial powers had to protect indigenous subjects. In the Netherlands East Indies, a newspaper published a letter urging the whites in the colony to remain calm. 'They should not forget that Europeans had a task to fulfil in the colony.' Millions of natives looked up to them: 'Our calm gives them composure. If we do lose our calm then the people who expect guidance from us will lose their heads and turn to excesses.'[13]

So as far as the imperial powers were concerned, then, in the light of those parental, patronizing attitudes towards non-whites, whether or not to recruit them for a war in Europe boiled down to a logical question: *would you trust a child with a gun?*

Some said yes. 'Is a black army desirable?' asked one British naval officer:

The real difficulty is white prestige, the most damnable doctrine in the Empire. The less certain a white man is of his superiority in brains and education and physique over the coloured man, the more he clings to the prestige of past, historic victories... the more anxious he becomes... 'After the war we have to live with these blacks... such life will be unbearable if they think themselves our equals.' That is the argument... of a coward who is not sure of himself... it neglects that very present fact that, unless we beat Germany, we (or those who are left of us) will be in the position of the coloured races... 'salaaming' before Prussian Junkers. Personally I would sooner be 'under' coloured men. So the first step towards a coloured army is to break the prejudice... Does anyone doubt that [they] would fight? They have given us proof of it in the past.[14]

The official responses to how ethnic and religious minorities might serve on the onset of war were less confident. Almost all of Britain's dominions wrestled with the issue, and mostly they stuck with their pre-war polices. Neither Canada nor New Zealand had any laws that forbade non-whites serving in the army. In terms of the latter, Maori were equal to whites under law, but they still eventually ran up against the colour bar, which prevented indigenous troops across the empire from facing white armies. In Canada, Mike Mountain Horse, a member of the Kainai Blood Tribe from Alberta, was miffed. 'From the outset of this colossal struggle the Red Man demonstrated his loyalty to the British Crown in a very convincing manner... When duty called, we were there and when we were called forth to fight for the cause of civilisation, our people showed all the bravery of our warriors of old.' But he would not be allowed to put on a uniform in 1914. Sam Hughes, the minister of militia in Canada, argued for the exclusion of First Nations men on the basis that the Germans would not 'extend to them the privileges of civilized warfare'.[15] It was a policy that would stand until the end of 1915, despite the long history of cooperation between the British army and Canada's indigenous peoples.

Australia's stance was brutal by comparison. By August 1914, Australia was already limiting the number of non-whites coming into the country in order to protect its 'whiteness'. Unsurprisingly, then, they refused to enlist aboriginal peoples into the army. At this point, they had more white recruits than they could deal with, and they neither wanted or needed minorities in uniform. A set of instructions for people at recruiting offices stated that: 'Aborigines and half-castes are not to be enlisted. This restriction is to be interpreted as applying to all coloured men.' Recruiters did bend the rules and enrol lighter skinned aboriginal peoples, but only two managed to enlist fully in 1914 without being later discarded for being too dark. Those who were dismissed received barbs such as: 'unsuitable physique', 'aboriginal' or 'unsuitable physical colour'.[16]

As for the rest of the empire, chiefs among the Zulu, Tomb and Pondo peoples in Africa offered to fight. None were accepted in 1914. The *Nigerian Pioneer* lamented in an editorial later on that for educated natives, 'the only outlet remaining for… loyalty was subscription to the various funds in aid of the war'.[17] In 1914, it was a similar story for Jamaicans wanting to pledge themselves to serve. In 1911, the Black population accounted for 75 per cent of the island's total. Most of them lived in abject poverty. People would leave for America, for plantations in Central America or Cuba, or to work on the Panama Canal. For those left behind, an escape by way of the army was perhaps extremely appealing. For Black men throughout Europe's imperial territories, their time might come later, but in the opening weeks of the war their services were declined, and not always politely.

This was far from an exclusively British problem. In Russia, the government was deeply suspicious of some subject peoples such as the Tatars who lived along the Volga River, about 750 miles southeast of Petrograd. Surveillance was carried out on Muslim activists. The fear was that the Tatars might gravitate towards another alliance, one that better represented their Islamic religion, such as with Turkey. So, Tatar religious activists were put under surveillance. Kazakhs, Uzbeks and Kyrgyz people in Asia were ruled out of service because they were considered to be too backward to display traits of honour and bravery. As for the groups that were recruited, including Latvians and Poles, just because they were white did not mean the government trusted them, either. In 1914, fears of insurrection saw some of those men limited to a quota in some units, or posted far away from their homes.

Imperial powers had particular ways of choosing which non-whites would be called forward at the beginning of war. For the British, everything about recruitment for the Indian army came down to martial race theory, the idea that some Indians were genetically suited for soldiering and others categorically were not. Sikhs were deemed to make excellent warriors. Sikhs only numbered 2 per cent of the population in India, but in 1904 they formed 20 per cent of the Indian army. The theory skewed the regional makeup of the force, too. Roughly half of all troops recruited in the First World War were recruited from the Punjab, in the north of the country. Bengal had a population of 123 million, and yet because the men were considered effeminate, it only provided only one fighting unit. Low-caste men or those from the plains further south were not permitted. Neither could a man join if he had previously had a menial job. Caste hierarchy meant that the other soldiers would not accept him.

France operated along similar lines of selection. North Africans had fought throughout the empire, as well as in the Crimea and during the Franco-Prussian War. Some 300,000 served on the Western Front at some stage during the First World War. Moroccans were regarded as warriors. The war ministry informed officers who would find them in their chain of command that they were 'intelligent, manoeuvrable, courageous, passionately warlike... tough, sober, and good marchers'.[18] The five battalions that took part in the opening throes of the war in Western Europe would suffer 80 per cent casualties by the end of September. It only fuelled legends about them among the enemy, too. The Germans referred to them as 'swallows of death'.[19]

Algerians were seen as decent enough soldiers, but the French viewed them primarily as shock troops: *Give them a weapon and send them running towards the enemy.* Despite these flattering opinions, however, France failed to train these North Africans for specialist roles because they did not credit them with the ability to do anything complex, such as fixing a telephone wire. The country, not to mention these indigenous troops, would pay for this stereotyping on the outbreak of war. Those five Moroccan battalions sailing for France in August 1914 did so without a single machine-gun, because they were deemed overly complicated for a non-white man to understand. As for the Tunisians, it was said that as soldiers, they might as well be women.

West Africans were to the French what Sikhs were to the British. The French army's leading proponent of non-white troops, General Charles Mangin, called them 'natural warriors'. Mangin effectively shaped the French army's stance on indigenous soldiers before the war. He had served extensively abroad and had absolutely no reservations about the effectiveness of non-white soldiers. He began promoting the idea of *la force noire*. He viewed these imperial subjects as an endless supply of men for France to send out into the world, including to use against the terrifying, ever-strengthening spectre of their German neighbours. By the time war broke out, he had managed to generate well over 4,000 articles drawing attention to his 1910 manifesto.

The fearsome West Africans that Mangin regarded so highly were largely referred to as *tirailleurs sénégalais* regardless of where they were from in the region. They were categorized as precisely the right combination of brave, ruthless and loyal. Just like the British in India, the French recruited in West Africa selectively, based on location. In the interior, the Bambara and Mossi were considered 'warrior races', while at the coast, the Fanti and Susu were classed as mediocre and less desirable. In 1914, the reputation of the tirailleurs preceded them to Europe. Their legend had previously spread so far as to terrify the Germans. In the field, they would respond to meeting Africans with 'an almost irrational fear'.[20] In German propaganda, the Black soldier would be accused of rape, murder, even mutilating the dead, and the Kaiser's government accused France of de-civilizing Europe by employing them.

Various responses of the minorities who were the subject of all of this conflicting sentiment exist sparsely. However, Africa is enormous. To try and apply one perspective, one attitude, one allegiance to Black Africans in the First World War is impossible. Their reactions and the ways that they viewed and contributed to the conflict were as diverse as those in Europe, which would fit into Africa three times. Across the continent, however, it is possible to paint a broad picture. There was a feeling that this was a white man's war. The Europeans were at it again, and the Black man would suffer for it. In British-controlled Nyasaland, Joseph Mandanda said what millions of Africans surely felt as economic deprivation and conscription forced them into uniform:

> Do you think you can work on the soil without anything inside your tummy? We were the women for the fighting Europeans. This is what we were doing... They just snatched [our country]... They had already snatched it from us. If you object, you should expect gunpowder somewhere inside you... If you objected, death was the only solution, and who could entertain the idea of dying? Life is sweet. Yes, bwana... So you give in.[21]

As such, indigenous troops in Africa did not necessarily care what had taken them to war. Some had a fatalistic view along the lines of: 'One of them will rule us, what does it matter as long as we eat?' Cultural appreciations of what war actually meant caused some amusement in what is now Mali. An old warhorse named Youkoullé Diawarra had been impoverished by the French conquest of West Africa. He was forced to beg for food. He was ecstatic when he heard that war was coming. He bounded home, retrieved his weapons and returned to the village. '[Someone] explained to him that it was not an African war, but a... war between light skins.' Diawarra had seen visions of loot and an escape from poverty, and the French had thwarted him again:

He began to curse all Europeans of all races and their 'civilization' with them. At the risk of being arrested for seditious statements, he wandered through the streets, proclaiming his fury: 'Let the "light skins"... get killed until there are no more. Not a single one left on the face of the earth!... O God!... Make the wombs of their women sterile and may they never bear fruit again.'[22]

Elsewhere in the village, Mamadou Daouda had fought for the French, and predicted that white men would ruin the world. 'It's going to be a mess! I saw how the light skins fought... I know them,' he said. 'They will destroy each other's cities and villages. Believe me, it's going to be a mess of fire and blood! They are so learnt that they have succeeded in enslaving matter; they make it work for them. Look at iron: they have made it their soulless captive, but endowed with such strength that it is capable of working faster and harder than man.'[23]

One evening men congregated in the square at Kérétel. Young Amadou Hampâté Ba Amkoullel watched them debate the causes of the war:

For some, it was surely because of a dispute over land, a boundary between fields, between hunting or gathering grounds, between fishing or grazing places or something else of that kind... For others, it could only be a women's issue. The leaders of the 'light skins', everyone knew, were ardent rabbits, their virile members retained heat well and became enthusiastic as soon as a beautiful woman came to swing her slender waist and rounded hips before their eyes. It was added that women were very rare in France (an opinion based on the fact that the colonials very rarely brought their wives to the colony and sought companions among the native population) and that, moreover, they were more of the temperament of the peaceful cow than that of the cat... In a country where there was such a great shortage of women, anything touching on this question could not fail to ignite war.[24]

Diawando Guéla M'Bouré, known locally as 'the great speaker', stood up and called for silence. He had no illusions about imperialism:

> Here it is... we constitute, for the light skins, a very important material asset... They are not apostles who have come to carry out a charitable mission without expecting immediate reward... Why did they... capture and domesticate us? Only to use us in times of need, just as the hunter uses his dog... to help them work or to fight their enemies.[25]

When it came to white motivations for war, M'Bouré was chillingly accurate:

> My brothers, I will tell you: the French entered the war to keep us, just to keep us, and the Germans to have us. We shouldn't look for another explanation. Besides, what's the point of wasting our time wondering about the reasons for their fight? It would be better to find a way to derail this calamity, because whatever the cause of this war, we will bear the brunt of it in one way or another... If the fire does not go out very quickly, then tomorrow, the day after tomorrow or in a year, the light skins will collect all our sons and our goods to maintain their war, because that is what we are here for.[26]

In British East Africa, a cross-section of people who were interviewed years later demonstrated that they did not care why they might have to fight, either. 'We were fools,' said Issa Lipende. 'We never even dared ask for the reasons of the war. We were just killing one another in ignorance of the motives.'[27] When Benjamin Kamanga was asked to list the nations pursuing victory, he excluded any Africans. 'The Africans were European slaves. I doubt if ever any African people knew why there was this war. They were told to go to war... That's why these innocent people should be excluded from the list.'[28]

Both British and German authorities fed propaganda to their indigenous forces. One man was told that the English were skin-flints who paid far less than Germany. On the other hand, Anusa Makumba's interpretation of the war was that he was 'helping the country by repelling the Germans… We wanted the British and not the Germans because they're the people whom we knew, and not the animal Germans.' Better the devil you know was a concept clearly demonstrated. 'We never knew the Germans,' he continued, 'and we never wanted them to come here. So it was better to get rid of them before they rooted themselves in our country.'[29]

The Germans had a fearsome reputation in East Africa. Benjamin Kamanga was rooting for Britain. 'I did pray earnestly that they would win the war… It was part of the German's scheme to kill all old people, useless people, and only the young should survive. The British, though bad people too, are quite sympathetic and compassionate.'[30] The silliest rumour in Nyasaland was that the Germans were cannibals. Tempi Makumba was convinced that they wanted him dead, and that he owed this knowledge to the British he served. 'We put much more effort in because they were some friends who were willing to help us in combatting against these people-eating Germans. When the Germans were driven away, we were very grateful that we were not eaten, that we were still with our friends who know how to live with people, the friends whom we're used to.'[31] In Kildon Wajiusa's village, the elders were convinced of the exact same danger. 'They said all sorts of terrible things, that the Germans would cut off our heads and cook our flesh in pots to feed the German soldiers.' Young Wajiusa believed them: 'I was very much afraid and I wondered what the Germans looked like so that I could run away from them when they came into our village. I did not want to die.'[32]

Imperialism and the war that it created also acted like a contagion, poisoning indigenous people against each other. In the villages of Nyasaland, the chiefs who convinced men to go to war were often reviled by their own people. 'Chiefs were puppets to the government,' said Karonga Nkhata. 'They suffered

intimidation so they helped the recruiters to take people to war.'[33]
There was outright opposition. In Useni Ghisa's village, two men
who fled during the night to evade war came back the next night
and burnt their chief's house down 'because they said it was him
who let the army people take men to war. They blamed him.'[34]
Of all of those interviewed, Benjamin Kamanga articulated the
bitterness which African people felt against their own as a result
of the war and imperial interference:

> Chiefs had betrayed their people… Our chiefs were crooks;
> they did not fend for their people but for their position. If
> they did not support the government they would be sacked,
> but they did not know that they were the people's repre-
> sentatives or mouthpieces. They did not know this, but of
> course they feared the government and suffered a lot of
> intimidation. People [went to] war because chiefs forced
> them to go there.[35]

*

Every single imperial power was guilty of absolute hypocrisy if
it pointed towards their national interests. It would be difficult
to find anybody who called out this hypocrisy at the beginning
of war better than Michel Lempicki. A Polish member of the
Russian State Duma, the parliamentary body forced upon the
tsar as recently as 1905. He produced and published an eloquent rant in 1915 that questioned the idea of Russia position-
ing herself as the saviour of Slavs against Austria–Hungary. He
demanded to know what entitled Serbia to a level of protection
that twelve million Poles who were part of Russia's own empire
did not receive. These Poles had endured a consistent policy of
denationalization from Russia. 'It is a chaos of violence, a brutal
force, which devastates and destroys everything in its path.'[36]
Prior to Russia's declaration of Slavic unity, Poles were denied
the right to buy land. No more than 10 per cent of the students
at any given university were permitted to be Poles. They could
not be schoolmasters, 'nor gymnasium or university teachers, nor

judges, nor magistrates'. They could not even be railroad conductors. Polish as a language was banned from public life and to speak it incurred harsh punishments. The number of Polish representatives in the Duma was much lower than promised. However, in Austria Poles had a diet at Lemberg, a political party and participated in government. Poles had acted as ministers of Home Affairs, Foreign Affairs, Finance and more. So for Polish people in Russia, who was the enemy?

Lempicki's crowning glory was an open letter to the Grand Duke Nikolai. As commander in-chief of the Russian armies, Nikolai had sent out a political message at the beginning of the war endeavouring to sweeten the idea of mobilization among the Poles ruled by his cousin, the tsar. Lempicki published a response that read: 'You invite the Slavic nations to side with the Russian Empire and all contribute to its victory because, you assert, there is no salvation and happiness for the Slavs except "in the maternal womb of Great Russia".' The fact that Russia now wanted to join hands with Poland was something Lempicki could not tolerate after all that had passed:

Under the sceptre of the Tsars, until now, there was no place for any nation except the Great Russian nation; no other had, strictly speaking, the right to exist... they became the object of religious persecutions... Poland, living happily under the sceptre of the Tsars, would have cleared the way for you to the Slavic world; you preferred to strive to make a corpse of it and lay it out on your road.[37]

4

Ukufunga

Africa

At the beginning of the war, with the exception of Liberia in the west and Ethiopia in the east, all of sub-Saharan Africa was under some form of European control. The imperial land grab had become so fraught that the Berlin Act of 1885 agreed that in the event of a war in Europe, all involved would broadly speaking leave each other alone in much of Africa. However, within a few days of war being declared, this agreement was in tatters. European powers started moving indigenous subjects about the planet like pawns on a giant imperial chessboard. Britain, Germany, Belgium and France would mobilize hundreds of thousands of men to fight, build, fetch and carry for the war effort in Africa. By the end of September 1914, blood on this continent had already been spilt across more than 4,000 miles.

Germany's late arrival on the imperial scene meant that although they possessed colonies or protectorates, they were invariably surrounded by rivals and isolated. Togoland in West Africa had been under German control since 1884. Home to a million Africans and about the size of Ireland, it was divided across the middle by mountains. Infrastructure such as railways and roads was mostly limited to the southern side of these, so any invasion would face difficulties the further inland it travelled. German interests were squashed between Britain's Gold Coast colony on one side and *l'Afrique-Occidentale française,* French West Africa on the other. The land to be fought over in southern Togoland was marshy before rising towards the mountains.

Criss-crossed by little rivers and streams which often dried up in summer, the terrain was covered with palms, forest, long grass and thick scrub. The climate was muggy, and many Europeans found it unhealthy. 'Even in peace times under normal conditions the physical and moral strain on Europeans necessitates frequent leave to a temperate climate.' All of this was protected by the *Schutztruppe,* or 'Protective Force'. These units were strewn throughout the Kaiser's empire. Led by white officers, the majority of the troops were indigenous recruits. Beneath them in the pecking order was a police force of some 500 more local men, commanded by more white officers.

Thanks to the Royal Navy, who carried out a rapid campaign to decimate Germany's global communications, by 5 August only the wireless station at Kamina, high in the mountains 100 miles inland from the city of Lomé on the coast, was connecting Togoland to the outside world. To save it, the acting governor contacted French and British officials in the neighbouring territories and suggested they act in accordance with the Berlin Act. It was a valiant effort, but it was in the Allies' global interests to destroy the installation at Kamina. They wanted to silence Germany on the world stage.

By midday on 7 August, it was apparent that the Germans had evacuated Lomé and fled north to defend their wireless station. Men of the British Gold Coast Regiment probed across the border and clashed with German police. Some of their equipment was ancient, but they did carry machine-guns and decent rifles. They had proven themselves locally, and their ranks were filled with formidable men of the Hausa, Fulani and Yoruba tribes. It was here that the acknowledged first British shot of the war was fired by a soldier named Alhaji Grunshi. Officials piled into Lomé that evening in a Ford lorry. They were greeted by a hapless German representative who had been left behind in order to formally surrender 75 miles of territory inland from the coast, and the British flag was raised.

The French then joined the push for Kamina. To the north, accompanied by more British troops, they closed in on the wireless installation. By 22 August, the Allies had reached the village of Khra, a rough enclosure next to the railway surrounded by dense bush, about 50 miles south of Kamina. Here the Germans had concentrated as many as five hundred men and four machine-guns, and had spent three days digging in, camouflaging trenches and clearing their field of fire. The dense nature of the countryside made defending it hard, but it also meant that attacking was difficult, too. Troops could not see what they were doing, or communicate with each other properly.

Twenty-four-year-old Lieutenant George Thompson had been born in Zululand, more than 3,000 miles south-east of Togo. He and his two dozen troops were placed with a group of French tirailleurs. Together they barely numbered some forty men. On 22 August they advanced to attack the left flank of the enemy defences. According to a German NCO, at first the defenders were scared, but they held their own. Thompson led his group through heavy fire before they were pinned down. There they remained for several hours until mid-afternoon, when Thompson thought that German fire was slackening. He decided to try to advance the last 50 yards to the enemy trenches. His group were decimated. The enemy had been saved by an additional company of native soldiers arriving by train from Kamina. Thompson was mortally wounded, some native troops fled, and almost all of them who stayed paid for that bravery with their lives. Thompson's body was found lying alongside that of Serjeant Asuri Moshi and several more men of the Gold Coast Regiment, in addition to most of the tirailleurs. The first British officer killed in action during the First World War, Thompson was buried next to his African soldiers where they fell.

As the British and French prepared to attack again the following day, the Germans had other ideas. They left their trenches and retired to Kamina, probably because they had heard that Allied troops were converging on the wireless station from the east and the west, threatening to cut them off. One German NCO present was unimpressed. They had held their own at Khra, with few casualties, and 'were by this time convinced of their ability to offer a prolonged resistance in this strong position'. On the night of 24 August, the Allies heard loud explosions to the north, the sound of the Kamina station being destroyed by the enemy. When daylight came, the wireless masts that had previously been visible from miles away were gone. Two days later, Governor von Doering surrendered Togoland to the Allies.

*

In East Africa, Germany went on the offensive. European colonists had scarcely made a dent in the potential for monetizing this vast region, or in defending their share of it. Both were complicated endeavours. The landscape was hugely varied: coastal stretches; vast lakes; mountains, including Kilimanjaro; arid, empty plains; and thick jungle. The area in play was enormous, more than 1,000 miles north to south, and more than 750 miles in from the coast. German East Africa alone was double the size of Germany itself.

Britain was originally content to sabotage German wireless communications along the coast, or attack a key port like Dar-es-Salaam. There was no intention of getting involved in a protracted campaign inland. A small force of three battalions was rustled up in India and set out for Mombasa on 19 August. Then, as they sailed away from Karachi on their 2,700-mile journey, bureaucracy lost its mind. Battalions in India had not finished mobilizing yet, there was no defined command structure, and to address any issue involved contacting not just India, but also the Colonial Office and other jealously interested government departments in London. It was from there that General Edmund Barrow, military secretary to the India Office, changed the plan: 'The object of the expedition under your command is to bring the whole of German East Africa under British authority.'

The man in charge of military operations in German East Africa did not intend to sit on his hands, either. Lieutenant-Colonel Paul von Lettow-Vorbeck was conscientious, intelligent and often charming, but he was also belligerent and uncompromising. At the beginning of August he not only called up reserves, but by the time he had finished pillaging the police force, he had something like 5,000 officers and men under his command and was determined to do something with them.

On 8 August, he woke to the sound of the Royal Navy attempting to shell a nearby wireless mast. Less than a week later his troops crossed the border into British territory near Kilimanjaro and occupied Taveta. From there, without the resources to do much else, the German and British contingents sat and stared at each other. Rather than one campaign, Lettow threw small punches all over Eastern Africa. It looked chaotic, but that was not necessarily the case: 'During the following period several enterprises were carried out by flying columns... the intention being to drive away the hostile detachments who were reported to be guarding the watering-places in the adjoining English territory, to inflict losses upon them, and so to open the way for our patrols to operate against the Uganda and Magad Railway.'[1]

On the north-western tip of Lake Malawi, the border with British-controlled Nyasaland was formed by the Songwe river. Here the Germans launched an incursion of almost 2,000 men. Janet Nyaunthali was about eight years old when news came that the *Schutztruppe* were across the river:

When the news swept our homes that the Germans were coming... our men told the women to take the children and run and hide far away. People were scattering everywhere. Some fled with their cattle... I remember clearly because that was the same week my mother... gave birth to my brother... We escaped to Ngosi where we hid in the bushes.

This was a journey of about 7 miles, and an incredible strain on her exhausted mother. The men remained behind, 'because it's not our custom for Ngonde men to run from war'. At nearby Mwangolera they collected around a sacred tree. 'They sat there silently, calling on spirits to ward off the evil of war... We call that *ukufunga*.'[2]

Nearby, as the enemy lay in long grass, Captain Griffiths of the King's African Rifles led his men onto the scene. His company was armed with machine-guns, and thanks to the cover from banana groves, the enemy did not realize how small his numbers were. The German troops fled back towards the Songwe and into the path of a main British force that was also concealed by trees. Less than half got away without being killed, wounded or taken prisoner. 'The moral effect of this engagement was immense,' wrote one indigenous observer. 'The German authorities had brought [to witness] their triumph the leading chiefs in the New Langenburg territory. These men, forced to crawl home like rats, never forgot what they saw... and when, later on, we in our turn became the invaders, the natural consequences of this folly overtook the Germans.'[3] Lettow would later claim that much valuable reconnaissance had been done in unknown terrain in the opening throes of his war; how to get around, where to find water, but for now, his campaign in East Africa was at a standstill.

5

You Have to Serve the Best You Can

The Royal Navy was expecting a rapid encounter with the enemy as soon as war began; a clash of titans. Britain and Germany had spent years battling for naval supremacy and both outclassed any other navy in the world. In August 1914, Britain had concentrated its Grand Fleet on the western edge of the confined North Sea, 'a grey-green expanse of smudgy waters'. On the opposite side was Scandinavia, and in the middle was Germany's only way out. Any route to freedom for the Kaiser's High Seas Fleet would involve crossing the Royal Navy's path, and so everything pointed to a showdown, and quickly.

From Scapa Flow the Royal Navy prowled the Germans' northern escape route. Instead of enemy battleships, they found fishermen. Not every boat was fitted with a wireless set, and smaller craft might not know a thing about world events until they reached a port. So, men on German trawlers they met cheered a hello and waved their caps, knowing nothing of the war. Innocent though these fishermen were, crews were taken aboard British ships and their battered boats were sunk. At the very least, their carrier pigeons and any wireless equipment were destroyed: they could not be allowed to relay information about British warships.

The fishing boats made for good target practice, but they were not the prey that the Grand Fleet wanted; Britain was searching for the German High Seas Fleet. As James Somerville sailed from Scapa aboard *Marlborough* on 15 August, excitement was building:

We are making a big sweep in force down the North Sea...
I should imagine that we are sure to meet some of their
destroyers and cruisers tonight, so we ought to get our
first crack at the enemy very soon. The fleet looks simply
immense as we steam along; long lines of battleships with
destroyers... I wonder if by this time tomorrow I shall have
something thrilling to record![1]

The German fleet, however, had no intention of venturing out.
Why would they? They knew they were the weaker force. Three
days later, *Marlborough* had encountered nothing and Somerville
was fed up. 'I'm getting <u>very</u> bored with this war, it's too deadly
monotonous for words at present.'[2] The monotony continued
for the Grand Fleet as it became clear that the enemy was not
interested in a battle to the death. 'We passed a dead whale and
fired the maxim at it,' wrote Bernard Colson aboard *King George
V*. 'Apparently the pope is dead.'[3] Somerville sulked after another
fruitless search in September: 'Sick as death to think that again
we have swept... and found nothing. They must sit like rats in
their holes.'[4]

*

Britain and France had formally agreed on dividing naval responsibilities in any European war. Broadly speaking, the Royal Navy
would patrol the North Sea and the English Channel. The bulk of
the work protecting commerce in the Mediterranean and keeping the Austrian navy confined to the Adriatic would rest upon
France's navy, the *Marine nationale*. They would also monitor
Gibraltar and the European end of the Suez Canal.

French naval officers sniped about being the poor sibling of
the army, for being asked to do too much in return for too little
investment. 'We have almost constantly waged naval warfare with
insufficient means,' complained one, 'in material even more than
in personnel.'[5] But while Britain's sailors were shooting at dead
whales and culling pigeons, their French counterparts had already
led a raid on the enemy. The French government did not care what

their ships did as long as they provided a show of force against Austria. At Malta, Admiral Augustin de Lapeyrère received a telegram with those vague instructions on 13 August. He decided that he was going to strike at Austrian ships blockading the friendly Montenegrin port of Antivari, about 80 miles south-east along the Adriatic from Dubrovnik. The blockade was intended to stop Montenegro from liaising with her allies, and comprised five small ships and a scattering of torpedo boats. Practically, freeing the port aided Montenegro, as well as potentially impressing a potential future ally in Italy across the Adriatic.

Admiral de Lapeyrère gathered every ship he could get his hands on, mostly French but with British representation, too. Aboard the French battleship *Vergniaud,* an unnamed sailor recorded that they arrived north of Antivari at sunrise on 16 August: 'There was a slight mist: so we did not immediately see the coast, which was merging with the clouds.' Impatiently they waited. 'Little by little, as we approached land... the panorama of the Montenegrin port soon unfolded... surrounded by its high mountains... the curtain of fog had melted under the heat of the sun.'[6]

At around 7.45 a.m. the Austro-Hungarian blockade spotted five columns of smoke. They had had no previous inkling that Allied ships had been converging in the vicinity, but it was now clear that this incoming force was far superior in size. In command of SMS *Zenta,* Captain Pachner ordered a swift return north to the safety of Cattaro. In the meantime, Allied lookouts had sighted. The *KuK Kriegsmarine* vessels were surrounded and the *Vergniaud* prepared to do battle: 'The wait was not long... *"Bran le bas de combat"* was greeted on board with overwhelming enthusiasm. The bugle began to sound throughout the ship, it was nothing but an indescribable chaos of men, each running to his combat post: then, a few seconds later, everything returned to the most absolute calm, waiting for the outcome.'[7] The new dreadnought *Courbet* opened fire. SMS *Ulan* escaped, but outgunned, the response from *Zenta* fell short. A direct hit smashed through her engine room, killing the crew members there, disabling both engines and striking a funnel. She slowed down, gamely still firing her port guns as fires broke out on deck and in the magazines. She began to vent steam, smoke pouring from her funnels. 'The forecastle was shot, the bridge was partially shattered and water burst into the first boiler room... Captain Pachner had to give the order to abandon ship.'[8]

'Successive explosions could be heard,' reported de Lapeyrère aboard *Courbet*. 'Like those that might be produced by mines, and a thick column of white smoke drifted out from the middle to the rear of the vessel.'[9] At 9.30 a.m., several stronger explosions occurred, and *Zenta* listed to 45 degrees, her bow sticking out of the water, before she slipped away. The whole unequal scrap had lasted just a few minutes, but the blockade of Antivari was broken. The brief battle resulted in an Allied victory, but it was very much a hit-and-run affair. De Lapeyrère was too far from his supplies, and at risk from Austro-Hungarian ships that could be sent south from established bases at Cattaro and Pula. He knew when he was ahead, and he cashed out and left.

*

Just as the war saw fighting on multiple continents almost immediately, so it continued to invade civilian life. In previous centuries, war's reach was shorter: fewer combatants, slower communications, fewer people reading about it. But in 1914 it would have been extremely difficult to remain oblivious as the world ignited. This war smothered populations and intruded on lives across the globe. The impact might have been felt because of the people who disappeared, the jobs that were lost, the food people ate, the prices they paid for it, where they went or how they got there. It might have been reflected in the freedoms that people now saw suddenly taken away: forced to fight, forced to move, forced to stay put, forced to ration their food. Few people in the world could boast that the First World War did not touch them at all.

As men departed for war, the authorities on the home fronts had to restore order. Patriotic demonstrations had, in some locations, turned into mischievous looting and generally bad behaviour. In Paris, Célestin Hennion, the chief of police, 'arranged for half a dozen auto-buses containing a dozen policemen to circulate different neighbourhoods at night. 'They stop now and then, and the police make a silent search for marauders. Anyone found with a revolver or a knife is arrested, put in handcuffs, and placed in the bus and taken to the station.'[10]

Elsewhere, silence descended where it did not belong. Before the war, sixty trains a day had crossed the *Kongeå*, the border between Denmark and Germany. People were used to the constant rumble of the heavy locomotives. Now the familiar sound of wheels screeching against rails was gone. It provoked curiosity rather than fear. At the border crossing point at Skodborghus, two Danish women ventured onto the bridge and asked the gendarmes posted there whether they would be allowed to cross the border and have a look about. The answer was prompt: 'No, no! Ladies are much too insidious!'[11] Who knew what international incident the two women might cause?

War remained the only topic of conversation. Outside Paris's bookshops, crowds gathered around maps that were posted for passers-by. They were of immense interest. So far, men had disappeared into the fog of war. The army's postal machinery was not yet functioning, and beyond knowing where they had been ordered to report to, the whereabouts of their loved ones and what danger they might be in was a mystery. It was not surprising then, that the subject of the conflict brought strangers together.

Those not required to fight found other ways to contribute. A few miles from the Franco-German frontier, it felt like the enemy was already at the gates. 'Nancy was surrounded by a ring of fire.' A group of men, those too young, too old or unsuitable for army service, formed a group to help keep order. 'Wearing a brassard and wielding a club were the only distinguishing signs of the guard,' but men of all classes were present. 'During the day, [they] walked the busiest arteries... or were stationed near public monuments and on squares. They mingled with groups... intervened in conversations and watched suspects... At nightfall, [they] patrolled, closing shops, worrying about unwanted lights. All these good people exercised their duties very zealously.'[12]

They were a little too zealous on occasion. Scuffles had to be broken up 'due to their lack of police skills', but people of all ages just wanted to be useful. They were willing to make the smallest contribution, and in Paris, journalist Anthoine Delecraz was moved by one scene in particular: 'Strolling through the main streets of my neighbourhood, I realize that some public services are completely disorganized by the mobilization which deprives them of any manpower. Refuse, foul smelling, sits on the edge of the pavement, abandoned.' In the August heat, the smell was nauseating. Then he saw a lorry with four men on it. The driver was a teenager, two others were well over forty. They appeared to be collecting rubbish, and so Delecraz asked the boy if they might swing past his street. '"Address yourself to the colonel," he replied, pointing out to me a man in an English cap walking alongside. I walk forward to meet him. "Are you the colonel, sir?" I examine him on the sly. Tall, straight, slim.' The elderly man had a pronounced regal bearing, and an imperious white moustache:

'I am indeed a retired colonel... I have two officer sons. Too old to return to the fire, at the age of seventy, I'm trying to be useful. You see, I am running temporary rubbish collection, while waiting for the business to be reorganized. You have to serve as best you can, at such a time...' And when he opens his jacket to take a note [of my street]... I see the rosette of an officer of the Légion d'Honneur.[13]

Just as men like the elderly colonel found things to do, children were by no means all passive observers as flames continued to engulf Europe. In Brussels, boy scouts were everywhere. 'If you called on a minister at his bureau a scout conducted you to his presence; if you went to a passport office... a scout scrutinized you. They were in the cafés... the hospitals and the railway stations, upon the tramway.'[14] Around Nancy, however, the boys from a local gymnasium took their participation to extremes. 'They roamed the battlefields and came back loaded with spiked... helmets, rifles, pockets stuffed with epaulettes, metallic buttons, straps, which they offered to their friends.' Soon they were doing a roaring trade in souvenirs, 'but accidents having occurred, young people having been killed or injured',[15] the military authorities soon clamped down on their antics.

An unfortunate manifestation of all of this nervous energy brought about by the war in its early days was that people continued to be obsessed by spies. In Brussels, word got out that somewhere, a boy scout had tracked a German spy and caught him trying to erect a wireless mast on a rooftop. Every scout in the Belgian capital set out to do the same.

The thing became a plague within 24 hours, for boys are terrible when their native instincts are enlisted and sanctioned... [They] had no pity and no humour... They... spread terror wherever they went. I saw an old gentleman of obviously innocent character being tracked along the main street of the town by a stealthy boy who conducted the operation in Red Indian style, dodging from shop door to shop door. His victim soon discovered the plight he was in and then his efforts to escape became ludicrous. He was too fat to hurry and so he tried the expedient of buying things he did not want in all manner of shops. He bought tobacco at least twice within the space of ten minutes. At last the boy ran out of his hiding-place and confronted the man, demanding to see his papers. In an instant a crowd collected. The unfortunate man had no papers. You heard the angry growl of the crowd rising in a crescendo above the expostulations of the victim and the shrill talk of the boy. The crowd began to jostle, to threaten, to abuse. The boy lost his head and shrieked the fatal word 'SPY'. A scuffle began which but for the arrival of a couple of gendarmes would have gone badly for the victim. The gendarmes knew the fat gentleman and released him.[16]

Adults were keen to distance themselves from suspicion. In Paris, shop owners were so terrified of looting that they began affixing notices and documents to their shutters and windows:

[A] jeweller, displaying his passport, announces that he is French-Russian... The Delion hat shop is 'French of French origin'. A chocolatier on *Boulevard des Capucines* announces that it is a Swiss-French house... The Rocca perfumery, [along the street], shows a portrait of its director, and shown on his jacket is the 1870 medal... Maxim's Shoes, *Boulevard Poissonnière*, had the most ingenuous idea. The owner stuck to the shop window a photographic print of his mobilization book showing his military record.[17]

*

Personal freedoms were attacked everywhere after the outbreak of war, with sweeping legislation being forced on populations, supposedly for the greater good. Austria–Hungary saw one of the harshest disruptions of democracy when parliament was shut down in Vienna for the duration of the war. In Britain, the Defence of the Realm Act flew through parliament and was passed on 8 August. One wit claimed that until August 1914 a sensible, law-abiding Englishman could pass through life and hardly notice the existence of the state, beyond the post office and the policeman. All of this would change during the war. The Act would come to be known, with little affection, as DORA, and the sheer range of powers 'she' gave the authorities immediately stifled normal activities. DORA allowed the government to requisition personal property and buildings, but it was in controlling the population that it went above and beyond anything that Brits were used to. It was forbidden to talk about the war in public, buy binoculars, light fireworks or even fly a kite. The ringing of church bells was suppressed, as was walking near railway lines, using invisible ink or buying brandy and whisky in railway refreshment rooms. Londoners were not even allowed to whistle for a taxi, lest it be mistaken for an air raid alarm.

Freedom of speech was obliterated across the planet. In Trieste, under Austrian control but coveted by Italy, people could be charged with insubordination and imprisoned if they made statements about the war that sounded questionable to the authorities. One Franz Bressano spoke innocently to three Bosnian soldiers in a brothel. They subsequently went to the authorities and reported him for being disrespectful to the emperor.

As well as policing what people said, authorities now controlled what they wrote, too. On 3 August military censorship came into force throughout Russia, even for civilians. Movement was also now regulated. On the east coast of England, Harwich, an important base for the Royal Navy, was shut off. Residents now needed passes to travel in or out of the town, to get to work or return home. Domestic lights had to be extinguished by 7.00 p.m., pubs had to close by 9.00 p.m. Civilians were no longer allowed near the seafront. In Karlsruhe, along Germany's border with France, the military importance of the town led to draconian regulations there, too. Soldiers guarded bridges, roads, stations and even the nearby forest. Charlotte Herder was indignant about the state's interference in her life. 'One has to have identity papers if one wants to take a walk into the outskirts of town. It is as if we are prisoners,' she complained.[18] The border with Switzerland 120 miles away was closed, automobiles were forbidden to exit the town, and all telephone and telegraphic lines that would have enabled the residents to communicate with the outside world were cut.

Internments also continued. Authorities were merciless. 'It was a terrible sight when the soldiers marched a little outside town to get an old man… who'd been an editor at one of the newspapers,' wrote a Dane in Schleswig . 'When they arrived at the house, the soldiers were commanded to surround [it] with loaded rifles and fixed bayonets, so that he couldn't sneak out.'[19] Three men went to get the old man, who could barely walk, and escorted him through the town to a prison cell. No corner of the planet was safe, it seemed. Germans who had been living in the Dutch East Indies, who considered themselves high society, were also seized. A planter from Sumatra complained about the camp he was transported to. The washing facilities were dreadful, they had to cook their own meals and do the dishes themselves. The camp beds on which the prisoners were expected to sleep were not provided with mosquito nets, and, because brushes and polish had not been handed out, they could not clean their shoes.

6

A Brief Autumn Stroll

The Balkans

As the Germans crossed the border into Belgium, her Austro-Hungarian allies had yet to join the conflict in earnest. On the night following the declaration of war against Serbia, river monitors of the Habsburg Danube Flotilla had fired at Belgrade, and artillery batteries repeatedly shelled the Serbian capital in the days that followed. But in terms of land operations, commanders were faced with a dilemma that had plagued Habsburg military planners for years: *how do we fight multiple enemies at once?*

The likelihood of having to wage war against both Serbia and Russia at the same time had caused serious headaches in peacetime. The *kaiserliche und königliche Armee,* the Imperial and Royal Army, simply did not possess the number of troops needed to conduct full-scale, simultaneous offensive operations on multiple fronts. In the event of a two-front war, Austria–Hungary would need to fight one enemy at a time, resigning itself to holding operations against the other. Where an offensive would be most sensible, however, would only be known once war began, meaning war plans needed enough built-in flexibility to allow for sudden developments.

A solution was found by dividing the armed forces into three separate deployment groups. Upon mobilization, A-Group, consisting of the First, Third and Fourth Armies, would face the Russians in Galicia, while the smaller *Minimalgruppe Balkan* Fifth and Sixth Armies would deploy along the empire's southern borders with Serbia and Montenegro. The all-important flex-ibility would be found in B-Group. This swing force consisted of the large Second Army comprising twelve infantry divisions and one of cavalry, and could deploy either against Russia or in the Balkans, depending on where the chief of the general staff wished to go on the offensive. While undoubtedly complicated, the plan nevertheless alleviated Austria–Hungary's concerns over a two-front war, at least on paper.

However, problems began to arise immediately upon the dec-laration of war. As late as 31 July, Chief of the General Staff Franz Conrad von Hötzendorf remained convinced that the war in the east could be contained to fighting Serbia, and that a quick victory was needed to deter Serbs within the empire from staging a revolt. Moreover, he also feared that an opportunistic Romania might decide to back Serbia in order to seize control over the contested region of Transylvania. As a result, Conrad made the fateful decision to deploy B-Group in the Balkans to support Minimalgruppe Balkan in an invasion of Serbia. This order defied reason. Russia presented by far the greater threat, and by late July, it should have been obvious to all that Russia would never just stand idly by and let Austria–Hungary crush Serbia. Furthermore, the Germans, who had sacrificed a strong defence in the east in order to deploy the bulk of their armies against France, were outraged at Conrad's decision to pursue an offensive against Serbia. While A-Group was by far the largest of Austria–Hungary's deployment forces, its twenty-eight infan-try and ten cavalry divisions would still likely be insufficient to overcome the feared 'Russian steamroller'.

Conrad had little choice but to comply with his German allies' wish to confront Russia, but with the Second Army already en route to the Balkans, this change of plan was awkward. Counting on a slow Russian mobilization, the Austro-Hungarians decided that instead of attempting to turn their large Serbian-bound force around, a better option would be to let the troops proceed to their original destination along the Serbian border before then sending them off to Galicia. It was a farce. In the end, only III

Corps and part of IX Corps would immediately be deployed in Galicia, while the rest of the Second Army would have only limited impact on early events in the Balkans, and instead spent much of August and early September traveling the length of the empire by rail.

The man in charge of the invasion of Serbia was General Oskar Potiorek, who had been a rival of Conrad's for the position of chief of the general staff and had served as governor of Bosnia and Herzegovina since 1911. The assassination of the Archduke Franz Ferdinand and his wife in Sarajevo that had proved the critical rupture in European diplomacy in the end had happened on his watch, largely because of his incompetence, and Potiorek hoped that a victorious campaign against Serbia would regain his prestige. Like Conrad, he thought little of the Serbian army, and the invasion was expected to be nothing more than 'a brief autumn stroll'.

On paper, Potiorek appeared to hold the advantage, with 370,000 men to the Serbs' 210,000. However, these figures did not account for several crucial factors. With the Second Army's departure for Galicia, which was scheduled to begin on 18 August, Austro-Hungarian strength would shrink dramatically. Meanwhile, the Serbian figures did not include large numbers of irregulars, *komitadji*, on whom the regular army could rely to boost its strength and cause chaos in the Austro-Hungarian rear. Including these, the actual Serbian strength was closer to 350,000 men. Additionally, once Montenegro joined the war on 6 August, yet another 40,000 to 60,000 men could be added to this number. Austria–Hungary's numerical advantage was merely an illusion.

Serbia's soldiers were also significantly more experienced than their Austro-Hungarian counterparts. Almost all were veterans of the Balkan Wars of 1912–13, so both officers and men possessed extensive combat experience, something none of Potiorek's men did. Years of war had also left the small Balkan kingdom much better equipped than might have been expected. In terms of the all-important number of guns with which the forces were supplied, once the Second Army left for Galicia, the Serbs would even enjoy a slight, but vital, superiority in firepower, too. Finally, the Serbs also had the advantage of an experienced, highly skilled command, led by the capable and tough Radomir Putnik. As chief of the general staff, sixty-seven-year-old Putnik had led the Serbians through both Balkan Wars, and his service in each and every one of Serbia's wars since 1876 had moulded him into an experienced tactician and strategist. All these factors combined to make the Serbs a much greater adversary than Austria–Hungary expected.

The first two weeks of the war were marked by a number of limited engagements and skirmishes along the border. Serbian, and, later, Montenegrin forces made several nuisance raids into Bosnia and Herzegovina. Montenegrin artillery batteries on Mount Lovcén also shelled the Austro-Hungarian naval base in the Bay of Kotor, some 40 miles from Dubrovnik, but the actual damage was limited.

On 9 August, Potiorek issued the order for an invasion of Serbia. The Fifth Army would carry out the main attack across the lower Drina near Loznica and Lešnica, while the Second Army would launch supporting attacks across the Sava river from the north. Once these rivers had been forged, the Fifth Army's two corps, VIII and XIII, would begin marching on Valjevo, some 60 miles south-west of Belgrade, where Potiorek envisioned a pincer movement encircling and defeating the Serbian centre by 18 August. To the south, on the upper Drina, the Sixth Army would attack Montenegrin and Serbian forces that had crossed into Bosnia, and once these had been pushed back across the border, the army would begin marching on the city of Užice in western Serbia. The Fifth and Sixth Armies would then move together on Kragujevac to crush the remainder of the Serbian Army. The plan looked simple from Potiorek's headquarters in Sarajevo, but given the terrain and distance between them, his armies would not be able to support each other until well into the advance, and the Second Army would only be available for a few days.

Still, Potiorek remained confident. In the days that followed, small Austro-Hungarian forces made several crossings of the lower Drina to probe Serbian defences. Eager to settle scores, some officers grew impatient. 'In my opinion', wrote Hungarian Lieutenant István Szakraida, 'our army is marching very slowly. We eagerly await the moment when our attack begins. Everyone knows why we are attacking Serbia; we have the mourning ribbon on our arm!'[1] He would not have to wait long. On the evening of 11 August, reports reached Serbian High Command that Austro-Hungarian forces seemed to be massing along the Drina and Sava rivers, indicating that a major crossing was imminent. However, Putnik was not convinced that this was the real invasion. Having believed that the most logical invasion route was from the north against Belgrade, it was only after a long meeting with his staff that Putnik agreed to move troops west. His smaller Third Army was ordered forward to occupy a line facing the Drina, while his Second Army was moved northwest to defend the Sava. In addition, the First Army would shift westwards to take up position behind the two others.

As the three Serbian armies received their marching orders in the early hours of 12 August, Austro-Hungarian preparations for forging their way across both rivers were in full force. Roads were packed with troops making their way to riverbanks, where pioneers were busy preparing crossings. Before long, the first pontoons began touching Serbian soil on the opposite banks. Juričič Houžvic was a Czech native living in Serbia in 1914, who had volunteered to defend his adopted homeland. 'We were attacked along the entire length of the front by strong artillery and machine-gun fire, under the protection of which the Austrians launched boats and pontoons into the Drina,' he recalled.[2]

One by one, Austro-Hungarian regiments were being rowed across. For those waiting their turn, the tension grew, as everyone knew that once on the opposite bank, they would be in enemy territory. 'Everyone feels that the time for games is now over,' wrote one soldier, 'the clock has struck! The baptism of fire is approaching. One cannot imagine that in a few hours, bullets carrying death will be flying around.'[3] Franz Schöttner, of k.u.k.

Infanterie Regiment Nr.73 (IR 73) described the terrifying cross-ing. 'We hear cracking over there and it hisses continuously, sst, sst... The Serbs had waited until we were in the middle of the river and started shooting at us... I can't describe what I was feeling. The pioneers rowed with all their might.'[4]

Sand deposits in the river prevented pontoons from getting all the way to the shore, and the men had to jump into knee-deep water and wade across while Serbian bullets continued to whizz by. Skirmish lines were immediately formed, and communications were established with neighbouring regiments before the advance inland began. The men first had to pass through a dense forest, and upon entering a small clearing, they were met by heavy fire from Serbian detachments who had taken up position along the opposite forest edge. 'The enemy just seemed to be waiting and showered us with shrapnel,' wrote Schöttner. 'The effect was ter-rible. Lieutenant Zipser was hit in the shoulder, some of our com-rades were wounded, one fell. I was lying behind a pile of wood, which was struck by the fuse from an exploding shrapnel shell. A couple of logs fell on my head, and I got a few bruises.'[5]

The order to attack the Serbian position was issued and the men charged forward. 'A mighty hurrah thundered through the air and we were already charging at them with our bayonets,' wrote another soldier of the k.u.k IR 73, František Petržíla:

However, many fell to the ground dead or wounded from the continuous Serbian fire. We finally chased them off, since they had to retreat in the face of our numerical superior-ity. We continued slowly through the thickets behind them. Now and then we collided in the forest, and then there was a hellish rifle fire on both sides, which was even more ter-rible, since the echo in the forest increased the thunder and rumble many-fold.[6]

A single Serbian soldier was caught alive, and his captors immediately pounced on him. 'They pushed him, kicked him, the poor man was shaking with fear and begged to be shot at once.'[7] However, with no time to waste, the prisoner was taken to the rear, and the order to continue the advance was given. Meanwhile, back across the river, those still waiting their turn to cross caught their first sight of the wounded being transported to field hospitals on the Austro-Hungarian bank. 'It was a sad sight to look at those wretches,' recalled Ewald Mácha of the k.k. Landwehr Infanterie Regiment Nr.8 (LIR 8). 'Everyone thought that perhaps tomorrow he too would be such a poor, crippled creature, and without knowing why and for what.'[8]

By the end of 12 August, about half of the Fifth Army had crossed the Drina. The rest followed the next day, and they probed Serbian defences, which, despite several sharp clashes, proved relatively weak. At Šabac, the Second Army had established bridgeheads across the Sava, but because of the army's anticipated departure for the Russian front, this could not be exploited. The advance inland began in earnest on 14 August, just four days before they were due to depart for Galicia.

As the Austro-Hungarians set off, they passed the site of the first day's fighting, which for many was their first contact with the reality of war. 'There were many felled trees and bushes, broken and blown apart by shells,' wrote Ewald Mácha:

> The ground was full of various items: rifles and bayonets, dead, bloody bodies. Everywhere was full of... shreds of tattered, blood-stained clothes, bandages, rags, pieces of underwear; all this was now lying on the ground, and flocks of crows were already circling over their prey, over the bodies of the poor victims who found premature release from their earthly torment.[9]

Progress inland proved painstakingly slow and difficult. The terrain was hilly and the sun burnt mercilessly in a cloudless sky. One soldier left a vivid account of the gruelling marches:

> There is nothing to be seen but corn so high that horse and rider disappear in it... The burden is getting heavier

and heavier. You feel as if you haven't slept for days. The thirst burns, the sweat runs down the forehead like a little stream and is collected by a dirty hand on the chin and drunk as the only precious liquid available... The infantry marches in the fields on both sides of the road, and a path first has to be made. Corn stalks, corn cobs... pumpkins are lying around. You don't see them, because the four of you are marching in close file, and your feet, which are already sore, bump into them, slip and step on them. Half the men have ailing feet. On the road, the artillery and the endless line of wagons rattle by, clouds whirl up from the bottomless dust and settle an inch thick on the infantry. The eyes become inflamed, the lungs gasp, the tongue sticks to the palate... The shoulders are bleeding from the cutting load, and the gun is held in a different position every moment; for the arms want to refuse service. [A] quarter of an hour passes, half an hour... The sun rises higher and higher. Air and sand are boiling.[10]

Before long, men began to fall out. 'Many soldiers' feet were bleeding because of the new, unbroken shoes,' wrote Croat soldier Frane Dubravčić. 'Some fell unconscious along the road and remained on the ground. There were also deaths along the way.'[11] Due to poor roads and a lack of railheads near the front, obtaining fresh drinking water proved difficult. Proper supply lines were never established. For the soldiers, marching uphill in the blistering heat, this meant empty canteens and parched mouths. 'Excruciating thirst, but no water or anything to drink anywhere,' wrote Jaroslav Míchal of k.k. LIR 8. 'I crawled behind the others, weakened until I fainted from exhaustion. A corporal found me and gave me a sip of water, which somehow revived me.'[12] Egon Erwin Kisch, a famous reporter from Prague, now conscripted as an infantryman with the k.u.k IR 73, described how the only water that could be obtained was a bucket of murky fluid, full of tiny organisms. 'I drank it through a blue neckerchief which I put to my mouth,' he wrote. 'The water tasted better than champagne through this neckerchief, which had previously been stuck to the neck of an infantryman and which half the platoon had already used as a filter in their mouths.'[13]

Much like the Germans in the west, the Austro-Hungarian forces were learning very early on that when invading their smaller neighbours, statistics did not necessarily give an accurate measure of how easily those countries could be overcome. This was becoming abundantly clear in Serbia as well as back in Belgium.

7

The Fist of a Colossus

Belgium

The second phase of the battle for Liège was for the ring of forts surrounding it. Contrary to German expectations, the fall of the city had not led to their automatic capitulation, which mattered most of all. The longer the Belgians held out in the forts, the more they delayed German progress into France. General Karl von Bülow, commanding the German Second Army, was not, however, about to give up. When the gaps between Liège's defences were overrun and the city fell, the twelve forts became isolated from each other, and so the simplest way to tackle them was to start in the east and work across to the other side of the city.

Until now, any fire directed at the forts had been desultory, mainly aimed at demoralizing the garrisons. Every now and again, the Germans stopped shelling and enquired whether the Belgians might like to surrender, but the garrisons declined. In terms of the heavy artillery required to pulverize concrete and Belgian resolve into submission, Bülow originally had just six Howitzers with which to attack twelve forts. The forts were dated, but their capture would require more than that. The Germans also suffered from a distinct lack of ammunition. As early as 6 August, artillerymen were already foraging for more shells back in Aachen. To take on Liège's forts, however, they were going to need serious, concentrated firepower.

While more big guns were on their way, the Germans turned the ones that they had to hand on the forts whose field of fire covered the road by which those bigger guns would arrive. Bülow needed them silenced to accomplish this in peace. Fort Barchon

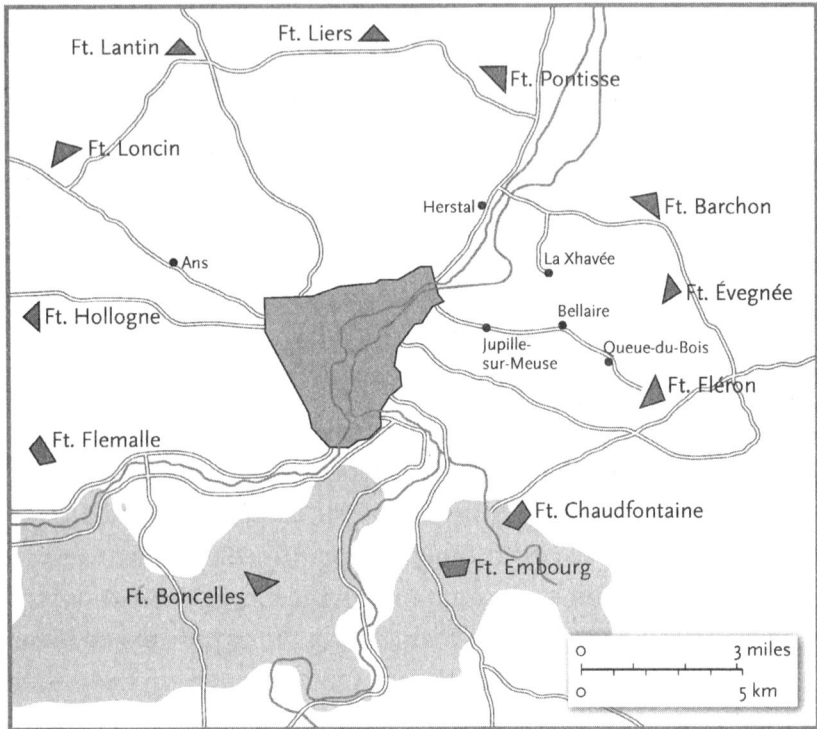

Defence of Liège

was the first fort to fall, on 9 August. Facing a mutiny, the overwhelmed commander surrendered despite minimal damage. This opened a breach in the Belgian line and also left a path open for the Germans to move back and forth to their comrades in Liège. Two days later, Fort Evegnée capitulated. The road now lay open and siege Howitzers rolled along it. The German heavy artillery on hand went from six pieces to a staggering ninety-four.

For General Leman's garrisons, fighting back was near impossible. A fort is a fort; attackers know exactly where it is and how to fire at it. On the other hand, the Belgians were facing mobile targets. They lacked consistent aerial observation, and razing villages like Boncelles to the ground did not solve the problem. They could see where they were shooting, but could not pick out an effective target. Added to that, even if they had had proper observation, the German invaders had done plenty of snooping in the years before the war and located blind spots. They promptly occupied them.

By now, German attentions had turned to Fort Chaudfontaine. Belgian officer Count Gaston de Ribaucourt watched, depressed, as the German heavy artillery was hauled up and unleashed on 12 August. 'The big pieces have begun their firing and the agony is approaching.' He found it demoralizing, plugging away with their own shells in response, despite having no idea what they were shooting at, just hoping to do some damage to the enemy. They sat all night with fixed bayonets, lest the Germans attack. As soon as dawn arrived, the German heavy artillery started bombarding them again. De Ribaucourt was in the officers' firing chamber when 'a tremor accompanied by a tremendous noise shook the fort... Thrown against the opposite wall, I dragged myself towards the door through the debris. With another officer, I crossed the vestibule... and an awful scene presented itself to my eyes.' The space had been converted into a sleeping area. 'At the moment of the explosion, one hundred and forty men of the garrison were there, stretched out on straw or on mattresses, and in tragic horror, I see this whole room on fire. Straw, mattresses, soldiers, everything is burning! In this brazier, the lucky ones are struggling, their clothes in flames, real living torches!'[1] Set on fire, the screams of the victims would never leave him.

Unsurprisingly, the resolve of the survivors was broken and Fort Chaudfontaine capitulated, but in terms of weaponry, the worst was still yet to come. Germany owned two 42-cm Howitzers. These monsters weighed 45 tons and could fire a 5-foot shell more than 6 miles. However, in August 1914 the guns were not finished, and so they had to be claimed directly from the factory. By 10 August the parts were being loaded onto trains and the following afternoon, both were on their way to Liège without ever having been test fired.

Nicknamed Big Berthas, when they reached the battlefield their first target was Fort Pontisse, almost at the limit of their range. Men who saw one in action did not forget. It took a full minute for one of the gargantuan shells to bend in an arc towards its target. 'The civilian population was very curious about these great guns and stood in close crowds around them, but five minutes after the first shot was fired, which rattled the roof tiles and window panes, not a human was left in sight.'[2] The damage, one soldier noted, was unforgiving: At the first shot, the glass from the nearest windows rattled down on the pavement… In a few places, the air pressure had caused the plaster ceilings to fall down on the floors.'[3] In the face of these beasts, with masonry crumbling around their ears, the garrison at Pontisse surrendered.

At Embourg, asphyxiation from the fumes of bursting shells and a shower of concrete falling from the vaults prompted the men inside the fort to throw in the towel. Fort Liers fell, then Fléron. With more than half of the Liège forts now out of action, the Germans moved west towards Fort Boncelles. Inside, the wounded commander lay delirious and still intent on mounting a defence. Within a day, his fort was filling with noxious fumes. The garrison threw in the towel. 'Three white flags were hoisted on the fort… the garrison flooded the powder magazines, broke the guns and rifles, and rendered unusable everything that might be of assistance to the enemy.'[4] The destruction of the village of Boncelles had been for nothing.

After Lantin also capitulated, that left three forts to the west of Liège. It was Fort Loncin, guarding the road to Brussels, that was now the focus of the German heavy artillery. In charge, Commander Naessens – 'short, stocky, with… steely blue eyes, a searching gaze' – was adored by his men.[5] General Leman had also ensconced himself at Loncin after fleeing his command post at Liège to conduct the overall defence of the fortress ring.

Before the arrival of the heavy guns, the impact of the German artillery on Fort Loncin had been minimal. But on 12 August, that changed. The garrison was forced to withdraw further and further underground to escape the lingering fumes from bursting shells. By the early hours of 14 August, Loncin was being bombarded by a variety of heavy guns. The impact of each shell was a terrifying experience for those inside. 'The fort trembles to its foundations,' wrote Serjeant Krantz, a Luxembourger. 'After each shaking, fragments of cracked, pulverized concrete drip over our heads. A grey dust, mixed with a thousand shards of glass, cracks underfoot, tickles and dries out the throat and the nostrils.'[6] When asked if he would like to surrender, Commander Naessens said he would rather die. Nonetheless, he was beginning to realize that Loncin was being squeezed on all sides. 'Soon, all our telephone lines were cut,' he wrote. 'In the evening, most of the premises serving as accommodation for the troops were evacuated and the soldiers sent, with their sleeping supplies, to the large central gallery located in the centre of the fort.'[7]

On 15 August, the barrage remained relentless. Naessens was an example to his men, always visible, always talking. 'He challenged some with a joke that relaxed the atmosphere, he comforted others with a friendly tap on the shoulder, and he urged them all to resist.' During a lull in the barrage, he gathered everybody in one place: 'Climbing on an ammunition box, he called out to them, shouting: "We won't surrender, will we?" "No, never!"' his men replied. *Long live Belgium!*'[8]

'From dawn, the bombardment redoubled in violence… shells… with frightful howls, from all points of the horizon and bursting, with a terrible din in the midst of flames and greenish smoke.'[9] Morale inside was not helped by the worsening conditions. It was dark, filthy and swelteringly hot. Men worked without shirts, their skins blackened by the conditions. They lost all concept of time. Sleep was out of the question. The toilets were not connected to the underground part of the structure, which meant that, under fire, the garrison could not access them. Bins filled up rapidly with human waste, the stench of which hung in the air and combined with explosive fumes. Men were subsisting on nothing but biscuits. The electricity had failed by now, and hundreds of kerosene lamps shook and went out with the impact of every shell. 'In the light of these lanterns, a light greatly dimmed by the smoke and dust which make the atmosphere almost opaque, our resting soldiers are playing cards, seated on empty ammunition boxes.'[10] Their games were interrupted every time the lamps went out. They would grunt, swear, then relight them all.

'To make matters worse, a fine concrete dust falls non-stop... Our maps and papers are covered every few minutes with such a layer... that we have to shake them before reading them.' Wreckage lay everywhere: 'The beds overturned; the windows... are broken; the infirmary, the operating room, the kitchen, the refectory, the General's room are swept away. Everything is destroyed.' By this point, the garrison was willing the enemy to come at them, to end it. At about 3.00 p.m. a flurry in the bombardment made Naessens sure that the German infantry was poised to strike: 'Immediately there was a veritable outburst of joy. It is because, for several days, all those... at the fort asked me incessantly: "Shall we not see them up close, these filthy pigs?"'[11]

The Germans still had one card left to play. Jozef Grofils was patrolling outside. He had a front-row seat to witness the effects of the two Big Berthas as they were repositioned to attack Fort Loncin: 'Suddenly, we hear a howl, as if an express train passed through the air.' It was hard to spot the shells, 'because they were coming at such speed that it was difficult to follow them with your eyes.' The first one fired 'struck like a thunderclap in a summer sky, making the whole atmosphere vibrate.' This one landed long, shaking houses in a nearby village. Then the Germans began correcting their aim: 'The fourth [shell] fell on the massif, raising a thick cloud of earth and rubble which rose very high in the sky, the central mound disappearing in a greyish plume filtered by dusted light. In the galleries, everything collapsed and the men were thrown to the ground... Everything is upside down.'[12] Where smoke lingered the men could see no more than a few inches ahead.

From an observation post in the medieval castle at Waroux, Serjeant Julien Adam witnessed German soldiers creeping through uncut wheat outside and made a last telephone call to General Leman. 'We are completely surrounded... I feel like this is the end.'[13] Inside the remains of the fort, Leman was hurriedly destroying papers and anything that might prove useful to the enemy. The food supply was ruined, the last three guns were disabled and the shells nearby detonated. Then, disaster struck. The whistle of another giant shell approached. By now, the men had taken to curling up into a foetal position, bracing themselves for the terrifying impact. German colonel Erich von Steinbach witnessed what happened from outside as it 'tore through the cracked and battered masonry and exploded in the magazine. With a thunderous crash, the mighty walls of the fort fell.'[14] Another German soldier said it looked like the fort had been wrecked under the fist of a colossus.

Serjeant Krantz was in the firing office with Leman and Naessens. 'A sheaf of flames and a tremendous jolt throw us all against the wall, then, nothing more, silence.' IR 165 would be among the first Germans to enter the fort. Private Gaston Damoiseau, sixteen years old and unsure whether he would be executed or taken captive, did not want to meet them. He had volunteered to join his father in defending Loncin. After the explosion, he found him collapsed in a gallery. 'I'm finished, I'm spitting blood,' he said.[15] His son tried to help him up, but the senior Damoiseau made it no more than a few steps before collapsing again. At this point Gaston lay down next to his father and played dead.

Many of those still inside Loncin were trapped, but some clawed their way to freedom. Exposed suddenly to daylight again, men blinked hard and shielded their eyes. The scene resembled the aftermath of a volcanic eruption. The survivors that could, ran. Felix Yans had burnt feet and so fled dragging himself on his hands and knees. Back at the fort, Steinbach was one of the first Germans to enter the chaos. 'When the dust and fumes passed away, we stormed the fort across ground literally strewn with bodies... Buried in the debris, and pinned beneath a massive beam, was General Leman.'[16] Along with Commander Naessens, plucked from a ditch outside, he was loaded onto a cart and taken to a hospital in Liège.

Travelling the other way were both Belgian and German doctors coming up from the city to help the wounded. Soldiers from both sides were working in the ruins. Now that the fight was over, bloodlust had been replaced by humanity. 'They cleared the concrete blocks with their bare hands, pushed aside heaps of smoking debris, lifted broken beams and, here and there, they pulled from the rubble a crushed body whose eyes were already dull.' Dr Defalle, a local resident, was mortified: 'From time to time there were still explosions... From the ruins came inhuman cries. They were wretched people who were burning and begging to be saved. It was necessary... sometimes to saw off a limb to extricate these brave men.'[17]

By the morning of 16 August, with General Leman captured and word spreading of the explosion, the last two forts surrendered. Meanwhile, the inhabitants of Loncin, hovering on their doorsteps, watched distraught as survivors hobbled away. 'Bruised men walk painfully, supporting each other on the cobblestones... After being pulled from the rubble and receiving some treatment, they stoically walk to the city's medical clinics and hospitals with blackened faces, hair scorched from the flames and dried blood crusted over their parched lips.' Dozens of men would remain entombed at Fort Loncin, but their suffering was finished.

When Dr Defalle returned to his clinic in Liège he faced harrowing scenes:

> The arrival of these wretches with frizzy hair, blackened hands and faces... The Germans took them for Senegalese! In the operating room, scenes took place that filled us with horror: when we took off clothes, we tore off shreds of flesh; the legs, the arms were disintegrating. Horrible wounds, burns of all degrees... In the atmosphere floated an awful smell of charred flesh and fat... Hardly had they recovered from the dizziness in which they had been plunged, when they were dragged through the pain caused by the washing of the wounds... in order to remove the dust, the smoke, the debris of all kinds.[18]

Hubert Stienert's son was so badly burnt that when he tracked his boy down, the Belgian civilian found himself looking at a mutilated stranger:

> We approached the bed. How can we imagine that we have before us our handsome and joyful boy! A thick layer of

wadding supported by strips conceals the form: the head, the neck, the arms, the legs, everything has disappeared, melted as in a block of plaster. Eyes, nose, no trace! In place of the mouth, a frightening wound, a real crack which would have been formed by the bursting of a rotting body...[19]

*

On 17 August King Albert and his advisors agreed that the Belgian government should flee Brussels. The king was approaching a landmark decision. If his army was annihilated, it would stay so. The Belgian population could not provide another. Albert had two options, neither of which were appealing. He could keep the army on the Gette and hope for a miracle. Alternatively, he could retire towards the national stronghold at Antwerp. His enemies would claim more Belgian soil, but Belgium would live to fight another day.

Matters came to a head the next day. Alexander von Kluck's First Army, which was to form the far right of the German line, joined the fray. At Louvain, where army headquarters had been established in the medieval town hall, King Albert wrestled with his conscience all day long. Finally, he made the agonising decision that the army would fall back on Antwerp, thus delivering thousands of his subjects into German hands. For how long, nobody knew. The people of Louvain suspected that something was afoot. Their resolve crumbled. 'Groups formed at the corners of the streets, trying to reassure one another... In the distance could be seen a light that stood out at first palely and then more clearly against a sky of thick gloom. Soon the horizon became red... Without doubt fires were burning there. Fires lit by whom? As yet no one knew.'[20]

As the night wore on, the wounded began arriving. The streets filled with soldiers, horses, artillery, wagons. 'Above the railway station a German aeroplane hovered... At dawn the noise of guns became more and more clearly perceptible, announcing to the anxious townsfolk that the invader was approaching.' Civilians loitered around the railway station. 'Towards 5.00 a.m. news... was circulating that the Belgian army was about to retire... Was that really true?… The last picket of gendarmes, which had until then formed the guard at headquarters, entered the railway station… and mounted a train which drew off in the direction of Antwerp. That was the end.'[21]

The people of Louvain began to realize that they had been left to their fate. They shared that fate with Brussels, whose authorities had grimly left that city to the invader, too. Brussels was of no strategic value, and there was nothing to be gained by sacrificing lives in defending it, so trenches were filled up and barricades removed. Soon, tens of thousands of German soldiers marched ceremoniously into the capital. They were fresh troops, unsullied by battle. Some of them even goose-stepped for effect. The Belgian crowd watched on, sullen. Protests were few, but at one point an old woman pushed through the crowd to get to the conquerors marching past. As a policeman attempted to stop her she screamed: 'I had a son. They killed him!' As she was manhandled away she cried: '"Down with the Prussians!" The words produced a momentary panic, but the German soldiers passed by looking, but not reacting.'[22]

Neither the Belgian army nor the German troops invading their country were the finished article in August 1914. Mobilization and concentration of soldiers were still in progress, and units were short of their proper numbers. They would remain so for the first fortnight of the war. Under the circumstances, which were largely of their own making, the Belgian army had done just about all they could. The Liège defences had failed spectacularly. While only Loncin and Chaudfontaine were actually destroyed, all of the other forts surrendered of their own volition and usually within a day of falling under bombardment by heavy artillery. The method of systematically attacking the forts bit by bit slowed the Germans down, but it achieved wholesale results. They had been delayed, but at no great strategic cost. Arguably, the First and Second Armies could not have proceeded any faster than they did in the early days of the war. The question on Belgian lips now though, was: 'Where are our allies?' For now surely only France and Britain could save them from oblivion.

8

Cerska Planina

The Balkans

A t Antwerp, King Albert was at least buoyed by the prospect of the imminent arrival of his allies. However, in the Balkans, the Serbian army was going to have to fight it out on their own. With the Austro-Hungarians already on their soil, they would need a miracle.

That is not to say that the Austro-Hungarians were finding matters easy. The further they advanced, the worse the terrain got. The Fifth Army's route through western Serbia led directly across Cer Mountain, known as *Cerska Planina* to the Serbs. It dominated a region devoid of roads and studded with numerous hills and ridges. This large, uneven plateau, surrounded by cornfields as far as the eye could see, was wholly unsuited for war. Nevertheless, it marked the most direct route to the city of Valjevo, which still lay more than 40 miles to the south-west.

Logistical problems mounted for the Austro-Hungarians and even more strenuous marches were inflicted on already exhausted soldiers. Some resorted to throwing away their equipment. Soon, the countryside was littered with discarded overcoats, knapsacks, spades and hatchets. On 15 August, the 21st Landwehr Division set off for the peak of the mountain. Dark storm clouds began to gather above. Just as they reached the heights late in the afternoon, the heavens opened and dumped a raging thunderstorm on them. In command, General Artur Przyborski considered this the last straw, and ordered his weary men to make camp for the night.

While the Austro-Hungarians made preparations for a much-needed night's rest, the Serbian Second Army had finally arrived at the front following a forced march in the August heat. Its capable commander, General Stepa Stepanović, had led these men through both Balkan Wars and was popular among the troops, whom he fully trusted in return. Stepanović knew the terrain well and while he was not aware of his enemy's exact location, he fully realized the importance of Cer Mountain. He ordered the Combined Division, with artillery support, to seize the heights of the plateau. Captain Ješa Topalović recalled the difficult approach through the storm:

> It was already night; a downpour began, accompanied by volcanic thunder and lightning. Water was pouring in from all sides. Mud and rain, which seemed to fall on the exhausted troops with some kind of malevolence, made it even more difficult for the artillery to move across the hilly terrain and the ruined road. A heavy and dark night descended... You couldn't see a hand in front of you. The unknown, unpaved, muddy road, the overworked livestock, the downpour; all combined to cause the kind of difficulties a person can only overcome in war...[1]

After hours of difficult marching, the 21st Landwehr Division's campfires could suddenly be made out through the darkness. The enemy had been located, the order to attack was issued, and two of the Combined Division's four regiments were soon making their way towards the unsuspecting Landwehrmen. Przyborski's exhausted troops were oblivious to the presence of a strong Serbian force closing in on their position. 'We were all asleep, officers undressed, all comfortable,' one soldier recalled.[2] A perimeter had been established around their encampment, but the tired sentries saw nothing through the darkness and the pouring rain.

Then all hell broke loose as the Serbian infantry emerged from the surrounding cornfields. The sentries were caught off guard and some of the Serbian soldiers yelled to the defenders not to shoot, lying that they were in fact friendly Croats, before opening fire at close range. 'They were blowing their bugles, shouting that they were ours,' remembered one Czech soldier.[3] Taking full advantage of the darkness, the Serbian officers led their men forward into the Austro-Hungarian positions, and many of the defenders were cut down before fully realizing what was happening. Some were even bayoneted to death in their sleep. 'Terrible rifle and machine-gun fire broke out,' recalled Serbian captain Milutin Nikolić. 'Neither the enemy's strength nor his disposition was known… Our soldiers literally ran into his trenches… It was hot as hell. They shouted at the top of their lungs, shots were fired in all directions, and the soldiers fell like mown sheaves.'[4]

Austro-Hungarian officers and NCOs struggled to control their terrified men. They fired blindly at anything that moved in the darkness. 'At such a moment you forget that you are human,' wrote Jaroslav Míchal of the k.k. LIR 8. 'You become an animal that senses death and defends itself as best it can.' One by one, their positions were being overrun. The deafening noise of battle, the terrible confusion in the darkness, and the sight of their comrades falling dead around them resulted in some of the defenders losing their nerve:

The worst was the young guys. They were the first to lose their composure… Boys, children really… Literal 'snots', as the Major had put it: 'Many of you snots should get a bottle of milk and a pacifier instead of a gun!' And here? Many of them fall, covered in blood, and cry, not out of fear or horror, but in pain: 'Mother, my dear mother!' Some of them are already speaking their last words.[5]

Fighting raged throughout the night with undiminished ferocity. 'Machine-guns, both ours and the enemy's, never ceased firing,' a Serbian soldier wrote.[6] By dawn, the Austro-Hungarians had suffered heavy losses, including many of their officers, yet they still clung on to some of their positions. The Serbs, too, had many casualties, and a steady stream of wounded made their way down the mountain to the dressing stations. By now, however, the Serbian artillery had finally caught up, and more infantry was being ordered forward to push the Austro-Hungarians off the mountain. 'The crack of thousands of rifles resounded throughout the country,' František Petržíla recalled. 'Shells whizzed and sizzled in the air; they exploded with a tremendous thud as they landed, digging into the ground... Woe to whoever was nearby. Shrapnel crackled in the air and masses of lead balls rained down on us... The screams... of the wounded could be heard everywhere.'[7] Jaroslav Michal also noted the deafening noise and destructive force of the guns: 'There was a row of oak trees in front of us... shells hit them and branches flew in all directions... Everything was shaking and falling... Entire trees and their roots flew through the air. There was a mad rush to dig in. Dread and horror descended upon the trenches.'[8] Austro-Hungarian batteries operated to little effect; the coordination between the artillery and infantry left much to be desired. Meanwhile, the Serbian guns kept up a steady fire. 'The cannons roared,' remembered Captain Topalović. 'The battery commanders could not meet all the infantry's demands, since there were more targets than there were guns.'[9]

Shelling took a heavy toll on the defenders. Shrapnel tore huge gaps in their ranks, and high explosive projectiles buried men alive. František Petržíla witnessed Serbian artillery score direct hits on their Austro-Hungarian counterparts. 'The gun flew apart like a toy, the wheels to the sides and the carriage to a tremendous height. The gunners were also killed immediately. The others stopped firing, left the guns and ran to hide.'[10] For many, this was their first time under fire, and they had not yet grown accustomed to the destructive power of modern artillery. Some broke down. Jaroslav Míchal intervened with one of his young comrades in a particularly heartrending scene:

> He had been sitting huddled and clutching a cross in his hand... Only his unnatural crying turned our attention to him: his lips were twisting strangely, his face was twitching,

tears were flowing from his wide eyes. He cried more and more and called out for his mummy! [Then] he didn't cry anymore. He screamed. He let out screams from his throat and jerked himself in all directions. We felt really sorry for him. Such a good boy, childlike nature... How can I calm him down at least a little? I thought. I took him in my arms, comforted him, caressed him, kissed him like a father would his child and rubbed his face and temples. [He] pressed himself to me. He hugged me, his crying subsided, but the expression on his face remained numb, eyes frightened, body shaking and trembling.[11]

The nocturnal attack had left Przyborski's division in a poor state, and his own nerves were shattered. His reports to VIII Corps headquarters painted a gloomy picture of the situation on Cer Mountain, which was corroborated by another senior officer, General Panesch. 'Half the men were dead or wounded,' he wrote. 'A few staff officers, company commanders and many young officers are dead. Captain Niehsner fell... Shot in the thigh, injury to the artery, bleeding to death, shot in the shoulder as well... I wanted to resign from military service right away, but it's not that easy to give up everything and resign in the event of war.'[12]

Clearly shaken by the ambush, Panesch ignored orders from corps headquarters to hold his position, and instead withdrew his battered units. Fortunately for the Austro-Hungarians, the Serbs had also suffered heavy losses and were in no position to exploit the enemy retreat. The Combined Division had suffered almost 3,000 casualties, and was forced to temporarily pull back when the Austro-Hungarians launched a counter-attack in the morning.

*

Meanwhile, the Austro-Hungarian 42nd Brigade, commanded by General Alois Podhajski, tried to advance from the north, but quickly came under fire from Serbian infantry and cavalry from the front and both flanks. Many of the Austro-Hungarian soldiers broke and ran. Ewald Mácha, who had been posted in the rear to protect the ammunition train, could hardly believe his eyes when large numbers of men came streaming back. 'Their clothes are tattered and dirty and their faces look strange. They have no weapons. "Where are you going?" we ask in amazement. "Oh, it's bad, bad," they reply.'[13] Before long, Podhajski's brigade was retreating in complete chaos towards the Drina and the pontoon bridges leading to safety. Panicked infantrymen fled in disorder and artillerymen abandoned their guns and ran. 'Frightened horses were running between us,' wrote Czech soldier Aloise Holeček of the 21st Landwehr Division's medical company. 'Wagons were overturned, sacks of food [rolled] into the ditch. In order to run more easily, the soldiers threw away or lost their equipment; the Austrian *"Tapfere Offiziere"* ["brave officers"] ran first. It was terrible.'[14]

As his division retreated, heavy fighting had also broken out further south. Here, the Austro-Hungarians attacked General Pavle Jurišić Šturm's Third Army, but a frontal attack by the 36th Division around the village of Jarebice was met with withering Serbian fire. 'People were dropping like flies,' wrote Lieutenant István Szakraida of the k.u.k. IR 37. 'Wailing and rattling mingled with the maddening noise of the explosions. Gravel, earth, human limbs flew everywhere. It was impossible to stand it... At this moment, the air pressure caused by the shells drilling into the ground next to me knocked me and Lieutenant Kiszlinger to the ground three times.'[15] Despite repeated charges, the Serbian lines held. Only when the Croatian 42nd Honvéd Division broke through the Third Army's weakly defended left flank, did Jurišić Šturm order a retirement.

The Serbians' 6-mile retreat by night would prove a harrowing experience. The storm still raged, turning the roads into rivers of mud in complete darkness. All the while, the fleeing columns were subjected to constant Austro-Hungarian fire. 'Shouting, shooting... horror! The ammunition train flees in fear,' wrote Serbian artilleryman Milorad Markovic. 'The commander and I went ahead, the battery followed behind us. Chaos on the road!

Supply trains, foot soldiers, horses, everything got stuck... We feel nothing but shame.'[16]

Evacuating the wounded proved so difficult that many of the most serious cases had to be left behind. 'An officer was left on the road, we nearly ran him over,' wrote Marković. Czech volunteer Juričič Houžvic later described a particularly haunting episode. 'Many of the wounded could not be cleared in this mountainous terrain, and heart-rending scenes therefore occurred. The seriously wounded had to be shot by their comrades and quickly buried under piles of stones, after all evidence of their identity had been destroyed as a precaution.'[17]

For the Austro-Hungarians, however, this local success would be of little actual value. Due to high casualties and exhaustion, the attack could not be pressed, and the following day was instead spent resting, regrouping and bringing up reinforcements.

Fighting continued along the entire front on 17 August. The demoralized men of the 21st Landwehr Division continued retreating to the Drina, and throughout the day Serbian irregulars and cavalry continued to harass the retreating columns, leading to several bloody clashes. 18 August did not bring Potiorek his expected victory. Deciding to concentrate on the enemy forces pursuing his retreating centre, Potiorek now ordered his flanks to envelop Stepanović's Second Army on Cer Mountain in a pincer movement. In the south, XIII Corps attacked the Serbian Third Army, but ultimately failed to break through. In the north, the Second Army's IV Corps attacked in the general direction of the town of Valjevo. This was the day originally scheduled for them to begin departing for Galicia, but given the increasingly dangerous situation, that would clearly have to wait. Faced with heavy Serbian fire, many of the Austro-Hungarian regiments barely managed to advance at all. One exception was the k.u.k. Bosnisch-Hercegovinische Infanterie Nr.3 (BH IR 3). Moving forward in dense columns, the fez-wearing *Bosniaken* suffered dearly as a result. 'The officers and NCOs made a lot of effort to hold back the men's brave, but suicidal, charge,' wrote officer Pero Blašković. 'The terrain was densely overgrown with crops, bushes and poplars. Patrols of Serbian soldiers were posted in the trees and they inflicted heavy losses on us with rifle or machine-gun fire.'[18] Soon, both the regimental commander and his replacement had been wounded and the attack collapsed.

As Potiorek's efforts on the flanks proved unsuccessful, the Serbs maintained the pressure on his centre. In vain, officers of the retreating 21st Landwehr Division desperately tried to organize rearguards. 'The confusion that prevails cannot be described,' wrote Ewald Mácha. 'A captain on horseback, revolver in hand, drives everyone back against the enemy, who is said to be approaching rapidly.' None of them wanted to comply, not even when the captain started shooting. The Austro-Hungarian 9th Division attempted to regain some lost positions, but without success. 'We attacked the hillside, but we didn't even get halfway before everyone was dead or wounded,' recalled František Petržíla of the k.u.k. IR 73. Serbian artillery covered the attackers with shrapnel and high explosive shells, and when Austro-Hungarian artillery fired short, hitting their own infantry, the order to retreat was finally given. The men fled, running over the bodies of their comrades, while the wounded begged and pleaded for help. Petržíla described horrifying scenes:

I found many soldiers who'd been killed and mutilated by the shells; their legs or arms had been torn off, many had their bodies torn in half and their intestines [spilled out]. Another had his head smashed beyond recognition. It was terrible to look at. I was so moved by the cries of the wounded that I bandaged one after the other and brought them to the dressing station. One poor fellow with his legs shot off begged me to take pity on him and shoot him. The wretch lay in his own blood. Another again begged me to cut off his arm from the very shoulder, because it hung only from his skin.[19]

It was now becoming increasingly clear to the Serbian high command that their opponent was wavering. Now was the time to strike. On the morning of 19 August, the Moravian Division launched a powerful attack against the Austro-Hungarian 9th Division, which soon broke. The panic-stricken invaders scrambled out of their positions and began a chaotic flight towards the Drina, only to become easy targets for the Serbian guns. Officers tried to maintain order, but had little choice but to follow their panicked men: 'A wild escape ensued. Everyone wanted to save themselves,' remembered František Petržíla.[20] Soldiers ran around without weapons. Horses broke free from their handlers and thrashed around, while wagons overturned and spilt their cargo of ammunition and food on the ground. Seeing this, some hungry soldiers, who'd had nothing to eat for days, frantically fell upon the sacks of bread and crates of canned meat to fill their pockets. Artillerymen abandoned their guns and stretcher-bearers dropped the wounded at a nearby brickworks and ran, leaving the desperate men to their fate and ignoring their pitiful pleas not to be forsaken.

Men flooded onto the single road leading to the river, which was soon packed solid with infantry, cavalry, artillery and supply trains. Horses, lashed too hard, reared and bit each other. Men were crushed beneath hoofs and wagon wheels. All the while, Serbian shrapnel shells exploded above, spraying their deadly clouds of lead balls down on the road and ripping through the dense columns. 'Sometimes the balls just rained down on the baggage wagons and smashed the barrels, chests, trunks and crates; sometimes they clattered against the cauldrons of the field kitchens or on guns,' wrote Egon Erwin Kisch. 'But sometimes they hit groups of soldiers, who screamed and groaned, called for help, or simply lay in pools of their own blood. Those who followed stumbled over them. If horses were caught by the explosives and detonators, they would fall down in their bridles, their necks dripping, their torsos pierced, their legs broken, but still alive.'[21] This was no longer an army, but a rampant horde running for the border in senseless fear. 'I was reminded of Zola's novel *The Debacle*, where Zola captured the escape of the French from the Germans,' concluded František Petržíla. 'This was almost exactly like that.'[22]

The gruelling retreat continued throughout the rest of the day and into the night. In its wake lay bodies as far as the eye could see. The commander of the Moravian Division, General Ilija Gojković, reported to Serbia's Second Army headquarters that the entire area before him was covered in corpses, still warm and oozing with blood. 'I see what bloody battles are being fought here, and I see that human life is nothing,' wrote Serbian artilleryman Mileta Prodanović. As his battery joined the pursuit he witnessed horrifying scenes. 'It was a terrible sight to see; corpse next to corpse, horses and enemy soldiers. Terrible stench. It seems that no one got out of here alive... The supply trains trample over dead bodies, because it's only possible to go around in some places.'[23]

The last remnants of the shattered VIII Corps reached the Drina during the morning of 20 August and began crossing the pontoon bridges back into Bosnia. By evening, the survivors of the 21st Landwehr Division had left Serbian territory. Over the following days, the rest of the Fifth Army followed. In places, the crossing descended into chaos. Frane Dubravčić of the k.u.k. IR 16 noted the tragedy that transpired when the pioneers blew up the pontoons before the last troops had got away:

> Despair reigned among those who remained on the right bank of the river. The Drina is deep and fast, and the enemy is at your back and will come any minute! Those who knew how to swim quickly undressed and swam. Those who did not know how to swim held each other's hands tightly, five to ten of them, then undressed and waded into the water until the current pulled them, wrapped them and tricked them. We saw how the water carried individuals away and they were heard calling for help, but they soon disappeared under the surface.[24]

Only now did the survivors fully realize just how terrible the cost of the failed invasion had been. In less than two weeks, Frane Dubravčić's regiment had lost fifty-four officers, including its commander, and more than 1,000 men were either killed, wounded or missing: 25 per cent of its strength. 'We mocked that Latin phrase, *Dulce et decorum est pro patria mori*,' he wrote.[25]

The Austro-Hungarian Sixth Army, which had been fighting Serbian and Montenegrin forces that had crossed the border in the first days of the war, also suspended any further offensive action and began withdrawing further south. With this, the only units still in Serbia were the three divisions of the Second Army's IV Corps, defending the bridgehead at Šabac. Holding the town now made little sense, and IV Corps was most needed in Galicia for the coming battle against Russia. Contrary to reason, however, it was decided that it was of the utmost importance to hold Šabac, so as to preserve a sliver of prestige in the face of a catastrophic defeat.

For days, desperate fighting raged for control of the town, before finally, on 23 August, the corps commander ordered one last massed bayonet charge. With no clearly defined objective, the attack quickly collapsed under a hail of Serbian rifles, machine-guns and artillery. Two divisions broke and retreated back across the Sava in complete disorder. 'They swarmed back across the narrow pontoon bridge until it could not accommodate them all,' remembered fifteen-year-old Stevan Idjidović, whose village of Jarak on the riverbank now became a thoroughfare for the retreating Austro-Hungarians. 'In contrast to the well-equipped, well-tailored soldiers we had seen marching smartly like con-querors across the bridge into Serbia, we now beheld a bedrag-gled, dishevelled, dirty mass of humanity almost all with torn clothing, some only half dressed, pantless or coatless, and bare-headed.'[26] By the following afternoon, the last Austro-Hungarian troops had left Serbian soil.

With this, Austria–Hungary's first invasion of Serbia came to an inglorious end. The operation had been a complete fail-ure. Potiorek's forces had been thrown back across the border in disorder, leaving thousands of their dead on the slopes of Cer Mountain and the banks of the Drina and the Sava. 'You wouldn't believe it,' recalled one Serbian soldier. 'So many... were killed that one could step from man to man, from corpse to corpse, for [nearly a mile].'[27] French war correspondent Henri Barbi described the entire area around Cer Mountain as 'nothing but a mass grave and decaying flesh' and recalled that 'a stench spread from the shadow of the forests, so foul that access to the top of Cer was impossible'.[28]

In total, the Austro-Hungarians suffered more than 23,000 killed, wounded and missing in less than two weeks of fighting. While these losses were relatively light compared to other clashes in the opening weeks of the war, Potiorek's disastrous 'autumn stroll' had been a severe blow to Habsburg military prestige. Worst of all, the fighting had caused significant delays to the transfer of the Second Army to Galicia, where the first major clashes with Russia were just about to commence.

Somehow, the Serbs had conjured up their miracle. Victory at Cer provided a significant boost to morale, both at the front and at home. A mighty enemy had attacked and been soundly defeated, providing the Allies with their first significant victory of the war. Furthermore, the Austro-Hungarian defeat deterred Bulgaria and Romania from entering the war on the side of the Central Powers, at least for now. Victory, however, had come at a cost. Serbian losses of 16,000 were considerable for the small nation. One observer described the sight of endless columns of carts transporting the wounded from the battlefields to field hospitals in Valjevo: 'In them lie pale and immobile bodies in torn and dirty uniforms and with bandages that are no longer clean... For four or five days they have been travelling like this... without comfort and without protection from rain and storms. Their wounds are infected; in some places, maggots are crawling on them.'[29]

It was a stark reminder of the high price of victory in modern war. But for now, Serbia had been defended, and on 22 August, General Stepanović began his orders for the day with the following words: 'The holy land of our homeland has been cleansed of the enemy, and those places that he desecrated with his heathen foot have been sprinkled with his blood.'[30]

9

Don't Talk to Me About the War

Neutrality was a sacrifice for a nation. It meant pandering to those at war so that they left you alone, and it meant having no seat at the table at the end of the conflict when the spoils were divided. To maintain a neutral stance in 1914 you had to isolate yourself, and put your own ambitions and your sovereignty below that of everyone around you for the privilege of being allowed to maintain it.

The nature of how the world worked in 1914 forced all countries to reappraise what they thought neutrality was. Neutrality was historically defined as not participating on either side, which was easy enough when a battle took place in a single field, or a war concerned small professional armies and it took weeks, even months, to communicate news of it across the globe. None of this applied anymore, and so new ideas constantly evolved during the war. Countries no longer fought each other in isolation, and global trade ruined anyone's chances of remaining insular. Nobody went to war without relying on supplies and materials brought in from abroad, and so at what point was a Swedish ship carrying iron ore for a combatant participating in the war? Sweden's economy relied on selling that ore to survive, so what should they do? What was participation? Did you have to actually fight in a battle? Or were you a participant if you shipped guns to those battles? Or merely the raw materials like that iron ore which would be used to manufacture war materials? Were you actively participating if you so much as exported food that sustained an army?

Each supposedly neutral nation approached questions like this differently, but they all faced a battle of a different kind to stay out of the war, and the outcome was not necessarily in their own hands. They could follow the rules that supposedly framed neutrality, but getting belligerent nations to respect their interpretation of those rules when they were more interested in their own survival was another matter entirely. Stakes were high, and some nations went all out to stay out of the war. They were willing to pass laws, take freedoms away from their own people, and, ironically, even mobilize their armies to maintain neutrality.

Some nations reasoned that they had nothing to gain from intervening on either side. This accounted for much of Latin America. Europe was a long way away. They had no shared military alliances, no political gains to pursue. Other nations stayed out because they lacked the means to get involved in a costly, industrialized war. For example, Spain was broke. The army, which had lost the best remnants of her global empire in 1898 in the Americas, was a mess. The political status quo was fragile, politicians did not want a civic meltdown, and King Alphonso XIII's hold on power was weak. Elsewhere, Norway had only come out from under Swedish control in 1905. With a small population of two and a half million people, they were still too busy establishing their government and industry to get involved in someone else's fight. Perched in a far corner of Europe, King Haakon and his people just wanted to be left alone.

For other nations, pragmatism be damned. The war presented opportunities they could only dream of from a world at peace, and therefore neutrality was not sustainable. For the Ottoman empire, European powers clawing at each other might leave the door open to claim back what they had lost. They might no longer be 'the sick man of Europe' if they picked the winning side. Nations like this would probably have to participate in the war, or at least commit to doing so eventually, but there could be huge rewards.

Government policy is one thing, but neutrality did not mean apathy for ordinary people, either. If your team is not in the game, you pick a side to support, at the very least. It's human nature, and the outbreak of war was the biggest 'game' transpiring anywhere on the planet. Japan was still neutral at the beginning of August 1914, and yet people flocked to stations and ports to wave off those leaving to fight: 'In Yokohama and Kobe were great crowds of Japanese at the stations shouting *banzai* and waving *sayonara* to their departing French, British, Austrian, and German friends, who were all going over to Europe on the same boat to fight each other.' Similar scenes in Shanghai had a little more spice running beneath the mood: 'Germans on one side of the pier or... the deck, the British on the other.'[1]

In Denmark, thoughts naturally turned to *what if?* If Germany was defeated, Denmark might be able to reclaim Schleswig, the disputed territory that had been formally ceded to Germany in 1864. 'It is a living hope... It's not only... a confirmation of the hope of reunification, no, deepest down it's the outcome of the feeling of cohesion that awakens everywhere, where Danish people become aware of their Danishness.'[2]

Some Americans were smart enough to have figured out that in a war, as surely as some people would die horribly, others got rich. Why not them? In the *New York American*, the most popular newspaper in the country, the tone was callous:

Action! Should be the watchword and the duty of the American Congress and the American People in this great commercial emergency. TWO [BILLION] in trade is the prize which world conditions have put before the American people. Europe's tragic extremity becomes, without any working of our own, America's golden opportunity not of a lifetime but of a century of national life.[3]

The allegiances of the American people varied hugely. America was a nation of immigrants, or for the later generations, at least people who still half thought of themselves in terms of where they originated from: Swedish-Americans, or Italian-Americans. With twelve million ethnic Germans living in the United States, and millions more Irish, a significant number of whom despised Britain, there was no easy decision for the government to make in picking a side.

Ethnicity aside, a banker in New York had nothing in common – politics, lifestyle, or anything else – with a German immigrant farmer in Texas hill country. Neither resembled a factory worker in Ohio. This meant that the opinions Americans formed about the conflict were wildly diverse.

The idea of a war to end all wars, making conflict obsolete, was a worldwide trope during the First World War as people tried to process the bloodshed. *When this is over, nobody will ever want to let it happen again.* But in America this concept had an added twist. The *New York Times* talked about the war as 'the dying gasp of a backward, aristocratic Europe' before it was replaced by democracy and modernity: the American way of doing things. In some cases, newspapers treated the war lightly, even with humour, as if the distance and the impossibility of having an enemy army of a million or more men marching across their own borders made it less comprehensible, perhaps even entertaining.

*

The upheaval and uncertainty that impacted neutral populations took its toll on ordinary people throughout the world. In Italy, Ferdinando Martini watched a restless public gradually slide towards civil disorder. 'A month ago the declaration of neutrality was welcomed with unanimous assent by Italians,' he wrote in mid-September. 'Today the condition of the public spirit has changed and the sensational restlessness of the few and the wavering restlessness of the many are equally worrying.'

In Constantinople, six-year-old Irfan Orga was baffled by his parents' behaviour. He watched his father talking to the women of the household:

He stood leaning against a console table, and for the first time I felt him to be old. I did not know he was only 26... He was essentially a man of peace, a good Muslim who feared his God... A man who was appalled by the poverty of his people... The carnage and brutality and utter senselessness of war tore his heart for the ordinary man who was caught up in the military machine.[4]

Their home had been sold. His father was adamant that they had to conserve their resources for the war to come. Outside, Irfan's world was changing too: 'More and more men were taken to be soldiers and presently one saw mainly women in the streets. Servants and mistresses and prostitutes, they all had to eat and would spend their days tramping the streets in search of an open shop. Bewilderment, resignation was to be seen in all their faces but no resentment. That came later.' At the new house, his father took him aside and said:

'I hope I shall see you here as a grown man, my son, and myself as an old man. But if anything happens to me, then you will have to take my place. Perhaps many times it will be difficult for you but it will be your duty to look after your mother and your grandmother.' I could not bear to hear my kindly father talk like this and I threw myself on him, weeping as if my heart would break.[5]

*

No country found a complete consensus of opinion among its people. The Argentine government did not want war, and there were official guidelines on how the country should behave, yet her people were inclined to support the Allies. Britain was her most important trading partner, and culturally, the Argentinian people had huge respect for anything French and an affinity with this fellow Latin nation on whose revolution they had modelled their own. Bastille Day was soon to be a national holiday in Argentina.

Spain was split, and some people got so tired of the constant back and forth that in Barcelona, people started wearing badges that said: 'Don't talk to me about the war.' In Italy, too, there was no definitive consensus of opinion. In the opening weeks of the war, Gino Frontali watched his fellow soldiers arguing. They represented the whole spectrum of Italian opinion sitting around one table. One had a law doctorate, and was a nationalist. 'Albi affected a great respect for everything that was German... discipline, hierarchy... He absolutely wanted us to take the field alongside them to "stab" France in the back.' The accountant in the room wanted Italy to remain neutral. 'Bega, incapable of enthusiasm, believed that as an intermediary Italy would be enriched at the expense of the belligerents.' The socialist music-lover, Ciceri, was a pacifist. 'In contrast to the atrocities attributed to the Germans, he reproached the Belgians for the Congo, above all he wanted to save the genius (and he thought implicitly of himself) from the obligations and risks of military service in war.' And then there was Gino himself, the doctor. He could not even work out what 'Italian' meant to him. Born and raised in Egypt, where he went to a German elementary school, he 'felt confusedly that the cause of the allies against the central empires involved a concept of life, of individual liberty, of the form of government, of international relations, which was in accord with my feelings'.[6]

And so there was a huge difference between a government declaring neutrality and achieving it. Nations struggled against their own people and a range of differing opinions. Neutrality in many cases had to be quite literally enforced, and for every potential issue the authorities solved, another sprung up. On 20 August, to protect American neutrality, President Wilson ordered that there must be no 'transaction that might be construed as a preference of one party'.[7] By the end of 1914, however, a senate committee would be bragging about America's munitions industry, referring to it as an 'auxiliary arsenal' for the likes of France and Britain.[8] With the latter dominating the seas, Germany could not shop equally in this market. The United States was defiant. 'Millions of dollars' worth of guns, ammunition, shells, horses, equipment, supplies, food, and gunpowder had been shipped to England, France, and Russia, amounting to a total of over $825 million dollars of material purchased... by the Allies alone.'[9]

Smaller nations were bullied into improper conduct for neutral countries. Denmark's geographical position meant that she could impact who sailed in and out of the Baltic Sea. On 5 August Germany demanded that the Danes assist in mine-laying operations. Denmark did not want the German army marching across its frontier, but the country also wanted no part of antagonizing the Royal Navy. They had no choice but to comply, but ingeniously, less than twenty-four hours later they also implemented a ban on exporting animal feed, potatoes, fuel and weapons that Germany would have wanted to buy, therefore levelling the score diplomatically.

Columbia was uncomfortably stuck in the middle of a spat over a wireless installation at Cartagena that Germany was allegedly still using to bounce messages across the globe. Neutrals were required to prevent belligerents from using their territory for military purposes, and that included communications. The British naval attaché in Washington was ordered to go and inspect the site. He found it completely under German influence, and reported that all of the German employees remained at their posts. The British government was soon harassing the Columbian government to shut the station down. The debate rumbled on into the autumn, by which time Britain was asking the United States to mediate on the basis that Columbia was not meeting its neutral obligations. By December, British persistence paid off and the station was defunct.

Enforcing neutrality often meant the loss of freedoms for neutral populations at the instigation of their own governments. In Switzerland, the government started issuing legislation on 4 August to keep the population in line for the 'application of Swiss neutrality, which the people must observe'. They regulated everything from dealing with refugees to banning recruiting for any other army. 'Swiss people who do not behave in a peaceful and neutral manner can be incarcerated and foreigners expelled.'[10] Freedom of the press was the most significant casualty worldwide. Publications had to remain impartial. The Spanish government mandated complete silence on the subject of the war, and did it so swiftly that the decision was taken without the input of parliament. The premise was that if Spain acted like the war was not happening, then the country could not be dragged into it.

Like Denmark, the geographic location of the Netherlands made life difficult for the authorities. Queen Wilhelmina began in August by urging her subjects to remain entirely impartial. This appeal was circulated on posters throughout the country, and a Belgian writer described the Dutch newspapers as 'ash-grey with so-called neutrality'.[11] Private wireless installations and radio transmitters were outlawed. Troops were sent to pull them down, or commandeer them for their own use. But for every editorial comment, public march or statement that was decapitated by the authorities before it caused trouble, the Dutch authorities soon faced another.

The Netherlands was just one of many nations balancing maintaining neutrality with being ready to defend themselves if someone decided to forcibly take it away from them. Dutch authorities had to combat people smuggling, leaking information or selling it to belligerents. Every waiter in The Hague was a suspected German agent; British and French spies were thought to have infiltrated the camps that had been opened to house German deserters. In addition, like any other nation monitoring its newspapers, the Dutch press also had to be mindful that both sides were actively trying to get propaganda distributed on their soil. Despite all of the efforts on the Dutch government's part, there is still evidence to show that German troops cut through Limburg along the Belgian border in the opening weeks of the war, therefore violating Dutch neutrality.

*

In August 1914, Italian ships began leaving South America carrying mobilized Italians home. This was permitted under the rules of neutrality. What was not permitted was also bringing German and Austrian men back to Europe carrying false papers and intending to join their respective armies and navies. But how was a neutral power supposed to police every passenger who embarked on a ship belonging to private merchant fleets? These men were only supposed to find passage on ships belonging to the Central Powers, but those ships were mostly bottled up in harbours all over the world and were unable to get out owing to Allied naval superiority. Even more threatening to neutrality was the fact that some citizens raced to join one side or the other. The Italian government had to contend with the grandsons of Giuseppe Garibaldi attempting to recruit their own legion of Italian volunteers to join the French. They even ran a newspaper campaign in Marseilles to find recruits. In Paris, the American ambassador Myron Herrick greeted a group of young men:

> They wanted to enlist in the French army… and they asked me if they had a right to do so, if it was legal. That moment remains impressed in my memory… it was one of the most trying in my whole official experience. I wanted to take those boys to my heart and cry, 'God bless you! Go!' But I was held back from doing so by the fact that I was an ambassador.

Herrick explained the laws concerning neutrality diligently, but finally snapped. 'I brought my fist down on the table saying, "That is the law, boys; but if I was young and stood in your shoes, by God I know… what I would do."' It was exactly what the young men wanted to hear. 'Each gripped me by the hand, and then they went rushing down the stairs as though every minute was now too precious to be lost.'[12]

Some countries, like the Netherlands, absolutely did not want to fight. Others had every intention of getting involved because they had scores to settle and territory to win. For those nations, neutrality did not mean sitting back. Whether they were yet to pick the side that was most likely to give them the spoils they wanted, or whether they needed time to be ready to send an army into battle, the period between the outbreak of war and when they joined the conflict officially was one of intense activity. There were no depths of dishonesty, intrigue and outright skulduggery that they would not stoop to in their own interests.

The tug of war over Italy's allegiance started immediately. Italy was not yet ready to fight, and so the government held back from overtly picking a side. There were ten months of complex diplomacy before Italy joined the war on the side of the Allies, however, once Britain went to war with France and Russia, Italy was never going to join the Central Powers. Taking on the Royal Navy in the Mediterranean would have been suicidal. Additionally, though she had a defensive alliance with the Central Powers, when Italy did go to war, it would be with a wish list of eventual spoils. Germany might have been a plausible ally when carving up Europe, but Austria–Hungary was not. Not unless they would give up the cities of Trento and Trieste, which the Habsburg empire had no intention of doing. Italy was already planning for the moment when she would reveal her allegiance to the Allies.

General Luigi Cadorna took the job as chief of the Italian general staff, as war commenced. Having been allied with Austria–Hungary for three decades, any war planning concerning them had been limited to sensibly plotting how to defend themselves in the event the Habsburgs breached the frontier. In a few days, this cautious scheme was in tatters. Having declared her neutrality on 6 August, three days later the Italian government was in talks with Britain and France about potentially joining the Allies, and by 21 August, Cadorna had fully reconstituted Italy's war plan with Austria–Hungary cast as the enemy. It was now purely offensive: Instead of resisting a hypothetical attack coming from the north, Italy was preparing to burst forward towards Trieste and Gorizia, a full nine months before she officially joined the war.

Neutral countries lied, too. All manner of secret agreements were signed. There was no essential reason for Turkey to go to war. The Ottoman empire scarcely existed in Europe by 1914, but despite having some of the most vehement opinions about non-white troops in Europe, Germany dreamt of Turkey declaring war on Britain. All of those angry Muslims unleashed, unified under German influence, calling on their Islamic brothers and spreading *jihad* across the world and into India, where millions would rise up and began the exsanguination of the British empire. The possibility of the Germans having the run of the Black Sea as an ally of Turkey was terrifying to Russia, too. If that became the case, Russia would be cut off from her own allies and would only have northern ports safely at her disposal, ports that were frozen solid for half the year.

On the outbreak of war, the dominant Committee of Union and Progress in the Ottoman empire launched a policy of *müsellah bîtaraflık*, 'armed neutrality', without discussing it or gathering a consensus of opinion. German military advisors had been coming and going from Constantinople for nearly a century, and this had led to German domination in supplying the empire with outside ammunition and equipment for the Ottoman army. All of this was viewed by Ottoman leaders as injecting modernity and efficiency into their armed forces. The intended Berlin to Baghdad railway also tied Turkey's economic prospects to Germany. And money was something the Ottomans desperately needed. On 2 August, Grand Vizier Said Halim signed a secret treaty with Germany. Only two other Turks knew about it. Everything now was about playing for time before sending the Ottoman army into battle. With luck, the war might even be over before that became a reality, and victory would still be theirs. As Germany protested about the delay, the Turks claimed that they needed to finish mobilization before they could do anything. Armed neutrality gave them breathing space to ready themselves for action.

Elsewhere, the Swedish people were wary of Russia to the east. This was not the only factor driving the country in the direction of the Central Powers. The king was married to the Kaiser's cousin, and upper-class Swedes admired Germany, and often considered themselves to be Germanic in ethnicity. Politically, the *Aktivister* group called for support to go to war with 'our admirable kinsmen'. They saw it as a racial struggle: Western civilization against 'the flood of real barbarians' to the east.[13] Sweden declared neutrality on 6 August 1914 and four days later made a secret agreement with Berlin, promising 'benevolent' neutrality. Swedes blacked out lighthouses and laid mines. They purposefully interrupted the flow of supplies going to and from Russia and her allies, while Swedish diplomats attempted to recruit Italy and Romania for the Central Powers. No mention of the atrocities occurring on the Western Front appeared in Swedish newspapers.

Not every attempt at an accord paid off, but few ended in the humiliation that King Carol of Romania suffered. He was a member of the Kaiser's Hohenzollern family and was pro-German. It would be fair to say he was desperate for his country to join the Central Powers. Unfortunately for Carol, his people had been utterly unimpressed with Austria–Hungary's conduct during the Balkan Wars. Added to that, several million Romanians were living under Habsburg control and had been subjected to brutal treatment, including 'Forced Magyarization' that tried to make them act as if they were Hungarian. King Carol, who had a secret pact with the Central Powers, was also pitched against most of his government, who agreed with the general public and wanted to join the Allies. Bullish, despite the constitutional limits of his powers, he decided to get up in front of senior advisors on 3 August and, ironically in French, condemn neutrality. The response to his speech was an embarrassed, lengthy silence.

Nations were not above telling tales, or even stealing from each other. In the summer of 1914, two warships were fortuitously due for completion in a British shipyard in the northeast. The only problem was that they had been ordered and paid for by Turkey. Churchill requisitioned them both for the Royal Navy on the premise of national security. The *Reshadieh* was already complete, and some 500 unfortunate Ottoman sailors, who were already on hand to collect her, were now stranded on the River Tyne. 'There seemed to be a great danger of their coming on board... and hoisting the Turkish flag, in which case a very difficult diplomatic situation would have been created,' wrote Churchill. 'I determined to run no risks.'[14]

On 1 August, it was announced that the two ships were now named *Agincourt* and *Erin*. The seizure might not have caused quite so much trouble had the Ottoman people not subscribed their own money to pay for the warships. The British embassy in Constantinople received large volumes of hate mail. One woman named Behiçe, apparently with a son in the army, wrote: 'Your seizure of our battleships, which we purchased by working hard and making self-sacrifices really hurt us... I hope God causes all your battleships to be crushed by the German navy. Amen.'[15]

Regardless of the debacle surrounding the two warships, Turkey had already nailed her colours to the wall early on. The German ship *Goeben* was in the Mediterranean on the outbreak of war. On 3 August, orders were sent for her to make a run past the Allied navies and strike for Constantinople. She made it, causing no end of recriminations among the British and the French as to how. When the *Goeben* sailed through the Dardanelles and into the Sea of Marmara, it was to a rapturous reception from the Turkish people, who hailed them as saviours, with the Sultan proudly watching on. The event was covered extensively in the press, and was captured on film so that people could see the arrival in cinemas. On 6 September the British ambassador wrote to his mother that: 'We are... having an exciting struggle to counteract German influence. [Turkey] is virtually a German protectorate since the *Goeben* got in.'[16]

The Ottoman government refused to intern German ships and disarm their crews. In the weeks that followed, 1,600 Germans were absorbed into the Ottoman navy, which was to be commanded by Admiral Wilhelm Souchon. As early as 16 August, Enver Pasha, the war minister and chief of the Ottoman general staff, had also requested more men to help defend the Dardanelles. In response, Germany formed the *Sonderkommando Kaiserliche Marine Türkei*, or 'Imperial Navy Special Unit Turkey', comprised of 26 officers and 520 men. By the end of August, they had landed secretly in small batches and were at their posts. This was not neutrality in any sense of the word.

Charles Lister and his colleagues at the British embassy felt utterly useless to influence anything. On 6 September, he complained that: 'Here we live in an atmosphere of lies and violently stirred up anti-English feeling.'[17] They received nothing but news that had originated in Germany, and could get nothing into print themselves. The British were not the only ones to have noticed. A Belgian national was stopped by a Turkish minister who said: 'I have news for you, the Germans have entered Brussels.' The Belgian was quick. 'I have news for you,' he shot back without a beat. 'The Germans have entered Constantinople.'[18]

*

Some neutral nations were even actively fighting in the opening weeks of war. Although Portugal did not officially join the Allies until 1916, like Turkey, her allegiance was clear for all to see. Since 1913, the Portuguese had been anticipating an eventual attack by Germany on either Mozambique on the East African coast, or Angola, on the other side of the continent. August and September 1914 saw skirmishing in both colonies. The first Portuguese soldiers to die in the First World War did so on African soil, three years before Portugal joined the Allies. The Kaiser's government, which had had men plough across the respective borders, had to issue an apology.

*

The war created huge amounts of work for countries that had declared neutrality. In August 1914, neutral embassies had to cope with their own displaced people who were being shipped home. As well as dealing with the baggage left all over the continent by their own subjects, men like the American ambassador James Gerard in Berlin then had to assume responsibility for international colleagues who had had to vacate their embassies on the outbreak of war. On 5 August, Gerard took over British interests. Seals were placed on the archives at the British embassy, and instructions were taken for dealing with any stranded British subjects as well as his own. Gerard immediately formed a team to organize British affairs. In Brussels, America's ambassador Brand Whitlock was performing similar duties for the Germans. Over the course of four nights, his volunteers sent some 9,000

Germans over the Dutch border by rail. Volunteering at the American embassy in Paris, Eric Fisher Wood was eventually assigned to look after stranded subjects of the Kaiser. 'Poor creatures,' he wrote. The French had given all Germans twenty-four hours to get out of Paris. Now they flung themselves at him:

> Last week they were everywhere treated with respect and politeness, today they are looked upon with hostility. They are hungry and they have no money. They are surrounded by looks of hatred and they are terror-stricken... They have no place to sleep as no hotel or lodging-house dares harbour them. Many of them have lost all their worldly goods... There are refined women who have slept in the streets and parks... There are rich men who literally have not an available copper and whose eyes have taken on the nervous look of hunted animals.[19]

The strain put upon neutral ambassadors proved too much for Ricardo Bollati, the Italian ambassador to Berlin, who found himself home for the summer. When Italy declined to join the Central Powers, Bollati declared to the Italian foreign minister that he would commit suicide rather than return to work in Germany. Nobody took him seriously. The following day Bollati returned to the Consulta and produced a doctor's note claiming that he had developed a stomach disease. The minister returned it to Bollati, and smiling, said: 'To avoid returning to Berlin, the first method was preferable.' 'The response was witty,' wrote Colonial Minister Ferdinando Martini. 'But what ambassadors does Italy have!'[20]

10

Revanche

France

The Battle of the Frontiers was not like the Somme or Passchendaele. This was not an offensive planned for months in advance on a huge scale. When it began in August 1914, it was the result of two massive armies trying to execute pre-existing war plans at the same time, and fighting random encounters wherever they happened to clash.

For the French army, the century or so before the First World War had been tumultuous, a contrast between the highs of Napoleon's dominance over Europe and the humiliation of Prussians marching into Paris. Determined never to suffer the latter again, France had not been idle. Military commanders had been generating various plans for a future war since 1875, and by 1914 they were on Plan XVII. The important thing about it, was that, unlike Germany's Schlieffen Plan, it did not dictate how to win a war; it was intended as a schedule to get the country mobilized and ready to fight.

France put five armies into the field in 1914, more than a million men, and most of them were to be deployed in the northeast, because Plan XVII only had one enemy in mind: Germany. In command was fifty-nine-year-old General Joseph 'Papa' Joffre, and by 5 August he had set up his *Grand Quartier Général* at Vitry-le-François on the River Marne. Just because Plan XVII did not dictate how to fight, this did not mean that Joffre didn't know what he planned to do. The First and Second Armies formed the French right, the southern end of an enormous front. The Third

Army faced daunting border forts known as the *Moselstellung* just across the border around the town of Metz, as well as the fortifications in Metz itself. The Fourth Army was positioned slightly to the rear, waiting to be of use as events transpired. Finally, on the left of the line was the Fifth Army, whose lengthy sector stretched all the way to the Belgian frontier.

So much for how the French deployed their armies, but how would they fight? The devastating results of the Franco-Prussian War of 1870–1 had led to much soul searching. New, motivated officers known as the 'Young Turks' had since made their mark on the French army, with the result that it was offensively minded: 'The laurels of victory float at the tips of enemy bayonets,' wrote future General Ferdinand Foch in 1904. 'You have to... conquer them through hand-to-hand combat... Rush, but rush in numbers and in mass... Throw yourself into the ranks of the adversary and settle the discussion with a cold weapon.'[1] In 1913 Joffre concurred. This was the way. Otherwise, what was the point of going to war in the first place? Even if one might have to defend on occasion, that scenario should be flipped as soon as possible, because it would never lead to victory and it just was not becoming of Frenchmen.

The Allies attempted to coordinate their attacks. On 6 August, in command of the Russian armies, Grand Duke Nikolai informed the French that he would be ready in mid-August. The plan was to bludgeon the Central Powers from both east and west at the same time, but that was more than a week away, and Joffre was impatient to score a quick, morale-boosting victory over the Germans. He wanted to demonstrate just how ready France was. Not only that, he was looking to score a quick, limited victory to impress not only his allies, but the French people, too. While Joffre waited for the Russians, and for mobilization to finish, he ordered an immediate attack in Alsace.

*

France had lost both Alsace and Lorraine to Germany thanks to the Franco-Prussian War. *Revanche* was the agony that followed, an obsessive desire for revenge, as a nation mourned the lost territories for more than four decades. Academic interrogation apparently shows that the desire for revenge had waned in the years before the First World War, yet among the First Army men advancing into Alsace to make Joffre's impatient demonstration, emotions ran high. A Chaplain on the march with VII Corps, who were fated to carry out Joffre's quick, interim attack, reached the frontier on 7 August. 'We are walking at night… Suddenly groups stop around a post; the border! No, it was never the frontier… it was only a wound made in the side of [France], still bleeding after 44 years. I approach; I read on one side *France*. On the other side, someone had already scratched out the words *Deutsch-Reich*… This… was nothing in itself; but it was a lot for us.'[2]

Captain Dupuy recounted someone ripping down the border post in the Oderen Pass, before the French occupied the town of Thann without firing a shot. 'Two officers… hoisted the tricolour flag on the roof of the town hall of the old Alsatian city… Everywhere our soldiers had trodden roads strewn with flowers… there had been distribution of wine… beer, boxes of cigars; we had seen a 70-year-old Alsatian sobbing with emotion.' Not everyone was joyous: That same day, as troops jubilantly marched through Oderen, an old priest had said, shaking his head, 'My children, be careful. There are a lot of them on the other side.'[3]

The scenery in Alsace was something to behold. Parisian Léon Riotor arrived with an artillery unit. 'Pine forests cover the hills, enclosing verdant valleys where sumptuous rivers water the meadows,' he wrote.[4] Mountainous beauty does not make logistics easy for an army, but by 8 August, the French had taken multiple Alsatian towns. Auguste Zûndel, a resident of Mulhouse long past military age, watched the Germans scatter. 'It was so rapid that the soldiers forgot rifles in their [barracks]; we saw artillery crews passing without their guns… Prince Max's staff left the Central Hotel without paying, but not without pillaging the cellar.'[5]

Spontaneous celebrations broke out in towns and villages all over France. Albert Carap had been a twelve-year-old boy in

1870. In August 1914, he thought he had finally seen justice. 'The French in Alsace! Can one imagine what these four words have of prestige for a Frenchman who remembers... our sadnesses of 1870... The Alsatians–Lorrainers, so faithful, will return to the French homeland!'[6]

French joy was short-lived. On 9 August, serving with IR 112, Dominik Richert and his comrades were instructed to help take Mulhouse back for Germany.

> Suddenly all laughter stopped and nobody felt like joking any more, because none of us felt that he would survive the night, and there was heartily little of the famed enthusiasm for battle or victory which you find described in patriotic writings. We had to march... and at the edge of the road we saw our first corpse, a French dragoon whose chest had been pierced by a lance. It looked horrible: the bleeding chest, the glazed eyes, the open mouth and the clawed hands. We all marched silently by.[7]

As they left the road and went into the forest, they saw six dead Germans lying face down. 'We were given the order to... advance to the edge of the woods and then lie down flat.' In front of them, Dominik could see a parade ground. 'I thought to myself: the Frenchmen will blow us away the moment we move.' He held his breath.

> The command came: 'On your feet!... March!' The first line got up and ran out of the wood. A warrant officer from the reserve remained lying there. I do not know whether it was cowardice, or whether he had fainted from fear. As soon as [they] left the woods, they came under fire... The bullets flew over us and whistled into the leaves or bounced off the trees. With thumping hearts we nestled as close as we could to the forest floor until the command came: 'Second line! On your feet!'... We got up and jumped out of the woods. Immediately the bullets whizzed past our ears. The soldiers

in the first line were now lying down and directing a steady fire at the bushes.[8]

Men with slight wounds ran back the other way. 'Our artillery was firing shrapnel into the [outskirts of Mulhouse]. The whoosh of the shells was a new experience for us. The crashing, crackling and whizzing sounds brought on a nervous excitement.' Opposite, Captain Dupuy watched French guns enfiladed on the road by machine-guns. 'The batteries could not advance any further and had to take up position near the cemetery... crowded by curious [civilians] who had come to witness the battle... In front of our lines, there are tremendous explosions raising clouds of dust and smoke... this is the first revelation of the adversary's heavy artillery. Our [guns] responded with fury.'[9]

'Suddenly we heard two shells whizzing very close to us,' recalled Dominik Richert, facing those guns. 'Two French shells exploded less than twenty metres behind us. While still running I took a quick look back and when I saw the smoke and the tufts of grass flying through the air, I thought to myself: if one of those should land between my legs, oh dear!' He threw himself to the ground. They opened fire. 'Ping', he wrote, 'a bullet shot past me along the ground and kicked up some grass. If it had been [a foot] to the left my life would have been over.' They worked their way forward. 'There were just too many of us. Our next task was to storm the vineyard on the hill... as soon as we got up there, the French troops fled among the vines and disappeared.'[10]

Richert and his comrades were more interested in the pile of bread and the wine the French had left behind. They fell on it. The men of IR 112, tired and scared, were beginning to lose their heads. 'Among the vines we found a young Frenchman. He was unconscious. By striking matches, we were able to see that he had been hit on his thigh. A chap from Mannheim wanted to beat him to death.' Dominik and another comrade managed to stop him, but they could do nothing as mayhem then erupted. Imaginary Frenchmen lurked everywhere: 'People started shooting wildly, hitting trees and everything, even chimneys became targets. Bullets were flying everywhere... Some of the houses had caught fire, and lit up the surroundings. The injured of both sides were brought in. The dead were left lying.' The men lay down, but sleep would not come. 'We were frightened into wakefulness by the sound of shot and shell. "What's up?" we called to each other in the darkness.' The firing continued to build, and again, panic broke out. 'Our officers ordered us to form a line, to lie down, and [shoot back]. We fired for several minutes, and then word came in that they were Germans.' Richert and his comrades were ordered to sing *Deutschland über alles* to show their 'enemy' that they were fighting for the same side. 'My God, how we sang! Almost all of us pressed our faces into the grass, to get as much cover as possible. The officers shouted and cursed, but they could not bring the poor people who had been hit back to life. We had lost as many men to the German bullets as we had lost to the French.'[11]

*

France had suffered a check in Alsace, but the main offensive was still fast approaching, and events such as those in towns like Mulhouse could still end up being mere temporary setbacks overall. Joffre meant business. The attack he launched on 14 August has been described as a jab with the right of his armies, before he attempted to deliver a knockout blow with his left. That day, the Germans withdrew in front of his advance. The French took Donon, commanding a vital pass through the Vosges mountains, and managed to advance some 10 miles towards Sarreboug too. The Germans continued to pull back, with isolated clashes occurring across the front. This, however, was far from a disorderly and panicked retreat. It was caution.

On 17 August, Joffre had de Castelnau's Second Army shift its angle away from the First Army on its right to face north. Though still joined in the middle, the French armies in Alsace and Lorraine were now pointing in different directions. The French did not know it, but they were being lured into a trap. Georges Bertrand was in Lorraine serving as a junior officer with the 6e Bataillon de

Chasseurs Alpins. In his mid-twenties, he was one of the Second Army men who changed direction. 'Suddenly, around four o'clock in the evening, the order is given to [turn] north... we feel worried, as a result of the atmosphere of uncertainty.' Had the enemy been defeated elsewhere? In wind and rain, they marched. 'We are told that the Prussians have abandoned Dieuze. It makes no sense! It's raining, it's still raining, and it's terrible. I say to myself: "How can we manage to support such a life, being continuously soaked?"'[12]

Before first light on 19 August, Bertrand's battalion advanced into battle 30 miles north-east of Nancy. The sun rose, revealing the village of Vergaville shrouded in mist. 'The bullets begin to hiss. We are advancing in leaps and bounds... The artillery finally goes into action.' This lifted their mood. 'It is interesting to emphasize the joy experienced by the infantryman when, engaged in the fight, he feels supported by artillery, when he sees behind him the guns forming up in action, or when he hears the French shells passing over his head.'[13] But the enemy was no longer in Vergaville when they got there. The battalion was ordered 5 miles further on to Bénestroff, located on the great German railway from Metz to Strasbourg. Bertrand could see why this was where they might have decided to make a stand; losing access to that line would have been a strategic catastrophe.

Opposite the chasseurs alpins, Lieutenant Hawickhorst was lying in wait with IR 173. They caught sight of the French approaching from about half a mile away. The battle began. 'Aim here, aim there at that burning heap, aim in the dip in the railroad embankment,' wrote Hawickhorst. 'My captain, Bühler falls. Captain Bockmann... is also dead... Lt Krevet's chin is crushed by a shell fragment. My neighbour on the right is bleeding from a mortal wound in [his] side. My neighbour on the left is badly injured in the head.'[14] Georges Bertrand and his men were attempting to approach methodically. 'Well-grouped by sections, we try to progress by leaps and bounds. The sections, lying down suddenly when the shell arrives, and the men, glued to each other, face against the ground, doing *the turtle*.' After half a mile they ground to a halt.

The earth is plowed by the shells on all sides, to the right, to the left, in front, behind us... they spray us with their shrapnel. My men are flattened on the ground, tight against each other... From time to time, a shell that had fallen near the section covered us with a rain of earth, of bullets, which fortunately, most of the time, riddled only the shell formed by the men"s knapsacks. If there is one that falls right in the middle, it will be a pretty sight.[15]

What was the point in caution? If Bertrand was going to die, it was out of his hands. He sat down in front of his men. 'I place my destiny in the hands of Providence... I light a cigarette. I watch my men... What are we waiting for in this hell? Night to come. But it's 9.00 a.m.!' Georges stared at his watch: 10.00 a.m., 11.00 a.m., noon.

*

Now, while I was listening to the cursing of my men, the cries of the wounded and the terrible song of the shells, I heard a sonorous snoring, which contrasted in a strange way with the noise of the combat: most of my men were asleep! In the course of the afternoon... I crawl to a stack of straw where my captain is. He smokes a cigarette, smiling and calm. I had never seen him so calm... What to do? Wait until nightfall, said the captain, to get out of this asylum.[16]

Under cover of darkness, they withdrew to Dieuze, 2 miles back towards Nancy. Stretcher-bearers roamed the plain while German searchlights swung through the sky. 'Methodically... stopping sometimes to scan the night and to detect our movement... *"We are still there watching."* And there was something hallucinating and terrible about it.'[17] Bertrand and his battalion were about to get a nasty surprise.

Crown Prince Rupprecht was the commander of the German Sixth Army. Opposite de Castelnau's Second Army, he had been told to tie up French manpower as much as possible. Since

14 August, Rupprecht had figured out that the force advancing against him was weaker than he had first thought, and he decided that attacking was going to be more effective than leading them forward and toying with them. After much wrangling with supreme commanders, Rupprecht's Sixth Army, and the Seventh on his left, were given permission to counter-attack on 20 August.

'The night of August 19th to 20th is one of the darkest I have had to spend,' wrote Georges Bertrand. 'Our company had sought shelter from the cold in a shed... While the men had fallen asleep, truly annihilated by the... day, we remained, my comrade and I, in an agonizing insomnia.' When morning came, they heard rifle fire coming from the outposts north of Vergaville. Rupprecht's counter-attack had begun. 'I throw myself with two sections behind a wall, and we wait for the enemy,' the Frenchman recalled. As the sun rose again on the battlefield, the Germans appeared on the ridge ahead:

> You could see the greyish infantry running... and tumbling down the slope as quickly as possible to seek shelter in a sunken road, advancing straight on us. There was something beautiful and special about the regular repetition of these deployments... You could feel the application of a studied method... It was a spectacle... It recalled the collective movements in which the dancers of a ballet perform on the stage.[18]

Bertrand's men were not just watching. 'Sheltered behind their wall, [they] fired non-stop at this veritable human avalanche... "It's coming from all sides," cries one of my chasseurs. "Did you notice," said my Serjeant: ... "It's funny, they manoeuvre like us!"'[19] Their position was rapidly becoming untenable. Advancing towards Vergaville with IR 174 was Captain Schneider:

> I had the whole company spread out... On the left wing people eagerly opened fire... The effect was great. The red

trousers of the dead Frenchmen on the green meadows...
shone like poppies. Now we were caught by enemy fire from
a westerly direction. The whole height was partially covered in dust so that nothing could be seen. Here I received
my wounds in fairly close succession. First left hand, then
right hand, then a ricochet into the left lung. After the last
bullet I thought it was the end. I was not afraid of death,
but an excessive sadness overcame me.[20]

The Second Army was retreating up and down the line in
Lorraine. Georges Bertrand, still in Vergaville, could do no more.
'I did not claim, with 60 men, to stop the German offensive.' All
he saw was disorder: infantry, artillerymen trying to drag their
guns, wagons with supplies and ammunition, automobiles carrying staff officers, 'all of [them]... passed each other, not knowing
what to do or where to go. It smelled if not of retreat, at least of
a hasty withdrawal.'[21]

As the French First and Second Armies fell back there was still
hope. If the jab with his right had failed, as his men in Alsace and
Lorraine were being driven back, at 8.30 p.m. on 20 August,
Joffre finally issued orders to unleash his powerful left hook.
The following day, the Third and Fourth Armies were ordered to
stage the main French offensive north of the fortifications around
Metz towards Belgium and Luxembourg. This is where Joffre
anticipated finding the concentrated strength of the German
army, and where he planned to crush it.

11

Plain, Dastardly Murder

East Prussia

War on the scale being waged in the west was slower to begin on the opposite side of Europe. The first weeks of the war there were characterized by border guards taking potshots at each other, and cavalry patrols occasionally charging when an opportunity arose.

This was the calm before the storm. Russian war planning called for a division of forces upon mobilization. The Southwestern Front, commanded by General Nikolai Ivanov, was deployed against the Austro-Hungarians in Galicia, while the Northwestern Front, commanded by General Yakov Zhilinsky, would oppose the Germans in East Prussia. In the event of the Germans sending the bulk of their forces against France, which it transpired that they would, 'Plan 19' called for the weight of the Russian army to be concentrated against Austria–Hungary, as they would therefore present the more immediate threat. Consequently, at the outset of war, Ivanov had the Third, Fourth, Fifth and Eighth Armies at his disposal, while only the First and Second were available to Zhilinsky.

Zhilinsky was not to remain passive, however. The north-west was where Russia intended to deploy in concert with France in the west. A successful invasion of East Prussia would force Germany to transfer troops east, easing the pressure on France, with luck while the Germans were already being battered by Joffre's two-punch strategy. With Germany's gaze firmly planted westward, it would be reasonable to assume that East Prussia would only be defended by a small force, and so Zhilinsky began planning an invasion. General Pavel von Rennenkampf's First Army was to advance from the east on 17 August, engaging the German defenders along the border and pinning them in place. Meanwhile, General Alexander Samsonov's Second Army would advance from the south, aiming to surround the enemy.

The plan looked reasonable on paper, but it was difficult to coordinate the two armies' movements. The main issue facing the Russians was geography. Right in the middle of Zhilinsky's front lay the vast Masurian lake region, with 2,000 bodies of water, which ruled out large-scale military operations. Instead, the two armies would advance on either side of this wet terrain, effectively splitting the front in two. The responsibility of making sure that vital contact did not break down lay with Zhilinsky, who would prove woefully inadequate in this role. Nicknamed 'the living corpse' by his troops, he was pompous, devoid of leadership qualities, and owed his position to personal connections, not merit. Ominous clouds hung over Russia's first major campaign of the war before it had even begun.

Defending East Prussia, Germany's Eighth Army stood alone, commanded by the competent if somewhat cautious Maximilian von Prittwitz und Gaffron. Prittwitz had just over 200,000 men, mainly infantry, but also a cavalry division and a mix of garrison and local Landwehr troops. While the advanced age of many of the latter would limit their value in an attack, they were motivated because they were defending their homes. Still, Prittwitz was significantly outnumbered. This was expected, however, and the German High Command was confident that the Eighth Army would only need to delay an enemy advance into East Prussia long enough for a victory to be won in the west.

Fully expecting that the first Russian attack would come from Rennenkampf in the east, Prittwitz had decided to concentrate his defences there, with three corps forming a line behind the River Angerapp, some 25 miles from the border. Only one corps was left to defend East Prussia's southern border against Samsonov's Second Army. It was a sound plan, but no plan ever survives first contact with the enemy. In Prittwitz's case, it did not even survive that long. Days before Rennenkampf moved, all of Prittwitz's plans were thrown into disarray by an officer immediately subordinate to him.

The aggressive and headstrong commander of I Corps, General Hermann von François, was itching for a fight and strongly opposed to the idea of letting Russia decide the course of events. On his own initiative, he abandoned the defensive line behind the Angerapp, and ordered his corps forward to meet the enemy head on. By evening on 16 August, François's 1st Division, commanded by General Richard Conta, had almost reached the border. Completely isolated from the rest of the Eighth Army, François's corps was about to unwittingly withstand the full brunt of the Russian invasion alone.

*

In the early hours of 17 August, Rennenkampf's army began its westward advance. First contact was made almost as soon as men crossed the border, and before long, one of François's heavily outnumbered divisions at the town of Stallupönen was being attacked from three sides. The whistling bullets, shrapnel and the burning farmsteads lighting up the horizon made a deep impression on the soldiers, most of whom were experiencing battle for the first time. 'With a disgusting howl, the Russian shells fell near us and set fire to the houses in the villages,' recalled a lieutenant in Grenadier Regiment Nr.1 (Gren.R1).[1]

Soon, large groups of excited spectators in Stallupönen were gathering along the edges of the town to get a first-hand view of the ongoing battle. 'Shells were followed with the greatest possible interest,' wrote the local priest.[2] The numerous small clouds in the sky were observed; the high-flying dark Russian ones and the light grey German ones with the brightly flashing core. At first, the Russian infantry held, letting the artillery do the work and leaving the Germans to fire wildly at any hedge, fence or ditch suspected of concealing them. As the day went on, however, rows of Russian infantrymen began breaking cover to charge. While strong in numbers, however, these attacks lacked coordination, and time and time again, the defenders managed to bring them to a halt with accurate rifle fire. 'The Russians burst out like mosquitoes from behind a hill in front of us,' recalled one NCO from IR 43. 'Now it was a pleasure to see how effectively our bullets hit. The ranks of our enemies thinned more and more until new ones appeared on the scene. Their numbers seemed endless.'[3]

All morning, IR 43 held on to its advanced positions outside the small village of Göritten, to the south of Stallupönen. Heavily outnumbered, lacking artillery support, and with ammunition beginning to run short, the men eventually began to feel the strain. Furthermore, Russian forces were soon spotted to the south, moving around the regiment's right flank, and even to the west, threatening their rear. By 11.30 a.m., every man still able to operate his rifle had been pushed into the firing line, but the sheer weight of the Russian attacks made the situation untenable. The regiment began pulling back into Göritten itself.

The same scene was being repeated all along 1st Division's front. The number of German casualties was growing, and every available company was being thrown into battle to shore up weak spots. Only through the failure of the Russian commanders to identify and exploit weaknesses in the German line was a breakthrough averted. Slowly but steadily, 1st Division was being pushed into a corner. François, observing the battle from a bell tower in Stallupönen, fully intended to hold his ground, and when an officer arrived with an order from the army commander for the corps to immediately retreat 17 miles west to the town of Gumbinnen, he refused. According to François, his actual reply to the officer was: 'Tell General von Prittwitz that General von François will break off the engagement when the Russians are defeated.' While later used as an example of his steadfastness in contrast to Prittwitz's timidity, the insubordinate general probably had very little actual choice in the matter. With the Russians maintaining the pressure on his embattled regiments, any attempt to disengage would most likely have had disastrous consequences. The reality was that retreat was no longer an option. François's corps would either have to win the day, or be overrun.

*

By mid-afternoon, Russian shells began to fall on Stallupönen itself, sending the curious inhabitants running for cover. It was clear that the invaders were closing in, and around Göritten, the situation was now becoming desperate. Finding themselves almost completely surrounded by the Russian 27th Division, and having suffered high casualties, including many of their officers and NCOs, the defenders were reaching their breaking point. A final attempt at a counter-attack faltered in the face of vastly superior enemy forces. 'Ultimate success seemed certain,' wrote General August Adaridi, commanding Russia's 27th Division. 'The resistance of the German right flank was broken; [They] began to hastily retreat.'[4] But just as the Russians were preparing to administer the coup de grâce, lines of infantry were spotted approaching from the south. Assuming that these were from the neighbouring Russian division, Colonel Petr Komarov, commanding the 105th Orenburg Infantry Regiment, decided to personally establish communications and galloped towards the newcomers. Suddenly, a shot rang out, and a bullet knocked him off his horse, fatally wounding him; the new arrivals were German.

General Falk's 2nd Division had spent all morning listening intently to the noise of battle coming from the north. Realizing a crisis was unfolding around Stallupönen, Falk decided to act independently and go to the aid of Conta's hard-pressed 1st Division. Around noon, he had ordered four battalions and most of his artillery to begin marching towards the sound of the guns. Now these fresh troops were attacking straight into the unprotected flank of Russia's 27th Division.

As artillery shells began to fall, and rifle and machine-gun fire ripped into their ranks, the Russians quickly collapsed. 'I cannot forget some of the officers and soldiers who were badly wounded near me, with torn entrails or broken legs, screaming and moaning terribly,' wrote Captain Alexander Uspensky of the 106th Ufa Infantry Regiment. 'Another, seriously wounded in the stomach (all his intestines were crawling out), fixed his terrible gaze on me and for some reason croaked one word: *"Comrade!"*'[5] As men were being hit from all sides, panic ensued, and officers found it impossible to maintain order. One was seen wandering around on the battlefield amid all the chaos yelling, 'The banner! The banner! Save the banner!' before he was killed.[6] Some scattered groups bravely tried to hold their ground, but to no avail. 'When there were no officers left in my company, I, being more intelligent, took over the command,' wrote one Russian soldier. 'I led half a company forward until I was badly wounded by shrapnel in my right side. In addition to this severe wound, I had contusions on my right arm and both legs… The shrapnel wound was very large and deep and the pain was unbearable.'[7]

Soon, the 105th Orenburg Infantry Regiment broke, and began fleeing the field, closely pursued by German shells. This caused a ripple effect as panic spread from one regiment to the next. It did not take long before the commander of the neighbouring 107th Troitsky Infantry Regiment reported that his troops were running too. Adaridi ordered his reserve, the 108th Saratov Infantry Regiment, forward to attack the Germans and stop the 27th Division's flight. A message was quickly received from the 108th's commander that 'despite the measures taken, including shooting at the retreating troops', nothing could be done to make them turn back.[8]

With this, the Russians halted all attacks, and as darkness began to descend, the fighting died out. In the first real clash of the campaign, François's I Corps had managed to achieve a narrow victory in the face of unfavourable odds. The field was littered with Russian dead and wounded. The 27th Division alone had lost nearly 7,000 men, including 62 officers. Luck had played a big part in François's success. If not for Falk's timely intervention and some glaring errors by the Russians, his outrageous insubordination could easily have resulted in the loss of an entire corps. Furthermore, reports were arriving of Russian forces moving north, around his corps' unprotected left flank. François received more orders to withdraw from Prittwitz. Deciding that he had done what he could, he finally instructed his divisions to pull back to Gumbinnen, north-east of the Angerapp river.

*

In the wake of Stallupönen, Prittwitz initially feared that the Russians would be hot on François's heels, but they were slow to respond, and on 18 August François's corps safely reached Gumbinnen.

Despite his close call, François was still eager for a fight. The bulk of Rennenkampf's First Army was advancing in his direction, so François suggested a surprise attack. His corps could swing north and attack Rennenkampf's right wing, while XVII and I Reserve Corps attacked the Russians head on. It was a daring plan. Prittwitz was hesitant at first, but when reports arrived that Samsonov's Second Army had crossed the southern border, he was forced to accept that waiting passively for Rennenkampf to come to him would only give Samsonov time to advance and cut off his line of retreat. Stuck between a rock and a hard place, he agreed to the unruly François's plan and issued the orders for his three corps to attack the following morning.

At 4.30 a.m. on 20 August, the northernmost of François's divisions opened the attack, slamming into the Russian XX Corps on Rennenkampf's right flank. Initially, François's predictions seemed to have been right. Taken by surprise, the Russians quickly panicked, with many simply throwing down their rifles and raising their hands. However, once the initial shock had subsided, resistance stiffened, and as Russian infantry took up positions in shallow trenches, farmsteads and villages, the attack began to slow down.

An hour after the first assault, General Conta's 1st Division joined the fight. 'At the signal to charge, the bayonets are fixed and the banners unfurled,' recalled an officer in Gren.R.1. 'The company stormed the forest to drum rolls and blaring bugles, banners waving. It was an encouraging vision of war.'[9] This was how men had imagined war would be, but visions from centuries past had no place on the modern battlefield, and Conta's men were met with fierce resistance by the Russians, who proved masters of utilizing the terrain. Every cluster of houses and every barn had been occupied by enemy infantry and had to be charged at the point of the bayonet. Casualties mounted. One officer, charging forward at the head of his company, yelled out: 'Onwards! The dogs can't hit anything!' No sooner had the words left his throat before a bullet struck him in his chest.[10] Similarly, a captain seeking to calm his men lit a cigar and mocked the Russian guns, only to be killed by shrapnel moments later. [11]

Just before noon, the Germans reached the village of Uszballen, which they found to be heavily occupied. IR 45's skirmish lines charged forward, pushing into the village streets. Here they were immediately met by Russian rifle and machine-gun fire coming from every house and basement. When they clashed at close quarters, both sides' artillery fired rapidly and bloody hand-to-hand fighting broke out. 'The fire was so strong that the soldiers literally turned black from powder smoke,' wrote a Russian officer.[12] Soon the entire village was ablaze. A few surviving Russians managed to flee, but many were burnt alive. German casualties were equally heavy, and the survivors were now thoroughly exhausted and reluctant to attack the next occupied hamlet.

Despite the fierce resistance put up by the Russians, François was still managing to keep his attack going. The same, however, could not be said about XVII Corps on his right. Its commander, August von Mackensen was known as a strict disciplinarian, eager to fight. Based on the reports that the enemy was concentrating against François's men to the north, Mackensen concluded that only weak Russian numbers were facing him, and based on this conviction, he drove his men hard against what he assumed was the enemy's exposed left flank.

At first everything went as expected. Encouraging reports kept arriving from François, and Mackensen was eying an opportunity to encircle the Russians. As it turned out though, the reports that he had so blindly trusted turned out to be wrong. In reality, his corps was marching straight into the enemy, who had dug in among the hills and forests. As the Germans came within range, they were immediately enveloped in a murderous cross-fire. The men were ordered to charge the enemy, and once again, scenes resembled something from wars gone by. The standard-bearer of IR 21 later recalled how he advanced towards the Russians 'with the flag unveiled and waving in the wind'. But while they were intended to inspire the long lines of exposed men during the attack, these banners presented clear targets for the Russian guns and now drew a devastating fire. It quickly became clear that they were doing more harm than good. 'Since the clearly visible flag offered too good a target, and our losses were increasing, the order was given to roll it up,' recalled the standard bearer. 'I myself now grabbed a rifle off a fallen comrade and joined in the infantry battle.'[13]

The Germans were being shot at from all sides. A Russian officer of the 106th Ufa Infantry Regiment recalled seeing an enemy column being hit by heavy machine-gun and shrapnel fire, which caused a large dust cloud to form. 'When it dispersed', he wrote, 'there was no longer any column, only black spots to remind you that it had been here. The lower ranks even stopped shooting for a while, leant out of the trenches and looked into the distance in surprise.' His comrade, Lieutenant Burlak, noted that the attacking Germans tended to drop to the ground when coming under fire, only to find themselves trapped in the open, where the Russians could easily pick them off.[14]

The only hope of German success was to keep advancing. Accomplishing this fell to junior officers. One of these, Lieutenant Ménard of IR 21, desperately tried to drive his men onwards. 'Heavy shellfire overwhelmed our advance and I saw many brave boys in my platoon sink to the ground,' he wrote. One shell exploded above them, and a shrapnel ball pierced the knapsack and mess-kit of Ménard's bugler. The man calmly turned to Ménard and said in a dry tone: 'Herr Oberleutnant, I believe the fellows are firing live rounds!' As they closed in on enemy trenches, their attacks began to fail. 'The Russian position was laid out very skilfully,' Ménard said. 'The trenches ran along a rising slope in a potato field. No Russian infantryman was to be seen, only the whizzing of the bullets indicated that the trenches were occupied.' The platoon got to within 1,000 feet of the enemy trench but could go no further, as the Russians were now shooting them down from three sides. Ménard was hit when he tried to jump forward. Anyone else who attempted to stand up went down almost instantly. All his men could do was stay put and keep their heads down. XVII Corps' attack was collapsing, [15]

Prittwitz's right wing, consisting of Otto von Below's I Reserve Corps, was about to enter the fight too. Just like his comrades, Below knew little about what he was facing, and his orders were simply to attack Russians. Cavalry patrols reported no sign of the enemy. Acting on this information, Below decided that rather than marching against a seemingly absent foe, his corps would be better utilized supporting Mackensen. He ordered his men to turn north. This change of direction ran contrary to Prittwitz's orders, and it would soon become obvious that German reconnaissance had once again failed miserably.

Having marched all night, the soldiers of Below's 1st Reserve Division were exhausted. Halting in the village of Garwaiten, no sooner had the men's thoughts turned towards the hot lunch being brought up by the field kitchens, than one of Mackensen's cavalry patrols came galloping into the village yelling: 'The Russians are coming!' At first, this was met with scepticism, but somehow Below's patrols had missed the entire Russian IV Corps that was marching directly into his right flank, which was now dangerously exposed by his northward turn. During the ensuing battle, once again the Russian artillery proved vastly superior, and only the timely intervention of another German division turned the battle in Below's favour. German reservists cleared one farm, hill or cluster of trees after the other. By evening, the Russians had been pushed back, and disaster had been narrowly averted.

While Below had managed to check the Russian IV Corps' advance, his successes did little to alleviate the unfolding disaster facing Mackensen. Jeppe Østergaard, a private from Grenadier Regiment Nr. 1, noted that entire companies seemed to melt away before the Russians:

> Of quite a large group, only eight are left, and after running the first [160 feet], myself and a one-year-volunteer fall; him from a stray shot to the head, me from a light wound in the thigh. We crawl on all fours back to the ditch, the wound is bandaged and there's a moment's rest. A short while later, Lieutenant Leopold returns unscathed. In the end, he had had only one man left.[16]

When the Germans tried to break the deadlock by bringing machine-guns and field guns forward, they were immediately targeted by Russian sharpshooters and artillery. Mackensen's own gunners struggled to even identify targets on the battlefield, let alone neutralize them. Any battery that dared to venture too close to the enemy in support of the infantry was quickly shot to pieces. Before long, the fields were littered with guns and carts, around which lay the dead and wounded crews and horses. One Russian officer recalled seeing a German battery shot down before it even had a chance to get into position. The guns were still rigged up for transport and the artillerymen, all of whom had been killed, were still seated on their dead horses.

Mackensen's men broke in the afternoon. At first, a few individual soldiers began running to the rear. Others followed suit, and the call 'Save yourselves if you can' erupted everywhere. Officers tried in vain to maintain order. 'Many threw away their knapsacks, no one listened to the commands. Everyone hurried back,' wrote Jeppe Østergaard.[17] This was no orderly retreat. Men ran away in a hail of Russian bullets and shrapnel. The wounded were predominantly left behind, although some soldiers did try to grab a fallen comrade as they ran past, dragging him along. On the way to a dressing station, Lieutenant Ménard cast a final glance over the scene. It was a depressing sight: 'The darkness of the night was illuminated by the burning villages.

Shot-up guns, overturned limbers and dead horses stood out ghostly from the ground in the glare of the fires. The rattling of the artillery rushing by and the sad sight of the many wounded added to the grisly image of the battlefield.'[18]

In a last, desperate attempt to restore order in his ranks, Mackensen left his headquarters and tried to rally his troops, but it was too late. He could do nothing to convince his exhausted and demoralized men to face the enemy again. Emotionally shaken by seeing his shattered regiments flee the field of battle in complete disorder, Mackensen finally realized that the situation was beyond saving and ordered a general retreat.

*

In Gumbinnen, the news that the Germans were preparing to retire stunned the remaining residents. Many people had been absolutely confident in their soldiers' ability to beat the Russians. The last trains had already left the town, so now huge crowds flooded every road leading west, causing traffic jams as far as the eye could see, blocking the movement of troops and hindering the evacuation of the wounded. 'The procession of the unfortunate populace rolled along on foot, in wagons, laden with every imaginable household item,' wrote one officer.[19] The confusion was made worse when some civilians were seen travelling against the westbound stream of refugees. These were inhabitants who had evacuated Gumbinnen before the battle and were now trying to return home after what they assumed had been a German victory. When told that this victory had not materialized, and that Gumbinnen was now being evacuated, these hapless people naturally wanted to reach their homes and retrieve all the valuables they had left behind. Only with great difficulty could they be persuaded to turn back.

News of XVII Corps' retreat reached Prittwitz in the evening. Throughout the day, he had received mostly positive reports, but what had seemed like certain victory was now looking like a defeat. Furthermore, concerning news was reaching him from the southern border. Intercepted Russian messages revealed the formidable strength of Samsonov's Second Army. Reconnaissance aircraft also reported seeing huge clouds of dust that suggested that Samsonov was advancing further west than had been anticipated. Prittwitz was unprepared for this eventuality and the threat of being cut off was growing. He was faced with a difficult decision: continue the attack against Rennenkampf and risk being cut off by Samsonov, or retreat? Still undecided, he telephoned François, informing him of Mackensen's failed attack and warning him that a retreat across the Vistula looked increasingly likely. This was no small matter. The Vistula was more than 125 miles away, and such an order would effectively mean giving up East Prussia to the Russians.

Inevitably, François protested profusely. His corps had the enemy on the run, he argued, and had captured large numbers of prisoners and guns. A continuation of the attack on 21 August would surely break resistance in the north and allow him to roll up the entire Russian line. If he was successful, Mackensen's failure would not matter. Prittwitz's own staff were adamant that Rennenkampf could (and should) be beaten, but Prittwitz was not convinced, and the order was issued to all units to disengage from the fight and await further orders.

As night fell on 20 August and fighting died out along the line, rumours about what had happened at Gumbinnen began to spread. In the north, François's I Corps had managed to push the Russians back, and officers and men alike had expected to resume the attack in the morning. Some men were seen weeping as they instead had to march west. In the south, Below's men had also bested the Russian IV Corps. Surely that meant success? But in the centre, Mackensen's XVII Corps had been soundly thrashed by the Russians and had suffered more than 8,000 casualties. His men, having fled the field of battle in disorder, leaving rifles, guns and wounded comrades behind, did not feel victorious. Asmus Jørgensen described his bewilderment when he first became aware of the way the battle was being described by the German press: 'When we later gathered in [Gumbinnen], it turned out that [there] were only 33 men left in the company.

Afterwards I read in a newspaper that the Germans were writing about the "Victory over the Russians at Gumbinnen and Walterkehmen." But I had actually experienced this "victory," and we had in fact been beaten.'[20]

The Russian soldiers of III Corps were also in no doubt as to who had won the day. As Mackensen's shattered corps retreated, cheering broke out in the Russian trenches. 'The heart was filled with joy and pride,' wrote Captain Uspensky. 'Jubilation was written on all our faces, exhausted by the horrors of battle! We won! And against whom? The Germans!'[21] The humiliating defeat at the hands of the Japanese less than a decade earlier loomed in the back of many minds. Now, Russia had bested the greatest army in the world. This was redemption. A captured German officer was even heard exclaiming in amazement: 'How well these Russians have learnt to shoot since the Japanese war!'[22]

Later in the day, officers and men emerged from the Russian trenches. 'Abandoned weapons, items of equipment, artillery shells and rifle cartridges, wagons loaded with military property of various kinds, the corpses of fallen horses… were encountered throughout the day,' wrote General Adaridi, whose 27th Division had been routed at Stallupönen and had now redeemed themselves. 'To sum up, all the signs were present to indicate that the retreat was disorderly and that the troops had sought to get to the rear as quickly as possible.'[23] Captain Uspensky was stunned by the grisly sight of an artillery battery that had been destroyed by the Russian guns:

> Here is a young officer with a raised sabre, his head thrown back and his mouth open, screaming… Here… a soldier has half inserted a shell into the gun. With his hands [still on] it, he's kneeling, with his eyes fixed upwards with some expression of surprise, as if asking: 'What's the matter?!' … From a distance, these figures seemed to be alive, but when we got closer, we saw that three-quarters of the officer's head had been torn off from behind and literally only a

mask remained, and the soldier's entire stomach had been ripped out.[24]

For many, this was their first real experience of combat, in a war that differed dramatically from what they had expected. German soldier Willy Tharann wrote on 20 August: 'No, this is not an honest fight, but just plain, dastardly murder. Poor fool, you let yourself be deceived like that! Full of strife, you turned away from life and joyfully went to war, which you believed would turn machines into people again. What a terrible mistake!'[25]

Back at Prittwitz's headquarters, no decision had been made about what to do next. But if the situation seemed uncertain in East Prussia, it appeared completely chaotic to Germany's supreme headquarters. The messages reaching General Moltke from Prittwitz changed repeatedly throughout the day. First, victory was apparently within grasp. Then, the situation was desperate. Some units were reported lost, only to then reappear in later messages. The increasingly frantic army commander asked Moltke for reinforcements, but was told to pull himself together. But how could he hold against such vastly superior enemy forces? That, the reply came, was his problem. Thanks to the Belgians, the Schlieffen Plan was already behind schedule, and no men could be spared from the west. The exact exchange between Moltke and Prittwitz remains unclear, and sources contradict each other. What is clear, however, is that by 21 August, Moltke was under the impression that the situation in East Prussia was out of control, and he had no confidence in Prittwitz to turn the situation around. A change of command was needed for the Eighth Army, and in the afternoon of 22 August, Prittwitz was informed that a special train was on its way with his replacement.

12

Stuck in the Middle

Wars have caused enormous upheaval for civilians caught in their midst for millennia. The normal rules of society no longer apply, and marching armies plunder and commit atrocities, with little regard for property or human life. The First World War was no exception, not least in the Balkans where the conflict began.

Officials in the city of Belgrade, located on the shores of the Danube, which marked the border between Serbia and Austria–Hungary, had received the declaration of war with great concern. It seemed only natural that the enemy would attempt to capture the Serbian capital immediately. Even before the first shots were fired, the streets were buzzing with activity. 'People swarmed about like bees in a hive,' wrote Sveta Milutinović, a Serbian journalist, about the immediate aftermath of the declaration of war on 28 July. 'Some were getting ready for military service, others were in a hurry to leave the city as soon as possible, since the news had spread with lightning speed that the Austrians would start bombarding Belgrade with heavy shells during the night.'[1] Before dark, three trains left Belgrade packed full of refugees, with people sitting on top of every car.

Shortly after midnight on 28–29 July, two river monitors of the Austro-Hungarian Danube Flotilla opened fire on the Serbian capital with their 12-cm guns. SMS *Bodrog* was credited with firing the first shot of the war – not on enemy troops, but against civilians. The bombardment was short-lived; as soon as the vessels came under return fire, the Austro-Hungarians retired.

However, in the following days, shells regularly fell on Belgrade, destroying houses, banks and hotels. A number of factories were hit too, as were the city's main post office, the state printing press, the train station, military offices, the National Museum, St Michael's Cathedral, the Academy of Science and the famous Terazije Square in the city centre. Crucially, the power plant and waterworks were damaged, depriving the city of lighting, fuel and running water. Civilians ran for shelter. As well as in basements, many also sought refuge in the large caves underneath Tašmajdan Park, which soon became crowded with people from all layers of society. 'They lay next to each other and trembled with fear: ladies from the most respectable houses and poor laundresses and day labourers from Palilula and its surroundings,' wrote Milutinović.[2] Meanwhile, wounded women and children, and others who had been dug out from beneath collapsed buildings, continued to arrive at the General State Hospital where twenty-six-year-old doctor Slavka Mihajlović and her colleagues were forced to work by the light of candles held by paramedics and sometimes even other patients. Then, on 7 August, two heavy shells landed in the hospital's courtyard. 'Shrapnel mowed down everything alive. It is difficult to describe the scene I found in the women's hospital. Mothers held newborns in their arms and ran frantically through the corridors. Their voices and the cries of the babies merged with the roar of the cannons.'[3]

It was inevitable that civilians would flee from scenes like this. In East Prussia, the inhabitants of the villages along the Russian frontier began leaving for cities in the west such as Danzig and Königsberg as early as 28 July, several days before Germany declared war on Russia. Some had no choice. Russia ordered the removal of large numbers of people considered 'suspicious' from border regions. German settlers were given five days to leave their homes, along with a large part of the Jewish population living in westernmost Russia. In official circles, where anti-Semitism ran deep, there were constant rumours of Jews openly expressing support for Germany. Russian officials did not register that much of the very real resentment that many Jews felt towards Russia was rooted in the tsarist government's own policies of persecution and discrimination. To render them 'harmless', entire Jewish communities were deported from the vicinity of the front further inside the enormous Russian empire.

Likewise, in Austria–Hungary, concerns about ethnicities and allegiances among their subjects kept officials awake at night. The military enjoyed almost unlimited power when it came to the removal of civilians. Tens of thousands were relocated, supposedly for their own safety, perhaps, but also on the pretext of stopping civilians from collaborating with the enemy. Close to Russia, cities such as Lemberg and Czernowitz were among the first to be 'evacuated', with some 40,000 people removed from the latter alone. More cities followed suit. By mid-September, nearly a third of the pre-war populations of the fortress towns of Przemyśl and Kraków had been evacuated. Entire villages in surrounding areas became ghost towns.

Once the fighting began in earnest, country roads and village train stations quickly filled to the brim with people fleeing of their own accord. Soon, millions were on the move; wherever an army advanced, it was preceded by an immense flood of terrified civilians. In East Prussia, stories of atrocities committed by Russian Cossacks caused a mass exodus. By the estimate of one government official, a quarter of the population, a total of 870,000 of the region's inhabitants, abandoned their homes during August 1914. In the German town of Schneidemühl, only 200 miles north-east of Berlin, twelve-year-old schoolgirl Piete Kuhr recorded the arrival of refugees on their way out of East Prussia:

> They all carry bundles and cases, bedding, coats and cloaks all tied together. [They] are looked after at our Red Cross depot at the station. One woman with noisy children kept crying out, 'Where can we go? Where can we go?' I wished her good luck and said, 'Don't worry, the [Kaiser] will look after us all!' 'Dear child,' said the woman… 'a child like you

can have no idea what it's like, can you?' And tears ran all over her chubby face.[4]

To the south-east, in Galicia, thousands more civilians sought refuge from the advancing Russians. Within three weeks of the outbreak of the war, Lemberg alone saw 100,000 refugees, while in the Carpathian mountains, the small Hungarian town of Bártfa nearly tripled in population when 10,000 people, mostly Galician Jews, arrived in the space of just seventy-two hours. 'Refugees come from outside with women and children, wagons and cattle,' wrote one eyewitness in Przemyśl. 'Frightened, they ask to be allowed into the fortress. A real panic has broken out and people are flocking to the outposts in large numbers. But the order is to turn everyone away. Force must be used to disperse the crowds. Their touching requests are in vain.'[5] By early autumn, there were 350,000 refugees in the Austrian half of the Dual Monarchy alone. By October, that number had almost doubled.

On the Russian side of the frontier, the picture was much the same. Here, thousands could be seen fleeing east from the fighting in border regions. A Russian officer travelling to the front recorded the pitiful sight that greeted him. 'Hundreds of men, cows, horses; women with loose hair, as if tousled by a hurricane; mothers painfully clutching swaddled babies to their chests; homeless dogs... Jews in wrinkled, torn caftans; old women sitting on bundles... All this runs before my eyes in a pitiful string of dumbfounded, submissive, helpless and hostile faces with an expression of horror, humiliation and wild fatigue in their eyes.'[6]

In Belgium, the German invasion caused another massive stream of refugees. In all, nearly a million and a half civilians, some 20 per cent of the country's population, fled their homes. At Ostende, a tram conductor wrote: 'Refugees from Mechelen, Louvain, Thienen arrive here by train at all hours with packs, bags, children, and wander through the city to find a place to sleep.'[7] Most Belgian refugees crossed the border into the Netherlands, while thousands made for France or Britain. Serbia, too, saw entire cities abandoned. Before the war, Belgrade had a population of some 90,000. Within a matter of weeks, more than 80,000 of those had abandoned the capital. It was the same in Valjevo, in the path of the invading Austro-Hungarian armies. By autumn, only 300 of the city's 10,000 inhabitants remained, the rest having vanished into the interior. 'It was as if the entire world had to move or was waiting to move,' wrote the director of the Civil Affairs Office of the Red Cross, Homer Folks.[8]

Tiredness, hunger and exhaustion were experienced by millions of people on the move, but life as a refugee was especially trying for the elderly and for those travelling with young children. Marin Mattioli was only nine years old when his family was forced to leave their home in Xeuilley, outside Nancy. His youthful account of the family's flight records the hardship faced by many families:

My brother Jean is seven, Marcel five and I am nine. My mother pushes my two-year-old little sister in a small cart... It's almost dark and mom says to us, 'We have to walk, little ones.' My youngest brother is crying, he can no longer move forward and to make matters worse, it's raining. What does mom do? She pushes the little cart a long way then comes back to get my brother who she is carrying on her back. I can't help her because I'm carrying a small bundle of belongings and I'm also tired.[9]

Stories of battles and atrocities accompanied the refugees everywhere. In Munkács, 140 miles south-west of Lemberg, the Hungarian lawyer, historian and archaeologist Lehoczky Tivadar heard frightening accounts from those arriving from Galicia. 'The Russian guns fire incessantly,' they told him. 'They say so much smoke was produced that people suffocated.'[10] Stories like these convinced more to join them in flight, adding to the ever-growing flood of people.

Those who remained behind ran a real risk of being caught in the crossfire. In Galicia, Austro-Hungarian artilleryman Pál Horváth described civilians falling foul of artillery exchanges with Russian batteries: 'The villages that fell within the line of fire were set ablaze by the shells… their cries and howls of terror chilled the blood in a man.'[11] Similarly, in Lorraine, at Fillières a local priest described the aftermath of the fighting between German and French troops on 22 August:

> I saw, resting in the grass, one beside the other after the battle, a man and a woman who, wanting to flee through their garden, had been hit by the shells. The woman, with long black hair, had her shoulder cut open and shattered! Her husband, lying on his stomach, had his head buried in the ground! Beside them, here and there, dead soldiers. What a frightening sight![12]

*

Beyond the danger of being caught up in battles, atrocities against civilians occurred from the moment war was declared. As soon as the German army crossed the Belgian frontier on 4 August, stories began to spread. What would soon become universally known as the 'Rape of Belgium', though many atrocities also occurred in France, and even in German Alsace and Lorraine, became one of the defining memories of August 1914. While tales of German brutality and barbarism towards civilians were often embellished as propaganda, it is clear that the invasion left a trail of unnecessary civilian suffering in its wake.

The vast majority of these atrocities were carried out as 'punishment' for civilians supposedly taking part in combat operations. The term *franc-tireur* was given to French civilians who took up arms after defeat at Sedan during the Franco-Prussian War. The memory of this guerrilla warfare against a vague enemy dogged the German military in 1914. They were adamant that it would not happen again. 'Disgraceful!' wrote one soldier. 'An honest bullet in honest battle; yes, then one has shed one's blood for the Fatherland. But to be shot in an ambush, from the window of a house, the gun-barrel hidden behind flower-pots; no, that is not a nice soldierly death.'[13] Furthermore, the Schlieffen Plan required speed, and flushing out covert operatives slowed an army on the march. On 12 August, Moltke issued a clear warning against any form of resistance or interference by the civilian population:

> Every non-uniformed person, if he is not designated as being justified in participating in fighting by clearly recognizable insignia, is to be treated as someone standing outside international law, if he takes part in the fighting, interferes with German communications with the rest, cuts telegraph lines, causes explosions, in short participates in any way in the act of war without permission. He will be treated as a franc-tireur and immediately shot according to martial law.[14]

Moltke's warning was supplemented by more, drastic measures. These included the shooting of any civilian found to be in possession of firearms, as well as anyone attempting to sabotage the German advance. Additional punishments ranged from hostage-taking to executions and the destruction of property.

Infamous massacres occurred where the German advance encountered unexpected resistance. Civilians were often accused of assisting the defending troops, and once these had withdrawn, the Germans took their revenge. At Malines, Belgian units repulsed several German attacks between 24 and 27 August, before retreating on 28 August, leaving the city undefended. Two days later, the Germans shelled the city's inhabitants in retaliation for their supposedly having aided the defenders. One German soldier later recalled the subsequent advance through the burning streets:

> It was as hot as an oven. We had to keep an eye on each other's clothes and equipment to prevent the embers from lighting us on fire. We advanced slowly, since the facades of houses had fallen out into the street. Furniture from the upper floors hovered between heaven and earth or had crashed down. Death and suffering hung over the entire city. It was war in all its horror.[15]

Friendly fire also saw civilians blamed for German casualties. The combination of nervous exhaustion, confusion, tiredness, inexperience and the frequent over-consumption of looted alcohol resulted in inevitable episodes of German soldiers shooting each other. Supposed franc-tireurs were easily blamed, and innocent locals punished as a result. On 20 August, in one Lorraine village, one shot in the night resulted in two companies mistaking each other for the enemy and opening fire. 'I do not know exactly how many losses our company suffered, but [another] lost six men and a horse,' a Bavarian NCO wrote. 'Next morning the word was put around that the civilian population had been shooting, so we had to search the whole village for weapons. No proof could be found, and I do not believe the story. I presume that it was the overexcited nerves of some of the men which was the cause.'[16]

The German press fanned the flames of the franc-tireur panic. As soon as the Belgian border was crossed, newspapers filled with accusations of treachery committed by civilians against advancing troops. A correspondent from the *Berliner Zeitung am Mittag* claimed that Belgian women 'attacked sleeping and wounded German soldiers, mutilating them in ways that could not be reproduced, and tortured them to death'.[17] That such stories influenced German soldiers is clear from their own writing. With IR 86, Hans Brodersen described his first night on sentry duty outside Liège: 'The mood was sombre. We've heard so much about the franc-tireur war, that this… is almost the sole topic of conversation.'[18] Stories of sleeping or wounded troops being mutilated by the population at large conditioned German soldiers to fear civilians, anticipate the worst, and suppress feelings of guilt.

One of the worst displays took place in Louvain, 18 miles east of Brussels. In the final days of August, this esteemed university town, home to some 40,000 people, became the scene of one of the invasion's most destructive and violent atrocities. Louvain was first occupied by the Germans on 19 August. The population knew what was coming and tried to mitigate potential anger. In the days that followed the departure of the Belgian army, a curfew was installed, and people were warned not to oppose the Germans. Posters informed the population that any weapon found in a house would result in harsh punishment, not only for the owner, but for other inhabitants too. The atmosphere remained tense, but relatively calm for the next six days.

This all changed on the evening of 25 August. An alarm was sounded, followed shortly afterwards by the sound of shots being fired. The Germans would later claim that franc-tireurs had launched an insurrection, however, the most likely explanation seems to have been yet another case of friendly fire. Whatever the cause, the results were the same. Shortly after the first shots were heard, all hell broke loose. German soldiers fired wildly through-out the town. Houses were charged and the inhabitants chased out onto the streets, where many were beaten, stabbed with bayonets or shot. 'All the inhabitants in the houses, from where we'd been fired upon, were shot, both men, women and children,' wrote Iver Clausen. 'The innocent had to suffer with the guilty, it was a terrible pity to witness... Burnt and shot people lay in the street... You had to pinch yourself in the arm to check if you were awake or not.'[19] Homes were set on fire, and as they escaped the flames, whole families were shot down by German soldiers waiting outside. Many of Louvain's important cultural buildings were also destroyed, including churches and parts of the university. Shortly before midnight, the latter's library was set on fire. By morning, all that remained of it and its 300,000 volumes and manuscripts was a smoking pile of ash. One of the professors stood in his garden as the glowing, charred remnants of his medieval manuscripts fluttered down around him.

It was not over. By 28 August, 2,000 of the town's buildings had been destroyed while 248 civilians had been killed. About 10,000 people fled to roam around the surrounding country-side, where German patrols continued to harass and even exe-cute them. Thousands more were captured and deported in cattle wagons to camps in Germany. The destruction of Louvain became a symbol of German brutality and caused outrage across the world. By the time the Western Front began emerging in mid-September, it is estimated that more than 6,400 civilians had been killed in Belgium and France in more than 500 recorded incidents.

The Rape of Belgium remains the best known of all the atrocities carried out in the opening months of the war. However, it was not only in the west that acts of brutality were carried out against civilians. More occurred in the east and in the Balkans, often the result of familiar claims that civilians were participating in the fighting or aiding the enemy. On the outset of war, the city of Kalisz, 150 miles east of Warsaw on Germany's border with Russia, was subjected to a nearly three-week orgy of destruction. Russian officials and soldiers evacuated the city immediately following the outbreak of war, with the first German cavalry patrol arriving promptly the next day. Having anticipated their arrival, the mayor submitted. Later on, more German troops arrived peacefully and in good order, bringing artillery and machine-guns. The local Poles displayed little animosity towards the invaders, many of whom were themselves Polish, but their German commander, Major Hermann Preusker, still put the city under martial law. Events took a dark turn the following evening, when scattered gunfire was heard throughout the city.

The exact reason for the subsequent firefight has never fully been determined. Nevertheless, by morning, twenty-one civilians and six soldiers lay dead. Heavy reprisals followed. Suspects were executed, local administrators and religious leaders were arrested and taken hostage. Finally, artillery was brought in to shell the city. 'About 70 cannon shots were fired,' wrote a local engineer named Oppman, 'Private houses, a hospital, a church and temples were fired upon equally. All residents of the city, gripped by panic, hid in the basements, from where many... did not come out for several days, enduring cold and hunger.'[20] German patrols spread throughout the city, stopping inhabitants in the streets. 'Passers-by were brutally searched, often beaten with rifle butts,' wrote another witness. 'At the slightest opposition, they were put against the wall and shot.'[21] Over the coming days, German troops carried out looting, arson, rape and indiscriminate murder.

The Polish novelist Maria Dąbrowska described the systematic destruction of her city by the Germans:

> New squadrons of troops have entered the city and they no longer shoot, but burn. Each soldier has a torch and straw in his hand, or a vessel with something smelly, kerosene or tar. Some burst into apartments and shout: raus, raus! and those with torches go straight to the hall and set fire to it. On the street near the cemetery, all the houses are on fire. One Jew did not allow the fire to be set, so the soldier bayoneted him on the spot.[22]

'They fired machine-guns all over the city,' continued Oppman. 'Soldiers broke into houses and shops, robbed, started fires and massacred entire families; women, children and elders... In the magistrate's building, where city employees had gathered... the city cashier Pashkevich and three watchmen were hacked to death with an axe.'[23] Estimates suggest that several hundred civilians were killed. By late August, most of the inhabitants had fled the city, and 95 per cent of its buildings and houses had been damaged or destroyed.

While Kalisz would prove to be the most violent single atrocity carried out in the east at the beginning of the war, it was far from an isolated incident. Neither were the Germans the only perpetrators. In the wake of its invasion of East Prussia, the Russian army deported thousands of civilians to the vast inner reaches of the Russian empire. Later, authorities would claim that they had only taken men of military age. In reality, half of them were women and children, and of the estimated 13,000 civilians who were deported, one third would never return.

As early as 11 August, residents of the East Prussian border village of Radszen reported to the local district administrator that a number of civilians had been beaten and shot following a clash between German and Russian troops in the village. Such incidents would become far more frequent once the Russians crossed the border in force. On 18 August, echoing Moltke,

General Rennenkampf issued a proclamation stating that any civilian opposition would be ruthlessly punished, regardless of gender and age, and that villages and hamlets where it took place would be burnt to the ground. Cultural differences played a part. In Russia, barbed wire was an anomaly outside the military, but in East Prussia it was widely used by civilians. Barbed wire fences lined fields, meadows and vegetable gardens, leading to accusations that this was deliberately done to disrupt cavalry operations. Innocent Germans with bicycles, another item not commonly owned by civilians in Russia, were also frequently accused of spying, and many were shot on the spot.

On 29 August, a mass killing of civilians took place in the village of Abschwangen. Here, a German patrol had shot a Russian officer. A local official wrote a detailed account of the Russian reprisals that were subsequently aimed at innocent civilians. According to him, some inhabitants such as the local teacher, a father of six, were shot immediately, while the rest of the villagers were divided into two groups and taken to each end of the village. Here, all males aged fifteen and above were ordered to form rows, while the women and children were made to stand a few feet away. A Russian officer then informed the villagers that because they had opened fire, all the males were to be summarily shot, with the women and children serving as witnesses to the punishment. The official who wrote the report was due to be shot along with his fifteen-year-old son but was able to present a letter signed by a Russian colonel who had passed through a few days prior, thanking him for his good hospitality. He was spared. However, by the time the issue had been resolved, a volley was heard from the other end of the village, signalling that the order had been carried out against the other group. 'A young woman who had only been married four weeks... went to the Russians after seeing the bloody, twitching bodies of her husband, her father and her father-in-law, asking them to shoot her too, as her life was now without purpose,' continued the official. 'But the Russians withdrew and left the surviving women and children in silent despair in the midst of their murdered fathers, husbands, brothers and sons.'[24] In total, sixty-one villagers were killed.

At least 1,491 civilians were killed in East Prussia. In proportion to the population, the level of violence against civilians was comparable to that in the west. Material damage was considerable, too. According to official German figures, the Russian invasion caused the destruction of 41,414 structures, too. In Gumbinnen county alone, one fifth of all buildings were destroyed, and local administrators estimated that reconstruction would require some 198 million bricks.

*

Civilians who saw the devastation left behind by war did not forget it. For some, the experience was life-changing. Rape was not uncommon in the opening weeks of war. The stigma attached to such crimes, however, means that primary sources are scarce. Asmus Jørgensen, a Dane serving with IR 61 in the east, heard about it: 'In the forest, where we were advancing, we met groups of people, who all wailed about the Russians, who had *visited* them, and especially the women had felt their *love*.'[25] During a later court hearing, a twenty-year-old woman from East Prussia provided a rare first-hand account of such crimes, when she described how she had been attacked by a group of Russian soldiers in her home in the village of Wysockem in 1914. 'One of the Russian soldiers pushed me violently from the hall into the room and demanded that I give myself to him,' she testified. 'I resisted and was then violently thrown to the floor by the soldier. After he had finished with me, a second Russian soldier, who had waited in front of the door and refused my mother entry, came in. This one threw me on the bed and also forced me to surrender myself to him.'[26] The young woman, who had been seven months pregnant when the assault happened, later gave birth to a stillborn child. Sexual assault occurred in the west, too. On the Charleroi front, there were allegations of gang rape. 'In Pont-à-Celles... a person aged over seventy was insulted on several occasions, as well as many women and young girls.'[27]

Some of the perpetrators, it was claimed, had not participated in the battle, and had only just arrived in the area. The heat of battle could not be blamed.

Some of the war's worst atrocities were committed by the Austro-Hungarians. In Galicia and Bukovina, the army was highly suspicious that their own Ruthenian subjects supported Russia. They made the accusation sound like a disease: *Russophilia*. '[The Russians] are of a common language and religion to them,' wrote one Hungarian hussar, '[while we] could neither speak to them nor look favourably upon them, as they were unimaginably dirty.'[28]

Austro-Hungarian officials suspected that a network of conspirators was at work along their eastern borders. Russian religious leaders, teachers and politicians were imprisoned, even executed on suspicion of recruiting soldiers for the Russian army and eagerly awaiting 'liberation'. Many other innocent Ruthenes, whose language was also easily mistaken for Russian by untrained ears, were also arrested, along with anyone with a Slavic name. Tens of thousands were interned in concentration camps. At Thalerhof in south-east Austria, 30,000 political prisoners endured gruelling conditions, marked by hunger and the spread of disease.

Hanging was a common punishment for those accused of collaboration. Slovenian soldier Boštjan Olip witnessed two civilians shot after being accused of cutting a telegraph wire, while Viktor Arlow, a Hungarian officer, noted on 8 September: '...the sad task fell on my regiment to hang 68 traitorous Russians'.[29] As with the German and Russian armies, orders for these ruthless acts came directly from the top. On 10 September 1914, a circular was issued stating that regarding incidents of treachery, the army was instructed to 'shoot guilty parties on the spot without a trial' and 'take hostages from the municipality who would be killed if the same subversive acts were committed in the same municipality, and to shoot every tenth inhabitant, and burn down the village'.[30]

As in Belgium, France and East Prussia, civilians in the border regions of Austria–Hungary were looked at with mistrust. The enemy was thought to be everywhere. 'Three women were brought before the major, and the major sentenced them mercilessly to the noose,' wrote one soldier. 'They knelt before him begging for mercy... They were innocent, but the major and other officers claimed that in Galicia everyone was a traitor, so a patrol hanged them... All night long, they are butchering the poor local people like cattle.'[31] The Austro-Hungarians were not alone in carrying out atrocities against the civilian population. Anti-Semitism permeated the Russian army, and Russian troops frequently attacked Jewish communities. In Brody, 65 miles north-east of Lemberg, Cossack troops attacked Jewish homes and businesses. Hundreds of buildings were burnt to the ground and six people were killed.

The exact number of civilians killed in Galicia and its neighbouring region of Bukovina is not known. Thousands were hanged in the opening weeks of the war. The sight of people hanging from trees, with signs around their necks saying 'spy', became commonplace. The issue was severe enough that in late August, the emperor's military chancellery challenged the methods the army was employing against civilians as positively 'ludicrous' and pointed out that they stirred up 'much lamentable ill feeling'.[32] The atrocities continued regardless, and before the end of 1914, the army was forced to recruit additional hangmen in order to carry out the vast number of death sentences being issued.

*

In the Balkans, tensions ran especially high. During the first invasion alone, Habsburg forces killed up to 4,000 Serbs, many of them Austro-Hungarian subjects. Like the Germans marching through Belgium, Austro-Hungarian soldiers had been taught to expect a hostile civilian population, armed and organized by the Serbian state. Unlike the franc-tireurs, however, who existed almost entirely in the imaginations of the German troops, the *komitadjis*, Serbian irregulars, were very real, and very active. Extensively employed during the Balkan Wars, these highly experienced bands of fighters varied in size, but they were expected to assist the Serbian army by collecting intelligence and harassing enemy troops and supply lines.

The problem was exacerbated by the Serbian army's poor logistics. Only first-line troops were issued full uniforms. Further back, men were often only issued a uniform jacket or an overcoat, while the third line were dressed in their civilian clothes. These men were easily mistaken for armed civilians by the Austro-Hungarians. However, evidence suggests that the Habsburg soldiers were not particularly concerned with who was guilty or innocent. František Vančury witnessed this in Lešnica on the Drina:

> This afternoon a shot was fired from a house during the transport of the wounded. Immediately the house was searched and the two elderly people, a married couple, were brought to court. Without much ado, the man was hanged and the woman tied up for the day. But who can say if they were definitely guilty or not? In the afternoon, 120 civilians were paraded. Elders, men and very young boys. It was already known in advance that they would all be shot, but still the captain asked the high command, which freed the boys and some others and condemned about 80 to death. They were guarded overnight and today, 19th August, they were shot in the morning. I also went to see the dead, however, it was a terrible sight. They were all tied up in rows and shot. Terrible.[33]

Like their German counterparts, Austro-Hungarian officers were furious at the thought of civilians blurring the line between combatants and non-combatants, and many expected to face large numbers of belligerent civilians. In early August, Richard Riedl articulated the unease that permeated through the invasion force: 'We are in Bjelina, a town on the Bosnian–Serbian border. In the middle of the market square is a gallows, newly erected. The residents are half Serbs, half Turks… Everything is so spooky. You suspect something treacherous about every farmer here.'[34]

Rumours escalated. It was said that boiling water and burning kerosene had been thrown at the soldiers from upstairs windows, that bodies of the fallen had been mutilated and the wounded had been tortured. 'If an Austrian fell, ten female devils jumped out, pierced his eyes and tore out his tongue, slashed his stomach and pulled out his intestines,' claimed one officer.[35] Richard Riedl alleged that a komitadji was found with a bag full of 'cut-off noses and ears from our soldiers'.[36] Stories of corpses being found without eyes and coat buttons placed in the empty sockets seemed particularly widespread. Czech soldier Fric Tonda claimed: 'We saw four Serbs shot dead, caught for gouging out the eyes of our dead soldiers and putting buttons inside, carving out hearts, etc.'[37] Accounts like these are impossible to substantiate, but tales of such savagery caused further anger and resentment towards the civilian population.

It was only after the Austro-Hungarian defeat on Mount Cer that people began to comprehend fully the scale of the bloodlust that was on display in occupied parts of Serbia. As Serbian forces advanced on the heels of their retreating foe, the number of reports of massacred civilians grew. A Serbian colonel gave the following account of what his regiment had found in a meadow near the village of Krivajica:

Children, girls, women and men, fifteen in all, were stretched out dead, fastened together by their hands. The majority had been killed with the bayonet. A young girl had been struck... in the left jaw, and the blade had come out by the right cheek bone. Many of the corpses had no teeth... The chemises of the little girls and young women were covered with blood, which seemed to prove that they had been violated before being killed.[38]

To document the atrocities, the Serbian government commissioned Rodolphe Archibald Reiss, a criminology professor at the University of Lausanne in neutral Switzerland. Reiss conducted investigations on the ground, gathering evidence, taking photos and interviewing Serbian witnesses and victims as well as Austro-Hungarian prisoners. He uncovered a litany of inhuman behaviour. People had been brutally killed in reprisals carried out by an army that convinced itself that there was no such thing in Serbia as a non-combatant. First published in 1916 at more than 250 pages, Reiss's report made for sobering reading. Its potential as a piece of propaganda was not lost, either, and it was soon distributed to Allied and neutral states to support Serbia's cause. As a seasoned criminologist, Reiss also attempted to answer the question of what could have driven people to engage in such atrocities. He reasoned that the Austro-Hungarian soldiers had been taught that their victims were barbarians, and had likely committed their first massacres out of fear of being massacred themselves. Once this threshold had been crossed, the floodgates were opened:

Man becomes changed into a bloodthirsty animal. A real outburst of collective sadism took possession of those troops – a sadism which those who have been present at a bull-fight have had an opportunity of observing on a small scale. Once the blood-thirsty and licentious animal was unloosed and set free by his superiors, the work of devastation was carried out by men who are fathers of families and probably gentle in their private life.[39]

Evidence supports Reiss's theory. For example, as artilleryman Rudolph Koch passed through burning villages, he was overcome by a sudden urge to partake in the destruction. He later offered an account of how violence spread like a disease within invading armies in the summer of 1914:

Everything was on fire, the houses, fences, fruit trees, every village was a sea of flames... Even in us, the desire to destroy took over, and I set fire to a cottage myself with Pista Riedl, so that it wouldn't stand so sad and dark among its flaming companions that were flying up to the clouds. There is a terrible smell of burning everywhere, the smell of burnt clothes, bed feathers, etc. I realized then that if war is like this, then it's very ugly.[40]

13

You Wanted the War!

France and Belgium

Hindsight shows that Joffre was mistaken when he planned the main thrust of his French offensive. He knew about the German march through Belgium, but he underestimated the scale of it. This meant that he expected to find the enemy at their strongest opposite the middle of his line and this was where he planned to attack. Though more information was emerging about the wheeling motion of the Schlieffen Plan in Belgium, Joffre convinced himself that even if that was where the Germans had invested their main effort, as opposed to where he was about to strike, then he would happily be attacking a smaller force and he could sever the German swing by breaking their line and then hitting Karl von Bülow and Alexander von Kluck from the rear. On 21 August, the French commander believed that the decisive moment of the war had arrived, and ordered his Third and Fourth Armies to advance. They were positioned along the border between Sedan and Thionville, ready to strike his knockout blow. They lacked adequate knowledge of the terrain and the enemy in front of them, and they were outnumbered. Isolated clashes took place on the first day of the battle, but it was the following day on which the anticipated significant action occured. It was a day that would be costly for the Germans, and nothing short of catastrophic for France.

As 22 August dawned, Charles Delvert was serving as an officer with the 101e Régiment d'Infanterie in Joffre's Third Army. He had been on the march for more than an hour when daylight came. 'The sun rose in a halo. Its rays pierce the fine mist with dazzling lines… This rugged country is marvellous, wooded hilltops, lowlands, swept up in the fog.' He crossed the border into Belgium, and anticipation built. A few miles away, on the road to the village of Ethe, another lieutenant was riding with his regiment of hussars. 'The fog was not dissipating yet, but it was causing a diffused light that gave us the impression of moving within a globe of frosted glass. The objects around us, trees, houses… stood out against the milky background in flat silhouettes.'[1]

Charles Delvert had just crossed a railway line when his battalion suddenly came under fire. 'Machine-guns crackle in the fog. A noise runs through the ranks. The Germans are [650 feet] away! Great commotion among the artillerymen. Orders overlap. The batteries want to turn around; but how? A gun overturns; drivers shout; the horses rear up. In the fog, the firing redoubles. Ahead!' Delvert led his men into the village of Gomery to find mayhem. '[It] is crowded with horses dripping with purple blood.'[2]

Meanwhile, 2 miles to the north-east, IR 124 was attacking French forces in the tiny Belgian hamlet of Bleid. Twenty-two-year-old Erwin Rommel was about to come under fire for the first time. 'The fog is clearing, the warm August sun is vividly lighting up the lovely hilly landscape with its rich pastures, beautiful cornfields,' he recalled of the farm in front of him. 'My plan of attack is as follows…'. One half-section would open fire on upper levels of the building, while the other half stormed it from the right. 'Quickly I have the assault group take beams lying here and there on the ground. They will be very useful for breaking down doors… Meanwhile, behind the hedge, the second half-section is ready to open fire… We can go. On my signal, with the [others], I rush to the attack.'[3]

Rommel and his men crossed the road, reached the farmhouse and found shelter underneath a wall. 'The gates shattered under the powerful blows of the musketeers. A barn door jumps off the hinges. Burning straw plugs are thrown into the area filled with grain and fodder. The farm is surrounded. Anyone who wants to get out will jump on our bayonets.' Unsurprisingly, the French surrendered. 'Our own losses are limited to a few minor injuries,' Rommel recorded. 'So, we continue the assault from farm to farm... Where we are close to the opponent, he surrenders immediately... or he hides in the corners... But there too the men flush out the enemy and, with the greatest intrepidity, bring the French out of their hiding places, one after the other.'[4]

The village was aflame, and Rommel considered his work done. 'I round up those I can reach, have the wounded removed, and head north-east. I want to get out of this inferno... The fire, thick suffocating smoke, glowing beams, collapsed houses and maddened cattle... bar the way. Finally, half asphyxiated, we head out.'[5]

*

Back across the border, 20 miles to the south-east, the French village of Fillières had been occupied by the Germans on 7 August. Supplies had been seized, while some civilians were killed and others taken hostage. Father Martin had met the general in charge, and watched the German break down in tears under the strain of it all. 'Tomorrow or the day after there will be a battle,' Martin heard from another. The invaders were apprehensive. '"If Germany loses", says a captain, "it will take fifty years to recover." And furious, he tears up the newspaper he is holding in his hand.'[6]

At 9.30 a.m. on 22 August, the sound of gunfire erupted from the direction of the station. The villagers had prayed for deliverance. 'Full of emotion, we run from the houses through the gardens in this direction; then what a pleasant surprise! Through the tall oats, you can see the French uniforms.' For the locals, the sight of the 154th RI was glorious. This was by no means the sterile battle environment encountered later in the war, when villages had been cleared of their occupants:

Immediately they are surrounded, they are served refreshments. Hidden wine bottles make an appearance; we serve coffee... Captain Lamothe, a handsome blond man, mounted on a handsome black horse, is happy in the midst of these people, who have become free again (for a moment), who nevertheless warn him that the enemy is not far away: 'Ah! Madame, don't be afraid; we'll see each other again!'[7]

Half an hour later, Captain Lamothe was dead.

*

Fighting in an urban environment meant that nasty surprises lurked around every corner, and brutal hand-to-hand fighting took place at close quarters. 'On the ground, two men struggle desperately, a third runs up with his bayonet,' wrote one German, who continued:

A handful of French soldiers are fighting for their lives. A gigantic young, handsome officer... defends himself like a desperate man... one of ours fell, drenched in his blood, then, like clubs, three or four rifle butts fell on the unfortunate man's head. The brave officer collapses to the ground, disfigured beyond recognition. Finally, silence falls.[8]

Maurice Chevalier was twenty-five in August 1914, and fighting with the 31st RI. A clash of bayonets was his worst fear. He was so tired, that when the order to join one came, he felt drunk:

I was advancing heavily, too exhausted to tremble. We stumbled over stones, on embankments... under my stupefaction a dull thought informed me that the war was beginning for me in exactly the way that repelled me the most!... Obscure pictures of crossed breasts and bellies, punctured like balloons by this slender weapon that we held firmly in front of us, presented themselves in succession to my horror.[9]

When the enemy in front of him retired without a fight, he breathed a huge sigh of relief, saved from a bayonet battle for the time being.

Back at Fillières, shells rained down. At lunchtime, Captain Marx of FAR 69 was ordered to open fire on the village. 'The blows burst on the roofs... The fire spreads.'[10] Then IR 67 crashed into the fray. Civilians found themselves in the line of fire. Carpenter Louis Norroy was struck down in a field looking for his eleven-year-old son, Léon. Father Martin witnessed one casualty being carried away. 'An arm was hanging sinisterly out of the stretcher! Little Paula Lefondeur, nine-years-old... shot by German bullets! And in the midst of these horrors a German captain was shouting, "You wanted the war! Here it is!"'[11]

So, deliverance did not come for Father Martin and the people of Fillières on 22 August 1914. In fact, it was turning out to be a disastrous day for the Third Army, as French and German troops clattered into each other up and down the line. Just to the west of Longwy, Captain Courtes of the 46th RI found his company being routed in the village of Villers-la-Chèvre. 'You have to scatter, run, zigzag, jump, lie flat on your stomachs.' The shellfire made it impossible to get to the main road. 'The companies are dispersed, each acting on its own account.' Courtes made for the woods and skirted the edge of the tree line, intending to come out on a less congested part of the main road a mile west of town, but the road was blood-soaked and thick with retreating traffic:

What a dreadful sight... completely enfiladed by enemy cannon, strewn with the corpses of men and horses, with gun-carriages exploding and blazing! The shells pursued us without respite and fell, terrifying, in pairs, in threes, sweeping everything away, mowing down everything... Visions of horror and dread. Just in front of my eyes, on the flap of the bag of the man in front of me, bits of brain come crashing down...... splat... My eyes do not blink, my heart does not beat faster. Drowned in horror, we have only one thought: to get out of it.[12]

*

The Fourth Army's ordeal in Belgium was also devastating. Much like the Third Army to their right, they had sketchy information about the enemy. The terrain was awkward too, heavily wooded, but marshy in places. It was ideal for ambushes and ripe for confusion. Commanded by seventy-seven-year-old Fernand de Langle de Cary, this army was also about to find itself outnumbered.

On 22 August there was arguably no worse place to be than in the village of Rossignol, at the southern edge of the Forest of Chiny. The unfortunate troops sent here belonged to the Colonial Corps, and included the 3e division d'infanterie coloniale, which was regarded as one of the finest divisions in the French army. It had experience fighting in the wilds of Africa and the humid forests of Southeast Asia. If any unit could make something of this dubious situation, they might. Their one potential flaw? The inexperience of the divisional commander, General Léon Raffenel, who had only been promoted to the role in June. His men, however, were seasoned, and his chief of staff, Jean Moreau, was too. The plan was to seize the crossings of the Semois river, pass through Rossignol, and take the forest and finally the town of Neufchâteau beyond. The commanders were not yet anticipating any contact in significant numbers, and much like those divisions further east fighting random encounter battles, the troops were told to just fight the enemy wherever they ran into them.

Experienced though they might have been, the men had already been pushed to their physical limits. They had marched nonstop for more than a day, alternately through oppressive heat and heavy rain. Thanks to aircraft surveillance, the German Fourth Army in front of them had spotted the Colonial Corps cheerfully coming along the road to the forest, singing. Cavalry went in first, but had only made it about a quarter of a mile through the dense foliage when they met their German counterparts, who jumped down from their mounts and opened fire. As they fought, it dawned on the French that this was not a mere smattering of the enemy. In fact, in front of the French was a full infantry regiment, IR 157, which included numbers of Poles from Upper Silesia who had been conscripted into the German army. IR 157 had been ordered south through the forest towards Rossignol and was lined up behind a bank with an excellent view of the oncoming colonial troops.

The French cavalry warned the infantry directly behind them of the threat, but their commanding officer decided to press on. Confused shooting broke out amongst the trees and a bloodbath ensued. A battalion of the 1er régiment d'infanterie coloniale (1st RIC) was ordered forward. In charge, Lieutenant-Colonel Vitart had a reputation for exceptional bravery from the colonies, and thanks to inaccurate intelligence, he was convinced that there were no massed enemy troops within 20 miles. 'We only have in front of us the filth of Uhlans who are fighting on foot to delay us, and who will have to be dislodged with the bayonet!'

His battalion spread out, on either side of the road; visibility was limited through the trees. The bugle sounded and immediately the French began suffering casualties, including three company commanders. Another, Captain Ignard, survived. When they came to a small clearing, he ordered his men to lie down in sections. The fire grew in intensity, and Ignard watched the other companies vanish among the trees. 'A few dragoons were flowing back towards us in disorder. Horses wandered without riders. Infantrymen were seen in the thickets on our right, they fall back running. A voice in the company shouts: "Don't shoot, they're French!"'

Lieutenant-Colonel Vitart summoned Ignard and, shouting in his face to be heard above the noise of battle, demanded a bayonet attack. Ignard went back to his men and did as he was told. He found one of his experienced NCOs going from man to man, encouraging them all. 'He says to me almost cheerfully: "Look my captain, it's like being in the Ivory Coast."' Forest fights, this man understood. Ignard continued:

'Stand up... bayonet fixed!' And followed by my four sections I enter the trees... But the wood is thick, the sections advance irregularly and soon it is no longer possible for me to see the whole of my company... This charge quickly turns into rapid fire at point-blank range from a concealed enemy. Several Germans wearing the shako of the Silesian troops were standing to see better. One of them took aim at me, his shot hit the Serjeant next to me, but he fell almost at the same time... The fight took a confused turn, the sections were scattered.[13]

Those Silesians were not having everything their own way. They could not deploy their artillery in the forest and were pinned down, as advancing in the confusion would have exposed them to considerable risk. However, they could see the results of their fire taking its toll on Frenchmen concealed among the trees. 'Our musketeers were especially delighted in shooting down those "tree shooters,"' wrote one.[14] Then IR 157's machine-guns rattled into action and showered the woods. The men of the 1st RIC were running out of places to shelter, and command had broken down in the confusion. Vitart made his way back and found General Raffenel's chief of staff, Commander Jean Moreau: 'It's not working at all,' Vitart declared. 'It's terrible, we've walked into a trap and have fallen onto enemy positions established in advance with machine-guns!'[15] Wounded, Vitart went to find a doctor, and by nightfall his left hand had been amputated.

In Rossignol, General Raffenel was aware of the disaster in the woods, but despite all of the evidence he had been presented with, he apparently remained convinced that there was only a sprinkling of cavalry in the forest. He ordered more colonial troops inside. Obediently, mid-morning, the 2nd RIC vanished among the trees and proceeded to suffer the same fate as their comrades.

Inside the forest, the consistent fighting was hurting IR 157 too. By 10.30 a.m., there were barely any officers left. Added to that, the language barrier was telling. Liaison officers were supposed to bridge the gap between German officers and Polish soldiers, but under stress, with many Poles only having weak

German to begin with, confusion reigned. 'Our units were completely pulverized,' wrote one. 'Many commanders died or were injured. The non-commissioned officers took over their tasks.'[16] The forest was filled with dead and wounded, and command structures had evaporated.

The French, in the meantime, were feeling the pressure of overwhelming numbers of enemy troops. Artillerymen looked on uselessly, unable to deploy their guns properly from where they were stuck on the road. The men in the forest had no option but to fall back towards Rossignol, which left the enemy space to encircle the village and strangle the life out of the remaining colonial troops.

Surrounded, the French had begun putting Rossignol in a state of defence. Charles Rondony, who had risen to the rank of general having enlisted as a private soldier in 1875, was ordered by Raffenel to hold the line just outside the village at all costs. At 12.30 p.m., the Silesians emerged at the tree line with their Uhlan comrades. Nine hundred men remained to hold them back, but they were augmented by a dozen machine-guns. For now, the line held. Casualties amongst the Silesian regiment mounted, but the 3rd Colonial Division's suffering also continued. Its chief of staff, Commander Moreau, wrote:

It is now a hail of shrapnel which is constantly falling around us... We do not receive any reports. No one comes to us... It seems that a fog of inevitability and helplessness descends... The state of mind is that of a man exposed to a violent storm and who, already feeling completely soaked, no longer thinks about taking shelter, lets the rain flood him and no longer avoids puddles of water.[17]

To make matters worse, General Raffenel, commanding the division, was about to implode. When Moreau glanced up and made eye contact with him, Raffenel was silent. There was no resolve in his expression:

I think I can see in his eyes what he's thinking. The unfortunate man had the revelation of his incapacity at the same time as the irremediable disaster. He questions me, he waits for me to offer him something again, but I too think that everything is lost; all that remains is to put on a good face, to give to all those we see, to the brave people who are going to be killed, the image and the illusion of command standing until the end. We obviously can no longer do anything and if I spoke, what other feeling could I express than the rage at my impotence, the bitterness... at having seen my efforts annihilated by the oblivious ignorance of a stubborn old man, at the disorganized staff, at the sabotaged command and just now at the supreme stupidity, at these troops... launched at the beginning of the day in the forest one behind another, at the useless butchery.[18]

Raffenel wandered off towards the woods. Moreau followed, because it was his job. 'We are now marching... without any kind of shelter, in front of the telescopes of the enemy artillery who have certainly seen the red trousers and the golden kepi of a general.' At this point Moreau was wounded. 'I feel a violent blow on my thigh... I continue hobbling after the general and soon we reach the road; my leg went numb, full of tingling... I warn the general that I can barely carry myself on my right leg... "Well! Sit there, I'm going to look in this direction... I'll pick you up as I pass by."' Raffenel disappeared into a field. 'What plan did he have at that moment? Whether he even had one, I don't know.'[19]

Back on the outskirts of Rossignol, there had been precious little time to organize defences. Among the men falling back from the forest were Lieutenant Chaumel and the remains of his section. He was ordered to hold the exit of the woods under fire to prevent the enemy coming out. 'I immediately gave my section the order... the men are placed... lying approximately [650 yards] from the edge of the woods.' There they waited, until a line of men wearing grey and holding rifles began creeping out of the tree line:

The artillery takes hold of us and keeps us under violent and uninterrupted fire. I am obliged to make the men who protect themselves with their knapsacks dig holes in the embankment, which is too weak to provide shelter... A shell landed; a very precise shot inflicted significant losses on us. To our left a [French] machine-gun fires relentlessly; she is admirably served, but soon the servants are all out of action, she must be abandoned.[20]

At 2.00 p.m. the artillery fire waned, 'and, at that moment', wrote Chaumel, 'heads of enemy columns emerged from the woods and offered a superb target'. His men were lying in a field yet to be harvested, and so the crops were in the way. They could not fire lying down. 'I command: "On your knees!", then: "Fire at will!"' They seemed to be making progress. 'The enemy groups hesitate, stop and disappear momentarily.' Then he received an order to retire into Rossignol. Chaumel thought he could do more remaining where they were, so he ran back to verify it: '"Captain, have you given the order to withdraw?" He then replied to me in his calmest voice: "We are going to be turned, we are being shot in the back, start the retreat in stages immediately."'[21]

Shortly afterwards, the Germans launched their first infantry attack on Rossignol itself. Half an hour later, about 500 men remained to hold the village and half the machine-guns were out of action. Six remained as high explosive shells began dropping on the houses.

FAR 57 had waited for the opportunity to set up their guns all day. Now, emerging from the trees and facing Rossignol, they got their chance. 'To our joy, at four in the afternoon we finally received the order to prepare the battery for the attack.' The French had a machine-gun in the church tower, so a battery immediately put down a Howitzer and fired off a round. Fire erupted from the church and the machine-gun fell silent. 'Happy with the success, the entire battery then bombarded the village... which started fires everywhere.'[22] By now, the Germans had sent up more infantry, and together with the gunners, they gradually overcame the defenders.

The French artillery attempted valiantly to combat this new menace, but they were running out of ammunition. As they did, they disabled their guns, then killed the transport horses to stop them falling into German hands before they surrendered. In all, some 800 dead animals were found in the vicinity after the battle. A few hundred men from various colonial units attempted to break out of the village on the eastern side. They ran into enemy troops, but a few managed to find their way to safety.

Commander Moreau was on a fruitless search for General Raffenel. In the woods, he found General Charles Montignault instead, and asked him what he could do, 'but the only words he addresses to me are to express his impotence and his discouragement: "We are surrounded and there is nothing to do." The poor man is visibly at the end of his physical and moral courage. He... remained hidden in the woods, slumped on the edge of a ditch and now unable to move.'[23]

For half an hour more, artillery fire poured into Rossignol. Then, at 5.30 p.m., the Germans came at the village from three directions. They found the southern end of the village being completely ravaged by fire. 'In the street,' wrote Lieutenant Humbert of the chasseurs d'Afrique:

An indescribable crowd of soldiers, artillerymen, most of them wounded, lying along the walls, the others unarmed, unresponsive, seeming to passively await their fate... exhausted, dead tired. I enter a building in front of the church. It's a bistro. In the corridor filled with soldiers, a horrible sight that I will never forget: a wounded, tall and athletic young man, stripped to the waist completely. The right arm is torn off at shoulder height. The pain must be so intense that, groaning, he rubs the bleeding stump against the rough wall. He certainly only has a few moments to live.[24]

Lieutenant Chaumel was making his escape: 'Unfortunately the ring of fire is tightening, the infantry has joined machine-guns. It's coming from the north, east, south… and we only have a handful of men left with little ammunition… I call the remaining men to me… Under concentrated fire, bayonets fixed, we try to make a way towards the south-west.'[25]

The Colonial Division suffered more than 10,000 casualties. Along with infantry units, some of which suffered 70 per cent casualties, both the artillery and the transport had also been obliterated. As for the hapless Raffenel, he was last seen walking with a muddy rifle in his hand. His body was found by the side of a road some distance from where he left Moreau. He bore a head wound, and it was never quite ascertained whether he had been killed, or whether he had taken his own life. He was one of the first two French generals to fall during the war. The survivors were in shock. 'All the many isolated people I met seemed more stunned by the day than truly demoralized.' The division, one of France's finest, had ceased to exist as a fighting force, leaving a 7-mile gap in the French line. Along with the Third Army, de Langle de Cary's Fourth had no choice but to retreat. Their flight was miserable, but on the far left of the Allied line, the day still had one more disaster to offer up.

14

War in All Its Horror

France and Belgium

By 15 August, about the time the last forts at Liège were falling, Joffre had begun conceding that the main German armies were in fact swinging much deeper into Belgium than he had anticipated. Until that point, he had expended less thought on General Charles Lanrezac and his Fifth Army than on any other. In Joffre's mind, Lanrezac was to ensure that the enemy did not cross the Meuse, which sounded simple enough; the German force in that area was initially predicted to be insignificant. Joffre was even less interested in the measly four British divisions. Britain's 80,000 strong expeditionary force (BEF) was not scaring anyone in a clash of millions. Joffre was not even going to wait for the BEF to arrive before he tried to win the war. When they turned up, he would just stick them on the left flank of the French line to extend it as far as possible. It could not hurt to have them there, but he did not believe for one second that they would make a difference.

As the reality of the German manoeuvre through Belgium began to dawn on Joffre, although he clung to the idea that his planned attack by the Third and Fourth Armies on 21 August could still be decisive for the Allies, he had no choice but to address the issue of Lanrezac's precarious situation. On 19 August, Joffre had the Fifth Army move up towards the Belgian city of Namur, where crucially the Meuse and the Sambre rivers meet at a right angle, the first flowing north to south, and the latter more or less east to west. His concession that the enemy might swing out far enough to bring the Sambre into play as well as the Meuse was timely. In order for the Schlieffen Plan to work, the German First and Second Armies would have to manoeuvre south. Lanrezac was the only thing stopping them, and as yet he was in a poor position. He had nobody on his left, and his line did not extend far enough to cover the oncoming right flank of Kluck's First Army. As well as Bülow's Second Army, he also foresaw that he was going to have to face General von Hausen's Third Army coming across the Meuse from the east. It was a numerical catastrophe waiting to bear down on him from all angles.

Suddenly the British seemed more important. They had said they could be ready to fight on 26 August, but now they accelerated their preparations at Joffre's request. In command, Sir John French said he might even be able to get some units to the front by 21 August. As a measure of his mounting concern, Joffre also had three French territorial divisions placed from Maubeuge, roughly where the British line was planned to end, all the way up to Dunkirk on the coast. These were divisions which were generally perceived as grizzled, portly old men in tight uniforms, far from fighting fit, but they were all he had. Finally, there was a French cavalry corps under General André Sordet, which Joffre deployed next to Lanrezac to bolster the line.

Troops from Bülow's Second Army began trickling across the River Sambre on 21 August as the right flank of the German armies began finally making contact with the French. This was the part of the Schlieffen Plan where they were to push down to Paris and kick France out of the war. Then, it was planned to deploy the terrifying might of the German army against Russia.

When troops began their crossing between Namur and the industrial town of Charleroi, Lanrezac initially thought that Bülow was just throwing outposts across and making a localized play for Namur. In reality, as disaster played out at Rossignol on 22 August, the French Fifth Army would be throwing its entire weight at trying to push the Germans back north across the Sambre.

*

For the troops fighting the Battle of the Frontiers here, the terrain was dramatically different to that faced by most of their comrades. Belgium was an industrial power prior to the war, and this is where much of that industry operated. A British general described Charleroi's surroundings, where Belgium's answer to Britain's Black Country was built up for 26 miles along the Sambre:

> … a confusion of mines, blast furnaces, and glassworks, connected by a network of cobbled streets and lanes, lined by close-packed, dull, uniform miners' cottages, between which rise tall chimneys, the headworks of mines, and great conical pyramids of smoking slag. Industry has added a new feature to the countryside in the form of a canal, which rims eastward, its waters black with slime and reeking of chemical refuse.[1]

Nobody would willingly set out to fight here, and yet this was the hand both Lanrezac and the BEF were dealt. On 22 August the right of Fifth Army was concentrated on the Meuse and the fortress town of Namur. To the left of Lanrezac's line, where the river began arching south-west, General Sordet was effectively plugging the gap between the Fifth Army and the British, who were further left, up at the Mons-Condé Canal. For reasons that have no rational explanation, Sordet's cavalry force had been ambling around the Belgian countryside since the beginning of August, exhausting men and horses alike. Now they found themselves outnumbered and faced with artillery, too.

At 3.00 a.m. the 24th RI, men from Paris, Normandy and Brittany, arrived at Fontaine-l'Evèque having marched 20 miles. Here, just west of Charleroi, there was a break in the endless industrial sprawl and the men found themselves in a steep, tree-covered area, intersected by two streams. They began to dig in. Local farmers were pulled out of bed to help, and ploughs and horses were dragged into action. Ready, the men settled down, ate and tried to sleep, praying that nothing more would be asked of them on 22 August.

At 8.30 a.m. it was already clear that it was going to be a scorching day when isolated German cavalry loomed on the horizon. French machine-gunners had them within range, and when the moment was right, they opened fire. The enemy scattered, but the 24th, with the 28th RI, prepared themselves for the inevitable attack that would follow now that they had revealed themselves. Instructed to take up a position in the village of Carnières and hold the enemy up as long as possible so that Sordet's cavalry could withdraw safely, within an hour they were in the thick of it.

Meanwhile, the centre of Lanrezac's army was bludgeoned. The 41st RI was having a miserable experience near Ham-sur-Sambre, 13 miles east of Charleroi. In the morning their division had been doing well enough that they were predicted to push the enemy clean across the Sambre, which only lay half a mile north of the town. The tide soon turned. One section rushed a German machine-gun only to be torn apart when they fell upon a wire entanglement put out by the enemy the night before. Nearby was a regiment of Algerian troops, including Mustafa Tabti. He had sailed from Oran full of bravado. 'Men, we thought to ourselves, no fear… We Arabs are made of magnanimity and gunpowder!'[2]

About 4 miles south of Ham, by midday Mustafa and his comrades were establishing themselves among trees and thickets on a ridge just to the north of Fosse, anticipating covering North African Zouave units ahead as they tried to fall back from the river. 'What an atrocious day for us at Charleroi, my brothers!' wrote Tabti. They were harassed nonstop,: 'with cannon and a torrential rain of bullets they shattered us from mid-afternoon prayer-time to sunset prayers'.[3] The Algerians were destined to sit for hours under a violent artillery fire.

*

Back at Carnières, as the oncoming enemy increased the intensity of their attack, the French began to lose their footing. At lunchtime a German artillery battery thundered into action and the village was pounded with shells. One of the battalion commanders begged for reinforcements, but the response from above was brutal: 'With equal numbers, there is no reason to withdraw: you have to counter-attack.'

Desperate fighting occurred on the streets and in houses at the point of a bayonet. Still the commander, General Alfred Hollender, refused to send in reserves. Another plea came just before 1.00 p.m. and he did not yield. 'You [have been] reinforced by two battalions... This should be enough for you with the support of our artillery (which will finally become active) to carry out a counter-attack.'[4] At the point when the battalion's machine-guns were running out of ammunition and their crews fending off German bayonets, the general finally relented and sent in a company to help.

Somehow, the 24th RI held the enemy off until 2.00 p.m. when the Germans sent yet another battalion and came crashing into Carnières. Men poured down the steep *Rue de la Rosière* and threw themselves on the French from behind. It was just about the last straw. As the French began a retreat, two soldiers stayed behind to cover their escape. One, 'Raymond' Lemeurtrier, was shot down by German rifle fire. The other, twenty-four-year-old Raoul Lemery, stayed at his post until he ran out of ammunition, then fled. Diving into one of the houses at the foot of the street, he was chased by the enemy, who discovered him under a bed. They stabbed through the mattress with their bayonets, killing him underneath.

At Fosse, finally, at 5.00 p.m. Mustafa Tabti and his battalion were ordered to fall back from their battered position on the ridge overlooking the Sambre. Tabti was about to become one of the first soldier poets of the First World War. In the weeks following the fighting at Charleroi, lying in a hospital, he dictated a poem that would resonate with North African troops across France in the struggle to come:

The dead lay in countless piles.
They laid the Muslim beside the non-believer in a common
    grave.

'Artillery, fired from afar, set aflame earth and stone alike,
      my Lords!
We perished in great numbers, by bayonets and bullets that
      buzzed from all sides.

Some of the North African units that participated in the Battle
of Charleroi lost more than half their strength.

They charged us with the impetuosity of a torrent, my
      Lords! In Belgium they give no respite.
The sight of so many young men mowed down has melted
      my heart.
My lords! Dead, these heroes remain in the solitude of the
      countryside.
They perished without anyone reciting the profession of
      faith for them, Lords!
They lay exposed to the wild beasts, eagles and birds of prey.
In their memory, I sing with sadness, Lords! Were you
      made of stone, you would spill tears for them.[5]

*

The planned, hinge-like movement of the German armies in the
west meant that the further to the right a unit was, the further
it had to travel, and the longer it would take to bear down and
meet the enemy. On 23 August, the swinging right flank finally
completed contact with the enemy when Alexander von Kluck's
First Army levered into action against the BEF. Its important
role was reflected by its theoretical size, some 320,000 men to
Bülow's 260,000 next to him. The neighbouring German generals were not on friendly terms. In fact, Kluck was seething about
being put under his neighbour's control. He had no idea where
the British were as his men began to approach them. He certainly
did not think they were massed right in front of him as the Battle
of the Frontiers raged around Charleroi on 22 August. He was
under the impression that his troops were only approaching scattered cavalry and a few infantrymen. He was wrong.

To the west of Lanrezac's sector, the terrain started to become industrialized again, 'another medley of mines, factories, and villages, ending still farther west... in an intricate area of small market gardens intersected by innumerable dykes'.[6] Here, outnumbered at Mons, the British Expeditionary Force fought its first battle of the First World War. It was another rotten place for an army to try to fight in. Houses and factories blocked their view. Added to that, the place was full of people, civilians trying to watch the war in person.

The BEF had not had time to construct any solid defences. 'Remember,' wrote one artillery officer, 'trenches were not those of later days... They had all been hastily dug in extremely hard and difficult ground, so that there were none of the niceties of snug dug-outs and bomb-proof shelters. In many places it was just a matter of scratching up the soil behind a hump of shale and cramming oneself in as far as one could go.'[7] Fighting with the Loyal North Lancashires, reservist Frank Boswell concurred: 'No good whatsoever against shell fire.'[8] Men holed up in cottages, or built barricades of whatever furniture and household debris they could get their hands on. Clumsy wire entanglements were thrown out across bridges.

Much of the Battle of Mons followed a similar pattern. Kluck's men emerged, overcame small outposts that had been thrown out on the north bank of the canal, opened fire across the black, slimy water, and then, preferably with the help of artillery being brought up, attempted to cross the bridges. The most perilous part of the line was at Nimy, which sat around a bend in the canal to the north of Mons itself. The 4th Royal Fusiliers were established here with machine-guns on a bridge, which was a bit odd, because it restricted their ability to swing their arc of fire up and down a German column advancing from the side causing maximum casualties. As the sun rose, the locals emerged in their Sunday best for church. In and around the British army with their rifles and machine-guns, people were going about their business as if it were a normal day.

Peering at the BEF from the woods beyond the opposite bank

was IR 84, which was stacked with unfortunate Danish conscripts from Schleswig. 'We marched across a large, green grassy
field towards a forest on the other side,' wrote Peter Aarup. 'The
bullets were already whistling in the treetops, and the further we
advanced, the worse it got. We passed a brick works; in front of
it was a row of houses, and the inhabitants were hiding in the
basements.'[9]

As they emerged at the canal, the intention was obvious. *Get
across.* IR 84 left the trees and opened fire. 'The enemy started to
advance in mass down the railway cutting about 800 yards off,'
wrote a British officer. In charge of two machine-guns, Maurice
Dease 'fired... into them and absolutely mowed them down'.[10] But
the Germans kept coming. They would dash up from their skirmishing line, run forward and then lay down to fire until they were
ready to repeat the manoeuvre. 'The British let us get real close to
their lines before they opened fire,' wrote Andreas Kylling.[11] 'We
were lying on a slope... and we suffered heavy casualties.'

Hans Christensen Toft had been told that there was nothing
to fear:

Before the signal to charge was given, our NCOs told us that
these were just the British, who had occupied this embankment, and we shouldn't fear them; they couldn't shoot.
They were just no-good sportsmen. But we soon saw something different... our people were mown down in droves.
They fell like flies; I was wounded when two machine-gun
bullets went through my back, but I got off easy compared
to all the tragedy and horror I was witness to.[12]

Peter Aarup saw Toft and others cut down: 'There were seven of
us from Southern Jutland in my squad,' he wrote:

All of us were young reservists, who'd been called up on
4th August. The first to be wounded in our squad was
Jørgen Mikkelsen... He was hit in the shoulder. Then it was
teacher Petersen's turn. He was hit by two bullets in the

arm. Thereafter it was the turn of Hans Toft... he was hit in the lung. The next was my neighbour, Mads Jessen... He was hit in the leg. We yelled: 'Mads, stay down!' But he wanted to take cover by a house in front of us. When he got up, he was unfortunately hit in the head. He fell. We were now only four left.[13]

The British fire took its toll as IR 84 advanced. 'Because we were silhouetted against the horizon to the enemy troops in their lower lying positions, our casualties here were... significant,' wrote Lieutenant Liebe. 'Death tore great gaps in our ranks, but help was on the way. In the heat of the battle, we had not noticed our comrades... filling in the gaps in the firing line.'[14] Gradually, in the oppressive summer heat, they began to make headway. Then the German artillery arrived. 'The British resistance ceased,' Peter Aarup claimed:

The [turning] bridge was open, but a small German jumped in the canal, swam across and closed [it]. Then things got moving. We were the first to get across. The machine-guns, which had so violently received us, had been placed on the bridge pillars. Now, both men and materiel were strewn to all sides. It was the first time I had experienced such fierce resistance.[15]

Then Aarup claimed that he saw something that he was not prepared for. 'A little dog ran out from a house,' he wrote bitterly.

A soldier hit it with the butt of his rifle, and it howled. Then a young woman came out the door. She wanted to save the dog, but she had a knife in the hand and was probably in the middle of peeling potatoes. When a stretcher-bearer saw the knife, he had such a shock that he, in his confusion, pulled out his revolver and shot the woman. It turned out she was heavily pregnant. It was war in all its horror.[16]

As the day wore on, more and more of Kluck's men folded down onto the British line. To the left of Nimy, Mons and the little salient formed by the canal, the waterway stretched out into a straight line. Stationed around Jemappes, the 1st Northumberland Fusiliers were defending the Mariette Bridge. Shells started falling in the vicinity at about midday. This was a completely urban environment, and officers had houses prepared for the men to duck into if the Germans got across. 'One or two of the men on the barrier were convinced that it was nicer to be in a house with all these nasty shells flying about in the open,' recalled Captain Beauchamp Tudor St John. 'The house on the right of the barrier was getting quite full when a high-explosive crumped right into it doing a lot of damage.' Men came tumbling out of it again and landed right in the middle of a vicious street fight. The Northumberlands had been told to retire as soon as there was any indication of the enemy getting round their flanks, but in the melee it was difficult to figure out what was going on. Regardless, the position was quite obviously untenable. 'I began to send men back in small driblets down a side street. When most of the men had gone... the Royal Engineer officer and a staff Serjeant arrived to blow up our bridge. He reported to me that the Germans were over the bridges on both our flanks so that things did not look too rosy.'[17]

*

The British Expeditionary Force suffered some 1,600 casualties on its first day in battle. As the attacking force, marching against barricades and across open ground, the Germans suffered slightly more. The BEF had put up a spirited defence, outnumbered four to one in some places, but not as one, unified force. Individual battalions had attempted to take care of themselves in small clashes. The Germans won most of them, despite the fact that Kluck did not have a firm grasp on the day either.

By nightfall, Sir John French was aware that there were four German corps chasing his two British corps. He was already proving to be out of his depth, and the reality of his dire situation was rapidly dawning on him.

*

Having been bludgeoned on 22 August, Joffre's Third and Fourth Armies were reeling backwards too, but this was nothing compared to the flight of the Fifth Army on 23 August. Lanrezac's men had had a short reprieve when von Hausen's Third Army did not cross the Meuse, but now that manoeuvre was inevitable.

For the people of Dinant, this was to be the worst day of the war, with the town suffering the largest single loss of civilian life in the west. Partly confused by the echo of their own shots bouncing off the sheer rock face astride the riverbank, Hausen's Third Army cried 'franc-tireur' and dealt out ruthless punishment on Dinant's inhabitants. In total, 674 civilians were killed and much of the town destroyed. Throughout the city, batches of victims were lined up and shot by firing squads. Camille Fivet, along with several members of her family, was among a group put against a wall by members of Grenadier Regiment 101. Shielded from the bullets by the body of seventy-four-year-old Alexandre Bourdon, Fivet was one of just thirteen out of eighty-nine to survive. She remembered the aftermath of the first German salvo:

> I heard a baby crying and asking for a drink; it was little Gilda Marchot, aged two. A German immediately approached, put the barrel of his rifle in the child's mouth and fired! Disgusted, I turned to the other side and saw a soldier carrying something at the end of his bayonet; I recognized the body of my little niece, Mariette Fivet, who was three weeks old. After playing with this child's corpse, the soldier laid it on the ground and put his foot on its stomach to remove his bayonet.[18]

In total, fifteen children under five years old were killed in Dinant, while the oldest victim was eighty-eight-year-old Marie Andre.

*

In Belgium, those wizened and maligned French territorials sent by Joffre to extend the Allied front saw action, too. Some found themselves in Tournai, just over the border from Lille. Barricades had been fashioned from an array of automobiles, sandbags and furniture. The viaduct had been rendered impassable by unrolling huge spools of electrical cable. These supposedly elderly men had marched to Tournai from Calvados just in time to meet the German army, and witness Joseph Boubée had nothing but pride having watched them in action. Even when his city was lost, the resolve of these supposedly second-class soldiers was evident. On the banks of the River Scheldt, a serjeant had remained behind with a few men to cover the retreat:

> He leant against one of the large cast iron uprights which serve as pillars for the drawbridge. Very self-possessed, he shouldered, aimed, fired with such precision that with each shot of his weapon we saw a Prussian fall. At the same time, he spoke to his men and calmly made them retreat, facing the enemy, down the steep, poorly paved street that runs from the bridge towards the main square. He left last, always calm, and when he disappeared, just as the Prussians were rushing onto the bridge en masse, he had shot down eleven of them.[19]

*

At the vital point where the Meuse met the Sambre, the fortress-ringed city of Namur was still holding out against the German army as the Battle of the Frontiers raged. It paid the price of every lesson that the enemy had learnt at Liège. Bülow avoided the bloodshed caused by sending infantry in between the forts to isolate them. Instead, he brought an overwhelming amount of heavy artillery, including batteries of Austro-Hungarian Škoda guns complete with their native crews, to reduce the forts to dust. At this point Austria–Hungary had not even declared war on Belgium.

On 15 August, the first shells fell on Namur. The city had already begun to be a lonely place to be. 'Soldiers conscious of their terrible losses,' wrote journalist Geoffrey Young, 'a populace half-believing itself deserted by its allies. French troops sent in, and again hurriedly withdrawn.' Public services were shutting down. 'No trains are running. The station is full of weeping women and children.'[20]

At 10.00 a.m. on 21 August, the Germans began bombarding the forts. The shellfire was immediately violent and brutal. 'During the bombardment, the German infantry did not move. It was sufficient to crush Namur by the giant projectiles of the siege guns.'[21] If there were risky tasks, in some cases they were delegated to civilians. At Warisoul and at Bierwart, Belgians were allegedly sent out under the fire of their own guns to dig trenches in front of forts for the invader.

Somehow, on 22 August some of the garrisons held. Three French battalions arrived to reinforce their allies, but 3 miles outside the city, Fort de Maizeret was reduced to rubble after more than 1,000 shells were fired at it. Inside the city, it was clear that it was only a matter of time before Namur fell. Artilleryman Captain Paulis was exhausted. 'After the hard fights of the previous days, overwhelmed with moral and physical fatigue, I had ended up falling into a restless sleep.' Then, at 3.00 a.m. on 23 August, he was woken up by an order to remove the last available batteries. Paulis was not a stupid man. If operations were now focused on the citadel in the heart of Namur, then the city was already lost; Paulis was to save his guns. 'In the radiant light of this beautiful summer morning, while the fusillade crackled and the cannon rumbled... my men were silent and gloomy. I saw the anguish of my soul reflected in their faces.'[22]

The 10e Régiment de Ligne, one of the Belgian units manning the intervals between the fortifications, had been devastated. Posted on a line between Fort Marchovelette and the Meuse, they had been attacked since 20 August. The enemy themselves did not come, but their shells did: 'The Boches were demolishing our trenches, destroying them, burying us in them,' wrote one officer:

At the same time they cut off our retreat by dropping shrapnel behind us. It is necessary to have lived in these torments to form an idea of them! At the beginning of the war we all dreamed of heroic charges with the bayonet, of positions taken by irresistible assaults to a cry of '*Vive le Roi!*'... And now we found ourselves obliged to hide ourselves at the bottom of a hole like moles, and without having seen a single enemy, were forced to swallow either earth or steel.[23]

This bombardment lasted for eight hours, and then the invaders added a new menace to the scene. 'Suddenly the soldiers would hear above their heads the whirring of the propellers and the noise of the motors,' wrote one German on the ground:

The Zeppelins came nearer and nearer, but not until they were in the immediate neighbourhood of the forts were they discovered by our opponents, who immediately brought all available searchlights into play in order to search the sky... The whirring of the propellers of the airships... suddenly ceased. Then, right up in the air, a blinding light appeared, the searchlight of the Zeppelin, which lit up the country beneath it for a short time. Just as suddenly it became dark and quiet until a few minutes later, powerful detonations brought the news that the Zeppelin had dropped its ballast. That continued for quite a while, explosion followed explosion, interrupted only by small fiery clouds, shrapnel which the Belgian artillery sent up to the airships, exploding in the air. Then the whirring of the propellers began again, first loud and coming from near, from right above our heads, then softer and softer until [it] had entirely disappeared.[24]

*

On 23 August, the troops at Namur began to learn the dire outcome of the fighting at Charleroi. A German shell had wiped out the telephone exchange, leaving General Augustin Michel, in command of the city's defence, unable to communicate with the forts. More forts had to surrender. Fort de Marchovelette did not, but suffered the same fate as Liège's Fort Loncin. A giant shell from Big Bertha struck the magazine and it exploded. The last fort surrendered on 25 August, at which point they had held out collectively for just three days. Nineteenth-century forts were proving utterly futile in the face of modern firepower.

Abandoning another city, this time having to leave Belgian soil, was heartbreaking. The 10th Regiment prepared to retire. Their commanding officer, Colonel Verbist, was determined that they would depart Namur with pride. 'My friends,' he said. 'Smart bearing while crossing the city!' They did not let him down. Exhausted, they marched away from the *Place d'Armes*. As they did so, they passed the French 45th RI, who were also about to leave. With a uniform movement of the shoulder, the Belgians adjusted their haversacks, straightened their backs and marched past with their heads held high. The two commanders, one French, one Belgian, paused to salute each other with their swords. 'It did not matter whether one was dirtier than beasts, in greatcoats of a colour that has no name; the people of Namur have not often witnessed so smart a march past.'[25] By the time the 10th crossed the border into France, they had suffered 1,250 casualties defending their homeland.

Belgium was crumbling under the weight of the German army. The scenes on the road from Namur were devastating. A French journalist was attempting to reach the city. The sight of one village en route that had been caught in the crossfire was enough to reduce him to tears:

> In the only street... [are] a few old men and women searching in these shapeless ruins for things that belonged to them... They look at me fearfully, then, probably judging me harmless, sadly resume their search among the scattered debris. I walk away with a heavy heart, my eyes moist, thinking that these poor people, who lived there happily a few days earlier, in their little houses acquired at the cost of so much labour and pain, now find themselves homeless, without asylum.[26]

Another sight 30 miles from Namur remained burnt into his brain. In the aftermath of his escape:

We... arrive at the river... The greenish water which runs, fast, carries from time to time the corpses of French and Germans. They seem... to pursue each other in a crazy, fantastic race, hitting the banks, rolling in the whirlwinds, sometimes stopping against the piles of the bridge where they seem to rise suddenly, frightful to see with their white faces and their dull eyes. Some still hold their weapons in their clenched hands, others still embrace in a supreme struggle which, until the last moment, was fierce and savage. Bodies stopped in the reeds sway with a regular movement, then, driven by the eddies, come to rest on the banks. There, all four of us feel a kind of uneasiness at the sight of these poor dead people continuing to run after their death.[27]

The Battle of the Frontiers was catastrophic for all sides. With well over 20,000 French soldiers killed, 22 August 1914 is an eminently viable candidate for the worst day in French military history. By the end of the year, a letter found its way from a German nurse to the Meunier family. It had been removed from the body of their son, Albert, who had been summoned to war as a corporal with the 28th RI. In it, the young man had written:

If I die, I write last words which will give you courage. Imagine that we are all together, the comrades... and that the only desire of all was to march forward: the hope of victory... pushed us all with a patriotic impulse... but, for that, we had to make sacrifices, and these sacrifices were our lives. Despite your pain, you will be happy to learn that your son walked with his head held high and did his duty to the end... Think of me, I always think of you, and think that I have always been a good son and that I will be a good soldier. Farewell my dear parents, and my dear Lucienne: these are the last thoughts I will have when a bullet hits me. Your darling son who embraces you very much.[28]

15

Blurred Lines

What happened at sea in the opening throes of war impacted millions of people, neutral as well as belligerent. By 1914, the world had shrunk. Both the rise of global trade and the sheer scale of the conflict obliterated traditional concepts of neutrality. Nobody could fight this war without an enormous, constant flow of supplies and materials, and nobody could produce it all themselves. To ensure that they had everything they needed, they had to purchase from other nations and then rely on foreign ships to transport it. Therefore, no neutral country could realistically claim that they carried nothing that belonged to any nation at war. Immediately who owned what, where it had come from, and where it was going became contentious issues. Was a captain from where he claimed? Was his ship genuinely on the journey detailed in its papers? Using Rotterdam as an example, if a ship full of munitions arrived at this Dutch city, where was it going to end up? Nations could not agree on whether it was Rotterdam, the *immediate destination* that was relevant, or the fact that it was certain that those munitions would end up in Germany. What even constituted a war was its cargo? Crates of rifles or artillery shells were easily defined. But what about raw materials? Who was going to decide where that line was?

In one example on 21 September, Britain put iron ore on a list of contraband that could be seized. This was a huge blow to neutral Sweden, who exported it. If they continued to do so, were they behaving as a true neutral? What about food that could feed an army? Implementing control over goods in transit was a legal, as well as an ethical minefield, and how Britain went about seizing so-called contraband led to a hugely controversial move: nations began withholding food supplies arguably bound for civilians. At sea, the Royal Navy's dominance was telling. Nobody else could achieve the same level of interruption to enemy shipping and Britain was ready, willing and able to exploit this dominance in 1914 by preventing as much cargo as possible reaching the Central Powers from overseas. The Germans would refer to this as 'The Starvation Blockade'.

Even if the majority of her ships were not cowering from the Allies in harbours the world over, Germany did not have enough sea power to harass her enemies in kind, or to defend cargoes bound for Europe. However, on the outbreak of war the *Kaiserliche Marine* had at least a few warships out on station in far-flung waters. It was with these that she fought back. Submarine warfare would soon supersede it, but at the beginning of the war, for a short time it was commerce raiding that struck fear into the hearts of the Allies.

The name that kept seamen in the east awake at night was that of Vice-Admiral Graf von Spee. He only possessed a small squadron operating off Asia and in the Pacific, but he did boast two modern armoured cruisers, his flagship *Scharnhorst* and her sister *Gneisenau*. In the opening weeks of the war these ships, both of which were entirely capable of running down most merchant vessels, were in the wind. He also had *Emden, Leipzig* and *Nürnberg*. Spee had a number of spots from China to the Pacific where he could open up communications and take on coal. In theory, he could bounce around continually with impunity, attacking Allied shipping, and nobody knew when or where he might pop up. His squadron could cause trouble anywhere from Australia and New Zealand to China, the Pacific or even India. It was imperative that the Royal Navy neutralize this threat as soon as possible.

For passengers aboard ships, a stop and search was a terrifying experience. Making his way home across the South Atlantic aboard the SS *Arlanza*, 'Tommy' Lascelles had been fed what would turn out to be wildly inaccurate information about the progress of the war. The crossing not been without drama. One woman, 'having caught her husband in the act of infidelity' threatened to jump overboard and caused the ship to slow and turn around. 'All very bad for our already *surexcités* nerves!' The whole completement of passengers was jumpy. 'We play pirates elaborately every night... all the decks [are] veiled, and port holes muffled lest our lights should betray us to some passing German gunboat.' It all seemed a bit ridiculous. 'I don't think there is one within several thousand miles.' And yet, fuelled by a lack of news, passengers panicked. 'The pessimists among them expected to be sunk without warning or captured and interned... somewhere in West Africa until the war was over.'[1]

Lascelles was wrong about the proximity of danger. On 16 August, the day that the Battle of Antivari took place in the Adriatic, the enemy found them. 'We were at luncheon today', wrote Lascelles, 'when a large four-funnelled steamer became visible through the port-holes of the saloon. She was overhauling us at a great pace.' Passengers jumped onto chairs:

> Soon afterwards we hove to, and the word went round that this was a German boat and that she carried guns. I got my glasses and went up on deck to find her lying about a couple of hundred yards from us, signalling busily. There was no doubt as to her nationality, and before long she was identified as the *Kaiser Wilhelm der Grosse*, of the Hamburg-Amerika line... As I came up on deck, the Union Jack at our stern was hauled down, we were prisoners of war.[2]

Well, thought Lascelles. That was that. '[I] saw myself spending the next six months or more in... the Cameroons. We were quite helpless.' The majestic 650-foot-long ocean liner circled them slowly, 'still flickering signal after signal'. Lascelles was expecting them to lower a boat and approach at any moment. 'Suddenly two large poles crashed into the sea, close to my head, it was

our [wireless] installation going overboard by German orders...
while we were still wondering, she started to steam straight away
from us.'[3]

Lascelles and the other passengers could not quite believe it.
'Ten minutes later she was... on the horizon, and we were pursu-
ing our original course.'[4] All aboard *Arlanza* remained vigilant
for the rest of the crossing, especially at night. As for the famous
German liner, ten days later her crew scuttled her off the West
African coast after a terminal scrap with HMS *Highflyer*.

The fact that the *Arlanza* was stopped by an armed German
ocean liner, not a *Kaiserliche Marine* ship is significant. In the
opening weeks of war, navies escorted troops, protected merchant shipping, enforced blockade measures and hunted the
enemy. With so many responsibilities, spread across vast oceans
in every corner of the world, not even the Royal Navy had
enough ships. Every major power had a contingency for pressing more tonnage into service, and that began with taking merchant vessels into service to carry troops, as hospitals, or even,
like the *Kaiser Wilhelm der Grosse*, as auxiliary cruisers. Taking
the Cunard line as an example, the British government had contributed towards the construction of part of their fleet of ocean
liners, provided that they could be used in the event of a war.
Some, like the *Lusitania* and *Mauretania,* were considered too
greedy in terms of their coal consumption and were left to ply
the depleted passenger run. Four, however, were designated for
immediate conversion to naval use.

More than 85 per cent of Cunard's deck officers held com-
missions in the Royal Naval Reserve, including James Bisset. His
ship *Caronia* was undergoing a refit when war was declared, and
along with hundreds of crew, he had been temporarily laid off.
On the outbreak of war, Bisset raced back aboard. He was not
about to wait for orders to find him:

On board... hundreds of men [were] carrying furniture,
beds, bedding, crockery, glassware, silverware, carpets,
curtains... and slinging it [all]... into horse-drawn wagons

on the wharf. Simultaneously, gangs were painting her hull and superstructure grey, and her funnels black. Below decks, carpenters, joiners, plumbers, and electricians were dismantling the passenger cabins, removing all wooden panelling and partitions, wash-basins, electric-light fittings, and almost everything else that was not part of her basic structure. The crew's quarters were left intact, and also the first-class smoke-room, which was to be used as a wardroom for officers. With those exceptions, the once luxurious floating hotel soon looked an empty steel shell… bare and desolate.[5]

Cunard relinquished control of *Caronia* on 8 August. A skeleton crew of Royal Navy men boarded, but new arrival Captain Litchfield was not precious. Having never commanded anything bigger than a light cruiser of 3,000 tons, he glanced around this 19,000-ton liner and immediately asked the Admiralty if he could keep the Cunard officers who were already experienced at handling her, including Bisset. More men arrived: fishermen reservists and seamen from Scotland. They were a mixed bag, some of them out of practice: 'One of the RNR officers, who had been retired for several years, arrived on board in a uniform coat that could not be buttoned by several inches,' wrote Bisset. 'He was unable to see his own boots, but he scented battle like an old warhorse. "The exercise will do me good," he said. "It will take some of the fat off me."'[6] As well as men, *Caronia* needed the ability to fire at the enemy:

While the ship was being gutted, gangs of shipwrights and metalworkers had been making preparations to receive eight guns. The deck planking was removed from the gun positions, and the steel underneath strengthened by means of stanchions, girders, and beams, to withstand the shock of gunnery discharge and recoil… The guns were then securely mounted… A large amount of ammunition was taken in… A range-finder was fitted… and searchlights were mounted on the wings of the bridge. Armoured plates were riveted into position over vulnerable parts of the ship. Other parts were reinforced with bags of coal [or] sand, and rope-screens as protection against flying splinters. Speaking-tubes... and control telephones were installed from one end of the ship to the other... Coal, fresh water, provisions and stores were loaded, sufficient to enable her to remain three weeks at sea.[7]

*

Trinidade is a few vertical rocks poking out of the South Atlantic, 500 miles off the coast of Brazil. Here, one of Germany's prized liners was undergoing a vastly different transformation. With ships pinned in ports far from home, the *Kaiserliche Marine* had to employ creative methods. The 19,000-ton *Cap Trafalgar* had only made her maiden voyage earlier in 1914. On the outbreak of war, she crept out of Buenos Aires, took on coal at the Uruguayan port of Montevideo and fled into the Atlantic. At Trinidade, the tiny *Eber* was waiting to supply the crew and convert her for war.

There were no large reserves of dockworkers for labour, no warehouses to store expensive trappings: 'With much difficulty and improvisation we transferred both... cannon and... machine-guns along with ammunition,' wrote Otto Steffan, who was about to join the liner as an officer. There was no opportunity to fix armour plating to the passenger liner for protection. Without a wharf alongside, even taking on coal was difficult: 'The swells were long, and the ship bobbed up and down, tugging at her long anchor chain.' It was a messy job, the motion of the unsecured ship complicating their task. 'Soon coal and coal dust had permeated the ship. It was everywhere.' Food supplies were a concern, too. When *Cap Trafalgar* sailed to patrol South American trade routes, Steffan and the rest of the crew were already hungry, dreaming of capturing a refrigerator ship carrying meat to Europe. Perversely, below decks luxury was evident. 'We had to get used to the silk sheets and the cabins still smelling of the perfume of the last passengers!'[8]

*

Back in England, Captain Litchfield retained the services of *Caronia*'s surgeon, along with her carpenter, blacksmith and plumber. Members of Cunard's catering department were also signed on as cooks, waiters and officers' servants, but Litchfield's most difficult challenge was convincing 140 grizzled, reluctant men from below decks to join the Royal Navy. 'These men had a natural horror of... any kind of discipline... A few of them walked off the ship... but most of them signed, though with a surly demeanour.' That demeanour did not always improve.

On 10 August, *Caronia* sailed under sealed orders. She was on her way into the Irish Sea, to help guard Britain's Western Approaches. It became distinctly apparent to 'The 'Black Squad' – the stokers and trimmers – that life was about to get serious. These men worked four hours on and eight hours off. They were used to doing whatever they wanted when they were not in the engine room:

> They made their own rules, lived rough, gambled and fought among themselves... They dressed as they pleased, usually in dirty moleskin pants and sweat-grimed singlets, with... rags knotted around their necks, and, wearing [heavy] boots, clumped along the deck to and from their quarters and the engine-room... There was no love lost between them and... the deck officers, who viewed the stokehold toilers as being little better than animals.[9]

James Bisset was kinder about these men than some. He recognized that people did not work deep in the bowels of an ocean liner, wheeling coal in barrows and shovelling it into furnaces for hours at a time – endless, backbreaking labour – through choice. Mainly, they did it because life had failed to provide them with any better opportunity by which to scrape a living. These men skirted the poverty line until their bodies could stand it no more. Forgotten or reviled as they were, they were the lifeblood of Britain's domination of the seas in 1914, and so they were given some leeway:

The engineer officers knew how to handle them, but of discipline in the ordinary sense there was none. They knew no fine words, only raucous yells for more coal, more steam, more speed, delivered in a jargon which was a mixture of Scotch, Irish and Lancashire dialects, with hoarse profanities which no one except themselves could understand. As long as they did their work, without shirking it, or causing too much trouble, no notice was taken of their crude behaviour or slovenly garb, provided that they kept themselves out of sight of the passengers.[10]

As a career navy man, Captain Litchfield was mortified by all of this. He was determined to do something about this unruly bunch. 'The ninety men concerned turned out on deck in a shambling mob, grumbling and muttering... They were mostly unshaven, and grimy with sweat and coal-dust.' Petty officers ushered them into two lines.

The Captain emerged with a grim look on his face... walking slowly up and down the lines, staring at each man with obvious disgust. Some of them were overawed, some were sullen, and a few stared back at him defiantly... The Captain... delivered an address that was short if not sweet. 'You are in the Royal Navy now,' he began, 'and don't forget it... Remember, this ship may be under the enemy's fire at any moment. You have volunteered for service, knowing that risk. All bunks will be taken out of your quarters, and hammocks slung instead. What's good enough for the navy is good enough for you. Every man must shave daily, keep himself and his clothes and boots neat and clean, obey orders promptly, move smartly, keep his eyes and ears open and his mouth shut...' The Black Squad were astounded at being spoken to in such a firm manner for the first time in their lives. They shuffled off to their quarters, muttering and grumbling, and no doubt there was mutinous talk among them... but they had to knuckle under, and they knew it.[11]

Uniforms were issued and from then on, the Gunner's Mate put them through a ruthless round of drill and exercise each day. 'If ever there were raw recruits and an awkward squad, there it was. But gradually they learnt how to stand at attention, stand at ease, right turn, left turn, about turn, and even to form fours and to salute.'

*

As the sun rose on 14 September, *Cap Trafalgar* was back at Trinidade, where the crew were busy with hammers and torches removing anything on the decks that obstructed their line of fire amidst complaining and swearing. At 7.00 a.m., wireless officer Otto Steffan raced to the bridge to report to Captain Wirth that there was apparently a non-German ship nearby. The captain appeared nervous. 'What do you think, stand fast or run?' Steffan was decisive. 'Get out of here as fast as we can raise anchor.' They began stuffing coal in the bunkers as quickly as possible. 'The light breeze rattled the blocks and tackles and swirled the coal dust about the open hatches. The bunkers were filled, but valuable time was lost.'[12] At 11.00 a.m., black smoke appeared on the horizon.

The grey ship coming towards Trinidade was *Caronia*'s sister ship, *Carmania*. As the distance between the vessels narrowed, two requisitioned ocean liners prepared to do battle for the first time in history. They were evenly matched in size, with similar improvised firepower. Otto Steffan described the buzz onboard *Cap Trafalgar*:

> It was time to move. A shrill whistle brought coaling to a halt. Shovels were thrown aside. Crewmen crawled out of the bunkers. The anchor was hauled in... The officers on the bridge studied the newcomer. Was she a merchantman, a warship? As yet, we could not make out her flags. Alarms rang. Buglers sounded battle stations! Clear the ship for action![13]

Aboard *Carmania*, they had spotted *Cap Trafalgar* lying on the west side of the island. She had removed a dummy funnel and so they did not know who they were looking at, but they knew she was not British. They did not yet know that she was alone. At noon, *Carmania*'s crew were readied for battle. From just over 5 miles away, the British ship sent a shell across the German bow. *Cap Trafalgar* had now come around to face them and had seen the Royal Navy's ensign flying: 'We were certain we had a fight on our hands,' wrote Steffan. 'A bright flash from the ship – a geyser of water off our bow. Soon a second shot. We turned towards our opponent… "*Hoist flags and pennants!*"… Our flags were unfurled at the forepeak… We opened fire at 5,000 yards. Shell after shell slammed from our guns towards the enemy.'[14]

According to Royal Navy tradition, aboard *Carmania*, Captain Grant was supposed to give a dignified order to commence fire. Carried away in the heat of the moment, instead he bellowed: 'Let him have it!'[15] At first the German shells went long, and the British shells fell short. Then gun crews began finding their range. 'The hits became frequent on both sides. A German shell burst… killing one of the gun's crew with the jagged fragments of the machinery.'[16] On board *Cap Trafalgar,* they could see that they were hitting the mark, but Captain Wirth was not convinced that his firepower had enough of an edge to make a difference at this range, so he continued to close in, and under the bridge of *Cap Trafalgar* a machine-gun was brought into action. Otto Steffan was at his action station to the rear:

> Looking ahead, I could soon see nothing on account of the brown smoke clouds. The first enemy blow had hit the foremast. The shell then rebounded onto the deck and exploded beside the gun and its [ammunition] boxes. No member of the gun crew escaped without injury. Assistant Helmsman Schneider become the first of our company to die in the action. His head was blown off.[17]

Fighting amid first-class luxury was an odd experience. 'Enemy shells and shrapnel tore to bits the flowers in our elegant Wintergarten... First Officer Rettberg was injured in the back and thigh by marble splinters.' *Carmania* pulled away. As the *Cap Trafalgar* turned too, the British sailors noticed that she was listing. They fired at her waterline. Her lack of improvised armour was beginning to tell. 'Rounds fell into the second cabin stateroom and petty officer's mess with deadly effect to the hammocks, beds and clothing.' At their closest, the two large liners were little more than a mile apart. They could not miss each other. 'The guns were fired as fast as they could be loaded, and got so hot that the paint blistered off them.'[18] The results were devastating. 'She... simply peppered us,' wrote a young sailor on board *Carmania* to his sister, 'wiping out a whole gun's crew and a mess they were too, one's skull bashed in like an over-crushed walnut, another chap with his left side torn out... a very unpleasant sight; and the language our men used fairly made your hair curl, I have added quite a number of words to my vocabulary.'[19]

'Soon', wrote Otto Steffan, 'we observed the bridge of our opponent burst into flames. But he was also scoring on us.' The fire was not the only concern aboard *Carmania*:

> The deck around the guns was knee-deep in expended cartridges, the port side of the main rigging was shot away and hanging... whilst the wireless telegraphy aerials had been shot away... Some of the ventilators were absolutely in ribbons, a large hole gaped in the port side of the upper deck, [a shell had gone] upwards against the side of the wheelhouse and then through the after bridge, twisting and crumpling the steel rails... whilst fragments of boats and davits were lying all about the decks.[20]

Captain Grant paused. The enemy was now 5 miles away and clearly in trouble. *Cap Trafalgar*'s list had worsened. She was 'on fire badly, and almost entirely enveloped in smoke'. Attention on both ships was now on survival. 'We both had so much to worry about,' said Otto Steffan. 'Water gushes over the deck. Steam comes up in clouds from the broken pipes... we kept listing more and more to starboard.' His ship was doomed. 'A lucky shot, piercing below the waterline, had knocked out a main bulkhead and flooded the engine and boiler rooms so badly that pumps could not control the inrush of water.' As they prepared to abandon ship, they were defiant. 'Through the smoke and steam, three cheers for the Kaiser! Hoarsely, we sang the National Anthem.'[21] The crew of *Carmania* watched the end from their own ship:

Some half-dozen boats had cleared her sides and were pulling towards one of the colliers, which, with commendable pluck, had stood by... Over fell the proud German liner until her funnels lapped the water. She seemed to hesitate; then, sinking slowly, she heaved herself upright once more... Suddenly she tilted to a greater angle, her stern came right out of the water, and she dived down... with the German ensign still streaming in the breeze. A few swirling eddies, a little debris, and the small white lifeboats were all that remained of a gallant ship and her crew.[22]

'As I climbed down the ladders on my way back to the boiler room,' wrote one British officer, 'an intense feeling of sorrow came over me and I said to myself, *poor beggars, it might have been us.*'[23]

*

The village of Backwell lies south-west of Bristol. There, in August 1914, ten-year old Vera Waite was keeping her mother company on laundry day when a young man emerged from the Fairfield Inn nearby. 'He came across the yard to my mother in the washhouse and he said to her: "Here you are, here's a cup of tea, this is the last you'll have now that the war's on," and it frightened me out of my wits. What was going to happen to us?'[24] Vera's childish fears were well founded, even if she did not know why. The impact of the First World War on maritime trade is not a sexy topic of conversation. And yet the subject is hugely important because it explains how every nation that was reliant on a single import, or sent out a single export by ship, was faced with imminent disaster in 1914.

Without her sea trade, Britain could not feed her people. Before 1914, the country was importing two-thirds of everything that the population ate. At any given time, Britain had four to eight weeks' supply on hand, which meant that if that supply was severed in August 1914, British subjects would begin to go hungry before the end of October. The country could not manufacture the goods that her people needed, either. Every bit of cotton, silk, petroleum and rubber that Britain used came in from overseas. Even in timber, Britain was reliant on foreign trade. Some seven million tons arrived each year, and if the supply suddenly ceased, the knock-on effect would be staggering. A third of the timber import was used for pit props in coal mines, and coal, nobody could do without.

As soon as hostilities broke out, countries like Britain required a never-ending supply of guns, shells, rifles and uniforms. Whether the country was buying it in, or making it at home from imported materials, sea trade was critical. All of these things considered, it is easy to see why it was just as important in August 1914 to make sure that existing shipping kept moving, as it was to stop a German invasion force from landing on the Kent coast.

But it did not end there. British ships did not only carry goods in and out of Britain. Almost half of the goods transported back and forth across the globe when war began were moved from A to B in British ships. Britain's allies were as dependent on the maintenance of her trade dominance as she was herself. They all needed imports to support their workers and their economies. As soon as war broke out, pulling men out of manufacturing and putting them into their armies made these allies less productive at home, and even more reliant on importing food and materials. Even without a war, France's fleets could only manage 40 per cent of their imports and exports. Russian ships accounted for moving only 21 per cent of the empire's imports and a tiny 11 per cent of goods going out. In 1914, Britain's allies needed Britain's ships to operate in order to fight and to survive.

The idea of the English running out of tea was unthinkable, but war made it a possibility because ships did stop moving. Docks were silent. British ships distributed globally waited for naval orders, or for protection from German cruisers. As for the Germans, their ships and cargoes had either been seized or they were too afraid to come out of harbours for fear of meeting the dominant Royal Navy. In Siam, steamers belonging to Norddeutscher Lloyd and Hansa that were in harbour at Ko Sichang were 'moored in a long line in the river, presenting a somewhat interesting spectacle'.[25] Standing on a pier at Callao, due west of Lima in Peru, a German merchant took in the sight of ships lifeless at anchor in large numbers and sighed: 'Fifty years' work gone in an hour.'[26]

The knock-on effect of this inertia crept across the planet and reached into the homes of ordinary people with seismic effects in August and September 1914. Latin America, where nobody was actually at war, was especially hard hit by the crisis. Countries like Argentina, Brazil and Peru had built their economies using foreign shipping. The availability of this now vanished. Nations needed their tonnage for themselves. Even if there was a ship available, suddenly merchants could not afford to use them. The cost of moving one ton of grain from Rosario in Argentina rose from $2.28 at the beginning of 1914 to $14.60 by the end of the year. Sugar and coffee lay rotting on quays with nowhere to go.

Of all of the cargos that moved back and forth, the most terrifying commodity to become suddenly sucked out of the world's moving economy was coal. Without it there was no power, functioning railways or shipping. Nations that usually exported it were terrified of running out themselves, so locked down and refused to release any. Warsaw was bereft. Electricity in the city was completely dependent on importing coal from a part of Silesia that was now inaccessible, and factory production was therefore crippled. Coal panic was just the beginning. In one example, Argentina also banned the export of gold and silver, and ensured that its people could eat by blocking meat, rye, wheat, corn and barley from leaving the country.

Argentina then had food, but if businesses were not able to sell their goods, no money was coming in. They could not pay their workers. Unemployment exploded in Latin America. In Argentina, there were 1,000 unemployed workers in Rosario in August. The number rose to 30,000 three weeks later. In Pernambuco, on the north-east coast of Brazil, 2,400 men were fired at the docks. 'Conditions… are daily growing worse,' wrote one observer. 'Foodstuffs and other necessities are becoming scarcer. The families of many men formerly employed on the railroads, tramways, [ports] and factories are suffering from hunger to which cause the increase in the daily number of robberies… in various parts of the city.'[27]

Chile suffered dramatically. The most important product that they exported was nitrate. Much of it went to Germany, where it was used in fertilizers to enrich soil. By the end of the year, only 25 per cent of nitrate producers were still in operation. As the industry collapsed, the workers suffered 'widespread suffering and misery'.[28] In the districts where nitrate was mined, there was no alternative employment 'in the waterless desert where all workers as well as food and other supplies had to be brought in from outside'. By 25 August, 10,000 were out of work in the Iquique area on the northern coast. Unemployed workers and their families slept on the docks waiting for someone to come and get them. Scenes like this were by no means limited to South America. On the other side of the world in Australia, unemployment more than doubled in New South Wales in the last three weeks of August as exports dried up. Workers were let go, or at best put on half pay.

*

One sector threatened with disaster in August 1914 – and it was an existential threat – was farming. In Europe, war had broken out just as harvest time was approaching. Men had been mobilized, and farm animals had been requisitioned by the authorities.

No harvest led to no food production, which led to more unemployment and more closed factories before famine kicked in. Even if the remaining civilians could find a way to carry out the harvest, they faced being stripped of the results. 'Women, children, old people had to do all the field work with the greatest difficulty and effort,' wrote Croat Pastor Galović in remote Bošnjaci. Then the results were taken from them. 'Grain and other food was requisitioned for the army.'[29] For fishermen of the Brittany coast, the war also changed everything. Fishing at night became prohibited. They were told to anticipate meeting warships, often, and that they fished at their own risk. Artisans who produced luxuries instead of necessities were even worse off. In Limoges, their business was porcelain and footwear. Of 12,500 people employed producing either of those, only 4,500 still had jobs after war came.

People were saving money where they could. Across Europe, domestic servants lost their jobs as people economized. In Germany, the Red Cross in Wiesbaden was overrun with desperate women, while up to 8,000 people regularly waited in a large crowd outside the unemployment office in Berlin. People hoarded cash, too, the movement of which was essential. Customers also wanted to trade paper money, which they thought might become useless, for actual gold. In Dijon, 200 miles south-east of Paris, on the morning of 31 July alone, seven million francs were withdrawn from the Banque de France. In Russia, people hoarded coinage, depositing it in 'land banks' by burying coins in the ground, or stashing money 'under the stove or in the bosom'.[30]

Europeans, Chinese and Arabs all emptied their accounts in the Dutch East Indies. 'Armed with chairs, mattresses and cushions they queued in the evening to make sure that they were served the following morning.' One newspaper begged them to reconsider their reaction: 'Large amounts of money in your own house is not safe, and should unrest occur the plundering of private houses is more likely.'[31] Even the Vatican was running out of currency. 'Nothing comes from abroad now,' wrote an Italian politician. 'Things are at such a point that an American bishop has been hastily sent to the United States. [He] promises to return at the end of September [with] a million lire collected from the Catholics of the various dioceses.'[32]

When people did spend, shops were battlegrounds. With the possibility of supplies running out, panic erupted. At the same time, traders put up their prices. 'Our bread was rising in such an alarming way that it was necessary to study astronomy to see it,'[33] said one Argentinian newspaper. In the Dutch East Indies, the indigenous population feared an imminent famine. From Batavia to Semarang, shops on the island of Java were besieged. Beer ran out. On the island of Sumatra, 200,000 workers on estates needed feeding. Normally they obtained almost all of their rice from abroad, but French Indochina, Siam and Burma were refusing to export it. With prices of any remaining stock rocketing, locals pawned their belongings to buy rice by the sack-load for hoarding. London saw similar scenes. In Kensington, one of the city's most affluent boroughs, people lost their heads:

> Taxis today are laden with provisions people are taking home… They are selling provisions over the counter at fancy prices. Bacon is scarce, and sugar, groceries and butter have risen in price… Among the very poor there is indignation at rich people laying in siege stores, and they say burglars, and people who may starve later, are marking the houses where it is done, in order to raid them later on.[34]

Governments and local authorities tried to intervene. In Copenhagen, a price cap and a minimum weight was dictated for loaves of bread. In the Netherlands, they relied on the *Onteigeningswer*, or requisitioning law, which allowed goods to be confiscated from people who were deemed to be profiteering or stockpiling.

Despite measures like these, violence broke out. In Norway, the army had to be called in to subdue rioters, and in Kyiv a crowd of poor people even set up an impromptu court to condemn or pardon vendors who had raised their prices. Just as a crisis can bring out the very best in people, so did it bring out the worst. War profiteering was rife everywhere, especially among neutrals. In the first twelve months of the conflict, the number of Dutch millionaires doubled. They were called *oorlogwinstmaker*. There was nothing palatable about becoming rich on the basis of everyone else's misery, and they were brutally taken apart both verbally and in print.

Some of the worst-hit people globally were about to get hit even harder by the impact of the war. In 1914, if working-class people owned a car, or a horse or even a bicycle, then it was likely for work: making deliveries or pulling heavy equipment and machinery. All of these were now being requisitioned.

Parting with horses was a particularly sad affair. Harry Day had reported as a reservist for the Leicestershire Yeomanry. His first job was to travel around the county collecting requisitioned horses. 'My Troop collected horses from the George Hotel at Hinckley and I felt sorry for a young lady... I promised [her] that if it was possible I would keep that horse and look after it.'[35] Not every horse had such a happy ending. Just to the south of Paris, six-year-old François waited sadly with Chérie, 'the beautiful Anglo-Norman mare that his father, a doctor, had bought... to make the daily rounds of the sick in the villages'. He was talking to her gently when the vet, a brigadier and an obnoxious Serjeant arrived. François kissed her muzzle, stroked her side. 'Chérie was gone. I knew immediately that she would not come back. But it took me long, long, to understand that a whole world was gone with her.'[36]

It was not only transport that was seized. Huge armies also needed huge quantities of food. From 21 to 25 August, the city of Varaždin, 50 miles north-east of Zagreb, was required to deliver 35,500 loaves of bread to feed Austro-Hungarian soldiers undergoing military training before being sent to the front. More demands would follow. The pressure of requirements even impacted French colonies in West Africa. At Bandiagara, orders had gone out demanding that crops and animals be handed over. One sensible resident apparently intervened: 'My commander, this is clumsy,' he began:

By sending an order without explanation, you will sow panic. For fear of losing everything, people will flee across the border, to the Gold Coast, taking all their belongings with them. There may also be revolts. What is needed is to summon those responsible, to explain to them that France needs of them and that everyone must make an effort to feed the troops fighting at the front, because in these troops there are Africans, perhaps relatives.[37]

This approach softened the blow: 'Instead of telling them: "Requisition!" they had been told: "We need you," a crucial nuance for the old Africans. And as many of them had sons who were soldiers in France, in their minds they were giving to feed their children.'[38]

Perhaps the hardest blow of all was that, as people handed over their automobiles, their horses, their food and their supplies, they were not necessarily paid, instead receiving a voucher of some sort. In western France, horse owners were issued a treasury bill, promising them payment at the end of the war with 5 per cent interest. People were being asked to give up their means of earning a living, or the food from their families' mouths, and being handed a vague slip of paper in return.

16

Bits of Cork in the Swirl of a Current

France

There is a reason that precise casualty numbers for the Battle of the Frontiers are hard to come by. Disposing of the dead often fell to the advancing German troops. These men were paying less attention to counting or removing identifications and effects, than to eliminating the stench and the gruesome spectacle of the fallen. There were no dedicated units or bureaucratic processes to accurately record the endless bodies and thousands of dying men in makeshift hospitals in August 1914.

In Rossignol, the main street was full of shattered carts, wounded soldiers and dead horses. The Poles among the ranks of IR 157 had been looting underwear. They did not care if it was men's or women's, as long as it was clean. As exhausted as they were, that night the Silesians could not sleep in the aftermath of the battle. 'All the time, one could hear the cries of the injured in the village.'[1] Some of those screaming were their own. As yet, their senses had not been dulled by years of bloodshed.

For soldiers, there was a fate worse than a quick death. That fate was mutilation: permanent, brutal, life-changing incapacity. At Chimay, artilleryman Gaston Pastre was mortified:

A lamentable spectacle met our eyes. The station is transformed into a vast hospital. Wounded everywhere, in wagons, in waiting rooms, on platforms, under sheds... The greater part [are] Black, Turkish or Senegalese... Poor people, who have come from so far to end up bruised

229

there... This horrible vision of poor bloody and mutilated people makes your heart ache more than on a battlefield.[2]

A Dane conscripted into the German army, Hans Toft had been evacuated from the battlefield with a gunshot wound to the lungs. The scene at the main dressing station was grim. Those who were not going to survive were laid out in rows in a tent where they would eventually die. Toft was spared that fate, and was taken to a church. 'We were placed in a bed of hay around the altar... I lay next to one, who had his entire mouth shot to pieces. He kept shoving me, since he couldn't speak, as if he wanted to say: "*Don't you know me?*" It was a soldier from my company, but unrecognizable.'[3]

The scene at this dressing station was common. The standard of care a man received was largely a matter of luck. The terrain did not help; wagons could not get all the way to the front line. 'The injured had to be transported through forests on one's shoulders or on stretchers.' Additionally, though, one hard lesson learnt by the Germans in August 1914 was that attacking units had to keep field ambulances up to date with their movements. In the aftermath of the Battle of the Frontiers, the ambulances could not find the wounded because 'the entire medical staff observed... from a distance, in the style of nineteenth-century battles'.[4]

Abandonment was a terrifying prospect. For those that had to wait helplessly for aid, it was a traumatic experience. Twenty-four-year-old Désiré Renault was a pastry chef. At 3.00 p.m. on 22 August, he was shot in his left side. 'I felt... as if my bones were being broken. The bullet passed through my entire length... through my pelvis and lodged above my knee.... Immediately I felt great pain and a burning fever. The bullets continue to rain around me, I risked being hit again, so I did everything possible to drag myself into a hole.' As the light faded and fighting died down, he was left on the battlefield 'without care. Dying of thirst... I tear up handfuls of oats which I chew... The night draws on... I think of my parents, especially my mother, like when I was sick and... very little, and I am not alone in thinking of my mother, because I hear the wounded and the dying calling for theirs too.'[5] He waited a day for rescue.

The aftermath of battle was harrowing for those attempting to help the wounded, too. Henry Lafontaine was working at a field ambulance, dealing with the men butchered during the Battle of Charleroi. 'A [man] arrives, covered with a bedsheet, from which escapes mournful groans interspersed at very short and regular intervals with a kind of strange and plaintive snoring.' The young man in question was twenty-one-year-old Paul Ullmann, a Parisian. When Lafontaine looked under the sheet, he was mortified:

Head pierced from one temple to the other by a bullet. His face must have been very beautiful, but now... The foam comes out of his mouth, his nose, with something whitish, milky, which the Doctor tells me is cerebral matter. He is going to die. He is a young Serjeant in his early twenties... I will always see it again, that atrociously mutilated head, lamentable ruin with frozen eyes, already lifeless.[6]

Paul lingered between life and death until 25 August, but he was at least cared for in his final days. Doctors and medical units made heartbreaking decisions about who could be saved and who was a waste of their limited manpower. Commander Moreau was limping away from Rossignol with a doctor when he saw an artilleryman lying in the road on his stomach:

His face blackened, he raises his head as we pass, from which the brains protrude, and moves his eyes and lips. I point this out to the doctor who raises his arms and lets them fall with a gesture of helplessness. He obviously expresses that we just have to let those for whom nothing can be done die where they are. They are as good there as elsewhere.[7]

*

Once the wounded were collected, work could begin on the dead. One Pole near Rossignol noticed that the heat of summer was turning the bodies black:

> We have the impression that they are n———ers. Puffed lips, eyes shine with whites, turgid bodies, bulging stomachs. Swarms of flies and worms all around the place. We do not have to look for them because the putrid smell can be sensed from afar. We usually bury them immediately… Two trowels deep – covered with ground, anonymous – only a clod of earth is a sign that there lies a soldier. We only take off his identity badge.[8]

Many civilians immediately went out to help clear the landscape. It was practical, but it was out of sense of duty, too. They felt acutely that they could be the last person who might be able to tell a man's loved ones what had happened to him, the last person who might remove personal effects and return them to families. It was an intensely intimate experience. At Fillières, Father Martin remembered them all. The villagers found thirty-two-year-old Private Julien Gaborit, his spine visible through the tattered blue remnants of his uniform and his head detached from his body. '[He] must have remained there for a long time… until one day, on approaching, we saw dogs running away from there… The remains were carefully collected and buried.'[9] Three wounded Frenchmen , Léon Varet, aged twenty-two, Gaston Sancier, twenty-four, and twenty-six-year-old Jules Compagnon either slid into a well to evade capture, or fell in and, wounded as they all were, were unable to get out again. Having buried them, Martin was tormented by the thought of their final hours trapped down there.

The Belgian population of Tournai came out to see to their allies, too. 'They were there… on the bloody sidewalks, our poor [French] territorials. On their stiffened limbs, the red pants and the big blue greatcoat seemed even heavier.' Some bodies had been looted. 'In many places, in fact, the pockets had been turned inside out; all around the corpse, poor objects lay on the ground, remains of a humble life or of an obscure tenderness: pages of notebook, fragments of biscuits, or shards of mirror, sections of rosary, photo stained with kisses or tears.'[10] They dug a mass grave and laid the men to rest.

The suffering caused by the Battle of the Frontiers did not always end quickly. In the Field Ambulance at Carnières where Henry Lafontaine continued to treat the wounded, they put the worst of the lingering cases in a ward that they dubbed the 'Room of Horrors'. Twenty-two-year-old 'Robert' Schor was admitted with 'his shoulder shattered, his neck torn and his right temple taken away by the same bullet'. He seemed to be getting better. '[He] recovered so well that... we carried him to a bed under the big lime trees in the courtyard. He chatted, joked with his friends who came to see him; smoked two cigarettes and even got up to put on his military clothes for a few moments.' It was not to last. 'His head was still open and the wound, leaving bare the brain that could be seen beating... could not close quickly enough. A cerebral abscess was declared.' Schor died on 7 September. 'During his last two days of agony in his delirium, he constantly called: "Dad." His father had been dead for two years.' In the same room, Lafontaine encountered more misery. 'One day I almost fell while slipping on something sticky,' he recalled. 'It was a clot of hardened blood.' Twenty-four-year-old Serjeant Jules Rehel had had part of his skull torn off by a bullet. '[He] was digging with his index finger in the wound and throwing away, with sudden jerks of the hand, the clots and the materials that adhered to it.... In his delirium, he had torn off his bandage! Until his death... he had to have someone on constant watch at his bedside.'[11]

*

In the aftermath of the Battle of the Frontiers, Germany was still attempting to effect the Schlieffen Plan. Their strategy hinged on Kluck and Bülow's ability to plough into France and march on Paris. As yet, Joffre was not panicking about his retreating men, because as the Allies suffered a reverse in the west, he received word from Russia that her armies were rampaging across East Prussia on their way to Berlin. This was a happy development. Joffre was aware that Germany had focused most of her resources on his front, so if the Russians could essentially beat them via the back door, the French the British, and the Belgian army in Antwerp might not even have to fight a decisive battle at all. But he still needed a new strategy. To rely on Russia taking care of everyone's business would have been negligent. The first call he made was to have his reeling armies fall back a considerable way to establish a new, solid line. To this end, as long as they did not break, losing some ground was satisfactory. When the French and the British got to these markers, they could form up, reorganize and mount a proper defence. They could play for time.

For the Allies on the ground, already exhausted, this meant a lot of marching. The BEF was about to cover some 150 miles in a week and a half. Disorder reigned from the outset on 24 August. Until then, everything had moved forward. Now, suddenly, they were fleeing the enemy and going the other way. If there were only the infantry battalions to consider, then this might have been less complicated, but the roughly 8,000 infantrymen per division were less than half the total manpower. The rest, no less crucial, consisted of artillery, engineers and the lines of communication, who kept the men in the front lines supplied with everything they needed to function. On the move, a division created a 15-mile traffic jam. On a rapid turnaround such as the one that took place for the Allies in the opening weeks of the war, practically, this meant that when those fighting troops turned around and retreated, they ran headlong into ammunition wagons, food supplies, fodder for the horses, guns, endless lorries and even baggage trains coming up behind them.

Keeping traffic moving efficiently was the responsibility of transport officers. For everyone to withdraw from Mons and Charleroi in an orderly fashion would have required exemplary planning: allocating routes supply points and detailing when and where men were to rest. In August 1914, this was an impossible task, because nobody knew their endgame. 'Staff work simply went to pieces,' wrote one officer. 'It was not that men lost their heads or anything like that, but the various HQs found it impossible to keep pace with events. Battalions loitered for want of orders. Many of those who did get clear did so because they retired entirely on their own initiative.'[12] Not everyone was so lucky. Units set off in different directions, got broken up or lost; some of them walked right up to the enemy by mistake and were captured. Added to the chaos was a never-ending stream of Belgian and French refugees on the move, dragging their worldly belongings with them.

In the century since the First World War, there has been a tendency for English-speaking historians to claim the 'Great Retreat' as a solely British endeavour. However, while it is true that the whole BEF was involved, there were also tens of thousands of Frenchmen retiring alongside them in the aftermath of the Battle of the Frontiers. As well as Lanrezac's Fifth Army, the French Fourth Army was forced to withdraw too, to keep the line intact. Paul Lintier was witnessing similar scenes to his British allies:

In the breathless... bustle of the retreat we had to make our way through the crowd by force... tossed about from right to left like bits of cork in the swirl of a current, dragged this way and that... the tattered remnants of troops surged down the road. Wounded, limping, many without rifle or pack, they made slow progress. Some made an effort to climb upon our carriages, and either hoisted themselves on to the ammunition wagons or let themselves be dragged along.[13]

All of this was enough of a strain on the men involved, but in addition, in order to delay the German advance, they also periodically had to turn around to fight off the oncoming enemy. An officer presented a simple explanation: 'It is... a cardinal principle in rearguard fights that you must not only check your enemy, but must also, whenever possible, make a counter-attack.'[14] He pointed out that under these circumstances, cavalry was infinitely useful.

August was a blur for General Sordet's Corps de Cavalerie. Etienne Letard, a veterinarian with the 3e Régiment de Hussards, was tired of the endless riding and the state of exhausted, starving horses as his regiment went back and forth across Belgium for no discernible reason. Cavalry were soon to be marginalized by industrialized, static warfare, so in some ways these weeks in France and Belgium proved to be their swansong in Western Europe. The most mobile of all the arms deployed along the retreat, they were often sent to meet suspected enemy formations.

The larger rearguard actions, however, were fought by the infantry, including the BEF. On 25 August, Smith-Dorrien's II Corps and Haig's I Corps streamed down either side of the Forest of Mormal. By the end of the day Haig's men found themselves around the hamlet of Landrecies. Civilians had already begun digging trenches and preparing the ground. Artillery officer Arthur Corbett-Smith had something to say about night fighting: 'Especially in the early morning... [they] are horribly uncomfortable things. The nerves are continuously on edge and you are apt to loose off guns or rifles at the merest suspicion of a movement.'[15] Having marched 30 miles from Mons in oppressive heat with no adequate rest, Haig's men remained diligent. They put Landrecies in some state of defence, at least, before the majority collapsed in a heap. The unlucky ones slept outside in the rain.

It was just getting dark when one of the outposts heard an enemy unit approaching. An officer quickly gave the order for a company of the 3rd Coldstream Guards to open fire, but the Germans were already on top of them, bayonets fixed. Various Guard units were being attacked all over town:

The outpost line was crushed... in a moment, like tissue paper, and before anyone could grasp what was happening the Germans were pouring their massed columns into the town. Tired out, the men tumbled out of the houses; three privates and a corporal here, a dozen men and a Serjeant there, a subaltern, a private and a machine-gun at another corner, half a dozen men at two first-floor windows somewhere else. And the only light came from the flash of the rifles.[16]

Eventually, burning houses lit up the town. Then the German artillery arrived and subjected the Guards to both shrapnel and high explosive fire. The British fought back. Captain Friedrich Wilhelm Ruebesamen of FAR 4 witnessed what happened next:

> Captain Horn, who was marching at the head of his battery with his squadron, was immediately seriously wounded by a shot in the back. Their horses fell dead or wounded and buried the riders beneath them, the first gun was unable to move due to the loss of them, the remaining ones bounced about. Loose horses galloped back, the infantry and parts of the gun crews sought cover in the deep trenches on both sides of the road – a complete mess.[17]

Bit by bit, the Guards beat the enemy back. The Germans made off. They were done for the night, but this was not a loss. There were limited attacks, 'at various points under cover of darkness with a great show of vigour, [which] though beaten off, succeeded in conveying the impression to the British commanders in this part of the field that they were engaged with a considerable force'. If this claim is true, it worked, for Haig's corps was kept on alert all night. 'It was a clever piece of work, well conceived and well executed.'[18] The 3rd Coldstream, fighting their first action since their formation in 1897, had suffered 120 casualties.

A much larger fight took place 7 miles west at Le Cateau. There, on 26 August, General Horace Smith-Dorrien ignored the orders of General Sir John French, commanding the BEF and had his men make a stand. Bleary-eyed, Corporal Doctor Harrop, with the 2nd Duke of Wellington's regiment, found himself digging on a road. 'We began to dig our trenches,' he recalled. 'But at the first streak of dawn, bang, bang, bang, now we are off again, over they came: shrapnel, high explosive... but we kept on digging and got down a bit.'[19] Another battalion came through to attack. 'We covered their advance, but were sure they were going to their doom. [On] they went and the last man hardly out of sight, *ere they were tumbling*.'[20] For their trouble, II Corps suffered nearly 8,000 casualties at Le Cateau. In addition, nearly forty priceless guns were left behind, a far higher price than that suffered by the enemy. Smith-Dorrien's corps got away, which has been spun as a victory of sorts amid what looks conspicuously like failure.

*

Joffre was unimpressed with the plight of the outnumbered BEF. On the night of 26 August, he sent out orders to shuffle his forces, forming a new Sixth Army with General Michel-Joseph Maunoury in command. This was to be sent to the left of the Allied line to shore it up against Kluck, but they needed time to get there. It was imperative that the rest of the line held, including the British. Sir John French was beginning to annoy Joffre with his vacillation. Sir John lacked the cool head required for such circumstances, his health broke down, and he may even have suffered a minor heart attack in the opening weeks of the war. For the French, the British commander was a frustrating, even rogue element, not fully under their influence. And the future of their country was at stake.

Joffre had tighter control over the Fifth Army, and so on the evening of 27 August he attempted to address the BEF's worrying situation. All day long he had heard disturbing reports about the British, and he was beginning to fear a rout of his allies. At 8.10 p.m., he instructed Lanrezac to plan an attack towards the city of Saint-Quentin, against the German flank pursuing the British. Lanrezac was furious, as this involved his army changing direction by 90 degrees while in the midst of a fight. The two Frenchmen had a furious row the following morning, though Lanrezac had already obediently issued provisional orders. Joffre's plan was actually fortuitous, because on that day the Germans had crossed the River Somme, where the Sixth Army was detraining on the

French left. If Kluck's army caught them out, it would blow Joffre's overall strategy away. At what might have been the worst point of the whole ordeal for the BEF, Sir John French refused to take part in what became the Battle of Guise, citing the fact that his troops were exhausted. He was not wrong, but this meant that on 29 August, Lanrezac's army fought alone.

The battle began at 6.00 a.m. As opposed to making a stand, like the British at Le Cateau, this was a large-scale attack against the oncoming Germans. It came as a complete surprise to the enemy, and yet it was a torrid morning, with the Germans already advancing hard past the River Oise south of Saint-Quentin. The French were forced back, and in the afternoon, the violence of the battle increased. Under Lanrezac's command, General Louis Franchet d'Espèrey's I Corps was waiting to the rear, ready to be deployed as Lanrezac needed. His divisions were subsequently split either side of the ailing X Corps and they roared into action with d'Espèrey himself on horseback. As the two corps pushed the Germans back towards the Oise, Captain Graf von Büdingen was with the Hanoverians of IR 77:

> The terrible fire from the front and from the flank forced the leading parts to retreat. [...] From my height, I could see how the riflemen kept moving forward, being torn apart by the terribly heavy artillery fire, until they lost their nerve and were mowed down by shrapnel fire as they ran back, and how, despite this, they kept finding leaders who brought the rest forward, until the evening slowly descended.[21]

This was not a victory, but d'Espèrey did help to avert a disaster. The Germans had at least been stayed, and every delay was beneficial to the retiring Allies. The Frenchman was soon to get his reward.

*

The retreat, however, continued. Unsurprisingly, as they tramped on and on in the summer heat, often without food or water, the mood of the men on the road declined. Paul Lintier described a kind of numbness, and how it eroded fear. 'The longer you are exposed to danger, over which you have no control, from which you have no escape, the less scared you feel. Therein lies the secret of all military courage,' he surmised at the end of August:

> One must live, on the field of battle just as elsewhere; it is necessary to become accustomed to this new existence, no matter how perilous or harsh it may be... At first fear makes one perspire and tremble... Death seems inevitable. The danger is unknown, and is magnified a thousandfold by the imagination... Soon, however, one learns to discriminate. The smoke is harmless, and the whistling of the shells indicates in what direction they are coming. One no longer crouches down unnecessarily, and only seeks shelter knowingly, when it is imperative to do so. Danger no longer masters but is mastered.[22]

Despite a certain acclimatisation, inevitably, frustration mounted. The all-consuming, universal theme of the retreat for French and British alike was exhaustion. 'The weather was terribly hot: and our boots felt as if they had been filled with hot marmalade. All our clothes stuck to us, and we had not got used to the weight [of our equipment].'[23] The chalky dust kicked up along the route coated men in a ghostly 'paste of dust and sweat'.[24] Equally important as food for most soldiers was tobacco, and men were running out of that, too. 'The usual substitute was dried tea-leaves rolled in the parchment paper of the emergency ration,' wrote Arthur Corbett-Smith. 'Tea-leaves are very nasty to smoke, but I am not sure that they are so nasty as brown paper or the seat of a cane-bottomed chair; and I have tried them all.'[25]

Men's health was inevitably breaking down in neglectful conditions. The scene was grim in Paul Lintier's French artillery regiment. They were 'tortured with diarrhoea'. And there was nothing anyone could do about it. 'The Medical Officer had [nothing] left, and we had no choice but to chew blackthorn bark.'[26] The British were no better off. 'Cases of bowel complaints were very common,' wrote Corbett-Smith. 'The lads really need looking after like children, bless them! Aromatic chalk-powder with opium I found an excellent remedy... and I saved much agony from bad wounds by doses of opium.'[27]

Having been obliterated at Rossignol, the survivors of the Colonial Corps marched day and night. Etienne Letard's cavalry regiment described troops dragging themselves along the interminable road:

[An] unforgettable vision of African soldiers toiling on the first evening of their campaign in France. They are there, a few hundred, tall or medium-sized brown men who can be seen as thin and nervous under their ill-fitting khaki linen blouses. Launched into the fray at the end of the arduous journey which brought them from Morocco to the Somme, exhausted this evening by a long stage, they go with their bodies leaning forward under the heavy packs... always dragging cripples behind them, because some, already injured by their boots, exhausted by enteritis, walk with difficulty, staggering.[28]

What must they have made of this strange country, of the language barrier and their baptism of fire? 'They are sad, fierce, almost all mute; barely here and there a voice rises chanting a melody which begins with the high notes and descends to the low tones... Intrigued... the hussars tried to get a good look at their African friends.' The Moroccans, for their part, ignored the cavalry and Letard was disappointed, but then something happened. 'While our regiment continues its journey, I stop for a moment among these lost people with our medical officer. He has just spent several years in Morocco and, in the language of their country, he addresses the riflemen. Immediately, the heads... turn towards us; the brown faces, all hairless or surrounded by a fine collar of black beard, light up... The doctor is bombarded with questions.'[29]

The thousands of horses being driven along the roads south suffered intensely, too. 'Many had been slightly injured... and their wounds were suppurating,' wrote Paul Lintier.

> No one seemed to trouble about them, and that was not the worst, for some of them had to suffer the stupid remedies applied by the ignorant drivers. I saw one man urinate on his horse... which had been cut by a shell splinter... Seldom taken out of the traces and hardly ever unharnessed, the straps... had made large sores on them which were covered all day long with flies. And, besides all this, the poor beasts, like the men, were weakened by incessant diarrhoea.[30]

Arthur Corbett-Smith witnessed some drop down dead. There was no time to mourn these faithful animals. 'Unhook or cut the traces; push the poor beast out of the road. An old pal, was he?... Nothing matters now but keeping on the move. Yes, better shoot him. He deserves a clean end.'[31]

*

In a few short weeks, parts of France had become full of troops, not just those already serving at the front. The trail went all the way back to the still arriving transports. Second Lieutenant Regie Fletcher was a twenty-two-year-old reservist who had rowed for Oxford in the Boat Race earlier in the summer. He arrived at Havre with his artillery unit a few hours before battle commenced at Mons. Regie did not suffer fools, or worry about their feelings. His men loved his approach, not least because when Regie lost his temper it was often over their welfare. The first thing he did at Havre was buy them footballs, then he raged at an Army Service Corps corporal interfering with him drawing rations to feed them. 'Swear at corporal for five minutes without repetition,' he recorded in a notebook stolen from the stores.[32]

His short fuse was in large part because of the utter frustration of languishing on the coast instead of riding into action with his guns. The wounded from Mons and the early part of the retreat were now arriving at Havre. On 29 August, Regie spent his whole day packing up and organizing his men, whereupon they promptly stood around waiting for further orders. It was not until the following day that he found out that he was not to go to the front at all, but that Havre was being rapidly evacuated. The British lines of communication were under threat all the way back to the docks, where everything they needed to function and to fight arrived. 'At present, though not dying, I am sitting here in a rage like a poisoned rat in a hole, and cursing my luck. If only I had joined some damned [infantry] regiment, at least I should be fighting now, instead of running away without firing a shot.'[33] There were hints everywhere at the severity of the retreat. 'Stores at Havre full of bloody rifles.' On 30 August the arrival of German cavalry at Havre was considered a very real threat. 'Quite possible we may have to fight here,' wrote Regie. 'I… have a baby pistol and a toothpick. Probably shall chuck latter away and use fist.'[34]

Regie and his men were ordered to go and sleep in a field. 'If we hear firing among our posts, we are to cut and run to Havre docks, and embark at once… Expecting an attack on camp tonight and really almost hoping for it. Anything better than this inaction.' Regie could not believe that an ailing army did not need him, did not need their guns and that instead he was kept sitting in a tent all day censoring letters. He despised the invasion of privacy, and the repetition. '"How's the old cow"… "I am keeping away from the girls here"… The worst are those who say: "I am standing up against all our troubles for Jesus's sake; but, dearest, I cannot get any woodbines…" I hate reading [their letters], but the men don't seem to mind.'[35]

All of the painstaking, exhausting work of offloading and arranging food, bandages, fodder, horseshoes and all of the other things the army needed to function was now reversed. Everything needed rescuing. Men slung it all back on any available ship in complete disorder to get it safely away from the oncoming German hordes.

The terror spread. 'Boulogne was utterly unprotected, and every hour her citizens expected the enemy… When men woke in the morning they looked first at the flag flying over the citadel to see whether it was still the Tricolour... and no man certainly would have been surprised if he had discovered the black, red and white of the enemy in [its] place.'[36]

St Nazaire, at the mouth of the Loire, was to replace Havre as the principal port of the BEF. Thankfully, the quartermaster general, Sir William Robertson, had been thinking well ahead when he stopped supplies and men arriving at Havre as early as 24 August. During four days at the beginning of September, 20,000 officers and men, 7,000 horses and all 60,000 tons of stores departed for St Nazaire.

If not knowing what was happening felt like torture for Regie Fletcher, civilians knew even less. As the British prepared to depart Boulogne for the Loire, it unsettled the whole town. At the Hotel Bristol, where officers had been quartered, it reminded journalist Wilson McNair of a country house in the Scottish Highlands at the end of the season. He watched this feeling of abandonment sink in with the locals as the BEF departed: 'A week [later]... Boulogne was a place of fear and silence. The hotels were empty... Not a uniform was to be seen... and the long rows of tables in the cafés stood forsaken and melancholy.' Talk kept coming back to the Franco-Prussian War. 'There were Frenchmen in these Boulogne cafes who remembered 1870,' reported McNair. 'They had dim eyes that held a smouldering fire, and when they talked... you saw their hands clench and their teeth set as the tide of memory carried them backwards. Their eyes blazed at a hundred grim recollections, and the deep note of passion made their voices strangely eloquent.'[37]

At his headquarters, 30 August was a miserable day for General Joffre. He had dropped a heavy hint to Sir John French about the need to stay in contact with the French units either side of him. At noon, the BEF commander replied that his men would not be ready to oblige the French for another ten days. Within forty-eight hours, Lord Kitchener, the secretary of state for war, would have to dash to France to literally order the British general into line. The Battle of Guise had not achieved the desired result;

the German armies were still coming, and Joffre was forced to admit to his government that he could no longer say with any conviction that the Germans would not reach Paris. Then, at midnight, his misery was compounded, for word arrived from Russia of a catastrophic setback that eliminated all possibility of a rapid deliverance from the other side of Europe.

17

The Mousetrap

East Prussia

ollowing the German withdrawal from Gumbinnen, troops in
the retreating Eighth Army were both confused and disheartened. 'It seems as if even the senior officers know little about
the true state of the current situation,' noted Willy Tharann.
'This seemingly aimless running around makes us disgruntled.
We should be told everything because we have a right [to know]
as defenders of the fatherland.'[1] In Danzig, the East Prussian
people had noticed that flags were repeatedly flown to celebrate
successes in the west, while reports of victories in their theatre
seemed disturbingly absent. Meanwhile, spirits in the Russian
ranks were high. 'We beat the German like a son of a bitch,' one
letter read, 'and we will beat him until we have smashed him
into dust, so that he won't fight anymore, and then we'll return
home.'[2] On the home front too, news of victory was spreading. When the first trains with German prisoners and wounded
Russian soldiers arrived in Moscow on 26 August, people gathered to ask questions. '[The wounded] are living newspapers,'
wrote Ekaterina Sayn-Wittgenstein, a nineteen-year-old from an
upper-class family with German roots. 'They tell us what they
saw, what they felt... They talk about the battle of Gumbinnen
as if it was a simple thing.'[3]

General Rennenkampf was pleased with the success of his First
Army. All signs pointed towards the Germans fleeing before him
in complete panic. Now was the time to finish the job and chase
down his opponent. Instead, the army commander awarded his

tired men two days of rest before resuming the advance beyond the River Angerapp. Additionally, Rennenkampf was shocked by the enormous expenditure of ammunition and shells he had incurred. On 23 August, his army wired the minister of war requesting 108,000 shrapnel and 17,100 high explosive shells, as well as a staggering 56,000,000 rifle cartridges, 'to make up what has been used.'[4] Once Rennenkampf finally resumed the advance, it lacked vigour. His infantry marched slowly, and his cavalry hung back instead of maintaining contact with the enemy. This failure by Russia to press the attack reduced a potentially important strategic victory at Gumbinnen to a fleeting, tactical one. Not capitalizing on it awarded the Germans an opportunity to turn the entire campaign around. But first, the issue of who was to command Germany's Eighth Army needed to be settled.

Moltke's choice of replacement for General Prittwitz in East Prussia fell on two vastly different individuals, whose partnership would nonetheless go down as one of the most successful of the war. On the morning of 22 August, Moltke summoned Erich Ludendorff, whose recent success at Liège had not gone unnoticed, and briefed him on the state of affairs in East Prussia. The situation, Moltke said, was 'serious but not impossible.' He ordered Ludendorff to immediately travel to Eighth Army headquarters as the army's new chief of staff. Ludendorff left on a special train, with orders to pick up the new army commander. At his home in Hanover, Paul von Hindenburg had received a telegram from Moltke telling him to prepare for immediate deployment. In 1911, Hindenburg had retired after forty-seven years in the army. Now, the sixty-six-year-old was being recalled to active service. Without knowing what his role was to be, Hindenburg promptly replied: 'I'm ready.' Three more telegrams arrived in quick succession, informing him that the Eighth Army was to be his. With less than twenty-four hours to prepare, Hindenburg had no time to acquire a new field uniform, and went to the station to meet Ludendorff's train dressed in his old Prussian blues.

*

Ludendorff possessed a brilliant tactical and operational mind, but he was abrasive, impulsive and chronically impatient. Hindenburg, on the other hand, was known for his cool head, a character trait desperately needed to steady the shaken Eighth Army following Prittwitz's loss of nerve. Surprisingly, these two opposite personalities quickly found that they made a perfect team.

Aboard their train, they began to make plans. Samsonov's Second Army, advancing from the south, was the main threat to the Germans, and it was clear to both men that their best course of action would be to disengage from Rennenkampf and redeploy as many of their troops as possible in Samsanov's direction to the South. Upon their arrival at Eighth Army headquarters, Ludendorff found the mood to be 'anything but cheerful'. However, they were pleased to find that several of the army's staff officers, including the very capable Max Hoffmann, had reached the same conclusions as they, and that many of the preliminary orders for a concentration of forces against Samsonov had already been issued.

The plan quickly taking form was simple, yet daring. A single division of cavalry would be spread out along the entire front before Rennenkampf's army as a screening force, creating the illusion that the bulk of the Eighth Army was still facing him. Meanwhile, François, Mackensen and Below would relocate their corps to the south by road and rail and deploy on both flanks of the solitary corps that was already there to meet Samsonov's army. It was hoped that this move would catch the Russians off guard, allowing the full strength of the Eighth Army to deal a decisive blow to Samsonov's invasion where he least expected it. This would only be possible if Rennenkampf remained passive and did not attack the screening force too hard. It was a gamble, but so far Rennenkampf had indeed proved unwilling or incapable of pressing the attack. It was this sluggishness that the Germans were now counting on to use to their advantage in East Prussia.

François's I Corps had the longest distance to cover, reaching its position on the right flank of the Eighth Army's new front on 26 August. Meanwhile, Mackensen's XVII and Below's I Reserve

Corps marched south-west to make up the left wing. The question was whether or not the three corps would arrive in time to meet the Russian advance. While they were in transit, it would be up to XX Corps, commanded by Friedrich von Scholtz, to delay Samsonov for as long as possible. Luckily for him, the Russian Second Army was exhausted even before it crossed the border into East Prussia. The men had spent days marching along dusty roads under a scorching August sun, and their supply lines were already becoming overextended. Furthermore, two corps had not kept up with the main army.

This was a problem for Samsonov, as speed was perceived as key to Russian success, and he was being urged on. He was told that he faced no significant opposition along the border, and to push north and cut off the German retreat. In overall command, Grand Duke Nikolai declared that 'the foremost task of the First and Second Armies is to finish as soon as possible with East Prussia'. Any halt to the Second Army's offensive would be 'extremely undesirable'.[5] This meant no rest days – a serious problem for those on the ground. Nikolai Klyuev, the commander of XIII Corps, warned: 'If we continue the offensive as we have done so far, then by the time of the collision [with the enemy], we will have reduced the troops to a state not fit for combat.'[6]

Many of the problems plaguing the Second Army stemmed from the fact that its advance was being conducted along too wide a front, which made coordination between units challenging. Furthermore, Samsonov was leading his men into an uncertain situation. The lay of the land made it difficult for his cavalry patrols to reconnoitre, and the few aeroplanes at the Second Army's disposal were so old and knackered that they were of little use. Instead, they were primarily used to plod about delivering messages to the rear. This was in sharp contrast to the Germans, who effecitvely used aerial reconnaissance to determine the movements of Samsonov's army, as well as to confirm that Rennenkampf had not accelerated his sluggish pursuit. The Russians did not enjoy this luxury. When Samsonov told his superiors that he intended to pause the advance in order to secure his flanks and obtain information about the enemy before continuing, he was told curtly that 'to see the enemy where he is not is cowardice'.[7] The message was clear: *Get on with it.*

*

The first major clash along the southern border happened on 23 August, as the French reeled in the west, Namur was bombarded, and the British debuted at Mons. Russia's XV Corps stumbled upon elements of Scholtz's force who were dug in around the villages of Lahna and Orlau. Blundering forward, the Russian regiments were still marching in columns when the first artillery shells landed in their tightly packed ranks. Only then, under heavy enemy fire, did they deploy into battle formations to try to attack. But the Germans were not sitting passively and waiting for their opponents to come to them; officers led their men forward to meet the advancing Russian infantry and the result was bloody. The fighting was chaotic, often done at close range with bayonets, officers' swords, rifle butts and fists. The 'Hurrahs' of the German soldiers mixed with Russian 'Urrahs'. While the sound of the Russian rifle volleys echoed across the field, and bugle signals sought to pierce through the deafening noise of battle.

On both sides, entire skirmish lines were shot to pieces as they tried to advance across open ground. Whole companies of *Jäger,* German light infantry, seemed to simply melt away under heavy enemy fire. Meanwhile, two Russian battalions from the 29th Chernigov Infantry Regiment, who had managed to reach Orlau, found themselves subjected to devastating rifle and machine-gun fire coming from seemingly every house. Colonel Vladimir Zhelondkovsky, a battery commander of the 6th Artillery Brigade, recalled the confusion:

> During the battle, the commander of the Chernigov Regiment, Colonel Alekseev, grabbed the regimental banner and rushed forward. [He] was killed and the banner fell into German hands; the [men] fought for it with everything they had. In the end, it was recaptured with the assistance

of the Poltava Regiment, but parts of the brigade were thrown into complete disarray. Individual runaways rushed back, spreading panic... General Bogatsky... didn't display the proper courage, didn't lead the battle, and, declaring himself shell-shocked, left for the rear.[8]

Despite their brigade commander's loss of nerve, the Russians held their ground at first, until in the evening when a rush by the Germans pushed the invaders out of the village.

In Lahna, the battle descended into a desperate struggle for each house. Two companies of the 1st Jäger Battalion fought off repeated Russian charges, but were almost completely annihilated in the process. By evening, every officer was gone, and a small group, many of them wounded, decided they had had enough. About 20 Jägers of the original 500 made it back to safety.

By nightfall, the fighting had died down, and the noise of rifle fire and artillery shells was replaced by the cries of the wounded. On the German side, things looked grim. Many companies had lost most if not all of their officers and NCOs. Those left began to view their situation as untenable, fearing that it would be impossible for the battered troops to stand against a renewed Russian attack in the morning. Some units were reported to have suffered 60 to 70 per cent casualties already, and several battalions were left extremely exposed. Meanwhile, General Scholtz had hoped that a night-time counter-attack might improve his position, but a message from army headquarters informed him that the three incoming German corps would not arrive before 26 August.

Scholtz was therefore instructed to conserve his strength, and ordered a retreat from Orlau and Lahna before the Russians resumed their attack. However, the distribution of the order to the various companies strewn across the battlefield did not go smoothly. Messengers got lost in the dark or were shot, while some isolated companies could not be located. This chaos made retreating difficult, and early the following day, the Russian guns opened up and the Russian infantry resumed its attack. Only thanks to suicidal actions fought by his rearguards did Scholtz manage finally to disengage and pull back to a new line of defence.

*

The hard fighting had left the Russians too exhausted to pursue their retreat. Instead, they halted. In total, some 3,000 had been either killed or wounded. While visiting a field hospital after the battle, colonel Zhelondkovsky was stunned by the sheer number of Russian wounded. 'I, a participant in the Japanese war, have never seen so many wounded,' he recalled. 'All the rooms, stairs, corridors of the large barracks were littered with them, there were also quite a few Germans.'[9]

Judging that his remaining troops needed to recuperate, General Nikolai Martos, commander of XV Corps, sent a request to Second Army headquarters for a day's rest. However, Samsonov was still being urged to advance with ever greater speed. He was forced to deny the request and instead order Martos to proceed without delay. In the following days, Martos's corps would fight a series of bloody engagements as the Germans conducted a fighting retreat, drawing the Russians further and further forward. Samsonov's men were being pushed to their limits. Moreover, by advancing his centre, Samsonov continued to extend and thin out the flanks, while putting further strain on his already over-stretched supply lines. The Second Army was sticking its head through a noose that was about to be wrung tight.

Meanwhile, both Mackensen's and Below's men were now in position facing Samsonov's right flank. On the evening of 25 August, Ludendorff informed both corps commanders that Russian forces were advancing on the town of Bischofsburg, and that they were to attack at once. The enemy in question was the Russian VI Corps, commanded by Alexander Blagoveshchensky, a man wholly unsuited for a field command and known for both being a desk jockey, and for extinguishing all forms of initiative shown by his subordinates. Until now, Blagoveshchensky had received contradictory orders, with Samsonov having vacillated between keeping VI Corps around Bischofsburg to secure his flank, or ordering it 25 miles south-west to Allenstein to participate in the middle of the developing battle. As a result, Blagoveshchensky's corps, already outnumbered, was not properly concentrated to withstand the enemy in force.

First contact was made on the morning of 26 August, when Mackensen's XVII Corps encountered the enemy dug in to the north of Bischofsburg. Unlike at Gumbinnen, there would be no head-on charge without proper artillery preparation. Mackensen had learnt his lesson. Once in position, his guns opened up with devastating effect. 'The heavy calibres gurgle incessantly towards their targets,' wrote Lieutenant Alfred Laeger. 'The gunners work like mad. The last red poppies of the summer of 1914 wilt from the never-ending gun smoke and sink to sudden death in front of [them].'[10] Here and there, the German gunners heard enormous explosions, and watched as flames shot skyward, indicating that their shells had struck a Russian artillery position and ignited its ammunition dump.

The shelling caused chaos in the Russian ranks. 'The men, unaccustomed to the noise and destructive force of the shells, became stunned and began rushing to the right, then to the left,' wrote one witness.[11] Deciding that the only escape was forward, the officers ordered their men to charge the German positions. However, instead of attacking in force, each regiment was sent forward in turn, only to be shot to pieces. One after the other, 'every Russian who came within reach was taken prisoner, and an entire mountain of captured rifles, cartridge pouches and ammunition was building up', wrote Asmus Jørgensen of IR 61.[12]

As the wounded began flooding back, panic spread through the Russian ranks. At this crucial moment, Blagoveshchensky's leadership fell short. While his 4th Division was being smashed, his second, the 16th Division, remained idle in and around Bischofsburg awaiting orders to come to the assistance of their comrades. Such orders never came, and as the day went on, reports began reaching him that the 4th Division had been completely defeated.

The arrival of Below's I Reserve Corps in the afternoon sealed German victory. His men, having marched around the Russian left flank, rushed forward against an unsuspecting enemy and eventually sent the Russians fleeing. Blagoveshchensky threw up his hands and ordered his corps to retreat. Once again, communications were lacking, and this order did not reach everyone. The men of the 14th Olensky Infantry Regiment heard nothing. Soon, isolated and surrounded, the regiment was pressed against the shores of Lake Gross-Bössau. Only a few of the men who managed to swim across the lake were saved, while more than 1,700 were forced to surrender.

The fighting around Bischofsburg was costly for the Russians. More than 5,000 officers and men were either dead, wounded or missing, and a total of sixteen guns and eighteen machine-guns were captured. In their first real meeting with the enemy, the men of VI Corps, whom one of the officers had described as 'excellent combat material, sufficiently trained and brought up in a military spirit', had been transformed into a scattered and disorderly mob, trudging aimlessly through East Prussia.[13] Blagoveshchensky failed to inform Samsonov of his decision to withdraw. This turned a defeat into a disaster, as it left Samsonov unaware that his right flank was now completely unprotected.

*

Things were not looking much better at the opposite end of Samsonov's front. By now, François's Corps had completed its redeployment and was ready to attack. As ignorant as their comrades to the sudden presence of strong German forces before them, Russia's I Corps was taken by complete surprise when François launched an attack.

The commander of I Corps, Leonid Artamonov, had a reputation as an unscrupulous careerist, a pompous braggart and a religious zealot. He was convinced that faith in God was the deciding factor on the battlefield, and he was more concerned about the number of religious icons in barracks than he was about preparing his men for war. Having not expected to face significant enemy troops, Artamonov was taken completely by surprise by François's attack.

Once again, a Russian general failed at his post, and once again, Samsonov was not informed that his troops were retreating. In fact, in his last message to headquarters, Artamonov had boasted that I Corps was standing 'like a rock' and that Samsonov could rely completely on him. Less than two hours later, his corps was in full retreat, despite the fact his men had actually managed to repel German attacks in several places. Artamonov also managed to issue a number of contradictory orders to his subordinates and failed to give proper directions for the withdrawal. As a result, the retreat gradually turned into a rout. In the middle of all the confusion, Artamonov was seen staggering among his fleeing troops, muttering repeatedly to his adjutant: 'Everything's lost, everything's lost.' One eyewitness recalled: 'He walked like a sleepwalker, not noticing his surroundings, one half-torn shoulder strap hanging on his chest. He was all covered with dust. It was difficult to recognize in him the former self-confident and formidable commander of the corps.'[14]

On the morning of 27 August, Samsonov had examined the battlefield. Still unaware of the critical situation on both his flanks, the army commander seemed generally pleased with the way the battle was progressing for his XV Corps, and ordered his centre to continue to push. Only upon his return to headquarters that evening did he learn about I Corp's retreat. At first he refused to believe it, given Artamonov's positive reports. Reality soon set in. Samsonov promptly removed Artamonov from his command and ordered his replacement, Alexander Dushkevich, to immediately mount a counter-attack. The chaotic nature of I Corps' retreat, however, meant that it would be days before this could be achieved.

The situation had quickly turned critical for Russia. Any advance at the Second Army's centre only served to widen the gaps that had been left in both flanks by the retreating corps. The Russians were playing right into enemy hands. Assistance from the First Army also seemed increasingly unlikely. Rennenkampf was not only still plodding, but part of his force had been drawn off in completely the opposite direction to the coast, to capture Königsberg with its twelve major roads, six rail lines and three intersecting waterways. For Hindenburg and Ludendorff, this meant that they could now fully focus on defeating Samsonov, without any risk of Rennenkampf suddenly advancing into their rear.

With reports of heavy German opposition flooding in, it was becoming increasingly clear to Samsonov that his foe was not retreating to the River Vistula, as had been assumed following Rennenkampf's victory at Gumbinnen. Instead, all signs now pointed towards the Germans having regrouped for a counter-offensive against him. A message he sent to Northwestern Front headquarters on the evening of 27 August reveals that Samsonov now knew that he was facing elements from all of the Eighth Army's corps. Despite this, neither Stavka – Russia's supreme high command – nor General Zhilinsky, who was in charge of this front, changed their orders. The latter continued berating Samsonov to advance.

To his credit, Samsonov was holding up better than some of his corps commanders. Even after learning that another of his corps had already retreated nearly 20 miles without his knowledge, he still believed that the battle could be salvaged. 'Today, the enemy is lucky,' he was supposed to have told his subordinates. 'Tomorrow, we will be lucky.'[15] For his men, a full retreat for the entire army would have been their best chance of survival, but Samsonov decided that a counter-attack was his next move. He ordered the two corps in his centre to swing south-west and strike the Germans who had just routed Artamonov's corps. He also decided that he needed to go forward and oversee this in person.

When Zhilinsky found out that Samsonov was commanding this attack himself, he finally realized the gravity of the situation and immediately ordered a general retreat to the Russian border. Simultaneously, Rennenkampf was told that the enemy he had been advancing against so carefully for nearly a week was long gone, and that he was to hasten to Samsonov's aid. Both orders came too late. Rennenkampf was too far away, and by the time the order to retreat reached Second Army headquarters, Samsonov had already left for the front.

The decisive day of the battle came on 28 August. Realizing that neither of the Russian corps on the flanks was in any state to launch a counter-attack, the Germans left a thin screen to protect themselves there, and raced to throttle Samsonov's centre. So confident were they that the Russian flanking corps no longer presented any threat, that just a single regiment was left to protect against one, while a few Landwehr regiments were deemed sufficient to hold the other. Hindenburg and Ludendorff were ready to finish off Russia's Second Army.

Meanwhile, Samsonov's counter-attack from his centre was off to a bad start. Throughout the morning, heavy fighting had taken place around the town of Hohenstein. The Russians fought hard, but many were beginning to lose faith in victory. With so many officer casualties, units were losing cohesion. Morale was in rapid decay. By the afternoon, the battle had broken up into a series of confused and uncoordinated skirmishes. Furthermore, soldiers who had received little food for nearly a week were now thoroughly exhausted. Fodder for the horses was also running dangerously low. Seeing that his army could no longer continue its offensive, Samsonov finally ordered a general retreat. While the battle was undoubtedly lost, Russia might just avert a complete catastrophe, but only through a speedy and organized withdrawal back over their own border.

This did not happen. Instead, the retreat quickly descended into yet more chaos. The men struggled through difficult terrain: lakes, swamps and forests. Every road was soon clogged with columns of infantry, artillery batteries, and supply trains all trying to escape south. Staff work was lamentable even allowing for the circumstances. One general completely failed to assign routes of retreat for the individual units of his corps, with the result that they all arrived at the few suitable thoroughfares simultaneously. Confusion was widespread. Tired soldiers mistook neighbouring units for the Germans in the darkness, leading to several episodes of friendly fire. Colonel Vladimir Zhelondkovsky was dismayed:

I remember gloomy, silent soldiers, sometimes groups of them with officers, walking beside the road... The rifles are still in their hands, but these men are no longer... an army, merely a mob. I remember the sudden cry of 'cavalry' in some village, then wild, random shooting, the whistle of bullets, then someone's embittered, rude abuse. It turned out that there was no German cavalry, and that the men had fired at... our own Cossacks.[16]

XV Corps was even worse off. General Martos had vanished. Only later was it discovered that he had been captured in the night with his entire staff by a German cavalry patrol, leaving his men leaderless. The ramshackle nature of the retreat persisted, while the two German spearheads finally linked up, completing the encirclement. The Russians were trapped, and Hindenburg felt confident enough to report victory to the Kaiser. By the evening of 29 August, the retreating forces entered the Kaltenborn Forest. Hardly a single regiment still functioned properly. One witness later recalled: 'It was not the Germans who finished us off, but we ourselves... After Kaltenborn, the corps, as an organized unit, no longer existed, only a mob of infantry and cavalrymen who were looking for whichever commander to stick to in order to break out.'[17]

Several attempts were made at bursting through the German lines to safety. However, the soldiers were done in. Thoroughly exhausted from the endless marching, running dangerously low on food and ammunition, and utterly demoralized by defeat and the collapse of leadership, all such attempts failed. Captain Alfred Bülowius of IR 41 later recalled seeing long columns of Russian infantry, cavalry and artillery coming out of the forest towards the waiting enemy. Excited to be presented with such a perfect target, the German soldiers opened up with rifles and machine-guns. 'The effect could not be imagined more terrible,' remembered Bülowius. 'Everyone tried to flee into the forest's protection, leaving vehicles and horses behind. The shredded and wounded animals raced [about] aimlessly... wagons rushed about, it was soon a wild chaos.'[18] The firing was stopped, and a dense mass of people soon emerged from the forest waving white rags.

Fighting was nevertheless sometimes desperate and bloody. One German NCO described seeing 'friend and foe [lying] in confusion, choking each other'.[19] Colonel Zhelondkovsky witnessed a Cossack rallying some 300 men who refused to be taken prisoners. 'The mob rushed south after [him]. A few minutes later, I heard a frequent rattle of rifles, then a united cry of "Urrah."'[20] Shortly afterwards, soldiers from the German skirmish lines appeared and captured those who had stayed behind, including Zhelondkovsky. As it slowly became clear that any attempt at reaching the border would be futile, Russian soldiers began surrendering in large groups, some in their thousands.

In command of the Northwestern Front, General Zhilinsky received little information about all this. All communications with Samsonov had been severed on 28 August, when the general had left his headquarters to lead from the front. Zhilinsky was therefore unaware of the encirclement by the Germans and assumed that the Second Army was still retreating south. The following day, the battered corps that had flanked the Second Army fought on to try and save their surrounded comrades. Dushkevich's I Corps managed to briefly overcome one German position, but was unable to consolidate the victory and soon retreated yet again. The same day, General Blagoveshchensky's VI Corps also attempted a counter-attack, but with even less success. One officer noted: 'The command and control of the troops was disappointing, communication between the corps was broken. The headquarters of our VI Corps is in total confusion.'[21] A witness of 4th Kharkov Lancers Regiment described total disarray: 'The sides of the road were strewn with abandoned carts, covered wagons, gigs, infirmary wagons, civilian carriages... and various kinds of objects... Broken and worn-out horses roamed along the road.'[22] The last hope of relief for the encircled troops expired.

Russian rearguards did what they could to repel enemy attacks, but to no avail. Around the village of Mörken, IR 150 continued to charge the Russian lines under heavy fire from the defenders, who had dug in along the edge of a forest. 'The enemy riflemen and machine-guns opened up, and the projectiles whizzed around our ears like sawdust, wounding someone here and there,' recalled an NCO of the regimental machine-gun company.[23] Despite this, the Germans pressed on and once their machine-guns were in position the Russian defence collapsed.

Scenes like this unfolded everywhere, as the German troops continued to tighten the noose. Russian soldiers fought heroically, often until either killed or wounded, but they could not hold out. Dejected and demoralized, they were aware that they were standing on the precipice of defeat. German Willy Tharann described the confused fighting:

You march from west to east, attack and march from east to west, fight back and run in the opposite direction again after the Russians running around in the mousetrap… That was hell itself, the night at Puchallowen. Flaming heaps of straw, bursting bullets, the rattle of machine-guns and gunfire, singing and attacking Russians and the pitiful cries and rattles of the wounded. It was crazy![24]

On the night of 30–31 August, as what was left of the Second Army rapidly disintegrated, so did its commander. Plagued by asthma attacks, Samsonov wandered aimlessly through the woods with the remnants of his staff, chattering to himself: 'The Tsar trusted me. How can I look him in the face again after such a misfortune?' He repeatedly told his chief of staff, Petr Postovsky, that 'his life as a leader was over'. As the hours passed, the general seemed to be deliberately lagging further and further behind his officers, before finally slipping out of sight of his subordinates in the darkness. Then, suddenly, a single gunshot was heard in the distance. 'Everyone understood,' wrote Postovsky.[25]

Leaderless and without any hope of rescue, Russian resistance died out once and for all. All there was left for the Germans to do was to round up the prisoners, and see to the dead and wounded who littered every field, road and village. A correspondent described the terrible scenes he witnessed:

> Further on towards Hohenstein the dead multiply... I finally entered the city... Everything around me was on fire, and the finest houses had been reduced to heaps of rubble. Nothing but dead Russians, mutilated beyond recognition, many of them half charred or still smouldering in the flames... The dead not only display gunshot wounds, but also multiple bayonet stabs and blows from rifle butts.[26]

*

On 31 August Zhilinsky still had no information about the Second Army's position. General Klyuev, who had assumed command following Samsonov's suicide, was captured too, along with nearly 30,000 of his men. The battle was over.

But what battle? A few days before, the German staff had already begun to discuss what name this victory should receive for posterity. The 'Battle of Gilgenstein and Ortelsburg', the 'Battle of Hohenstein' and the 'Battle of Allenstein' all lacked something. The matter was settled when Hindenburg sent a different proposal to the Kaiser. The name he offered had been suggested by Ludendorff, despite the fact that it had little actual relevance to where the fighting had taken place. The name held a deep symbolic meaning, linked to historical enmity between Germans on one hand and Russians and Slavs on the other. Five centuries earlier, this was where Germanic eastward expansion had ended, when the Teutonic Knights were defeated by King Vladislav II's Polish–Lithuanian army. The Kaiser agreed with Hindenburg, and the battle was christened: Tannenberg.

The invasion of East Prussia had been an unmitigated disaster for the Russians. The question now remained whether the tsar's enormous empire could still achieve victory further south in Galicia. There, on Russia's other front, battle was already in full swing.

18

The Northern Thrust

Galicia

As the invasion of Serbia was coming to a disappointing end for Austria–Hungary, the Habsburg empire's war against Russia was about to begin. Both Russia and the Dual Monarchy planned a large-scale offensive across their shared border in Galicia, which today stretches across southern Poland and western Ukraine.

The Austro-Hungarian chief of the general staff, Franz Conrad von Hötzendorf, envisioned a powerful drive by his First and Fourth Armies north into Poland, a *Nordstoß* or 'northern thrust' aimed at defeating the Russians around the cities of Lublin and Cholm, midway between Warsaw and Lemberg. A victory here, he hoped, could lead to a linkup with the Germans in East Prussia, thereby cutting off Russia's Polish salient. His Third Army would be deployed around Lemberg, the capital of Galicia. Here they would protect the right flank of the advance and fend off any Russian attacks until the arrival of the Second Army from the Balkans.

For Conrad's plan to be successful, it required full German participation in East Prussia at the same time. However, his allies were focused on winning the war in the west. Until France was defeated, the Germans did not intend to do anything but defend in the east, and so, when it began, the northern thrust in Galicia did not have any real aim.

Unfortunately for Conrad, at the same time the Russians knew exactly what they wanted to achieve in the region. The commander of the Russian Southwestern Front, General Nikolai Ivanov,

was planning to launch a massive offensive with four armies converging on Lemberg. The Fourth and Fifth would attack from the
north, and the Third and Eighth from the north-east. The result
would be a series of enormous encounter battles, involving more
than two million soldiers, fought along a 280-mile front that ran
in a great arc bending towards Russia, from the River Vistula in
the north to near the Romanian border in the east.

*

Although Galicia was the focus of both belligerent powers,
deployment in the region proved time-consuming. For Russia, it
was a matter of bringing in troops from the far reaches of a vast
empire, while for Austria–Hungary, it was the lack of railways
through the Carpathian Mountains, running along the border
between Galicia and Hungary, that forced troops on lengthy
detours. Existing lines petered out far from the border, so both
sides had to travel long distances on foot to their staging areas.
Gruelling marches along dirt roads and through near impassable
swamps and marshes meant that by the time the soldiers finally
met the enemy, they were already exhausted.

Thousands of soldiers, along with countless supply trains,
horses, artillery batteries and ammunition wagons, filled the
sandy roads and earthen tracks of Galicia. 'Already at a short
distance one could see nothing,' recalled one Austro-Hungarian
soldier, '...only a long cloud of dust moving slowly on the road.
Soon we were disfigured beyond recognition, our uniforms
were ash grey and our faces were black and wrinkled.'[1] Soldiers
struggled with carrying their kit, rifles and ammunition in the
heat. 'The men's heads strained forward now, and I gave them
permission to undo their collars and hang their caps on the ends
of their rifles,' wrote one Hungarian junior officer. 'They were
loaded down all right: a rifle weighing [4.5 pounds], 120 rounds
of ammunition, bits and pieces in their knapsacks, bread bag,
spade, hatchet, mess tin, rolled-up cape, and so on.'[2]

Worst of all, however, was the thirst, exacerbated by the
burning heat. In the villages and hamlets that dotted the region,

residents brought out what water they could spare, but rumours of poisoned wells were widespread, and water offered by the locals, whom both sides suspected of aiding the enemy, was only accepted with great hesitation. As water bottles ran dry, however, parched-mouthed men soon cast aside previous cautions. Austro-Hungarian soldier Kurt Popper vividly recorded:

> For days there have been marches on desolate Galician roads and paths, through wretched Polish and Ruthenian villages. Dust, dust and more dust. In addition, the heat was unbearable. In front of, behind, next to us, endless columns of troops everywhere, striving to the north-east, man, horse, wagon, rider, everything thick with white-grey dust. No water! The tongue sticks to the palate, sand crunches between the teeth, thick dust sticks in the corners of the mouth, swallowing is an effort. The columns are enveloped in thick fumes, smelling acrid and stuffy of sweat. Flies plague us, settling on sweaty, dust-streaked faces.[3]

As in East Prussia, the fighting in Galicia in the first weeks of the war consisted mostly of border skirmishes between border guards and cavalry patrols, but on 22 August, the Austro-Hungarian First Army, commanded by General Viktor Dankl, crossed the border into Russia. That same day, General Ivanov ordered the Russian Fourth Army, commanded by Baron Anton Yegorovich von Salza, and Fifth Army, under General Pavel von Plehve, to begin marching south. The first major clashes occurred on the morning of 23 August when the lead elements of Dankl's and Salza's armies collided on the heights south of the town of Kraśnik, some 130 miles north-west of Lemberg. The Austro-Hungarian troops sought to secure the roads leading out of the marshes along the river Tanew, which marked the border between the two empires. At the village of Gościeradów they charged forward, only to be met by devastating fire from Russian positions to the north of the village. One Austro-Hungarian soldier described the fighting:

Through the howling projectiles, huge clouds of earth and dust rise towards the sky and thousands of splinters look for their victim. There, where the shells hit, all the noise of the battle suddenly falls silent, and anxious eyes full of mortal distress attempt to predict the path of the hail of lead. [The men] press themselves against mother earth and seek her protection. It's a relief to stand back up, when Death's scythe again whizzes by, and splinters and fragments smash into the earth all around... Then quickly shoulder the rifle, aim and shoot and shoot again.[4]

Just like the Germans at Gumbinnen, the Austro-Hungarians quickly became aware of the Russians' skills in digging in and fighting from entrenched positions. Only with the arrival of reinforcements and artillery did they finally manage to dislodge them.

Casualties were high. The village hospital overflowed with hundreds of wounded, many of whom had to be piled up in the hallways and even outside in the streets. '[They] lay on the beds, between and under them, on stretchers, on straw, in the rooms, in the corridors, everywhere, friend and foe, officer and man, mixed with each other, without distinction, brothers in pain,' wrote an eyewitness. 'On the floor were faeces, dirt, straw, bloody bandages and everywhere, a smell of sweat and clotted blood, plus a sultry heat and an army of flies. The few doctors did what they could... The two nurses in the hospital ran helplessly around... The hospital was only intended for thirty patients.'[5]

The hardest fighting of 23 August took place around Polichna. The Austro-Hungarian k.u.k. IR 76 had dug in on a hill just south of this village, having spotted a large Russian force marching south from Kraśnik. At dawn, enemy infantry and cavalry emerged from a forest. As Russian skirmish lines moved forward, Austro-Hungarian artillery began shelling the village. 'The artillery was ordered to light up Polichna in its entirety,' wrote Gusztáv Renner, a company commander with the 76th. 'Shortly afterwards, flames erupted from several parts of the village and huge columns of smoke burst into the sky. The order to shell the village was necessary, as the rows of houses and dense clusters of trees barely 1,000 paces in front of our positions greatly obscured our line of sight into the village and to the area immediately behind it.'[6]

Despite the heavy shelling, the Russians kept pushing south. 'The villages had caught fire,' wrote one Russian officer. 'Our infantry rushed towards an enemy position well fortified with trenches. The indescribable bravery was not rewarded: our infantry did not find support in time because we had no reserves and had to give way and retreat in the face of terrible machine-gun fire.'[7] Advancing Russians quickly took up positions along the southern edge of Polichna and a vicious firefight broke out. 'The Russians had soon established themselves in... houses, barns and attics, and from there heaped fire upon the regiment,' recalled Captain Josef Kö, another of the 76th's company commanders.[8]

A seesaw battle raged throughout the day, as soldiers fought hand-to-hand in the village streets, gardens and houses, many of which had been set ablaze by the artillery. 'The Russians barricaded the houses, gates and barns and poured a devastating fire on the attackers from [within],' wrote Gusztáv Renner. '[We] had to besiege the buildings so speak, one by one. The Russians defended themselves desperately and only left their hiding places when our soldiers managed to set fire to them. [Those] who endured to the end became prey to the flames.'[9] Josef Kö witnessed these gruesome scenes too. 'The Russians were smoked out like vermin. Loud wailing, calls for help, curses, animal-like roars shook the air. Many tried to escape the heat by jumping out of the windows.' The Austro-Hungarians forced them back inside with blows from their rifles:

The buildings collapsed with a crash; bodies lay burnt to coals under the glowing beams. Unrecognizable figures climbed out of the pile of rubble, bloody, torn and panting and stretched out their hands. Others only surrendered upon special demand, and even then only through gritted teeth. Many inquired before giving up, whether they would ever see their wives and children again.[10]

Both sides threw every last man into the fray, and the burning village changed hands multiple times. 'The fight was really fierce, the bullets fell like raindrops,' remembered one participant.[11] An Austro-Hungarian soldier described the terrible scenes of suffering he witnessed:

> Horses, cows, pigs, flocks of sheep, fowl of all kinds ran wildly about. Our path led us over burning, smoking beams, pieces of furniture, corpses, the wounded lamenting with pain. Everywhere we encounter dehumanized death... The earth was coloured red, because many a man had drawn his last breath here... On the parapet lay a man with a bullet through his skull and blood spurting from his mouth. But I immediately controlled myself. He formed a welcome cover for me, and, supporting my rifle between his head and knapsack, I did my duty.[12]

A short respite in the fighting was caused by a sudden downpour. The rifle fire died down, and on both sides, tired and thirsty men, whose canteens had long since been emptied, looked to the sky for a few refreshing drops of water. The impromptu ceasefire did not last long, however. Austro-Hungarian bugle signals sounded the attack, and in a final charge, the exhausted soldiers threw themselves forward. 'No orderly skirmish line, just a mass, a mighty knot, rolled on with burning faces, staring eyes and panting lungs,' recalled Josef Kö. 'Hundreds of throats rang out the "Hurrah!" Some shouted it loud and excited, others whispered it faintly with pale, quivering lips.'[13]

By evening, the Austro-Hungarians had gained control of most of the village, and with no reserves left, the Russians finally withdrew back towards Kraśnik. 'The flames of... Polichna illuminated the battlefield far and wide,' wrote Gusztáv Renner. 'In the spooky [twilight] you could see the enemy leaving the field at a messy run, giving up the fight all along the line.'[14] For some time after, scattered rifle fire could be heard throughout the village, as isolated groups of Russians, cut off and unable to retreat, desperately fought a doomed last stand. Anyone trying to make a run for the forest was quickly gunned down.

Victory for the Austro-Hungarians had come at an extraordinarily high cost. The k.u.k. IR 76 alone had suffered 1,200 casualties, including 500 dead – a loss of nearly 50 per cent on the first day of battle. Crucially, eleven officers had been killed and twenty-four wounded. Newspapers were quick to boast claims that the regiment's losses at Polichna constituted 'a new world record'.[15] But nobody in the empire seemed to register that this sleepy Galician hamlet, now razed to the ground, was merely a bump on the road to Kraśnik without any significant strategic value of its own. What mattered was that a victory had been won at great cost, and thus it must have been won with great honour, as well.

*

While the newspapers were celebrating early victories in places that few in Vienna or Budapest had ever heard of, soldiers in the field were dealing with the realities of war, some for the first time. Riding up behind the advancing infantry, Artillery officer Alfred Michael Schoß, crossed battlefields ripe with the debris and human wreckage after a single day's fighting. 'Horrible images appear before the eye along the way,' he wrote. 'Bloated, wax-pale Russians lie in the... fields. There, one sits in a trench, his rifle still at the ready, but his soul has already passed over to the better hereafter. A shrapnel shell has opened the back of his head and countless flies are sitting and feeding on his brain.' As his battery continued, they passed the bodies of comrades too:

> I find a dashing, blond platoon leader of the 20th Infantry Regiment lying in a field. His right arm rests under his face as if he was just sleeping... He has a small hole in the middle of his forehead from which the blood had seeped

out and dried up... He must have slept almost painlessly, because his facial features did not reveal the slightest struggle with death. On the other hand, lying right next to him is an infantryman who'd fought... He has dug entire holes with his hands, which are still cramped deep in the ground, and his clothes are like rags dragged around in the quagmire. Poor devil, I think to myself, how your pain must have been infinitely severe when the unfortunate projectile hit you. His face is completely unrecognisable with soil that has already dried in this heat.[16]

Fighting continued on 24 August along the entire line, as both sides went at each other with everything they had. Again, Dankl's troops repeatedly threw themselves at the Russians in enthusiastic yet costly bayonet charges for control of individual villages, heights and woods. What they lacked in tactical sophistication, they made up for in spirit. Austro-Hungarian infantry regulations stated that any difficult conditions on the battlefield could be overcome by aggressive action and moral perseverance; battles were to be decided at close quarters, at the tip of the bayonet. The Habsburg troops charged forward accordingly, but what had constituted 'difficult conditions' in wars of the past was nothing compared to what soldiers had to face in 1914. One Russian soldier wrote excitedly home: 'The Austrians advanced in tight rows, in platoon columns, and we mowed them down immaculately.'[17] Still, at least for now, this impressive *elan* seemed to be sufficient for Austria–Hungary to progress. On the morning of 25 August, Dankl's men managed to turn Salza's right flank. Panic set in among the Russian ranks, and the entire Fourth Army was soon retreating north towards Lublin.

The Battle of Kraśnik awarded Austria–Hungary its first victory of the war. Losses, however, were frightening. In a few days, Dankl's casualties had amounted to some 15,000 men, the result of an inexperienced army relying heavily on frontal attacks. 'The most characteristic feature of this first battle: total ignorance on all fronts,' wrote one participant. 'We did not know the terrain;

we had no idea of the enemy's location.'[18] Furthermore, while hailed as a major victory, it was no more than a local one, and the retreat of Salza's Fourth Army was temporary. That said, news of the retreat caused much anger in Petrograd. The Russian minister of war, Vladimir Sukhomlinov, scolded Stavka's chief of staff, Nikolai Yanushkevich: 'We need a victory over Austria. The Serbs beat them, and suddenly we will be beaten by them. This is unacceptable.'[19]

As a result, commanding the Southwestern Front, General Ivanov ordered Pavel von Plehve's Fifth Army to immediately go on the offensive to relieve the pressure on Salza's beaten army. Meanwhile, the Austro-Hungarian Fourth Army was also preparing to enter the fight. Its commander, General Moritz von Auffenberg, ordered two corps to attack north. At the same time, Archduke Joseph Ferdinand's XIV Corps from the Third Army, deployed around Lemberg, advanced in a north-easterly direction. This meant that nearly 400,000 men were now marching directly towards each other, with only a vague idea of where their enemies were. When they began to encounter each other on 26 August, a massive battle took place.

*

First blood in the Battle of Komarów, as it was known in Austria–Hungary, occurred along the eastern bank of the Wieprz river. Here, cavalry patrols encountered Russian forces preparing to strike. Realizing the danger, Auffenberg ordered his II Corps to launch a pre-emptive attack without delay. The result was a day of intense fighting, often at very close quarters, across the rolling hills and dense woodlands that characterized the landscape to the west of the city of Zamość.

Just as at Kraśnik, the Austro-Hungarians relied heavily on soldiers launching themselves forward in deathly bayonet charges. In the woods to the east of Kąty, men of the 13th Landwehr Division took on the Siberians of the 9th Grenadier Regiment at close quarters. One soldier recounted the moment his regiment charged forward: 'A hurrah of several hundred voices is heard and the two companies rush at the enemy with true berserker-like fury. Anyone who doesn't seek salvation in flight is killed.'[20]

Surprised by the ferocity with which the Austro-Hungarians were throwing themselves at them, the Siberian grenadiers soon began to waver, and in the dark forest innumerable confused and disoriented grenadiers roamed. 'By evening, there was such confusion inside that the men began to shoot at their own,' recalled a Russian battalion commander.[21] In the crossfire of Austrian and Russian machine-guns, the grenadiers were forced to retreat. Panic set in, and when their machine-gun officers were killed, the crews simply abandoned their weapons and ran away. The regimental commander, Colonel Vladimir Tokarev, desperately tried to rally his men around an artillery battery, but no more than a hundred were willing to stay and protect the guns:

> The grenadiers crowded in groups near the battery… All of them were deeply shocked… all attempts made… to rally the men and form consolidated companies did not lead to any positive results. The men gathered in one place, scattered uncontrollably in others, deliberately mixed up, hid their rank, company insignia, and so on. It was felt that the test of the first battle was too difficult.[22]

Only by ordering the gunners to open fire with canister shot through the trees, directly at the Austro-Hungarian attackers, did the Russian commander buy himself enough time to disengage from the fight and retreat with the remains of his shattered regiment. However, the Landwehr regiments had also suffered horrific casualties. One had been reduced to just 600 men, having started the day with nearly 3,000. The following day, the Austro-Hungarians would continue their push, ending with a chaotic Russian retreat north. The 3rd Grenadier Division, still shocked by the defeat near Kąty, broke again. The men were so shaken that it would take several days before the scattered regiments, some now reduced to just a few hundred men, could be regrouped. Some elements had retreated more than 30 miles.

Further east, Svetozar Boroević's VI Corps was also engaged in bloody fighting just north of the city of Tomaszów. Fiercely loyal to the monarchy, and well liked and respected by those who served under him, Boroević was both strict and demanding of his men. He would prove himself an aggressive commander in the field. On 26 August, his k.u.k. IR 85 comprising a nearly equal mix of Romanians, Ruthenes and Magyars, charged and threw the Russians off Pawłówka hill without artillery support, losing 35 officers and 1,250 men killed or wounded.

Even worse, however, were the casualties suffered by 15th Division the following night. Having reached the swampy banks of the river Huczwa and driven the Russians away, the division made camp near the hamlet of Pukarzów. But the enemy had not retreated. Instead, they had merely regrouped, and when the Austro-Hungarian officers, drunk on their first victory, failed to establish a proper perimeter around the camp, the approach of a strong Russian force went undetected.

'The mood among the Austrians was upbeat,' remembered Colonel Dmitry Nadezhny of the Russian 10th Division which was advancing towards them. 'Music could be heard from the area where they were located.'[23] Then the Russian artillery began firing. In the course of a ten-hour battle that raged throughout the night, those guns fired more than 3,000 shrapnel shells against the Austro-Hungarian positions. 'Blood flowed in torrents.' one survivor recalled. 'Shrapnel shattered my Captain's arm. He shouted to me: "Servus!... I've already had it!" At that same moment the poor man was hit by a large splinter that broke his back, and he fell silently to the ground.'[24] Meanwhile, Russian machine-guns kept up a steady fire on anything that moved. Panic set in when the Russian infantry launched an attack from the west, and entire Austro-Hungarian battalions were soon laying down their arms and raising their hands in surrender. Others ran. Forced to cross the Huczwa over a narrow dam, which quickly became packed with troops, those men presented easy targets for the Russian guns. 'A disorganized mass of people, seized with panic, rushed back towards Pukarzów,' wrote Colonel Nadezhny, 'overturning carts and guns into the swamp.'[25]

The Austro-Hungarian 15th Division had evaporated. Casualties were generally between 60 and 70 per cent. The Russians claimed to have taken 4,000 prisoners, 20 guns, a significant number of machine-guns, supplies and two regimental colours. The divisional commander, realizing that he had led his men into an ambush and having witnessed its near complete annihilation as a result, shot himself. Survivors fled west towards the neighbouring 27th Division to alert them of the situation, and, together, the two divisions managed to halt the Russian attack in another hard-fought scrap.

*

The morning of 28 August presented opportunities for both sides on the battlefront. North of Zamość, the Austro-Hungarians began to believe that they might be able to turn the Russian flank. However, in the centre, the picture looked very different. IX Corps was scattered along a wide front, and while it managed to occupy the heights east of Zamość, it only did so because the Russians had already abandoned their positions. Meanwhile, attempts to take Komarów proved unsuccessful. VI Corps was also in trouble. The defeat of 15th Division and mounting Russian pressure forced Boroević to pull his forces back towards Tomaszów. Seeing his opponent's centre start to waver, Plehve ordered his men to launch a massed attack southwest towards the city. Plehve was so confident that this attack would succeed that in the afternoon of 28 August, he informed Southwestern Front headquarters that victory was now imminent. He was wrong.

Sensing mounting danger, Auffenberg urged Archduke Joseph Ferdinand's XIV Corps on his right to launch a counter-attack. Supporting the Archduke was 19th Division, which was only just now reaching the front. Having spent the previous week marching, many of the soldiers were footsore and some set off towards their battle debut with their boots hanging around their neck. Ominously, they soon encountered broken groups from the previous days' fighting. 'There are whole rows of them, poor wounded and bloodied soldiers of all possible regiments and different nationalities,' remembered Alois Praveček, leader of the k.u.k. IR 75's regimental band. 'It pains us to look at them. Everyone says that the Russians are evil, terrible, that they're invisible and shoot from anywhere without being seen. Many are crying, others are contorted in pain beyond recognition. Others still are laughing with joy through the pain, because their injuries free them from further hardships of war.'[26] A month earlier, Praveček had been entertaining guests at Salzburg's Mirabell Hotel. Now he was leading his musicians, armed with nothing but their instruments, towards the sound of guns.

Opening the counter-attack, 19th Division charged the Russian V Corps in the flank with bayonets fixed. Russian artillery fire tore gaping holes in their columns. Fighting raged throughout the day, and while Austro-Hungarian elan once again triumphed, casualties were horrendous. The musicians of Praveček's band, tasked with caring for the wounded, soon had their hands full.

> They arrive in whole columns. Here comes one, it is terrible to look at him, with a painful, indescribable expression on his face, deathly pale... he is shaking all over with fright and cannot utter a word! He was speechless! ... At the tables, the doctors are working feverishly, operating, cutting, bandaging, then we carefully place them all on straw, one next to the other, in long rows around the building.[27]

*

Meanwhile, to 19th Division's right, Archduke Joseph Ferdinand's corps attacked the Russian XVII Corps in force. His 41st Honvéd Division rushed forward without waiting for artillery support and was stopped in its tracks, but the Kaiserjäger regiments of General Johann von Kirchbach's 8th Division fared better. That morning, the troops had been told by the military chaplain: 'Soldiers! The fatherland demands the greatest sacrifice from you. You must shield it with your blood, in a few hours many will stand before the judgement seat of God. Repent for your sins and pray a devout Lord's Prayer.'[28] Recruited exclusively from the mountainous Austrian states of Tyrol and Vorarlberg, and considered to be elite forces, the Kaiserjägers were eager to finally enter the fight, and the fury and spirit with which they launched themselves at the Russians was unparalleled.

The k.u.k. Kaiserjäger Regiment Nr.1 (KJR 1) charged the woods south of the village of Tarnoczyn, where the Russian 35th Division had just stopped for lunch. Not believing the enemy to be in the vicinity, the division's officers had failed to post sufficient sentries, and when the commander of the 137th Nezhin Infantry Regiment received word from nearby cavalry that a large enemy force had been detected to the south, the colonel replied that the report could not be trusted. As a result, his regiment was taken by complete surprise when the first shots rang out.

The men, many settled down to eat, rushed to their weapons and began searching for their units. 'There was panic everywhere,' wrote Captain Alexander Oboznenko.[29] Forty men from his company, along with various other scattered troops gathered around him, and after first calming the excited men down, Oboznenko ordered them to follow him towards the attacking Austro-Hungarians. However, as soon as the men left the protective cover of the forest they were met by heavy fire. Oboznenko was forced to return back among the trees for cover, where he found some 200 more soldiers from various companies taking cover in a ditch running along the tree line. He quickly organized the men into a proper firing line and ordered them to engage the attackers.

Among the Kaiserjägers who found themselves caught in a murderous fire was Lieutenant Josef 'Sepp' Engerisser:

Branches whirl in the air, the sky and earth spits iron; death and destruction all around! Our artillery is still deploying. Seconds of violent horror and then let's go forward! A line of riflemen lies in front of us. Can't tell if they're friend or foe. Forward! Down! Go! Down! Shoot, opponents at the edge of the forest!... Howling, a roaring, rattling and hammering makes every command imperceptible! But each individual feels that he cannot remain lying here, and in leaps and bounds things proceed forward. The legs threaten to give way. The chest is panting, the face full of dust and earth, sweat pours from every pore! You can't go on anymore. You aim and shoot and stay rooted to the ground. Charge!!! How the bugles blare![30]

Despite the heavy Russian fire, the Kaiserjägers charged again and continued to push forward towards the forest, where enemy officers were desperately trying to rally their men for another counter-attack, albeit with little success. 'I ordered Lieutenant Yaroshevsky... to leave the edge of the forest and advance,' wrote Oboznenko. 'But only three people jumped out with him. Then I began threatening them with a revolver and beating them with the handle, but the men stayed down and did not move.'[31]

The situation worsened further when the neighbouring 140th Zaraysk Infantry Regiment broke. Seeing them retreat, the commander of the 35th Division ordered his men to withdraw as well. Shortly afterwards, the Kaiserjägers reached the forest and entered Tarnoczyn later that evening. The village had been set on fire by the retreating Russians. On their first day in battle, the regiment had lived up to its reputation, inflicting more than 1,000 casualties on the enemy and capturing sixteen guns, while their own losses were relatively light. To the right, the k.u.k. KJR 3 and 4 also attacked with great spirit, but there the Russians were better prepared and the progress was slow and costly.

The decisive blow of the day, however, was struck by the Archduke's 3rd Division around the villages of Wasylów and Przewodów. Ján Hrušovský, a Slovak and a rarity in the almost entirely Germanic k.u.k. IR 59 from Salzburg, remembered the moment the first order to attack was issued:

We looked at one another, pale-faced and speechless. Then we slowly turned away and quietly looked down, heads bowed toward the ground. Corporal Oberleutner couldn't quite get the pipe to his mouth, and our small Lieutenant Holzinger clumsily pulled a cigarette case out of his pocket and lit one with trembling fingers. I really don't know if I am supposed to feel ashamed, but suddenly and without warning, my left ear filled with noise, and I felt a cold, unpleasant sweat under my armpits.[32]

The regiment was advancing towards Przewodów through fields of wheat as tall as the men themselves. At first, it was easy, but then the Russians suddenly opened up with rifles and machine-guns. 'Above us, something whistled, buzzed, not unlike the buzz of a mosquito,' remembered Hrušovský. 'Again and again. A whole swarm of mosquitoes seemed to be buzzing over our heads. Pa-pa-pa-pa-pa-pa... a shrill crackling began somewhere from the distant beet fields to our left. A machine-gun.' The officers and NCOs urged their men forward, but the Russian bullets soon found their mark:

Suddenly, something whistled close by with a ridiculously tiny squeal and landed with a dull thud. I looked up and saw a soldier with a child-like face looking at us full of surprise, then his face filled with fear as he fell, grabbing at strands of wheat, wanting to stand back up with great effort, coughing, the stalks under him turning red with drops of blood – falling again. I heard a somewhat shaky, small, and silent crying, as when a baby cries. I turned my head away with horror and ran on.[33]

The men involuntarily threw themselves to the ground, pressing their heads down as low as possible, but a lieutenant yelled out the order to fix bayonets and charge the village:

We stuck our short, sharp bayonets onto the muzzles of our rifles, and somewhat slowly, with great effort, we lifted ourselves up, looking into each other's faces in disbelief. Yes, there are times when everyone feels the same and we can express it with our eyes. It happens at lightning speed, but everyone understands how his comrade feels. I don't know how it happened, but I completely stopped thinking and feeling. I didn't want to think at all... I only remember that we rushed down the hill like an avalanche... We flew forward, wild, unstoppable.[34]

Soon they found the enemy. 'In front of me, out of the fog', wrote Hrušovský, 'rose greenish uniforms with green hats. I remember one such uniform taking aim at me. The bullet whizzed right by my ear.' The instinct to survive took over:

From our throats came a wild... inhuman roar... A figure in [that] greenish uniform and a peaked cap with a crazed... look jumped up as if from the ground itself, jabbing his bayonet around in front of my chest; I parried and immediately stuck my entire bayonet into his stomach. He looked at me quite closely, with wide uncomprehending eyes, and when I pulled [it out], he flailed his hands about and fell... disappearing into the fog... The village was ours.[35]

Nearby, Wasylów fell too, but casualties were customarily high. The k.u.k. IR 14 had so many wounded that its medical detachment ran out of bandages. The Russian XVII Corps broke and began retreating north, leading Plehve to abandon all hopes of a massed offensive. Instead, Auffenberg now began to detect the possibility of a double encirclement of his enemy. He thus ordered his flanks to resume the offensive in the morning, creating a pincer movement, while the remainder of his army should keep pressure on the Russian centre, pinning it in place. His Fourth Army was preparing to wrest an impressive victory from the Russians, but as orders were being issued on the evening of 28 August, further east a disaster was already unfolding, threatening not only to undo the early successes in Poland, but the entire Austro-Hungarian campaign.

19

Not Exactly Winning

France

After word arrived of the Russian disaster at Tannenberg, the Allies in the west lost any hope of deliverance from the other side of Europe. As their retreating armies crept further south with the Germans in pursuit, Paris watched with increasing consternation. Government officials were wondering if they should flee the city by 29 August, and the mood of uncertainty was already evident among the population, too. Felix Klein witnessed the scene at Montparnasse, one of the city's main train stations, where people clambered to get out of Paris. The suddenness of it all was jarring. Rumour had it that the Germans were now at Reims, some 90 miles north-east of the capital. The last Klein had heard, they were still in Namur. 'We feel the victims of a horrible dream,' he wrote.[1]

Joffre had no jurisdiction in Paris. He oversaw the war zone, and the city was designated within the zone of the interior. The responsibility for the defence of the capital lay with two new men: one was the returning minister of war, Alexandre Millerand. The other was the military-governor, General Joseph Gallieni, a sixty-five-year-old, walrus-moustached veteran of colonial campaigns. When they arrived to replace their axed predecessors, it was 26 August, and about 100 miles away, the British were being defeated at Le Cateau.

The scheme for defending Paris revolved around turning the city into a giant entrenched camp, but to achieve this would require forty days. The reason why so little of the work had been done in advance was that to construct a circle of trenches, concrete shelters and wire entanglements in an uninterrupted ring around the capital would require a vast amount of destruction, much of it to private property. Before the work could begin, the authorities had to decide that it was absolutely necessary.

Clearly this threshold had long since been reached when Gallieni began work. The Entrenched Camp was supposed to cover a radius of nearly 20 miles from the Eiffel Tower, but once the line was instigated, it still had fifty-nine gates, five main railway lines, two canals and four sewer systems where the enemy might breach it. The men that Gallieni had to seal all of this were territorials, and they had been at their posts a little over a week. He was unimpressed. Meanwhile, the President of the Republic, Raymond Poincaré, was panicking. When he asked Gallieni how long Paris could hold out, and should the government leave, Gallieni pulled no punches:

> I answer... that the Entrenched Camp... is by no means prepared to receive the shock of an enterprising enemy, that the batteries are not armed, that the ammunition is not in place, that infantry works are barely started, that supplies do not match the mobilization directions, that the territorial troops making up the garrison are in insufficient number and without serious military education; in short, that Paris is by no means prepared to support a siege.[2]

Gallieni was fixated on obtaining some 16 per cent of France's regular soldiers to defend the city. Such a demand appeared ludicrous to Joffre, who was charged with repelling the German army from the whole of France, and was dealing with a disorderly retreat. 'In any case,' Gallieni advised that, 'the government was to be ready to leave Paris as soon as possible.'[3]

His problems multiplied. Labour was one. In some places each man was responsible for constructing 600 feet of the line. Since the best available men had been sent to the front, those left tended to be too old or too young to be the most efficient workers. Supply was worrying, too. For example, cement was an essential component of putting Paris in a state of defence, yet nobody kept huge supplies of it in the city, and factories near Paris were rare. Even if items were available, requisitioning them from stores was turgid. On 16 August an engineering officer had asked for eight automobiles to move materials. He was granted his request immediately, but by the time Gallieni took over ten days later, there was still no sign of his vehicles.

*

Gallieni's new regime came like 'a thunderclap' as the threat hardened. Without delay, trenches were dug, and positions for gun batteries and barricades put up. There were plenty of civilians in a city of two and a half million people, many of them out of work since the start of the war. Gallieni used the labour exchange to mobilize them, and the unions became involved. Those organizations began motivating thousands of men, telling them which yards and workshops to report to. 'Each workman was told that he had to take a blanket or a coat, a bowl, cutlery.'[4] There were 23,000 of them toiling by the end of September, grouped together where possible by their place of civilian employment for the sake of efficiency.

This work left immediate scars upon Paris. The first victims were trees. In some areas, this was not just a case of clearing a field of fire for guns. To defend a city this size, sometimes full-scale deforestation was needed; the equivalent of wiping out Sherwood Forest three times over. However, it was not possible to simply bulldoze the whole lot; in some areas, trees needed to be cut down carefully to form stakes and defensive barriers. Georges Ohnet, the French novelist, owned a property at Emrainville just beyond Paris's eastern suburbs. He received word that 400 men had turned up with shovels and machinery and dug trenches throughout his park, hacking down his trees with impunity. He was lucky. In all, 12,000 homes were slated for complete destruction, but even then the work was not finished. Once the buildings were demolished, instead of a house blocking a field of fire, there was a pile of rubble. Where was it all going? Who was going to move it? Using what? The impact on property owners was catastrophic, and the best that Gallieni could organize to compensate them in the immediate aftermath was a system whereby local mayors were given time to warn their constituents about what was about to happen, so that they might organize some kind of shelter for Parisians made brutally homeless by their own government.

What did civilians make of all of this? The city was not of any strategic value to Joffre's war plans, but it was incredibly symbolic. For Paris to fall again, less than fifty years after Prussians marched into the streets, would have been devastating. Parisians had also heard rumours about German atrocities occurring in Belgium. On 30 August, as the Allies were reeling and Joffre was about to learn of the Russian shock at Tannenberg, Gallieni again asked for troops and again Joffre would not provide them. 'I have the impression that he considers Paris as sacrificed,' wrote the military governor.[5]

For Parisians, that day also marked the first occasion when a German pilot swanned into view and dropped bombs on them. Until then, war had just caused life in the capital to be dull. No more coffee on the pavement, no theatre, no cinema, no music. 'We know that many of the treasures of the Louvre have been safely put away in iron or steel cases, so that if a German aeroplane should drop bombs there is every chance that they will not be injured,' wrote one Parisian.[6] Notices had gone up all over the city proclaiming that military traffic had priority, everywhere. 'We now slow down at all corners to avoid being crushed by some motor-car… going at breakneck speed.'[7] By 28 August, however, there was a burgeoning panic, much of it caused by a lack of official information:

> The communiques tell us nothing… The man who serves you with coffee mutters angrily that it is useless to provision yourself, for all Paris will be in the flames of revolutionary fire before another week has gone. A letter from

England says that it is rumoured in London that the flower of the British Army is already 'wiped out'. How I have learnt to hate that phrase since the war began![8]

One of the first things Gallieni did with his sweeping powers was put an end to this press hysteria. The content of Paris's newspapers was already regulated, but he went much further. In the pre-internet world, extra editions were a profitable way to keep news cycling. In August 1914, editors turned out multiple extras a day to make money, each full of more fantastic rumours than the last, because they did not actually have any new information to print. 'The hawkers appear,' wrote George Ohnet, 'running along the sidewalks, shouting, waving their printed junk at all hours. *"Ask for the latest news! Important operations!"'* Most of the time, the reader's money was spent in vain. 'Fooled... nothing but the same information that has already been given in a previous edition.'[9] Gallieni banned extras. He also banned vendors from shouting out their headlines. 'The difference this order has made to the life of the city is extraordinary,' wrote one journalist.[10]

Some Parisians were defiant about a siege. 'People began to say... "Let them come! One does not enter Paris so easily. And if you get in, you'll have to get out. The women of Paris would have only to throw [their furniture], through the windows, on the head of the invaders, to crush them!"' Underneath this bravado, though, was 'a note of acute anxiety... The steady advance of the enemy, the obstinate silence of the War Office, the rumours... and the [aerial] bomb-throwing episode, were all disquieting factors... pessimism was gradually mounting in many hearts.'[11] As yet, the people in the capital did not know if their city would be defended, or given up to the enemy like Brussels. On 30 August, as the Germans raced south towards Paris, those living close to her outdated forts were given an hour's notice to leave their homes. In affluent suburbs like Saint Germain and Versailles, they fled.

The enemy was expected imminently and civilian anxiety peaked at the news that their government was abandoning them. At a council of ministers, the war minister told his colleagues it was time to go. German planes had bombed Paris, the news from Tannenberg meant there would be no deliverance from the east, and the German artillery was nearly within range of the city. On 2 September the government departed for Bordeaux in the south-west. Gallieni arrived at the ministry of war early in the morning that day. 'The courtyard is full of huge moving [lorries] that transport the archives... A bailiff introduces me to Mr. Millerand, alone in his completely empty office.' The two men shook hands. 'I cannot prevent myself', wrote Gallieni, from 'still insisting on the precarious situation in which the entrenched camp is found and on the need... to increase defence troops by all possible means.'[12] Millerand's parting gift as he left Gallieni to defend the city in the government's absence was to put the new Sixth Army Joffre had formed at his disposal. The catch? Millerand had given a parting gift to Joffre too: he placed Gallieni under Joffre's command.

On 3 September Paris awoke to a proclamation from Gallieni. He believed in keeping it short:

Members of the government of the Republic have left Paris to give new impetus to the national defence.

I received the mandate to defend Paris against the invader.

I will fulfil this mandate to the end.[13]

The knowledge, finally, that the army would stand and fight sent a surge of relief passing through the city. In the Entrenched Camp, all of the soldiers were at their posts. The city was sealed off. Joffre had given permission for the bridges approaching the capital to be blown, and artillery was pointed in the direction of the invader. The city would surely fall, but Gallieni intended to fight to the death, tying up German resources and disrupting the enemy for the benefit of the rest of France. Paris waited.

*

Meanwhile, among the retreating Allied forces, a man would have to have been blind not to realize that things were going badly. 'I remember particularly the date 1st September', wrote Arthur Corbett-Smith, 'because we then realized for the first time that something was wrong about that *"strategical retirement"* business. Our maps included Belgium and north-eastern France, but Compiegne was the farthest point south.'[14] As they passed through that town and out the other side, and marched off the map, he realized that nobody had planned for this.

The longer the retreat went on, the more gruesome it became. Seriously wounded men faced a desperate fate. Casualties were being evacuated from a hospital in Saint-Quentin. 'The movable cases were hastily got into ambulances... and carried off.' For some patients, this was their third flight, and not everyone found transport. Those who missed out could choose: wait for the enemy, or try to keep up with the rest of the BEF. 'So, mingled with the retreating army were the ghosts of men swathed in bloody bandages, some clinging to vehicles on which they had found a seat.' More staggered blindly along. 'Others, again, just dropping out, to huddle exhausted by the roadside.'[15]

With his French cavalry regiment, one night Étienne Letard came across a convoy of wounded in basic forage trucks.

They are *chasseurs alpins*, reservists, who fought on the Somme; some... horribly mutilated, are dying. To escape the enemy they allowed themselves to be hoisted into these improvised ambulances not even lined with a bale of straw, and they endured the journey without a murmur... By the light of a lamp the cars are emptied; blackish bloodstains appear on the floor, where the bodies had been; the wounded are taken to a basic aid station... This night, we note a new horror... these mutilated limbs, these scalped heads... this tattered flesh.[16]

At the end of August, the terrain became much more difficult to traverse. Paul Lintier spent a day climbing to the top of a steep plateau with his guns, and at the top he found stragglers.

Many of them looked as though they would never get up again... There was already something skull-like about their faces; the eyes, wide open and bright with fever, stared fixedly from out their sunken sockets... Their matted hair was glued to their foreheads with sweat, which slowly trickled down the drawn, emaciated faces, leaving white zigzag furrows in the dirt of dust and smoke... Hardly one of the wounded was bandaged... [Some] still managed to hobble along with the aid of their rifles, which they used as crutches. They begged us to find a place for them on the gun carriages.[17]

Not all survived the ordeal. Etienne Letard got a nasty shock when he jumped a low, loose stone wall and his horse reared in horror. 'I drew rein. A sob burst from my lips.' He had stumbled across a gruesome scene:

A score of corpses lay scattered on that sloping stubble-field. They were Zouaves. They seemed almost to have been placed there deliberately, for the bodies were lying at about an equal distance from one another... Their rifles were still by their side, with the bayonets fixed. The one nearest to us was lying with his face to the ground and was still grasping his weapon... . He was a handsome fellow, thin and dark. No wound was visible, but his face was strikingly pale under the red chéchia which had been pulled down over his ears...[18]

*

Just because they were advancing, these days were no easier for hundreds of thousands of Germans who were getting further from their supply lines as they marched far into enemy territory. This was anything but a triumphant procession. With the most ground to cover, at one point Kluck's First Army left their nearest railhead nearly 90 miles behind them as they marched 17 hours a day. More than half of their lorries and motorized transport had broken down, and fodder was not getting to the horses. With IR 84, Andreas Kylling was exhausted:

> Up in the morning at around four o'clock, a shot of thin coffee and a piece of dry bread, if you have some, and then it's onwards... The rifle hangs in its sling around the neck, the hands grasp the straps of the knapsack, the head bends downwards. One only sees the sole of the man's boot in front... The night is spent on the naked ground. The knapsack is used as a pillow, the rifle lies ready in the arm.[19]

For one unit of sappers, the ordeal started on 24 August when they began pursuing the French Fourth Army: 'Dust was covering our uniforms and skin to the depth of almost an inch.' Like the French and British in front of them, Germany's troops were also suffering 'a great tobacco famine'.[20] Drinking water was more of a problem than for the Allies, too. There were concerns that their enemies, including civilians, would have poisoned the supply and left it waiting for the oncoming German armies. They were ordered not to drink. 'The natural consequence was that the soldiers began to hate the population which they now considered their bitterest enemies.'[21]

Following the route of the Allied retreat meant that German soldiers also had to clear away debris so that their own armies could get through. Arriving in the town of Château Thierry on the Marne on 3 September, a terrible sight met the men of IR 86. French troops had arrived the night before. The inhabitants cheered and showered them with gifts, until a nearby German artillery battery opened fire. 'We saw piles of dead civilians among those in uniform,' wrote Hans Christian Brodersen. 'Torn-off limbs lay among the people who'd been shot to pieces, and splashes of blood had coloured the walls and windows. It was a terrible scene of destruction that will never leave my memory.'[22] Another Dane with the regiment described 'a feeling, like I was about to cry, [which] rose from the chest to the throat'.[23] He turned away in horror.

Back on the heights above the Meuse, the unit of sappers was ordered to clear obstructions, including moving bodies off the road in the worst heat of the day. 'Two men would take a dead soldier by his head and feet and fling him in a ditch. Human corpses were here treated... as a board in bridge building. Severed arms and legs were flung through the air... in the same manner.' It sickened one witness to think about this afterwards:

> We were not strong enough to get the bodies of the horses out of the way so we procured some horse roaming about without a master, and fastened it to a dead one to whose leg we had attached a noose, and thus we cleared the carcass out of the road. The portions of human bodies hanging in the trees we left... undisturbed.[24]

Supply lines were being stretched further and further, and so the Germans also looted the dead. 'We searched the bottles and knapsacks... for eatable and drinkable things, and enjoyed [them] with the heartiest appetite imaginable. Hunger and thirst are pitiless customers that cannot be turned away by fits of sentimentality.' As they marched on, they found dehydrated and dying Frenchmen by the roadside. 'Even if we had wanted to help them we should not have been allowed to do so, for the order was "Forward!"'[25]

Later in the war, this German asked himself 'whether I thought those things improper or immoral at the time?' Should he feel bad for all that he had been made to do? Should he apologize for the black humour that sustained them all? 'Why were we joyful and why did we crack jokes? Because it was the others and not ourselves who had to lose their lives that time. Because it was a life and death struggle. It was either we or they. We had a right to be glad and chase all sentimentality to the devil. Were we not soldiers, mass murderers, barbarians?' He did not want war, he did not want to kill people, this was not on him: 'It was a world in which [soldiers] were mere marionettes, guided and controlled by a superior power.'[26]

*

2 September marked the beginning of the end for the Schlieffen Plan, and by now this was dawning on Kluck. At this point, he knew surprisingly little about how events were playing out elsewhere. He 'imagined... that all the armies were advancing from victory to victory, and that the enemy was being decisively beaten along the whole front'.[27] Things had now taken a turn for the better in the east for the Germans but Moltke had to compromise in France, because in the panic following the fighting at Gumbinnen he had shipped two corps to East Prussia. He no longer planned to surround Paris. Instead, at the end of the day on 2 September, he ordered his armies to pass to the eastern side of the French capital, pushing the Allies south-east between Paris and Verdun. The worst aspect of this for Kluck was that he was now to drop back and follow behind Bülow. Fuelled by dislike for his comrade, Kluck was also a firebrand, and so the idea of plodding along behind his more cautious comrade was abhorrent to him.

So Kluck disobeyed orders, turned his force south-east and drove the enemy towards the Marne. He believed that the French and the British were there for the taking. His excuse was that if he waited the necessary time to get in line behind Bülow's Second Army, 'the [enemy] would regain the complete freedom of action of which it had been deprived. Should the First Army hold back, the great success for which the Supreme Command was confidently striving... could no longer be hoped for.'[28] The First Army marched on.

Out on the road, the strain was becoming too much for the hollow men still trudging away from the oncoming enemy. The BEF was a wretched sight:

They were complete wrecks, these batches of stragglers. Often we came across them huddled up by a signpost... like a little flock of sheep... Some we put up in the wagons, those too weak to shuffle along; and others we marched along till we could find a regiment to tack them onto. 'Cook's Tourists' we called them, till the term with us became almost an official one.[29]

The Allies knew how close the enemy was getting to Paris since French and British airmen had spotted the German columns. The importance of aerial reconnaissance in this, the first major conflict to see airborne warfare, was pivotal, but ground crews – the mechanics and riggers – could barely keep the machines in the air anymore. The aircraft were feeble constructions to begin with: wood, doped canvas and wires, and they did not react well to being run at all hours of the day and night in hot, dry weather, with only minimal maintenance, or being kept outside for want of hangars or tents.

James McCudden was responsible for some of the engines of the Royal Flying Corps's 3 Squadron. All he could do was patch up the machines as best he could: 'We were away from our transport... for days, and the mechanics who flew with the flight therefore had their hands very full in order to keep the machines serviceable under difficulties, for we only carried a small tool kit [in the air].'[30]

Often they tied the machines down out in the open. They weighed so little, that one gust of wind could spell disaster, and McCudden frequently worked through the night before going to sleep under a wing. He was sharp, and he had soon queried the need for these constant retirements. 'Captain Charlton was sitting in the Blériot and I noticed that he was looking very grave, so I asked if we were retiring. "No!" he replied! "We are just drawing the Germans on, and when we have got them far enough we will encircle them and capture the whole German Army."' McCudden had a nose for bullshit. 'Of course it was very necessary for our officers to keep our spirits up as much as possible, as it was quite obvious to us all that we were not exactly winning.'[31]

By 2 September, the BEF's railheads were only 15 miles north-east of Paris, and troops were about to retire across the Marne, some 150 miles from where the Battle of Mons had been fought ten days earlier. At Germigny-l'Evêque, 40 miles east of Paris, a local watched throughout the night, forlorn, 'the English army, in full retreat... I will never forget this endless and sad procession. A mournful silence hovered, disturbed only by the cadenced steps of the soldiers.'[32] That day British and then French intelligence confirmed that three corps from Kluck's army were moving south-east towards Château Thierry. Something had to be done, and an idea was starting to evolve in Joffre's head.

His plan involved letting Kluck continue to overextend his army, marching out into a salient that the Allies could then surround from three sides and attack. However, Joffre knew that he was going to have just one single shot at a massive counteroffensive. His army commanders were counselling patience. Their men were exhausted, and everyone was mindful of the worst-case scenario. If they attacked too soon and the line collapsed, France would be left wide open. So, for now, Joffre would let Kluck come, his force weakening by the day, as the Allies gathered their strength.

In the meantime, he got his house in order. His most significant move was to sack Charles Lanrezac as commander of the Fifth Army and replace him with General Louis Franchet d'Espèrey of I Corps. It was not a decision he enjoyed making, and there was a certain amount of scapegoating going on, but in his defence Joffre said: 'You can wage war only with men who have faith in their success, who by their mastery of themselves know how to impose their will on their subordinates and dominate events.'[33] At the time, he did not believe that Lanrezac was one of those men.

In Paris, Gallieni was in harmony with Joffre's strategy. In fact, he had already begun sending the Sixth Army east to find Kluck's flank. These men would attack the Germans from another river, the Ourcq. From yet another direction would come the BEF, who finally appeared ready to slot into the gap between the Fifth and Sixth Armies. Joffre was most proud of his new man, d'Espèrey, when the latter said that he too would be ready to fight. In fact, Joffre was almost in awe:

Barely 24 hours ago, [he] had just taken command of a retreating army… It was feared that the combat capacity of this army… would be considerably reduced. With an intelligent audacity which is only found in the soul of true warlords, admirably understanding the situation, [he] did not hesitate to answer 'yes' to a question which would have made many others cringe. Furthermore, the initiative of the new commander of the Fifth Army had succeeded in re-establishing understanding between his army and the British… The role of Franchet d'Espèrey on 4th September, 1914 deserves to be highlighted in history.[34]

Joffre could breathe. The interminable uncertainty was almost over, and he was seizing back control of France's fate. Even the population of Paris was ready for the reckoning that they knew was coming. 'Nowhere do I find real anxiety,' wrote Felix Klein. 'The only sentiment… is curiosity; I believe that if the Prussians go away without attacking us there will be a certain amount of disappointment.'[35]

At his headquarters, as 4 September came to a close, Kluck had little idea of the French scheme. 'The First Army will continue its march… tomorrow, so as to force the French away eastwards. If the British offer opposition they are to be driven back.'[36] What he did not know was that his army had come as close to conquering France as it would ever get. That chance had already passed him by, and the stage was now set for the miracle on the Marne.

20

Live Bait

War at Sea

I f the scale of the First World War inflicted a brutal learning curve upon armies, it was every bit as mind-blowing for those at sea. Since the last great clash of nations, several factors had changed naval warfare beyond all recognition: steam, electricity, weapons and shipping design. Technological advances challenged not only tactics that had been sound for centuries, but also ethics as well.

These changes dragged neutral seamen into the line of fire. On any given merchant ship, the crew was made up of myriad nationalities. Scandinavian seamen were prolific throughout the world, and a war memorial in Copenhagen commemorates almost 650 sailors who were killed on Danish ships. The list includes seamen from Scandinavia, Iceland and more than thirty additional countries. Many fell victim to an invention that Germany had embraced widely: mines. The British saw mines as a defensive tool, and they were not defensively minded. They were confident of victory if push came to shove. Germany, however, had lost the naval arms race, and mines were a weapon perfect for the underdog. It did not matter that the Allies had more ships and more firepower if new weapons could be employed at comparatively minimal risk to somewhat level the odds.

On the outbreak of war German ships had gone straight out to lay minefields across major trade routes. More were deposited to bob free on the seas. Just as Britain's blockade would fall outside accepted legal parameters, so did laying mines beyond the entrance to your own harbours for protection. There was no way to control which ship might sail into your mine, or to whom the vessel might belong. Situated in between Britain and Germany in sea terms, Scandinavia was immediately impacted by German mines. The first Danish ship lost in the war, *Maryland*, foundered as early as 22 August 1914 when she approached the end of her journey home from Argentina carrying maize. She hit a mine, and then so did the *Christian Broberg*, on her way home from Portugal, as she searched for survivors. Five days later the Norwegian ship *Ena* was sunk 30 miles off Newcastle-upon-Tyne. Less than a week later, Sweden joined this lamentable club. In the same area, the *St Paul* was 28 miles to the north-east of England when she struck yet another mine and sank. In all, forty-two neutral ships were lost to mines in 1914 alone.

Having not considered using minefields in this way, the Royal Navy had not invested in combating them, either. At the beginning of the war, Britain only had ten minesweepers, all old, roughly converted boats. The navy began immediately seizing fishing trawlers to plug the gap. These were tough boats with powerful engines, capable of dragging heavy equipment. By 8 August, almost 100 trawlers, along with their regular civilian crews, were already setting off in pairs to sweep the seas clear of mines.

On 3 August, the *Königin Luise*, a commandeered German ferry, was put to work as a minelayer. After a poor attempt to disguise her as a British ship, she left Emden in north-west Germany with 200 mines and made for the Thames Estuary. Spotted by ships from Harwich, she fled, jettisoning her mines as she went, but was chased down by a flotilla led by the light cruiser *Amphion* and attacked. By 12.15 p.m. on 5 August, her crew had begun abandoning ship. The *Königin Luise* rolled over and disappeared beneath the waves.

The next day, making for home, Captain Fox of *Amphion* attempted to steer clear of the area where he thought the *Königin Luise* had dropped her mines, but at 6.35 a.m. his ship struck one of them and exploded. *Amphion* became the first ship of the Royal Navy sunk in the First World War. Survivors, some of them badly burnt, were rescued by the destroyers sailing with her. Four men had lost legs, two more both of their arms. One hundred and forty-eight British sailors were killed, along with eighteen survivors of the *Königin Luise*. Plucked from the water when their ship sank, they had now been killed by their own weapons.

Fox survived, and when he assumed his next command, he was out for revenge. 'I don't want no honour and glory,' he told the crew of *Undaunted*, 'all I'm out for is blood.' He went on: 'For every man I lost on my last ship I mean to have ten in return.' 'He'd had the decks painted red,' recalled one crewman. 'In action I see a lot of blood sculling about,' he said. 'People get upset with seeing it.'... We boys, we thought the world of that.'[1]

*

As terrifying as the spectre of unseen mines was, their threat paled in comparison to the one posed by submarines. Once again, the Royal Navy had been ambivalent on the subject. The laws of the sea dating back centuries required that crews be allowed to safely evacuate their ship before it was destroyed or taken. A concealed attack from a submarine did not allow for that, and so the idea was regarded as barbaric. Surely nobody would resort to this? Sailors were terrified by the thought. However, at very beginning of the war, fear tended to far outweigh the actual threat. There were no depth charges yet to attack them, no method of detecting if they were beneath you. 'Had a bad attack of *submarinitis* at 4.00 p.m.,' recalled an officer aboard *Marlborough* on 6 August. 'Periscopes seen everywhere.'[2] The constant worry was exhausting. Two days later, they encountered miserable weather:

I shall be glad of it! Because it will keep off the submarines and we've had a filthy time with them today. About noon, ships reported sighting periscopes and eventually *Monarch* reported that a submarine had fired a torpedo... under her stern... it's rather unpleasant expecting to be torpedoed at any moment and makes me rather shy of using my cabin as I should be shut in like a cat if anything happened.[3]

At Scapa Flow, Charles Heald was serving as a surgeon aboard the dreadnought *Conqueror* on 1 September:

> Sudden lights far out... followed immediately by siren sounded rapidly. Very shortly news came that one or more submarines were actually in the harbour where they would be in a position to do infinite damage as the whole of our fleet was at anchor... Shortly after the siren, deliberate single shots were heard and an endless stream of picket boats dashed out to ram the enemy or at least break her periscope.[4]

*

For all of the energy wasted on false alarms, the threat of the submarine menace soon became violently real. The Royal Navy had a cruiser force made up of ships so slow that they were nicknamed the 'Live Bait Squadron'. In late September, three of its members, *Hogue*, *Aboukir* and *Cressy*, were bobbing off the Dutch coast without much purpose, and fatefully, two days earlier a German *Unterseeboot*, U-9, had nosed her way out into the North Sea under the command of Captain Otto Weddigen.

She was buffeted along by rough seas and high winds. 'Although 30 metres was sounded,' wrote watch officer Johannes Speiss, 'the boat was tossed about to such an extent on the bottom that we feared... damage to the hull and made haste to come to the surface.' After a tortuous journey, on 22 September the German submarine surfaced to examine her surroundings. 'Shortly before sunrise, the tanks were blown,' Speiss continued. 'I had the watch and was observing the horizon.' Crawling along, the only ships in sight were Dutch fishermen in the distance. Then, a way off, Speiss spotted the mast of what looked like a warship: 'Seeing a smoke cloud nearby all doubt disappeared: I had the motors stopped, and called Weddigen... He came immediately up to the conning tower and gave the order to submerge. Shortly afterwards the seas closed over us.'[5] It was not long before the captain confirmed that he could see three light cruisers through the periscope: *live bait.*

In the submarine crew rushed about fuelled by nervous energy, because they did not yet know what firing a torpedo would do to *them*. Another boat had only fired the first armed torpedo shortly before, and in the opening weeks of the war it was still believed that firing at close enough range might cave in the bow of a U-boat and destroy it. Speiss unscrewed the safety cover from the firing button and aimed at the middle of a ship. They were going to fire and then immediately dive. 'Under the greatest suspense everyone in the boat was counting the seconds... I pressed the firing button... and ran the periscope in with my left hand while calling down through the voice tube: "First tube fired."' Speiss was convinced that they were all going to die. He clung to the periscope fiercely with both hands. 'At once we heard a dull blow followed by a clear crash. Could that be the torpedo hit? Below, three cheers broke out and we in the conning tower joined in spontaneously. Nothing could be seen as we were at a depth of [50 feet] and the periscope was run in.'[6]

They were not dead. It had taken thirty seconds for their torpedo to reach *Aboukir* and for the sound to bounce back to *U-9*. As soon as they realized that their craft was still intact, the submariners shot to the surface to judge their work. The British ship was stricken. 'I noticed that the stern was down in the water considerably,' wrote Speiss. 'White smoke was pouring out of the four funnels, the bow was somewhat out of water, and the life boats had been lowered.' Slowly, *Aboukir* rolled over and vanished beneath the waves, taking 900 men with her.

Meanwhile I had gone below to the torpedo room to reload the first tube... Between times part of the crew were running back and forth in the boat to keep the boat in a horizontal position with the weight of their bodies... insofar as they were not occupied with the engines or torpedoes, [they] were chased back and forth in the boat continually by the order – 'All forward' or 'All aft', so that after about an hour everyone was 'done in'.[7]

Hogue was hit next, as she lowered boats to save survivors from *Aboukir*. Through the periscope, Speiss did not enjoy 'the gruesome impression made on us, by the drowning and struggling men who were in the midst of the mass of floating wreckage and clinging to the overturned lifeboats'.[8] *Cressy* was hit last. For good measure, Weddigen had their last torpedo fired at her as she listed in the water, 'bringing forth a large black cloud and then a gigantic white fountain. The giant with four stacks fell slowly but surely over to port, and like ants, the crew crawled first over the side and then on to the broad flat keel, until they disappeared under the waves. A tragic sight for seamen.'[9]

Weddigen now had to guide his boat home with hardly any current left in the batteries. They would have to travel on the surface most of the way. 'There was no enemy in sight, the sea had closed over the three cruisers. In the distance we saw a number of Dutch sail fishing vessels, which had spread all canvas to get clear of the accursed spot in haste. The weather was radiantly beautiful and even the swell had gone down considerably.'[10]

Admiral Reginald Tyrwhitt, commander at Harwich, raced to the scene. He found lifeboats and small craft drifting in the water. 'We went first up to a small English trawler which was loaded with men. They looked just like rows and rows of swallows on a telegraph line, all huddled together to keep themselves warm, they were all naked or nearly so.' In all, sixty-two officers and almost 1,400 men were lost. The Royal Navy had learnt a hard lesson. The next day, a message went out to all ships from the Admiralty: 'If a ship is torpedoed or struck by mines the disabled ship must be left to her fate and other large ships [must] clear out of the danger zone, calling up minor vessels to render assistance.'[11]

*

It does not matter if you have the most terrifying navy in the world if your opponent hides from you so that you cannot attack him. The British public had been expecting to defeat the *Kaiserliche Marine* quickly in the opening weeks of the war, and in epic, bloody fashion. The reality had proved very different. 'People have become... morose,' wrote an officer. 'The first cheerfulness has disappeared.'[12] Despite a flurry of success at Antivari, the French were no happier. 'The campaign is really off to a bad start,' wrote Vice-Amiral Amédée Bienaimé. Several ships were already under repair or run aground, 'and we are only on the fifteenth day of the war!'[13] To him, in the Adriatic, it seemed all immense risk and little reward.

21

The Avalanche

Galicia

I n Galicia, Conrad's northern thrust into Poland appeared to be proceeding well. His Fourth Army was in the process of encircling the Russian Fifth at Komarów, while his First Army had thrown the Russian Fourth back to Lublin. It was events in East Galicia, however, that were about to determine the outcome of the campaign. On 22 August, Conrad ordered the Third Army, commanded by General Rudolf von Brudermann, to advance east out of the Galician capital, Lemberg. Supporting troops were busy elsewhere or still en route, so Conrad only intended this to be a cautious probe. Brudermann, however, had other plans. A cavalryman hailing from an established military family, the fifty-six-year-old general was eager for glory.

As his men marched east, they had little intelligence about what lay ahead. They passed a steady stream of refugees moving in the opposite direction, recounting strong Russian forces around the village of Złoczów, some 37 miles east of Lemberg. Mixed in with the refugees were wounded soldiers, remnants of units that had already engaged the oncoming Russians in the borderlands. Sorry-looking cavalrymen who had crossed swords with Cossacks passed Fritz Lederhaas, an NCO of the k.u.k. IR 27, serving as a frightful preview of what might be in store. 'Many of the dragoons had lost their helmets... some 30 wounded horses with terrible lance and gunshot wounds dragged themselves behind. The poor animals suffered terribly. According to the dragoons, the fight raged just three hours from us. Well, in God's name!'[1]

Brudermann's understrength army was marching against a massive Russian force bearing down on Lemberg. This was where the Russians had expected the main Austro-Hungarian offensive to be conducted, not north into Poland, and they had stacked their Third and Eighth Armies here to meet it. As well as being heavily outnumbered, Brudermann was about to make a catastrophic error. The Russians had expected the Austro-Hungarians to take up a defensive position behind the river Gniła Lipa some 25 miles east of Lemberg. It was madness to cross and have the water at his back, but Brudermann did exactly that, pushing his troops over the river and straight towards the advancing Russians.

At daybreak on 26 August, a thick layer of mist covered the ground. Austro-Hungarian soldiers continued their march east. As the men passed through small Galician villages, they were greeted by kind civilians who offered them soda water, raspberries and tobacco. This heightened their spirits, but they suspected that the enemy was close. For officers of the k.k. Landsturm Infanterie Regiment Nr. 3 from Graz, the response to the announcement by their colonel that they might imminently cross swords with the tsar's armies was mixed. At first, they were 'thunderstruck at the sudden realization that the Russians had penetrated so deeply into Galicia'. However, the initial shock was quickly replaced with 'excitement of meeting the enemy so soon'.[2]

In the Russian camp, they were also not sure where they would find the enemy. One soldier about to enter battle for the first time wrote: 'We're counting the hours and minutes when, at last, we'll take part in the war, and we are only waiting for the command to go into battle. I'm not scared, [but] as soon as I think that I'll have to face a hail of bullets and bayonets, goosebumps cover my body.'[3] Another wrote about the moment his captain had told them that they would go into battle in the morning: 'The short word "*battle*", filled the soul with some strange trepidation, together with those passionate desires to quickly unravel it, see it firsthand, experience it and feel it.'[4] He would get his chance soon enough.

In the centre of Brudermann's line, General Emil Colerus von Geldern's III Corps was advancing on both sides of the Lemberg–Zoczów road. Everywhere, companies of infantry were marching across open fields or in columns down dusty thoroughfares, while despatch riders on horseback galloped to and fro. At first, there seemed to be no sign of the enemy, but as they passed the village of Bortków, the forward elements soon came under fire from a railway embankment, on which advanced posts of General Rusky's Third Army had taken up position.

Bullets whistled overhead and the soldiers quickly threw themselves to the ground. 'We gasp, bury our heads in the furrows, hold the rifle with bayonet fixed in our hands,' wrote Fritz Lederhaas. Then the order to attack was sounded, and the men rose to begin a bayonet charge towards the embankment. No sooner had they stood up than Russian artillery batteries opened fire. 'The enemy showers us with shells and shrapnel. Volley after volley!' continued Lederhaas. 'I'm already hearing the screams and sighs of the first wounded, seeing the first blood! My comrade is lying badly wounded in a potato field, filling me with rage, and I rush forward with eight men, the best marksmen of my squad.'[5] A platoon leader in the k.u.k. IR 27 described similar chaos as shells exploded and they were showered with earth: 'It's a hell of a racket. The crack of our shots, the thunderous burst of shrapnel mixes with the screams of the wounded... Everything indicates to us that we're dealing with vastly superior opposition on the Russian side.'[6] There were more Austro-Hungarian bayonet charges, and more devastating casualties.

Somehow, the Austro-Hungarian infantrymen pressed onwards, firing furiously. Such tactics had worked at Kraśnik and Komarów, when the two forces had been evenly matched, or when the Habsburg armies had outnumbered their opponents. At Złoczów it was a different matter. Here, Brudermann's troops faced enemy numbers that no amount of elan could overcome. 'The closer we get to the Russians, the more casualties we have,' noted Filip Kosmač of the k.u.k. IR 97. 'We saw Russian losses as well, but much fewer than ours, since they were mostly dug in.'[7] 'Hit by several bullets at once, I collapsed,' wrote Hans Weiland, a junior officer of the k.u.k. IR 87. 'I still remember the second I jumped up to charge, felt several blows, how my eyes turned blue, and with shouts of hurrah all around me and then falling with fading consciousness, the thought shot through my brain lightning-fast: death.'[8]

The hopelessness of the Austro-Hungarian attacks was perhaps best summed up by a young Slovenian soldier of the 87th: 'I will tell you things that you'll think are impossible,' he wrote to a teacher at home. 'Singing and screaming, we went into battle… without support, across an open field, against a hidden enemy, showered with bullets and shrapnel on both flanks; but we went on, the officers, among them the general himself and several majors, themselves with rifles in their hands, were in the front ranks. And death had a harvest, a terrible harvest!'[9]

General Alfred von Hinke was indeed in the front ranks of his brigade, which included the 87th. Seriously wounded in the leg, he had to crawl and drag himself along the ground before being grabbed and carried off the battlefield under Russian shrapnel fire. Pre-war honour codes called for officers to personally lead their men into battle, resulting in extraordinarily high casualties. Such foolhardy displays of gallantry were a waste of these men and their years of training and experience. Brandishing shiny sabres and wearing yellow sashes, the officers presented easy and tempting targets for the Russians. 'We follow the lessons of the [Russo-Japanese War] by always targeting the officers first,' a captured Russian officer told an Austrian journalist:

The more so because they're not difficult to pick out. First, the Austrian officer, contrary to us, does not carry a knapsack or a rifle; secondly, he's usually identified by the black strap of his binoculars… and thirdly, he is normally way in front when his men advance. Accordingly, we shoot primarily at everyone who precedes the skirmish line, at everyone who doesn't carry a rifle or knapsack, and… at those who are conspicuous because of any straps... And now you will understand your relatively high officer losses.[10]

To the south of the Lemberg–Złoczów road, the fighting continued until dusk in dense forests which caused great confusion. 'In some places [it] turned into a bayonet fight,' recalled a Russian officer. 'Due to the density of the forest, the shooting was carried out point-blank in some places, and after a short time we approached the main enemy forces at a distance of 450 paces.'[11] Often, any gains had to be won in desperate hand-to-hand combat. 'How fierce the battle in the forest was can be judged by the fact that the [58th Division] met the enemy with the bayonet eight times,' wrote General Dimitry Shcherbachev, commander of the Russian IX Corps.[12] A Slovenian soldier later attempted to describe such a fight, which he likened to a pub brawl with blades:

In front of you, you see a cluster of bayonets... Some hesitate, some waver, the cluster breaks, our knives sink into the flesh, blood splatters. In front of you, your comrade falls to the ground, you jump over him... Pounding, raging, moaning, and screaming. This is not just a noise anymore, it's howling. And in the midst of it, you don't know whether we are winning or losing... this unawareness pushes you forward... You care for your life less than you do for a cigarette. Only one thought keeps you going: to do as much damage as possible and to kill as many as you can.[13]

Despite some minor Austro-Hungarian successes, mounting casualties and stiffening Russian resistance soon caused III Corps' attacks to fall apart. 'At 11 o'clock, our line was so broken that we could go on no further,' wrote Filip Kosmač. 'We received reinforcements... and together we made a couple more jumps forward towards a hill... We started digging in... The enemy fire was as close to us as it could possibly be, with machine-guns and cannons. The crashing and banging was hellish.'[14] By now, the physical strain of the continuous marching and fighting, the burning August heat, the dust being thrown up by boots, horses and artillery shells, and the violent Russian fire preventing supplies from reaching the men in the front line, all began to take a toll on Austro-Hungarian soldiers. 'My eyes go black, hunger and a raging thirst plague me,' wrote Fritz Lederhaas.[15] The countless wounded now littering the battlefield also suffered greatly from unbearable thirst: 'Their first request when wounded was always "Water, water, oh please water,"' remembered Filip Kosmač. But no water could be brought forward. Russian fire also prevented the stretcher-bearers from doing their work. 'The wounded, covered in blood... they called on God and Mary for help, they called for their mother, father, or wife, but in the afternoon, towards evening, everything fell silent.'[16] In many units, ammunition was running low, as inexperienced troops had completely emptied their cartridge pouches during the first attack, firing wildly at a well-entrenched enemy.

By afternoon, the battle was entering its final stage and when the 22nd Landwehr Division, which got off to a slow start, finally entered the fight on III Corps' right, it met such strong Russian resistance that all attacks fell apart immediately. 'Our troops went forward like calves to the slaughterhouse,' wrote Ivan Matičič of the k.k. LIR 27:

Before, we always thought that everything would go as well as it had done on the training ground and at the parades... But now... Everything was crashing, whistling, flying about and the Galician fields were covered in blood. We had not imagined such a war, and were never told about it by our officers, who were now all surprised and headless as well and hiding by any means, leaving the leadership to young cadets who weren't much better.[17]

The divisional retreat turned into a rout which was exploited by the Russians, who launched an attack against III Corps' centre. With his flank turned, Colerus was forced to order his corps to retreat. By evening, the tattered remains of most of Brudermann's regiments were running back under a hail of enemy fire. 'They shot as if hell itself had opened up. But we ran and dropped like crazed and frightened beasts. The best of our soldiers were destroyed there,' wrote Filip Kosmač with scorn. 'For the Emperor and the homeland, in the field of honour and glory!'[18] Behind them remained a ghastly scene. 'The rising moon casts its ghostly shadows upon the battlefield,' recalled Fritz Lederhaas. 'The sight of the mortally wounded lying around is horrific. Scattered farmsteads overflowing with wounded are in flames.'[19] Lying by the side of the road, one man with a broken leg cried out: 'Help, help comrades, have mercy on me!'[20] But no one stopped. 'We tiredly pulled back along the road we'd so proudly walked down in the afternoon,' wrote one soldier in his diary. 'Retreat.'[21]

Brudermann's Third Army had no clear picture of casualties at the end of day, just the realization that the outcome was bad. The Russians collected the wounded. Among them was Hans Weiland of k.u.k. IR 87, who had received a bayonet wound and nine bullet wounds, one piercing his larynx. Cossacks found him, threw water in his face to see if he was alive, and after relieving him of all personal belongings, including his footwear, transported him to a dressing station, where a horrible scene awaited:

Thousands of wounded Austrians and Russians lay… moaning, wailing, whimpering, dying. The Slovenes and Germans kept quiet, the Russians moaned dully, the Italians from the 97th Infantry Regiment yelled: madonna! madonna!… A Russian lay in the dust next to me. A shot had ripped out his jaw and tongue. Still wanting to speak with the stub of his tongue, he gurgled, vomited blood, wrestled with his hands and feet.[22]

Soon, Weiland was transported to Złoczów 'with two Styrians, one of whom had received seventeen stabs in a bayonet fight, I was loaded hand and foot onto a dung wagon, and a Ruthenian peasant, accompanied by a Landsturm man, drove off with us… A painful, bitter journey. The jolting and banging tore the bandages open, the wounds began to bleed again.' Crossing the battlefield, Weiland witnessed the remains of III Corps' shattered units. 'The corpses lay on top of each other in the ditch by the railway embankment, along the road lay entire platoons... side by side, aligned and arranged as on the parade ground. This picture of the dead brothers hurt more than any wounds... On the first day of battle! What a terrible thought!'[23]

*

Meanwhile, further south along the Złota Lipa river, XII Corps had also been engaged in heavy fighting with Alexei Brusilov's Eighth Army, and had suffered equally terrible losses. Kálmán Tulics was a gendarme attached to the 38th Honvéd Division. Witnessing a field hospital in action, he recalled: 'I didn't know what to do with myself. My eyes just filled with tears when I saw all those many, many wounded. There was one whose hands were missing, another whose legs were missing. Many had their heads bandaged so that only their eyes were visible. And through great moans, growls, and wailing, they awaited the transport to the hospital... It was awful to see that many people suffer.'[24]

*

On 27 August Brudermann attempted another attack, but his men were spent and it was disastrous. His Third Army's offensive strength was completely expended, and the following day Conrad ordered Brudermann to retreat to a defensive line behind the Gniła Lipa to protect Lemberg. Meanwhile, the Second Army, which was still arriving from the Balkans, was urged to move quickly into position on their right.

Once behind the river, Brudermann's battered troops began digging in, but soon, in the early morning of 29 August, Russian guns begun shelling III Corps' new positions. A few Austro-Hungarian batteries replied, but with little impact as most were suffering shell shortages. Again, the Russians enjoyed significant artillery superiority, sometimes even to their own surprise. One Russian officer wrote excitedly: 'You have no idea how good our artillery is! It's simply incredible! I attribute 90 per cent of our victories to it.'[25]

The Russians were about to attempt to finish their enemy in Galicia. The task of breaking through the new Gniła Lipa line would fall to Brusilov's Eighth Army, which struck Austria–Hungary's XII Corps with three of its own. Predominantly a mix of Magyars and Romanians, XII Corps put up some resistance, but morale was spent. Many officers were already convinced that they were in the middle of an unfolding catastrophe and ordered their men to retreat. To prevent a complete Russian breakthrough, elements of the incoming Second Army were ordered forward to hold the line. 'Each unit, as it arrived in Galicia, was hastily thrown into action and the men attacked as at manoeuvres, advancing all together in open formation,' wrote a Romanian junior officer:

> The Russians, usually entrenched at the edge of a wood, let us approach within three or four hundred paces and, just as we yelled our 'Hurrah!' for the final assault with the bayonet, opened rapid fire with rifles and machine-guns which decimated our ranks in a few seconds. The few who survived wandered panic-stricken all over Galicia and soon lost any military identity they ever had.[26]

The following day, Brusilov's guns hammered the Austro-Hungarian positions with even greater intensity. Behind the artillery barrage followed dense columns of infantry. 'My battalion had been assigned the task of crossing the Gniła Lipa,' wrote a Russian officer. 'From morning till night I was exposed to a fierce fire. The shrapnel fell before me within my lines and killed my men, while the bullets squealed and made a horrible noise… By a true miracle I was not killed.'[27]

Despite attempts to repel the Russian attacks, the defenders, lacking both artillery support and reserves, could do little in the face of overwhelming opposition. Panic broke out as troops ran away from their trenches without order. 'Suddenly some Russian shrapnel come whizzing by,' wrote a cavalry officer. 'The usual panic immediately follows; everyone hurries to claim the road. In the mad throng, wagons are overturned, horses are knocked down, people are trampled and run over by senseless drivers.'[28]

Further south, the Second Army's VII Corps was thrown into the fight around the village of Rohatyn. Charging forward, the men quickly fell victim to more Russian artillery. 'The shells rained down around us, throwing the ground high where they hit,' wrote Kornél Szojka, a Hungarian of the k.u.k. IR 46. 'You could almost see the glint of the infantry bullets in the blazing sun... The Russians' firepower was far superior to that of the Austro-Hungarian troops in every respect. Our cannons barely fired. Only occasionally did a red cloud of our shrapnel appear high in the sky. This had a depressing effect on the morale and fighting ability of the troops.'[29] With counter-attacks ending in bloody failure, all hopes of halting Brusilov's offensive were crushed. That evening, Brudermann ordered his army to retreat to Lemberg and abandoned the Gniła Lipa line.

By now, the situation in East Galicia was greatly concerning Conrad. However, he was still hoping for a grand victory around Komarów in the north. While Brudermann was retreating, General Auffenberg had continued his drive to close the circle around Plehve's Fifth Army, and Conrad hoped that this could be achieved before he would be forced to order Auffenberg to come to Brudermann's aid. Perhaps, Lemberg might be saved.

This gamble did not pay off. In the last days of August, hopes of victory at Komarów quickly began to evaporate. On Auffenberg's left, troops were spooked by reports that Russian cavalry might turn their flank, while on his right, a wide gap had formed between Archduke Joseph Ferdinand and the retreating Third Army. Fearing that the Russians might exploit this and envelop his group, the Archduke shifted forces from his main advance to defend his rear. As both Auffenberg's pincers were pulled back, Plehve was able to narrowly escape encirclement, which put an end to Austro-Hungarian hopes of a decisive victory like the one their German allies were achieving at Tannenberg. Furthermore, it began to look increasingly unlikely that Auffenberg could shift his forces south in time to save Lemberg.

On 1 September, the Russians continued their westward drive towards the Galician capital. They met little resistance from the broken Austro-Hungarian armies. Some of them had now lost so many officers that entire regiments were being led by captains. 'Apparently, the Austrians' spirit collapsed completely,' wrote General Shcherbachev. 'They hurried to withdraw as soon as possible, abandoning guns, ammunition boxes, shells, wagons and weapons.'[30] The Russians were also beginning to feel the strain after days of marching and fighting, but a sense of victory invigorated them. 'The enemy makes a stand against us for a time, then we advance like a storm and beat every living obstacle that resists to the ground,' wrote one officer. 'Our armies are still growing: it's like an avalanche, and although I have taken part in the Japanese war, I didn't think that we could gather such masses of soldiers.'[31] 'The mysterious lights of [Lemberg] shine in the distance,' wrote another.[32] The road into the city appeared wide open.

The following morning, Brudermann reached the same conclusion. Realizing that his army could not hold Lemberg, he requested permission to retreat to a new position along the Wereszyca river, some 15 miles to the west. Conrad had little choice but to agree, although it was a devastating blow to have to abandon Lemberg to the Russians without a fight. By 3 September, the last Austro-Hungarian troops had left the city, and the Russian cavalry arrived. In a matter of days, the situation in Galicia had been turned on its head. Brudermann was retreating to take up a new defensive line. In addition, to prevent a complete collapse of the entire front, Auffenberg's Fourth Army was ordered to turn around and begin marching south towards Lemberg to take up a new position next to the Third Army around the important railroad junction at Rawa Ruska. Many soldiers knew very well what this meant. 'We are to turn back!' one Hungarian soldier wrote. 'Then our advance had failed! Those fields strewn with dead were for nothing!'[33] Not quite. At least, not yet. The enormous Battle of Galicia was about to enter its final, bloodiest phase.

22

Kesshitai

Beyond Europe

I n Africa, at the beginning of the war fighting was by no means confined to the imperial possessions clustered around the equator. Instead, the conflict spread more than 4,000 miles from north to south, too.

Italy had been building an empire since 1882, and had a tendency to see itself as the most benevolent of the imperial powers. 'Italians never leave hateful memories behind them,' claimed one military newspaper with a staggering lack of self-awareness in 1909. 'Because of all the superior races ours is the least rapacious, the least overbearing, the most equal towards the inferior or subject race.'[1] Throughout Italy's period of so-called neutrality, the country was already fighting a war against German interference in what is now Libya. The strategy of stoking existing discord instead of creating it from scratch, especially in areas that might encourage a potential ally, was heavily employed by Germany in multiple locations. In this theatre, existing counter-insurgency was exacerbated as soon as the war began; fuelled by German support.

As early as 22 August, Italian Colonial Minister Ferdinando Martini was panicking about Germans crossing the border into Tunisia from Tripolitania to provoke sedition against France among the indigenous populations. This was potentially embarrassing for Italy, who already favoured joining the Allies. Italy was not behaving like a neutral, but Germany was openly not treating her like one, either. A week later, there were reports of

Germans entering Tripoli and consorting with one of Italy's 'worst and most constant enemies' in the region, Caimacam Ali Bey Seyalati of the Sahel. In response, the Italian governor had this opponent to imperial rule immediately arrested and shipped to Italy to get him out of the way. The effects of this aspect of the war were already telling:

> German victories known to the Arabs have already pro-
> duced a bad effect: Germany is considered the protec-
> tor of Islam and therefore our neutrality is frowned upon
> in Libya: if we had moved in war against Germany and
> Austria an insurrection in Tripolitania would certainly have
> occurred... We need assiduous, careful vigilance and, at the
> slightest sign, [to decree] a state of siege in Tripoli.[2]

In early September, Berlin was still denying having sent any agents to Tripolitania. The Germans claimed that the suspects were simply carrying passports to their representative there. Nonetheless, their consul was called home. In the autumn of 1914, German and Ottoman interference in parts of North Africa came to fruition and the Sultan proclaimed a jihad. Italy's interests became engulfed in revolt, proving that Italy was at war long before officially entering the conflict in May 1915.

*

The early months of the First World War on the global stage were shaped by the fact that Britain had dominions in the southern hemisphere which were militarily organized. The question raised by the loyal declarations of South Africa, Australia and New Zealand was what could troops from those countries do to support Britain's war? The 'colour bar principle' that gave pause for thought about deploying imperial troops to fight white men did not apply, since the troops being offered in their tens of thousands were white themselves. This was unique among far flung empires in 1914. The capacity of these dominions to supply units without any racial conundrum, quickly, thousands of miles from any other concentration of British forces was potentially of huge benefit for the Allies.

Britain asked for intervention immediately and after a few weeks' preparation, all three dominions were ready to carry out operations to disrupt Germany's imperial possessions. On the Orange River, at the request of the British government, the Union of South Africa attacked their border with German South West Africa.

A group of three wells on a main route through inhospitable terrain, Sandfontein was midway between the settlements of Steinkopf in South Africa and Warmbad across the border. Near this spot, at Ramansdrift, sat a British South African column under General Henry Lukin. He had nearly 2,000 men and was the vanguard for the invasion of modern Namibia. The water made possession of Sandfontein essential for both sides, and so German troops were making for exactly the same location from the other direction. It was otherwise a barren spot. 'Ridges and groups of rugged ironstone hills intersected by narrow sandy passes, the... wells commanded by isolated conical-shaped kopjes of about 150ft in height.' Any force marching in this area was confined to thin, sandy tracks carved naturally between these hills. In turn, these would be the only means of escape, and Lukin's force, which arrived at Sandfontein first, found themselves occupying an inaccessible, isolated area where it was easy to be cut off. Retreat would be extremely difficult under fire.

On the evening of 25 September, an intelligence report informed Lukin that German troops were approaching Sandfontein. He decided to reinforce the wells and despatched artillery, a machine-gun section and cavalry from Ramansdrift. Their rapid departure meant that the men were not even issued with rations. The transport behind would just have to keep pace. When they arrived at their destination, the detachment would stand at about 250 men. Moving towards them were 2,000 of the enemy, including artillery and machine-guns. At dawn on 26 September, the German force commanded the high ground as well as the three passes from the north. There was even a dry riverbed that gave excellent cover for attackers. The situation was already untenable for the South Africans, who held the low ground and were surrounded. Their rear was open, and there was no established line for the transport to support them. The reinforcements had marched all night. Men and animals were exhausted, and they had walked into a trap.

Shortly after dawn an officer noticed dust rising from the north-east. The telephone line back to Ramansdrift was cut, and the situation was starting to look ominous. A patrol was sent out to investigate and now, from that direction, rifle fire was heard back at the wells. Leading the patrol, Serjeant Spottiswood and his men came into view, followed by a mass of German troops coming across the plain from two directions; From atop one of the hills, the South Africans saw enemy cavalry pouring into Sandfontein. Lukin's force contracted around the base of one of the pointed hills, when suddenly troops appeared from the direction of Ramansdrift. The South Africans were confused. The reinforcements had just arrived from that direction. Could this be more? But these were not friendly riders. The enemy had got around their rear.

Spirits rose when two guns of the Transvaal Horse Artillery rapidly unlimbered at the site of this new development and prepared to fire. It was barely 8.00 a.m. 'As matters now stood, there was no doubt whatever that the situation of the force at the wells was quite hopeless tactically, and no amount of re-adjustment of the meagre numbers available could have brought about an improvement.' But they had to try. The Transvaal artillerymen fired off a round each. 'The two guns echoed again and again among the surrounding hills, followed a few moments later by the burst of shrapnel.' They soon found their range, and the enemy fanned out and sought cover.

Back at Ramansdrift, General Lukin heard the guns and immediately sent more reinforcements. They were sorely needed, for the men at Sandfontein estimated that at least four guns were firing at them:

The enemy... shells began to drop with precision around
our guns. At this point the natives working with the transport fled, abandoning the animals... The horses then scattered in all directions, and soon fell victims to the murderous
fire. Some succeeded in gaining the plain, where they started
grazing between the opposing firing lines undisturbed by
the fearful medley of sounds.[3]

Any check delivered on the Germans was temporary. They
brought a machine-gun into action on the Ramansdrift road and
it ripped into the South African artillery position. In the early
afternoon a lull occurred. The Germans were even seen stopping
for lunch. The original reinforcements were still without rations
and watched on enviously. 'No such relief for our men. They had
passed a sleepless night marching, and were hungry and thirsty.
Owing to the sudden commencement of the action they had had
no time to fill their water bottles. The heat of the sun on the
ironstone rocks was terrific, and the situation was made almost
unbearable owing to the absence of shade.'[4]

The artillery fire resumed, but it was not until 5.00 p.m. that
Lukin learnt of the guns being employed by the enemy. He immediately led everyone left at Ramansdrift, about 130 men, out
towards Sandfontein. It would be in vain. At roughly the same
time, the white flag was being run up. 'There was little or no
demonstration on the part of the enemy. The last rays of the setting sun showed both sides making one dash for the well at the
foot of the kopje, where British and Germans mingled together to
quench their terrible thirsts.' Lukin arrived at daybreak and saw
the white flag fluttering and ambulances leading in the direction
of Warmbad. The cost of this scrap was sixty-seven casualties,
while the Germans also lost sixty men. Those who had died were
buried together. Looking around at the number of enemy troops,
Lukin quietly rounded up the men closest to him and made a dis-
creet withdrawal before anyone thought about capturing them.

*

Britain's Australian and New Zealand Army Corps (ANZAC) is synonymous with its troops' baptism of fire at Gallipoli in 1915, but that was not its debut. That occurred in 1914, on the other side of the planet.

Germany's foothold in the Far East was Kiaochao Bay, which was leased from China and administered from the port of Tsingtao. Germany also occupied a scattering of more remote territories in the Pacific, including German New Guinea and Samoa, and all three of these came under attack within weeks of the outbreak of war.

The actions of Australia and New Zealand were not completely selfless. There was a level of sub-imperialism at play, because both of these British dominions already administered territory outside their own. Although some 1,700 miles from Queensland, German New Guinea was the conjoined twin of the Territory of Papua, which had been under Australian control for a number of years. As for New Zealand, it had inherited the Cook Islands, a chain that had originally asked to become part of the British empire to avoid German occupation.

When war looked increasingly likely, the prime minister of New Zealand, William Massey, formed a war council with British-born General Alexander Godley, commander of the country's military force. With Admiral von Spee and his naval squadron at large, on 6 August the British government asked the dominion to undertake a 4,000-mile round trip to German Samoa to destroy the wireless mast there. Samoa was some 2,000 miles from Wellington, but it was 950 miles from the Cook Islands. In the vast and mostly empty Pacific, Samoa was absolutely inside the sphere of New Zealand's interests.

Godley's force numbered nearly 1,400 men and a handful of nurses. 'The enthusiasm throughout the Dominion, and the response to the call for volunteers, was most remarkable.'[5] He could afford to be choosy, so he gave preference to existing territorials and former servicemen. Initially told that Australia would take care of nursing, and that their girls could stay at home, the reaction of New Zealand's nurses was predictable. Hundreds volunteered. Matron-in-Chief Hester Maclean had the pick of them, and with just a few days to prepare, colleagues rallied around them to help them pack – despite their envy – and department stores knocked up some uniforms as no official patterns were available. Equipped with canvas stretchers and crates of supplies, the seven women chosen for the New Zealand Army Medical Corps left for war.

Officially, none of these men and women knew where they were going, though rumours were rife. Two hundred and fifty engineers paraded smartly through Wellington, unsure of what equipment they might need. The secrecy caused problems for medical personnel too, because there was a huge difference between preparing for the mundane climate of Europe and the challenges of that on a tropical island. Their destination would wholly shape the cases they would be dealing with.

*

Australia was slightly behind in its deployment, but was not about to be outdone. Britain had politely asked if the Australians might like to seize wireless installations such as the one at Rabaul, in German New Guinea. A camp opened in Sydney and the officers and NCOs, many of them Boer War veterans, 'worked night and day at getting their newly formed companies into shape'. On 17 August the scene off Sydney was frenzied:

Above the clamour of great machines in a score of sheds, the shrill… steam-whistle, the ceaseless clanging of steel on iron, the whine and rattle of cranes rose continually; the dry shuffle of hundreds… of feet, the abrupt shouting of orders, as the long, dust-coloured lines of men halted or moved forward by sections to the gangways of the big liner that loomed beyond them out of the dock basin… Everywhere was chaos, but chaos resolving itself into cosmos… From all sides food, medicines, hammocks, waterproof sheeting, sewing-machines, motor-cycles, and a myriad other things were poured into the holds... One saw everywhere big boxes of clothing, bundles of mosquito-netting... medicines, surgical equipment, and innumerable other essentials marked with a large red cross.[6]

Five days earlier New Zealanders departed for war with a rapturous send off from the people of Wellington:

Heralded by the band, they were soon attended by a cheering crowd, which grew larger and more enthusiastic as the news of their approach preceded the troops through the city... the column of khaki was bordered by dense masses of people. Enthusiasm reached its height about 7.00 p.m. when, with night throwing its shadows over the port, the transports moved... the crowds ashore, who had lingered all day to see the ships off... found expression in loud cheering, singing, [and] hakas.[7]

As they passed Pencarrow lighthouse outside Wellington and turned east away from Europe, the men knew for certain that they were going out into the Pacific. Bad weather threw the transports back and forth. 'Parades became a farce and were abandoned.' The cooks who remained upright found that few wanted to eat. 'I was one of the first to hang over the side,' wrote one soldier. 'No breakfast, no dinner, no tea, and a night that was worse than the day.'[8]

Their Australian neighbours departed in a similar direction and were chased all the way by a violent wind. They, too, tried valiantly to keep their military discipline:

It is not easy for... fifty men, all hampered with overcoats and rifles, to stand in a beautifully unbroken line on a deck whose angle of incidence perpetually shifts and veers... Sometimes even for the men who were well, drill was rendered practically impossible by the sea's antics, and it was a ludicrous spectacle to see a whole half-company, as a

huge wave rolled the liner on her side, go sliding and staggering across the deck, wildly embracing each other or
anything else, before fetching up with a bump against the
bulwarks.[9]

The weather improved, and soon the New Zealanders were in
better humour:

Meals of very poor quality and a few sacks of onions
stowed aft on the *Monowai*'s top deck were surreptitiously
raided and eaten raw with ships' biscuits with great relish
by a fortunate few. Of fresh water there was none for washing purposes and very little for drinking. The benefits of the
early morning hose parade, when all hands doubled naked
around the decks and received each in turn a hurried salt
water splash, were enjoyed to the full.[10]

By 27 August, the mood aboard had changed: 'The happy care-
free boys of yesterday became serious men. Water-bottles were
sterilized... bayonets ground... metal identity discs were issued,
together with 150 rounds of ammunition.' At Samoa, commanders were not expecting to walk ashore. They knew that there was
a permanent force stationed with the wireless installation on the
island of Upolu under European officers. The men aboard the
transports waited as heavy seas flung them about. 'A vivid recollection is the stillness on board. Most of us were thinking hard;
some were praying silently.'[11] The spine of the island emerged out
of the mist at dawn on 29 August.

Along with the New Zealand transports were six Allied ships
under the command of Admiral Sir George Patey, an old sea dog
who had joined the Royal Navy at thirteen and whose active service went all the way back to the Peruvian civil war in 1877. He
had given precise orders. HMS *Psyche* would approach Upolu at
daylight flying a white flag. There everyone would pause. 'Should
the German authorities refuse to surrender the town, or should
no answer to the summons to do so be forthcoming, *Psyche* will

order *Philomel* and *Pyramus* to enter the harbour, and they are to be prepared to open fire.'[12]

Psyche became a distant blur out in front of the fleet. She stood off the Samoan capital, Apia, with a flag of truce fluttering at her mast. 'At the wireless station they had picked out our approach and immediately tried to send out a distress call.' With naval guns pointed at the island, Patey had 'cease signalling instantly' tapped out. The station shrewdly complied. A landing crew carried a message for the governor of the island. More than an hour passed. *Psyche* ominously lowered her white flag. *Philomel* and *Pyramus* prepared to open fire. The troops, in breathless expectation, waited to see hostilities commenced. But almost immediately the signal flags again fluttered and like wildfire the news ran through the fleet that no resistance would be offered to the landing party.[13] Within twenty-five days of the outbreak of war, New Zealand had hauled down the German flag at Samoa without firing a shot.

*

The Royal Navy was playing its part elsewhere too. Yap Island, a tiny speck in the emptiness of the western Pacific Ocean, actually played a critical role in the Kaiser's empire. It was a junction for undersea cables, and the Germans had installed a wireless mast there, meaning that they no longer needed to rely on British communications. However, it took just a week of war for a British ship to deny the Germans this lifeline. The enemy station was given a chance to surrender, which the men stationed there ignored.

At [9.40 a.m. we] opened fire on the wireless house at a range of about 4,500 yards. The first shot went short and rather left, the next two went over. Then the fourth went in and set the building on fire. There appeared to be oil there which burnt furiously. I was then told to endeavour to bring the wireless mast down. I... plumped the fifth shot into the building. My sixth went left of the mast, seven, eight and nine missed it, and the tenth just burst short. [The mast] fell over the building in a more or less leisurely manner and crumpled up.[14]

*

When the station at Apia in Samoa was taken apart by the New Zealanders at the end of August and an installation at Nauru, a third of the way to Hawaii, was also silenced, German New Guinea's isolation was complete. A two-week pause off the coast of Queensland had given Australian officers time to try to knock their new recruits into shape. 'At the beginning of the cruise', wrote one observer, 'it may be doubted whether 20 per cent of the force had ever seen a modern service rifle before, and it is even alleged by some ribald humorists that more than one man was caught in the act of trying to load his rifle by poking the cartridges down the barrel!'[15] Ready or not, the Australians sailed around from their side of the island to German territory. The main town of Rabaul sat in a large, safe harbour surrounded by volcanoes. Above, on the opposite side of the bay, high up at Bitapaka, was the wireless station.

On 11 September, Australian soldiers awoke to find themselves looking at their first battlefield of the First World War, a 'long curving line of coast... half-veiled in pale blue mists... All about us in a great green arc... swept lofty hills covered from base to skyline with the nodding plumes of coconut-palms.'[16] The main landing would take place at Kaba Kaul, below Bitapaka, and their first job was to actually find the wireless station.

Kaba Kaul turned out to be a few houses, sheds and an insignificant little pier with two abandoned boats tied to it. There was nobody in sight. The Australian naval reservists promptly landed, hauling a machine-gun with them, and vanished into the thick rainforest. The Germans, however, had been anticipating their arrival. In command of the landing force, thirty-five-year-old naval Lieutenant Rowland Bowen pressed more than 2 miles inland plagued by snipers lurking high in the tropical vegetation. As they probed the way to up to Bitapaka, shots rained down from this invisible menace, or from trenches dug along the road. 'It is devilish country to fight in,' said Bowen:

> While the road is clear enough, on each side is a jungle of thorny palms, coconuts, long grass, and great hooked vines, impossible to see through for a yard ahead and exceedingly difficult to penetrate... I suppose it took us about two hours to do a mile and a half. They brought me a German whom they had wounded and captured. I... told him to call out to the others ahead to surrender, and that we had a large force. Nothing like bluff! He hesitated for a moment, then, seeing that I was going to shoot him if he refused, he yelled out...[17]

With this landing party was a medical officer named Brian Pockley. The twenty-four-year-old had been working at Sydney Hospital when war was declared. He volunteered for the Australian Army Medical Corps immediately and now, on the way to Bitapaka, he found he had his work cut out. Treating a man who had had been shot in the stomach, he called on a nearby sailor to carry the wounded man to safety. Pockley noticed that the sailor was not wearing a red cross armband that denoted: *I'm unarmed, don't shoot me.* He quickly removed his own and tied it on his comrade's helmet in the hope that it would keep him safe, and sent him on his way. 'Poor Pockley!' said Rowland Bowen. 'He... then insisted upon going back to help one of our fellows who was badly hit.'[18] Without his armband, Pockley was struck down and seriously wounded.

Bowen sent for reinforcements, as fire continued to rain down from concealed shooters. Sailors were rushed ashore. 'Even [a] ship's butcher, his apron still tied to his waist and a formidable cleaver in his hand, marched off with the rest, grinning with delight at the prospect of *having a go* at the Germans.'[19] Admiral Patey sent another of his polite telegrams to the German governor at Rabaul, inviting them to end their resistance immediately. 'I will point out to Your Excellency', he said, 'that the force at my command is so large as to render useless any opposition on your part.'[20]

Having braved the snipers on the road, reinforcements arrived. Bowen himself 'was lying almost insensible, his head roughly bandaged and his face covered with flies and blood, under cover of a fallen tree. 'So few were their numbers that it was all they could do to hold their position in face of the fire directed upon them literally from every side at once.'[21] At about 3.00 p.m., the remaining officers were debating what to do next when two machine-guns arrived. Their approach had been torrid, but Lieutenant Bond had set the example: 'He strolled along the road', said another officer, '…talking about the various plants we were passing at the side of the road. He's an enthusiastic botanist. There he was, discoursing on *Lepidoptera* and such, with the imminent risk at every moment of being picked off by some n– – – –r up a tree.'[22]

In the Germans' scratch trenches, their indigenous troops had suffered heavier casualties than the Australians had, and machine-guns were the last straw. 'The enemy's fire first slackened, and then stopped entirely, and suddenly a white flag was hoisted.'[23] With a German officer leading the way, Australian troops advanced along the road to claim their prize. The wireless station held a commanding position. Cliffs dropped off on three sides, and trenches covered the only approach. Two huge towers soared upwards into the night. 'Besides about 26 natives, seven German wireless officials were found, quietly seated at dinner in complete ignorance of the turn events had taken. With a philosophic shrug, they all surrendered the station without resistance, giving their word of honour not to escape.'[24]

In just six weeks of war, South Africa, Australia and New Zealand had pledged their loyalty and delivered. On the *Berrima*, Brian Pockley had been hoisted aboard in a miserable state. 'The bullet… had entered the stomach and turned… tearing away part of the spine, and leaving a wound in his back as large as a man's clenched fist. A murmured reference to his mother in Sydney was his last coherent utterance.' He was the first Australian officer killed in action during the war.

Further north, ordinary Japanese people could be unfamiliar with Europe. Some confused Austria with Australia. The latter had introduced new legislation to prevent Asian immigration diluting the white proportion of the dominion, and some Japanese people assumed that Germany had declared war because it objected to this 'White Australia' policy. Japanese leaders, however, were better informed. Japan was a long-term ally of Britain, and from the outset in 1914, her politicians would show incredible shrewdness in manipulating European allies to try to get what they wanted out of the conflict. Prime Minister Ōkuma Shigenobu, 'architect of many a previous cunning plan', referred to the war as 'the chance of a millennium'.[25]

The West had learnt not to underestimate Japanese forces during the 1905 Russo-Japanese War, which simultaneously bludgeoned Russian, European and white prestige. Now, in 1914, Japan began softly on 3 August by offering naval assistance in the Pacific. Britain wanted Japanese support, but only if they could control it. If not, Japan's imperial ambitions might become difficult to check. To that end, Japan was asked to limit operations to locating and reporting on German convoys and relaying the information back to Britain, but Japan wanted much more than a bit part like this.

Japan wanted to build an empire. Ordinarily, to achieve this would involve provoking the wrath of a European power and taking something from one of them that had already been claimed as an imperial possession. That or an act of aggression against, say, China, which would be viewed negatively. To that end, Japan hadn't yet tried. Now, with imperial powers fighting among themselves, there would be losers. What was taken from them, if Japan played her cards right, might end up in her hands. The war was therefore an unexpected, opportune moment for expansion with the least possible risk.

Independent of its offer to Britain and without consultation, Japan presented Germany with an ultimatum in mid-August. Among the demands, Japan wanted all German warships removed from Japanese *and* Chinese waters, or at least the disarming of the ones that were immobile. By 15 September, the Japanese wanted Kiaochao Bay handed over too, but they were too savvy to imply that they would claim it. The ultimatum claimed that this would be 'with a view to the eventual restoration of the same to China'.[26] This last phrase was a lie, but it calmed America down. After all, the United States had nearly 8,000 miles of Pacific coastline and her own imperial designs on the region. In 1914, the United States controlled the Philippines, Guam and Hawaii, and was nervous of Japanese expansion.

To be fair, what Britain asked of Japan threatened her status as a neutral nation. Declaring war on Germany was the honest thing to do and one that would not tarnish Japan's international reputation when she had clearly picked a side. The declaration came on 23 August, and Japan's navy put to sea. Ships patrolled the Pacific searching for von Spee's raiders, but what became clear very quickly was that statements about Japan having no territorial aspirations in this war were farcical. Within a few weeks, Japan had given up its ruse. More than anything, Japanese prime minister Ōkuma wanted to attack the German base at Tsingtao, inside Kiaochao Bay; to seize the best harbour in the region from the Kaiser. It was the only specific piece of land mentioned in Japan's ultimatum.

For their part, the Germans would have known that their hold on the bay was doomed as soon as Japan entered the war. This would be a theatre of war where Japan would employ all of her strength, both naval and military. The Far East might have been a sideshow for Europeans when it came to spreading their resources around the globe, but for Japan it was everything.

The Germans were as prepared as they could be. The East Asiatic Marine Detachment had been called to Tsingtao on the outbreak of war. Any warships in range were also commanded to return, and all German men of military age in the Far East were to be mobilized and instructed to travel to Tsingtao. The governor ordered as many mines as he could get his hands on laid across the entrance into the bay. At 425 feet high, Bismarck

Hill above Tsingtao gave the Germans a comprehensive view of Kiaochao and out to sea. There was a multi-levelled bunker already dug underneath, along with a trench system known as the Boxer Line. The Germans also had Howitzers. For all this effort, however, it has been estimated by some historians that Germany would have needed 40,000 men to hold on to Tsingtao and Kiaochao Bay. They had about 700.

*

At dawn on 27 August, Jakob Neumaier was on watch on a hilltop overlooking the bay. Out of the haze he saw spots on the horizon, ran to the speaking tube and screamed that the Japanese were coming. The Germans were expecting a full-scale naval bombardment, but the Allied fleet stopped out of range. Admiral Sadakichi Kato sent a wireless message ashore declaring a blockade of the whole area and had his ships commence sweeping for mines. Tsingtao lost almost all contact with the outside world.

The Japanese did not intend to land in the bay. Sailing through the mines was too risky. Instead, they landed on the opposite side of the peninsula at Lungkou. In principle it was a good idea, but the terrain meant that the 120-mile or so journey by land they would need to make might as well have been double for the effort it would take troops to cross it. Secondly, it was in China, and China was neutral, so Japan was basically invading her neighbour, confident that the Chinese government was too weak to do anything about it. The Germans knew it was a feasible plan, but they never expected the Japanese to try it. It was a nasty surprise. Instead of starving them out, the enemy was going to come at them in force with some 20,000 men.

Lungkou was a diversion. While the Germans were focused on the initial force coming south from there, the Japanese would make the real landing at Laoshan, along the coast from Tsingtao. Admiral Kato's squadron would deal with the mines blocking the entrance to the bay before protecting the landing of a larger group moving on Tsingtao. It sounded simple enough. The first landing party was ashore at Lungkou by 7.30 a.m. on 2 September. Then the heavens opened and an epic storm drenched the bay. Men had to wade the last 300 yards to shore through rough surf, as the rain turned to sleet and high winds pummelled them as they tried to build piers and bring supplies ashore. The next day, the whole operation was suspended until the weather improved. Rivers burst their banks, roads and railway lines were torn, the rails left broken and twisted when the water subsided. Buildings collapsed, and bridges that engineers had estimated they had built six feet above maximum flood levels were swept away. The Chinese people living in the region saw their lives destroyed:

> The villages in Shandong suffered appalling damage. They lacked even the simplest defences against flooding, having depended upon the visible water tracts and human memory for their protection. The natives hastily tossed up sand dykes, but the rushing water quickly eroded them and attacked the stone foundations. Within a short time the flimsy houses were careening around like whirling toys, only to collapse into soiled piles of household goods. The ruins, partially filled with sand, gave the townships the eerie unreality of another world. The Chinese must have perished in large numbers, but no one kept records.[27]

German infrastructure was flooded too. Troops donned bathing suits and high boots and got to work to save what they could. 'The officers joined the men in this coolie labour, forgetting all protocol in the battle to save their installations for the coming campaign.' To add to German misery, the Japanese launched seaplanes from out on the water and began dropping bombs on them, including the first ever air–sea attack in history. It was a miserable fortnight:

> The soldiers... could not see [six feet] in front of them, could not stay dry... The air [was] oppressively humid outside, and dank, sticky, and unbearable inside the fortifications. Nearly everyone suffered from colds or bronchial

congestion. In the evening the mosquitoes rose to attack, and anyone caught in an area belonging to these fearsome flying daggers had little respite. Many men looked like human pincushions and swelled up like elongated balloons under the ferocious assault.[28]

At Lungkou, on 7 September a night storm washed away Japanese piers and most of the landing craft. The cavalry arriving at Pingdu on the way south did so having lost 30 per cent of their horses. The troops lurched forward whenever there was a break in the weather. As for the men: 'They were a sorry sight after a week in the field, without even sighting the enemy. The uniforms were faded and full of gaping… holes… Most of [them] were listless from fatigue and lack of provisions.' Rations were unfit for use. When they staggered into town, they collapsed in a heap. There was no option but to suspend the advance. 'Morale was too low to achieve anything.'[29]

On 11 September finally, after a fortnight, the skies cleared. The invasion force probed forward and a week later finally clashed with the enemy. Dismounted cavalry struggled through soybean and millet crops. In command, Captain Sakuma's aim was to capture some prisoners, but as they circled the village one of his men accidentally shot his rifle and the game was up. 'A general melee opened between the two parties as both sides underwent their baptism of fire. The small German patrol faded into the fields and the Japanese started after them.'[30] As they moved out, twenty more enemy troops opened fire from the side. The resulting firefight lasted about twenty minutes. Sakuma was hit in the chest. The bullet severed an artery and he became the first Japanese soldier killed in action in the First World War. Retiring, the Germans did not get away unscathed. One of their officers, Baron Riedesel zu Eisenbach, was shot through both legs. He ordered his men back with the intention of covering their withdrawal. When a small party returned to collect him, he had bled to death.

In the meantime, the Japanese government was determined that the main landing on 18 September at Laoshan was going to take place, despite the harrowing experiences of the campaign so far. It was a callous order. After all of their hardships, the men at Lungkou were ordered back on transports and sailed around the peninsula.

The Kaiser once said: 'it would shame me more to surrender Tsingtao to the Japanese than Berlin to the Russians'.[31] That quote belongs on a list of his sillier utterances, but for Germany, with its little empire and big ambitions, Tsingtao was not *un*important. Inside the fortifications, German nerves were shot. If the Japanese were coming, they just wanted it over with. Add forays by Japanese airmen in their flimsy looking Maurice Farman aircraft, torpedo boats racing in and bombarding the shore and disappearing before the Germans could react, and it all amounted to a terrifying uncertainty.

The German plan was simple: massively outnumbered as they were, they would try to hold the Japanese up as long as possible then retire before they were overrun. Unsurprisingly, this plan did not appeal to those outnumbered men in exposed positions on the hillsides outside Tsingtao. The only possible outcome was failure, and possibly death. Everything hinged on a few unconnected lines running along a ridge to a high point known as Heinrich Hill. The very top of the mountain was isolated by steep rock walls. German engineers attempted to destroy what access there was. For the unlucky troops there, when the Japanese managed to get up to them, it would be game over. They dubbed it the Eagle's Nest, stocked it with brandy and cigars, and awaited the inevitable outcome of their suicide mission.

*

At Laoshan the sea was rough but the skies clear when Japanese troops set off on the morning of 18 September. It was important to get the men ashore quickly because there was nowhere for them to shelter if they came under sustained fire. The Japanese fleet in the bay had already been shelling the hills above the landing site, and the first troops got ashore and rigged up a wireless station without any trouble. In the days following, there were isolated skirmishes with Germans, most of which ended with the defenders retiring to Tsingtao. All the while, the Japanese were securing their positions and gathering information.

In overall command, by 25 September, the eminently sensible General Kamio finally deemed his force ready to breach the frontier. His men crossed the following day, despite a bombardment from the German torpedo boat *S90* in the harbour. German commanders watched an efficient and smooth advance by the enemy. Like Russia, Japan had learnt invaluable lessons in modern warfare a decade before. '[They] moved like professionals, presenting few targets. They used the terrain properly, dug in immediately, and avoided any contact with the defenders... The enemy infantry demonstrated a speed and agility in advancing over rough ground which far exceeded German endeavours.'[32] Not knowing that the Japanese had halted for the night, the Germans were afraid to sleep for fear of a night attack. When they did lie down, they did so cradling their rifles in their arms, just in case.

The *S-90* and *Jaguar*, aided by the Austro-Hungarian *Kaiserin Elisabeth,* fired on the Japanese advance from the water. The Japanese responded by deftly turning their artillery on the ships. If it was disappointing, it was exactly what the Germans had anticipated. From the Eagle's Nest on top of Heinrich Hill, the defenders watched events play out. Overnight, they threw out barbed wire, laid mines and repositioned their guns. They knew the assault was coming, and as the rain began to fall again, Kamio decided that the time had come to push towards them.

On 28 September, the day began with precise Japanese artillery fire smashing into the hillsides. The infantry moved forward. Then, however, the German and Austro-Hungarian ships returned and battered the Japanese guns. One by one they knocked them out of action and the attack began to waver. In the bay, however, the crews on those ships were about to get a rude awakening. They began taking hits. 'The ear-shattering bangs dumbfounded the crews for a short time.'[33] Then they caught on: they were not just being shot at from land, these shells were coming from elsewhere on the water. Backup had arrived, and an Allied fleet was now firing on them. The Japanese ships *Suwo* and *Iwami*, together with HMS *Triumph* and HMS *Tango*, had come to the rescue. After fixing their aim, on the second run their shells smashed into German positions ashore. They got off 148 rounds, then withdrew to safety before the enemy could respond.

The German gunners were stunned. 'The mood of the gun crews had switched within a few minutes from the excitement of entering the war to the abject terror of perishing in it. The earth quaked as the… shells came in with an unnerving sound.' On impact the 'crack of flying metal, hiss of compacted air, and ensuing smoke column' was terrifying. 'Inside the gun turrets the concussion of the exploding shells precluded all talk, all activity.' A cook preparing soup knew nothing 'until a huge shell came through the wall, tearing the doors off their hinges and passing out the other wall before it exploded in the yard'.[34] He paused for a moment, then apparently went back to the soup. Under the circumstances, the Germans thought it might be prudent to retire. Kamio observed the situation, but was reluctant to let his men rush headlong after the enemy and incur unnecessary casualties. He was not about to start wasting lives now.

By mid-afternoon the bulk of the German force was inside Tsingtao, with the exception of the men in the Eagle's Nest, and this is where Kamio looked to next. A reinforced company from his 46th Regiment, along with some sappers, were assigned the challenge of taking the top of Heinrich Hill and depriving the enemy of their priceless observation over Kiaochao Bay. This force of some 300 men would be dubbed *Kesshitai*, men resolved to die. In command, Captain Sato gave a rousing speech that ended with a cheer for the emperor, and off they went.

Arriving after dark, they began the climb with straw matting fastened to the bottom of their boots to muffle the sound. At dawn, the men in the Eagle's Nest had just begun their day when the Japanese blew out a lamp with a rifle shot and announced their arrival. In the firefight that followed, Captain Sato was mortally wounded along with his second in command. A frenzied battle continued all morning. Pinned down, without their leader, the Japanese attack stalled, but at the bottom of Heinrich Hill, the now-dead Sato won the day with a crucial decision he had made earlier on. He had divided his force. A second group of soldiers now surged up the hill waving the Japanese flag, and attacked the Germans from the opposite side. Their fire was not significant, but the impact of their arrival finished the defenders off. Resolve crumbled. Still cautious of wasting men, Kamio refrained from running his fleeing enemy down. Further progress could wait until heavy artillery arrived.

The Japanese had basically bluffed their way to the top of Heinrich Hill, thanks to the timely intervention of the Allied fleet early in the day. They now held a commanding view of everything the Germans were doing in Kiaochao Bay. The ships in the harbour were sunk to keep them out of Japanese hands. On nearby Moltke Hill, German Serjeant Eugen Ruddier led his men to a large hole in the ground. He gave a disturbing speech to the men perched on piles of dirt about him. 'What you see here is... an anticipated mass grave. It is surely for me, for you, for all of us. Drive the thoughts of seeing father and mother out of your heads. We cannot obtain victory here; only die. Still, before it reaches that point, take as many of the yellow apes with you as you can.'[35] As they made for their quarters, he ordered them to sing. They ignored him. Twice. He finally received a sad rendition of a patriotic German song. After that there was just the miserable sound of their tramping boots marching towards Tsingtao, where they now faced a siege.

23

Without Holding Anything Back

France

On 5 September, as Joffre's armies prepared to try to save France, the impending battle line stretched eastward more than 150 miles from Paris to Verdun. In the centre lay the town of Vitry-le-François. By now, most of the inhabitants had fled, including the mayor, leaving Father Leopold Nottin unimpressed. Shells were now bursting in the suburbs, and he found he was now responsible for everything from feeding the remaining population to organizing the disposal of dead horses abandoned by the passing French army. 'Our soldiers are retreating,' he wrote. 'The wounded fall in our streets, exhausted.'[1] Local nuns did what they could. Nottin reopened the recently abandoned hospital, but there was no doctor to be had, not even a pharmacist. As the last Frenchman passed through, the Germans arrived. Soon looting had begun and hostages, Nottin among them, were held at the Café des Oiseaux, where they glumly watched enemy soldiers drink everything behind the bar.

To the west of Father Leopold was another new army. General Foch had taken the retreat well, all things considered. On 4 September, André Tardieu, one of his staff officers, noted a building anticipation at their headquarters. As well as finding out that their detachment now had the official status of being an army, they learnt over dinner that Lanrezac had been removed as commander of the Fifth Army. 'CQFD,' Foch said laconically as he slurped his soup.[2] *I rest my case.*

*

Foch's new Ninth Army was tasked with holding the southern exits from the Saint-Gond Marshes. A strip of dense, rugged land stretching some 10 miles east to west and up to 4 miles in width, the marshes were passable by four roads running north to south. Foch did not need to allocate many men away from the roads, but there was certainly work for them elsewhere. His front extended on another dozen miles to the east towards Vitry, where the terrain became much more problematic: open, chalky plains with the odd copse of trees, with a stream or a village here and there. Idyllically French it might have been, but as Foch wryly pointed out, it was easy for an enemy army to cross and almost impossible to defend. Yet there was no room for failure. If the Ninth Army was split from the Fourth on his right, Joffre's offensive might be doomed.

Franchet d'Espèrey's Fifth Army was west of Foch, and on 5 September elements of his cavalry went out to reconnoitre the enemy positions in front of them. Marcel Dupont and his comrades were about to get a surprise when their colonel lined them up with a piece of paper in his hand. 'Men and beasts were half asleep,' he wrote.

> On hearing the first few sentences we drew closer around him as by instinct. We could not believe our ears... Had we not been told the day before... that we were going to retire to the Seine? And now in a few... simple words the Commander-in-Chief told us that the trials of that hideous retreat were over, and that the day had come to take the offensive.[3]

Dupont was ordered to examine a road leading to the village of Courgivaux. He chose his men, 'a corporal and four reliable fellows who had already given a good account of themselves'. Right out in front rode a trooper by the name of Vercherin, mounted on his faithful horse Cabri. Dupont had complete faith in him. They had already learnt the hard way that they had to spread out. 'We knew what ravages they made [if] our troopers were imprudent enough to cluster together.' Up ahead the road became dangerous. 'I called out to Vercherin to stop.' None of this new, cautious way of doing things made Dupont's heart sing:

> How much more dashing it would have been... to ride full gallop, brandishing my sword... into the nearest copse! But I knew then that if it were occupied by the enemy, their men would be lying down, buried in the soil, using the trees and bushes as cover, till the last moment. Then not one of us would have come out alive... The good old times of hussar charges are gone, together with plumes, pelisses waving in the wind... It would be senseless to continue to be a horseman in order to fight men who are no longer cavalrymen and do not wish to be so.[4]

Courgivaux itself appeared deserted. No locals, no enemy defences. In front of them 'a large farm protruded, like the prow of a ship'. The silence was almost worse than the noise of a battle. Suddenly Dupont saw Vercherin stand up in his stirrups. 'I understood that he saw something, and I galloped up to him at once... "Mon Lieutenant... there behind that stack... I thought I saw a head rise above the grass."' Then their horses were startled, 'suddenly seized with a simultaneous terror'. As he raised his glasses, Dupont saw them, less than 100 yards in front:

> A whole line of sharpshooters, dressed in grey, rise quickly in front of me. For one short moment a terrible pang shot through us. How many were there? Almost at the same time a formidable volley of rifle shots rang out. They had been watching us for a long time. Lying in the grass that lined the road leading to the farm or else behind the stacks... Not one of them had shown himself... We had to be off.[5]

On Dupont's signal they galloped away. 'I suddenly saw to the right of me Ramier, Lemaître's horse, fall like a log.' He saw horse and rider flail on the ground, 'forming a confused mixture of hooves in the air and waving arms'. Ramier got up and limped off. As for Lemaître, he was on his feet, setting his battered shako back on his head. The trooper skipped to safety, 'striding along with his short legs and heavy boots, jumping ditches and banks with a nimbleness of which I declare I should not have thought him capable'. A comrade managed to catch Ramier. 'It was painful to see the poor animal,' wrote Dupont. 'His lameness had already become more marked. He could only get along with great difficulty, and his eyes showed he was in pain.' They established that Courgivaux was impassable and there was nothing they could do for the horse.

> Lemaître was standing in great grief over poor Ramier, lying inert on the ground and struggling feebly with death. His eyes were already dull and his legs convulsed. Every now and then he shuddered violently. I looked at Lemaître, who felt as if he were losing his best friend. I dismounted... 'Don't grieve, my good fellow; it is a fine end for Ramier. He might, like so many others, have died worn out with work or suffering under some hedgerow. He has a soldier's death. All we can do is to cut short his sufferings and send him quickly to rejoin his many good comrades in the paradise of noble animals.'[6]

Lemaître looked utterly unconvinced as Dupont pulled out his revolver. His hand was shaking:

> One less horse in a troop is the same as one child less in a family. And, besides, it means one trooper unmounted and the loss of a sword in battle. Lemaître was right. Ramier was a good old servant, one of the kind that never goes lame, can feed on anything or on nothing, and never hurts anybody. It was hard to put an end to him; but since he was done for, I put the muzzle of my revolver into his ear. I did not wish him to feel the cold metal; but his whole body shuddered, and his

eye, lighting up for a moment, seemed to reproach me. Paff!
A short, sharp report, and Ramier quivered for a moment.
Then his sufferings ceased, and his stiffening carcass added
one more to the many that strewed the country.[7]

*

Next along the Allied line, the British rank and file found out that
their retreat was finally over late on 5 September. Near Melun,
30 miles south-east of the Eiffel Tower, the BEF's requisitioned
lorries were a grubby sight. 'Right down to Fontainebleau they
have displayed Mr. Johnnie Walker and his eyeglass, Mr. Pulltite
and his corsets, Mr. Mayflower and his margarine.' Soon the
men were stuffing the lorries full of shells, as well as spare parts
for much needed maintenance. 'The colours are not so brilliant
as they were a month ago. Some of the pictures... are chipped
by bullet marks, but Mr. Walker smiles serenely... and brings a
feeling of peace to our excitable French friends.'[8] Civilians as well
as troops felt as if the tide was turning. This was positive activity
instead of constantly running away.

On the far left of the Allied line, Victor Boudon was with
the 276e RI. They had been pulled out of the line and sent west
to join General Maunoury's newly formed Sixth Army. Joining
the retreat, the men had no idea why. They only knew that they
were being driven further and further south. When they halted
finally at Luzarches, they were just over 20 miles from the Eiffel
Tower. 'Our brains are annihilated by fatigue.' It seemed surreal,
to see Paris again a month after leaving; to have returned to
defend it. 'We see in the distance... from time to time, through
the foliage, the lights of the capital. Our hearts beat violently, at
the same time with emotion, joy and fear.'[9] Proudly, they stood
ready to fight, symbolic of the thousands of reservists who helped
make up General Maunoury's Sixth Army. Behind them, General
Gallieni was taking nothing for granted in Paris. His men were
working hard to put the capital in some state of defence in case
the worst should happen. 'Our workers, both soldiers and civilians, even worked at night, by torchlight,' he wrote.[10]

Within Kluck's First Army, there was a certain smugness. 'We continue to move south and push ourselves between the French Army and Paris,' wrote one man. 'The strategic situation is great.'[11] Another equally optimistic officer also wrote that the French seem 'completely stunned'.[12] Though this was true, Germany was about to find fortune turned on its head.

Early on 5 September, Maunoury's Sixth Army had begun marching north-east from Paris. The intention was to inflict a surprise attack on the Germans along the north bank of the Marne the following day, as part of Joffre's grand offensive. There was no expectation that they would meet with the enemy on 5 September, but there was risk involved in getting a head start. If they marched early, they might risk showing Joffre's hand. In fact, Kluck had learnt of the Sixth Army's existence already and swivelled part of his force around to face Paris. A day early, elements from the two armies were about to collide.

Kluck's infantry was probing forward. Having set out from just outside Paris, Victor Boudon and the 276th RI approached the same area. 'Opposite us… stretch the wooded hills, where the Germans lie in wait, invisible, holed up in their entrenchments.' In front of them, those Germans were about to pounce. Men like Boudon had no idea what was coming. Exhausted, famished, sweating, his company had halted on a shrub-lined path overlooking a village to eat soup. Then enemy guns announced themselves. 'Suddenly, abruptly, around us… German shells burst. "They serve us an aperitif!" some exclaim.' Boudon's company deployed south-east. 'We… arrive at the edge of Villeroy… in a sort of sunken road, from where we can follow the artillery duel.' Nearby, he spotted a fierce exchange of rifle fire, 'and the deafening tac-tac of machine-guns'.[13]

Moroccan units were striking out for the high ground in front, and so from here on, the 276th advanced with caution. Captain Pierre Guérin and forty-one-year-old Lieutenant Charles Péguy, a renowned socialist poet and writer, both held revolvers. 'No firing without orders! The Moroccans are in front of us!' They advanced through fields of oats. 'Many fall,' wrote Boudon. 'Another leap, a shift to the left, and here we are sheltered behind [an] embankment… panting and puffing. Bullets whistle past our heads.' The Germans were 500 yards away, 'entrenched behind the trees and shrubs… almost invisible'. Boudon's company were all sweating profusely, 'climbing the embankment and skimming the ground, weapon in hand, bent double, so as to offer less of a target to the bullets, stumbling in the beets'.[14]

'The terrible harvest continues,' wrote Boudon. He was beginning to lose heart as they went on in a single wave, 'without a line of support behind, on a terrain where the declining slope and the high visibility of our uniforms make us superb targets, with barely 150 cartridges per man and in the impossibility of being supplied with them, it is madness, a certain massacre'. Officers fell, but the company was galvanized. 'We shoot like madmen, black with gunpowder; the rifle burning our fingers, each digging his hands in the earth, between two shots, to fashion a woeful shelter. At every moment, there are cries, complaints, filth.' Lieutenant Péguy was still on his feet, despite the cries of his men imploring him to take cover. He did not listen, and a bullet cut him down.

Nearby, Reserve Infanterie Regiment Nr.27 (RIR 27) was relieved to see reinforcements arriving in force as dusk fell. 'We stormed the railway line and the village of Saint-Soupplets,' recalled one officer. 'The enemy was gone, but many dead red-trousers told us that we too had learnt to shoot… Impressions of the day were exchanged. Some are missing… Melancholy wants to creep up on us, but the work of defending the positions… helps us overcome it.'[15]

*

The fight was a draw of sorts. The French had been checked a day before their grand counter-offensive was due to commence, and Kluck was now scrambling large bodies of troops to face the Sixth Army. Their early appearance had given the German general time and intelligence to head off French troops coming from Paris.

When Kluck had part of his force swung around to face the Sixth Army, it meant that Maunoury's men were unable to make the decisive breakthrough that Joffre had planned. But what of the gap those scrambling German soldiers had now left elsewhere?

This gap meant that on 6 September, a different opportunity for a crashing blow on the German right was beginning to present itself. The more men Kluck siphoned off to face the Sixth Army, the more a fissure began to widen between his force and that of Bülow's Second Army next to him. A fissure that was not addressed, and which presented an outstanding opportunity to both the British Expeditionary Force and Franchet d'Espèrey's Fifth Army. The broadening gap invited them to pour into it. German communications were in disarray; armies were not talking to each other or to their supreme headquarters. Part of this lack of communication was the effect of the rapid advance through Belgium and northern France and disruption to infrastructure like telephone lines, but Moltke, who was supposed to be overseeing the whole of the war in the west at this point, ended up issuing no orders from the German Supreme Command during most of the battle to come. Neither did he receive any reports from Kluck or Bülow between 7 and 9 September. This was less than ideal in any battle, but it was about to have catastrophic consequences for the dying Schlieffen Plan.

For now, though, all this was to come. On the eve of his great offensive, Joffre despatched a note to France's war minister:

> The struggle that is about to commence might have a decisive outcome, but it might also have the gravest consequences for the country should it end in failure. In order to gain the victory, I am resolved to commit all our forces to the full, without holding anything back.[16]

*

Battle commenced at dawn on 6 September. Nearly two million men were involved. At Esternay, some 70 miles east of Paris, the German troops had no inclination of what was to come.

Tired soldiers were expecting a rest day. As they got up, many began bathing for the first time since they had left Germany. 'I am sitting on a chopping block and have had a shave,' wrote Hans Christian Brodersen with IR 86. He and his comrades were in good spirits. 'We've all slept.... like we would never wake up again. Oh, how lovely it is. There's a hustle and a bustle all around like in an anthill. Everyone is occupied. Some are washing shirts or socks... Some are cleaning rifles and others are treating their ruined feet.'[17] Suddenly, the peace and quiet was shattered by the howl of bugles sounding the alarm. French troops had been spotted advancing on Esternay, and soon the first shrapnel shells were exploding above them.

That day, elements of d'Espèrey's Fifth Army advanced as far as 3 miles. For IR 86, confusion reigned. Officers panicked and the men were ordered to dig shelters in an open field. 'Those who had spades were now envied by those who did not, and there was nothing left to do but employ fingers, bayonets and boot heels,' Brodersen wrote. He continued:

Shrapnel and high explosive shells flew about incessantly and swirled lumps of earth in all directions as they landed... we had our first taste of the accuracy of the French artillery. Down, down into the hard clay soil we needed to go, if we wanted to avoid too much exposure to the whirling shell splinters. Blood spurted from the fingertips, but since each handful of dirt provided increased protection, we continued the work without noticing it.[18]

Around noon, the order was given for the Germans to attack, but they were met with fierce resistance. 'With fear, I saw that the forward skirmish line was becoming uncannily thin,' recalled Hans Petersen. 'When they leapt forward, nearly half of them remained lying on the ground; they were either wounded or dead. Completely breathless, I threw myself down into a fresh shell crater.' As he tried to catch his breath, a wounded soldier grabbed him by the neck. 'He had been half covered by dirt and grime… He pulled my ear to his mouth and whispered, barely audible: "Help me, dear comrade… in the name of God, so that I will not lie here and die so far from home. What… would… my mother say", he groaned, "if she saw me lying here? Bandage me… quick… or I will die from blood loss. One of my arms has been torn off!" A slight shudder ran through me, a shell fragment had really torn off the arm close to the shoulder, and the blood poured out unceasingly… I bandaged the stump as best I could.'[19]

To the right, IR 84 was trying to advance across an open field. 'The concussion of an exploding shell caused me to tumble to the ground,' recalled Andreas Kylling. 'I was hit by a piece of shell in the arm. Soon after, a bullet entered the heel of my left boot.' When the French infantry was seen advancing in force, resolve crumbled and men began to run. 'I could not get out of the ditch, as two men had fallen dead on top of me, and they had probably saved my life,' Kylling continued. 'One of my comrades helped me up, but when we were about to join the retreat, a young lieutenant jumped up and shouted: "No, not back, but forward!" However, no one listened to him… our retreat began. It was our first, and it was carried out in complete disorder.'[20]

Back with IR 86, Hans Petersen had fallen behind the attack. As he tried to catch up, he saw ten men from his skirmish line running back towards him. '"What's the matter?" I shouted to Nis Abrahamsen. He waved his hand eagerly, warding me off, and shouted: "Back! We have no more men, it's certain death over there."' Realising that his company was retreating, Petersen quickly turned around and joined his friends in flight. 'We ran back like wild men, but only a few hundred [feet], then my lungs gave way. I became completely indifferent. What is the use, I thought; if I'm getting a bullet anyway, it might just as well hit me walking.' He slowed down and strolled, 'just as indifferently as on the street at home. Whenever I passed a wounded man, he shouted: "Take me with you, comrade, take me with you," or "Come and bandage me." But the emotions were almost dead, I paid no attention to them.'[21]

*

Isolated little victories were hard to come by. A mass of German cavalry regiments were rapidly allocated to try to bridge the burgeoning gap between Kluck and Bülow's armies. A ragged-looking force, they were required to fight for their lives on weary, emaciated horses. Reports kept filtering back that both British cavalry and French infantrymen were advancing on the front of the 1. Garde Dragoner Regiment. They appeared to be coming from all directions. First there was infantry on their left. As soon as that had been addressed by the German dragoons, British cavalry popped up on their right. The Kaiser's horsemen ran into them in the village of Dagny, 50 miles east of Paris:

> The squadron forms up for attack and gallops off, as a fresh outburst of firing comes from the village… The English cavalry, who were standing there, did not seem to think much of our attacking squadron. They awaited the charge standing still, firing from the saddle. Some of our men, struck by the bullets, roll out of their saddles. Before the actual shock the English wheel their horses about and flee. The squadron dashes into the village after them.[22]

There, the dragoons found French infantry, evidently just arrived. 'On one of the side streets, at the entrance to the village, machine-guns were being prepared for action. Serjeant Mehlis, a platoon leader, noticed this, swung his men around and charged into them with the lance. Not one of them was able to fire a shot'. What followed was gruesome: 'An English officer, a cool young fellow, made a cut at him. Buddenbrock, leaning over from his… horse, struck him with his heavy sabre square across the face.'[23] The outnumbered German cavalry then swung round and retraced their steps to avoid being scythed down.

*

On 7 September, the Sixth Army ran into Kluck's bolstered rear-guard and their advance stalled, but reinforcements were on the way. Among them was Paul Lintier, whose artillery unit had been transferred west. The roads from Paris out to the front were thick with traffic. Reinforcements were mixed with ammunition convoys rushing up to the front line. A morbid display of humanity flowed the other way. There were terrified refugees, the wounded and groups of German prisoners, 'one of which was made up of men so pleased to be marching away from the carnage in front that they marched towards Paris unescorted and in perfect order'.[24]

As Lintier walked, the more depressed he became. He had been on the march for more than ten hours without halting. Behind was Paris and in the distance, 'Montmartre reared its black silhouette against the western sky. The fields were lit up by the stars, which were exceptionally brilliant, but the road remained dark under the vault of tall trees planted in double rows on either side, between which floated a suffocating cloud of dust.' As night fell on 7 September, he was physically numb:

> The vehicles jolted and bumped so that it was veritable torture to sit on them... Our aching backs seemed no longer capable of sustaining our shoulders, and the breath came in gasps from our shaken chests. Our hearts thumped against our ribs, our heads swam, we perspired with pain. Should we never stop? Hour after hour we followed the same dark road.[25]

They finally stopped and began watering the horses next to a marshy river. Other batteries joined them, and then they saw something mesmerizing:

> A motor, showing no lights, forced its way through the herd of horses... Another car followed, then another, hundreds of them, silently and interminably. By the light of the moon, which had now risen, I was able to recognize the oil-skin caps usually worn by taxi-drivers. Inside the cabs I caught a glimpse of soldiers sleeping, their heads thrown back. 'Wounded?' asked somebody. 'No,' came the answer from

a passing car. 'It's the 7th Division from Paris. They're off to the front!'[26]

This unbelievable spectacle was all down to General Gallieni in Paris. He had been dealing with mayhem in both directions all day on 7 September. On the one hand, his job was to be ready to defend Paris. On the other, his role was also to support Joffre's offensive to the best of his ability and help drive the enemy away from Paris altogether. To send up reinforcements late in the day, he commandeered automobiles and wagons. He had already been using taxis to transport ammunition, but now he resolved to have as many as possible rounded up in order to rush more troops to the front. The military governor had ordered police officers and the Republican Guard, who were prowling the main streets of Paris, to flag down taxis, turn out their passengers, and send them off to military depots for orders.

Jean Jauffret was one of hundreds of drivers pressed into service. He was hailed by an official on the Champs Élysées. 'General Gallieni has requisitioned you to leave immediately,' he was told.[27] A little later at Porte de Pantin, four soldiers climbed into the back of his vehicle, destined for a 30-mile drive north-east. Their packs were stashed next to him in the front. One witness claimed that some drivers made off loudly singing the *Marseillaise*. 'Our taxis, who would have thought it?' recalled Parisian Georges Drouilly. 'The meters were running. What a bourgeois way to race to war,' he exclaimed. On their return, the taxi drivers said nothing. Civilians tried desperately to extract information from them, but the drivers were proud and tight-lipped about their role in defending their city. 'We can barely extract from them the confidence that they led soldiers as far as Dammartin,' complained Drouilly.[28] To Gallieni's credit, the city paid out more than 70,000 francs in fares, and when the sun rose, the reinforcements the taxi drivers had transported would join the battle.

24

Judgement

Galicia

News of the capture of Lemberg had spread quickly across the Russian empire. 'The Austrians are retreating in complete disorder, abandoning light and heavy guns, entire artillery parks and carts,' wrote an artillery officer as far away as Lithuania on 4 September.[1] There was a sense of euphoria in the air. However, while successes against the Austro-Hungarians were being celebrated, more sobering tales were beginning to seep out of East Prussia. 'Alongside the festive rejoicing comes sad news,' wrote one Russian doctor. 'In a subdued whisper it is conveyed from mouth to mouth that the Prussians unexpectedly threw a huge army at us, that in two days they... smashed us to pieces near Königsberg. They say that General Samsonov has been killed.'[2]

While news about Tannenberg somewhat dampened the victorious mood in Russia, it offered only scant consolation in Austria–Hungary. On the home front, people were whispering about the awful cost of the war. In mid-August, the first casualty lists had been published, and the growing number of women wearing black in the streets indicated that the number of losses at the front was significantly higher than officially reported. As the proclamation of victory at Kraśnik was being read aloud in Munkács in north-eastern Hungary, people were suspicious. Private correspondence with troops at the front revealed heavy casualties, and whispers spread that an entire regiment of hussars had been wiped out.

There was no spin that could be placed on the loss of Lemberg. '[It] frightened me,' wrote Jan Oeltjen, a Slovenian painter, on 6 September. 'The regiments of... Marburg and Graz... in particular are said to have been almost destroyed. If all this blood was shed for nothing, that would be terrible.'[3]

He just hoped the abandonment of the city was part a strategic move. Oeltjen had excitedly followed newspaper coverage of the war and celebrated numerous reports of victories. Now, he despaired that 'the Russians are now as far inside Austria as the Germans are in France'.[4] Things looked even worse at the front. Following the loss of the Galician capital, the retreat behind the River Wereszyca and the failure to encircle the Russian Fifth Army at Komarów, Conrad's armies were destabilized and evidence of carnage was everywhere. Farmhouses, barns and churches were overflowing with the wounded.

For Austria-Hungary, Brudermann's Third Army in particular was a complete shambles. The costly battles east of Lemberg and the subsequent retreat had left his men disheartened. Discipline had evaporated. He could not possibly remain in his post, and he was replaced by Svetozar Boroević, commander of VI Corps, who had proven himself at Komarów to be one of the Austro-Hungarian army's finest field commanders. Brudermann was shoved onto the first train to Vienna and unceremoniously retired, while Boroević set about the arduous task of restoring order and raising morale. His confidence proved contagious, and those under his command slowly but surely began to regain the belief that victory might be yet possible. Landsturm officer Viktor Arlow noted: 'From now on, we knew that we had a clever boss.'[5]

As Boroević took command of the Third Army and began to whip the routed troops back into shape, Auffenberg's Fourth Army was marching to their newly designated positions north of Lemberg. Their route led them back across the fields and through the forests and villages for which they had already shed so much blood. 'We marched towards Rawa Ruska,' recalled one cavalryman. 'In the area are hundreds of blackened... corpses of infantrymen, bloated to the thickness of a barrel.'[6] Pál Horváth, a

Hungarian artilleryman, concurred: 'They led us along a path of death... We were greeted by an indescribable stench... a few hundred [corpses] are still lying unburied in the hot sand.'[7] Frightened civilians emerged from doorways and windows to watch the long columns of exhausted men marching off to yet another battle.

Perplexed and dejected, Austro-Hungarian troops crossed the border out of Russian territory. By the end of the first day's march, enemy forces were also reported to be moving towards Rawa Ruska. The soldiers would have to press on. 'I jerked myself several times from dreams which told me that I had slept as I marched,' wrote one soldier.[8] 'Others I heard snoring as they walked beside me.' Béla Zombory-Moldován, a platoon leader in the k.u. Honvéd Infanterie Regiment Nr.31, recalled the toll the endless marching took on the soldiers' blistered feet, still unused to their stiff leather boots: 'All those dusty, sweaty feet; a pretty sight and a treat for the nose... Many of them limped, not daring to report [their pain] for fear of punishment.' When sorely needed halts were made, the exhausted men threw themselves on the ground. 'They removed their boots and fished out filthy, sweaty, decaying foot cloths. Those who had spares wrapped their feet in them; their poor, blistered, raw feet.'[9]

By 6 September, Auffenberg's Fourth Army was finally in position. His ailing men would be allowed no time to rest, as clashes with the Russians had already commenced. Marching in reserve, Zombory-Moldován approached the wooded heights north of the village of Magierów, east of Rawa Ruska. 'Suddenly a fountain of earth erupts; amid the flying fragments, three figures, limbs flailing. Then, further along, another cone-shaped fountain, men tumbling from it. Shelling! Our troops are advancing against artillery!'[10] Despite heavy losses, the Austro-Hungarians managed to seize the heights. However, the following morning, Russian guns began a devastating barrage in preparation for an infantry attack. Stupefied, Zombory-Moldován watched as, between salvos, his men frantically dug themselves deeper into the earth. Then, suddenly, a shell exploded near him:

Something has hit my knapsack and I'm almost suffocated under falling sand. My sole thought now, like an animal, is to save myself. Utterly helpless, I give myself up to my fate... I am reduced to a reflex; I no longer care whether I'm hit or not. I am completely cut off from everything around me. I have no idea how many are still alive out of the multitude behind me, or how many have run for their lives... I put my weight on my hands, like a runner, give the order: Pull back! My voice is cracked and carries no distance. I jump to my feet, and dimly see a few shadowy figures stand up and start to run. Summoning all my strength, I set off for the top of the slope in a crouching run: we'll be safe once we get to the other side... Over cartridge cases, scattered kit, dead bodies.[11]

Everywhere, the limited gains won by the Austro-Hungarians on 6 September were lost, as the Russians launched one strong counter-attack after the other. The bloodiest fighting took place at the northern end of the front. Here, Archduke Joseph Ferdinand was tasked with protecting the left and rear of Auffenberg's army, while strong Russian forces were seeking to outflank the entire Austro-Hungarian front. The Archduke's Kaiserjäger regiments attacked at sunrise on 7 September, aiming for the villages of Radostów and Telantyn. Meeting two entire Russian divisions, the Kaiserjägers had only just left their starting positions when they were battered by a murderous fire. Angelo Paoli was an Italian serving with the k.u.k. KJR 1:

It seemed like the end of the world: cannon fire, gunshots, the rapid fire of machine-guns, the bullets whistling everywhere; the dead and wounded were heaped around: some with no legs, some with no arms, those with heads split open, those wounded in the belly who were losing their intestines. The situation was impossible to describe. Little by little we reached a trench filled with our guys... It was all blood and corpses, you didn't even know where to step.

The order to advance was given. I made it maybe 300 paces and found a hole dug in the earth. I threw myself in it like a dead man; I couldn't advance any further.[12]

Blinded by the morning sun rising in the east behind the Russian positions, the Kaiserjägers struggled to locate the enemy. Firing wildly, ammunition quickly began to run short, and cries of *Munitionsmangel!* ('ammunition shortage'), began to sound from the forward companies. Nearly all those bearing supplies were killed or wounded trying to reach them. 'It was only with great difficulty that I was able to reach the foremost skirmish line with a few unwounded ammunition carriers,' wrote one officer:

The Jägers' defensive fire was noticeably weak. I dug into the ground next to a skirmisher and shoved ammo at him. He didn't move. I ordered him to toss the ammunition to his neighbour. When he still didn't pay attention, I gave him a shove and his head lolled to one side. Only then did I notice a small entry hole on the bridge of his nose - the skirmisher was dead. I crawled to the next one; this one was missing his skull cap.[13]

Before noon it was already clear that the attack had faltered all along the line, that the Russian artillery was dominant and that their Austro-Hungarian counterparts were being rendered impotent. With casualties mounting, many Kaiserjägers fled to the rear. Then cavalry patrols reported strong Russian forces advancing to the north, and with no troops available to fight them off, the order was given to withdraw some 3 miles west. However, due to the lack of communication with the forward troops, many units never received the order, and several were cut off and forced to surrender. Those who did retire were not much better off. With the enemy rapidly closing in and their fire continuing with undiminished strength, many were shot in the back as they retreated. Angelo Paoli remembered the terrifying flight:

I heard a voice to my left. I raised my eyes and saw a German from my company, who told me that all our guys were getting out. He had no sooner gotten those words out than a bullet cut through his throat. He fell back, screaming. I lifted my eyes a bit and saw the Russians, about 250 feet from me... I was desperate; I didn't know what to do. 'If I stay here', I told myself, 'they'll kill me. If I flee I'm as good as dead.' I couldn't even look at that poor guy they'd shot; I gathered what courage I could, lifted myself a bit and wriggled like a snake across the ground, then I got up and ran and entered another of our trenches: There, the dead and wounded were piling up on one another... The wounded yelled, 'For pity's sake, don't walk on me!'... I got hit slightly in my left hand and in my thigh. But once I got out of the trench, from among the dead and wounded, I set off running like a desperate man.[14]

Neither side could achieve more than localized success in four days of fighting. The number of casualties among the exhausted, ill-supplied troops was staggering. The k.u.k. KJR 1 suffered 1,000 in just a few hours. Due to the hasty retreat, many of the wounded were left on the battlefield, while others were piled up in barns and farms and left behind to be captured. The Russian 175th Baturinsky Infantry Regiment alone claimed to have taken some 2,400 Austro-Hungarian soldiers at Radostów.

*

The following days brought only further tragedy for the Kaiserjägers. These elite alpine troops were being squandered in droves on the flat plains of Galicia. During the night of 7 September, they pulled back to a new position around the village of Machnów, from where it was hoped the attack could be renewed. The march, conducted in depressing, pouring rain, led the exhausted men back across the Austro-Hungarian border and out of Russian territory. Defensive positions were prepared and stragglers picked up and quickly pushed into the gaping holes in the ranks.

On 9 September, enemy infantry could be seen advancing everywhere along their front, and Russian artillery soon began shelling their new defences. The Austro-Hungarians possessed little artillery for counter-battery work, and all they could do was wait for the Russians to come within range of their rifles and machine-guns. However, their enemy's recent experience during the Russo-Japanese War bore fruit again. The Russians crept slowly, letting the artillery do its deadly work. By midday, the situation had become untenable, and orders for another retreat were issued, but when the Kaiserjägers scrambled out of their defensive positions they were engulfed in more Russian artillery fire. As hopes of a renewed attack evaporated, Archduke Joseph Ferdinand was instead ordered to withdraw his battered group to a better position, to protect the Fourth Army's left flank. Victory would have to be won somewhere else.

*

The Austro-Hungarians had one last hope. On 8 September, Conrad had ordered Boroević's Third and Böhm-Ermolli's Second Army, now fully arrived from the Balkans, to attack across the River Wereszyca in support of Auffenberg's attack around Rawa Ruska. Almost immediately, they clashed with Brusilov's Eighth Army. Men were blown away by artillery, and officers' commands were completely drowned out by the noise of exploding shells. One lieutenant from the predominantly Croatian k.u.k. IR 96 wrote that the shrapnel 'flew as thick as schoolboys' snowballs'.[15]

Every available soldier was flung into action. Among them were all three of the Third Army's Landesschützen regiments, mountain troops recruited exclusively from Tyrol and Vorarlberg. One of them, Fioravanti Gottardi, a farmer from near Trient, remembered the scene that met him as his battalion entered the fray:

The thunder of cannon, the explosions of the bombs, the agonizing cries of the wounded blend together with the rolling groans of the dying! My mind is like a mill; it's impossible to think or form a clear thought. In a moment my family springs to my mind, but the commander's yell makes me forget everything. Forward to the assault! Coming out of the woods, we advance, mixing with the other lines, and at the sound of the drum and the bugle we attack the Russians. The yelling was tremendous, so much so that the enemy turned tail and ran.[16]

The first day brought some successes for the Austro-Hungarians, however, every inch of ground taken was paid for in copious amounts of blood. The battle that resumed the following day was marked by intense artillery duels. Once again, the Russians completely out-gunned their opponents. Kornél Szojka of the Austro-Hungarian k.u.k. IR 46 recalled: 'Here, too, we felt the Russians' superiority of fire and… it was discouraging, demoralizing. How can a soldier go into battle with enthusiasm if he feels and experiences first-hand that he is not being helped or supported enough by his own side?'[17] Fioravanti Gottardi suffered too:

While we are advancing on the plains… the enemy artillery targets us and begins the extermination. My poor battalion! The projectiles fall like rain… Death was circling all around me. The commander of my company, seeing the dangerous situation, raises his voice and shouts: 'Save yourself if you can!' Poor guy! It may have been his last shout, inasmuch as I never saw him again that day… With luck I saved myself, or maybe it wasn't my time, given that a grenade burst two steps from me and threw me… I got up feeling a bit beaten down, but fortunately unharmed.[18]

Every limited success came at incredible cost. The *Bosniaken* of k.u.k. BH IR 3, newly arrived from Serbia, managed to take a Russian position capturing both prisoners and guns, but casualties were heavy. In the course of just one hour, command of the regiment changed hands twice. By the end of the day, it was led by a captain. The battlefield was covered in tortured humanity.

'The terrain we were marching over was all covered with cadavers, with their faces all distorted, splashed with blood and mud, with the eyes open from the pain and probably also from terror,' wrote Giacomo Sommavilla, an Italian assigned to transport duty. 'The wounded pass by, pale and dripping with blood, staring at us with bewildered expressions, almost all of them asking for something to drink. Some were trembling with fear, some swearing at their fate in a thousand ways.'[19]

Conrad's troops had reached breaking point. Despite this, he still maintained hopes of reversing the unfolding disaster, and his orders for 10 September were for the Second, Third and Fourth Armies to resume attacking in the direction of Lemberg. The Austro-Hungarian troops were exhausted from weeks of uninterrupted marching and fighting, yet they continued to throw themselves at the Russians in desperate attempts to force a breakthrough. 'At 2 o'clock in the morning, it began to crackle as if it was judgement day,' wrote Boštjan Olip, a Slovenian.[20]

That night, the sound of gunfire died out, replaced by the cries of the wounded, begging for help and pleading for water. The following day the battle resumed. 'Again, I was in mortal danger,' Olip continued. 'Shrapnel tore my knapsack and one bullet went through my coat and hit my best friend right next to me in the arm. I bandaged him and he walked off. I felt terrible. I thought to myself, but he is going to my home. I told him to greet them, and I nearly cried… the bullets whistled around me like flies, but none of them hit me. I do not know why. I was in such terrible agony that I almost wanted a bullet to hit me.'[21]

25

Miracle on the Marne

France

Kluck's reinforcements were preventing Maunoury's Sixth Army from crossing the River Ourcq. Instead of a starring role in Joffre's grand offensive, these Frenchmen faced a thankless fight in a supporting role and badly needed the men being sent up by Gallieni on the night of 7 September. At Nanteuil-le-Haudouin, Paul Lintier and his artillery unit strongly suspected that Paris was under threat. They were enjoying a morning coffee in companionable silence when suddenly, the ground was crawling with infantry. 'Companies and battalions were emerging from the woods and from behind the hedges... Orders came for us to go and take up position... We were seized with a fit of wild rage. Would they manage to pass us, and get to Paris? To Paris, to our homes... to kill, sack, rape?' The artillerymen watched, incredulous as their comrades streamed past them. Guns should never be in front of the infantry. If they are, the battle has gone very wrong. But things got even worse when suddenly, rifle fire broke out behind them: 'We had been outflanked!' wrote Lintier.[1]

The gunners spent the day blasting away at the oncoming enemy. 'The guns became roaring monsters, raging dragons, and from their gaping mouths belched fire... Piles of smoking cartridges-cases mounted up behind [them].' Inside, Lintier was panicking. 'Night fell... Some mounted *chasseurs* passed by at a trot, followed by a whole brigade of *cuirassiers*. It was the retreat! We were beaten!... beaten!... The enemy was marching on Paris!'[2] It seemed there was no escape. Nearby, Charles Delvert was with the 101st RI and lamenting his bright red trousers, visible a mile off. 'We were', said General de Fonclare, 'dressed like parrots'... 'a dream target.'[3]

*

Kluck and Bülow were not the only German army commanders attempting to press forward. In Crown Prince Wilhelm's sector at the eastern end of the battlefield, General Sarrail's Third Army had pummelled his front on 6 September. A violent artillery duel followed. In the following days, outnumbered Frenchmen performed admirably on their right flank next to Verdun, which Sarrail refused to give up. This was not the only flashpoint that he had to worry about. On Sarrail's left, the line ruptured between the Third and Fourth Armies and chaos ensued. At 8.00 p.m. on 8 September, Joffre gave Sarrail permission to relinquish Verdun if he had to favour one flank. It was not a choice any general would want to have to face, and though the burden of making it had been lifted from Sarrail's shoulders, he refused to let the connection to Verdun be severed. It might yet prove to be a foolhardy decision.

Georges Bertrand and his regiment of chasseurs alpins had been abruptly pulled from the Second Army and sent west. They had no idea why they were moving, or where to, as they trudged night after night. 'At first, curious to know where we were going, we tried to overhear information.' The further they walked, the less they cared. These were men already exhausted after fighting the Battle of the Frontiers in Lorraine. To compound their misery, many of the ranks were suffering from dysentery. 'Every moment we saw men falling to the side of the road and groaning in pain.' By the time they reached the rear of the battle on the morning of 7 September, they were greeted by the locals, who were shocked at the state of them:

Walking more with heart than with feet... [we] continued to advance. The people of Bar-le-Duc watched us pass with painful emotion. There was no reproach in their eyes; because they felt that we could not make a greater effort. They imagined… bold and tireless *Chasseurs Alpins*, climbing peaks, crossing glaciers, and constantly hanging on ropes which prevent them from falling into the abyss… And here they saw them simply marching by in front of them as a ghost battalion.[4]

The following day, this same battalion was launched into action to try to maintain the link between the Third and Fourth Armies before the eastern end of the French line was severed from Paris and encircled. Strategically, this should have been Sarrail's ultimate priority, not Verdun. If those armies lost touch, it would leave the way open for the Germans to plough into the rear of de Castelnau's Second Army to the right, which was embroiled in its own nightmare struggle for survival facing east. If Joffre's right crumbled and his armies were divided, it mattered little what was achieved on the left.

At 3.00 a.m. on 8 September, Georges Bertrand and his men moved off in the direction of Vassincourt. A formation of German troops from Württemberg had worked hard to put this village in a state of defence. It was surrounded by a number of ridges, and Bertrand's company was ordered to take one of them. The German artillery had marked this high ground, and any Frenchman who tried to venture up onto it was met with heavy shellfire. Once they made it, men's nerves started to fray. Bertrand watched with surprise as a soldier destined for the church spied a German attempting to crawl away from the vicinity of a nearby farm and took aim, furiously shooting at him. Another man tried to stop him: 'You shoot a wounded person!' The churchman was not convinced. '"Oh! No," he replies, "he pretends to be"… And my chasseur, future priest… takes aim at his fellow one last time and shoots him, adding: "Besides, so much the better. I will kill him more easily." This is how the mentality of man changes in the heat of battle.'[5]

Opposite, Hugo Birkner of RIR 88 had also set off before dawn down a road to Vassincourt. As his company emerged from a forest, they spotted an enemy patrol. 'The first shots had barely been fired when the hammering tak, tak, tak of the French machine-guns began from the town and the bullets whistled over our heads.' The famous French 75s had registered their presence. 'In the murderous French machine-gun fire, the attack progressed slowly across the open terrain and came to a standstill.' Here, Birkner and his comrades were forced to wait for reinforcements. At 10.00 a.m., 'a line of riflemen from the 6th Silesian Jägers appeared to the left behind us... The command "fix bayonets" runs through the ranks. We watch as individual Frenchmen jump up [and] run away. Once again there is shooting!... Then "Onwards, march-march" with a beating drum against the village.'[6]

Outside Vassincourt, Georges Bertrand watched as a German regiment with fixed bayonets were mown down. 'Every time one of them makes a move, the machine-gun starts, and it is a pleasure to see enemies fall, sink to the ground, making gestures of suffering, sounding a death rattle, dying. It truly warms the heart.' Bertrand felt good about their own progress. 'We only have a depression to cross, the opposite slope to climb, and we will enter the village. I am ruminating over this project within myself, and I am looking forward to being the first to enter Vassincourt with my men. I shout, joyfully, to [a comrade] "If I advance, support me with your fire!"' Then the situation rapidly changed:

Now, at this moment, we hear... singing in the distance. This noise increases, becomes more rapid, disordered, breathless. This song, at first rather slow like a chant or a funeral march, gradually gives way to wild cries... What is it, my God, what is it?... I then see in the valley a spectacle... With physical words, how can we convey the impression of physical enormity! An entire German brigade, at a running pace, launched a counter-attack on our left... We are overwhelmed. The grey uniforms sweep across the meadow. They seem to be driven by an invisible force, and although they begin to fall in large numbers, we always see others replacing them. It's both beautiful and terrifying.[7]

Bertrand ordered his men to open fire, useless as it seemed:

> Everything starts moving, everyone tumbles down the slope, everyone screams... the blue uniforms rush and fall into the German mass. What happened in that minute, I really don't know. I can still see some details, but the whole thing is drowned out like a fog. I see my brave little Chasseur Cabannes, having passed us all by a few feet, brandishing his weapon, crazy, glorious, epic. I can still see him, driving his bayonet into the stomachs of the Germans surrounding him.[8]

The spectacle only grew more horrifying. He watched one of his men turn and run from the enemy, only to get skewered in the backside by a German soldier. 'My chasseur turns around, furious and angry,' wrote Bertrand, 'and... plants his bayonet right in his mouth.' Somewhere in his mind he had a recollection of two men, 'rolling on the ground, and using their bayonets as daggers'. There was more to come. Again, his men fell upon the enemy:

> It is once again brutal and intoxicating hand-to-hand combat... My two revolvers are empty. I grab the bayonet of one of my men who fell at my side, and in my turn, with a drunken soul, I play the bladed weapon. There are no more officers, there are no more soldiers, there are only men who defend their own skin, who rush forward, their mouths open, their features contracted.[9]

Once again they had earned a reprieve, but Georges Bertrand had no desire to outrun his luck. With his men he made for a small wood. 'We jump a stream. But the Germans... opened hellfire on us, and I received a bullet in the arm.' This time, the enemy succeeded in pushing the French away from Vassincourt. Having been bandaged up, Bertrand returned to his men. 'We read in their eyes the fatigue. They drag themselves along miserably. The failure of this day takes away the courage they need to continue the fight. Night falls, and the melancholy of the evening seems to penetrate them.'[10]

Opposite, Hugo Birkner had also survived the day. 'Over 200 prisoners fell into our hands when we entered [Vassincourt],' he claimed. 'Several barns were set on fire and soon the entire village was aflame.' The last thing the men of RIR 88 wanted was to begin again in the morning, but their enemy was insistent. 'An early morning counter-attack by the French, who wanted to surprise us in the dark, collapsed bloodily in the fire of our rifles and machine-guns.' Birkner recalled that the artillery fire of 9 September was 'the likes of which we had never encountered before'.[11]

Georges Bertrand, with his arm wound, wavered. He got permission to stay behind and rest. 'I'm going to find the commander to ask permission to stay in the ambulance. My arm hurts and I have a fever.'[12] However, his conscience could not stand it, and he decided to rejoin his men. He rounded up supplies to take with him, and managed to scrounge up some bread and some English sweets. He found his chasseurs embroiled in the fighting, and Creutzer, their machine-gun officer, up a tree directing his men's fire by telephone. 'They soon located our poor trench and shot it up,' wrote Hugo Birkner, 'so that the battalion gave the order to vacate the position around midday.' Bertrand's company kept a depressing vigil all night in the rain, in case the enemy attacked:

> Our men have fixed bayonets and are standing, wrapped in their large coats... The rain still falls... In the night, like a funeral echo, desperate calls resound... wounded Germans calling for help from their brothers in arms... The whole night passes like this, in expectation, in fever and suffering. I am leaning against a tree with my comrade, and at times he bends over me, asking me solicitously: 'Aren't you in pain?'... All that night, in the rain, waiting for the attack, we sucked English sweets.[13]

*

With a front of more than 20 miles, General Foch viewed the Ninth Army's situation with trepidation. His main concern was the far right of his line, and the yawning 23-mile gap between where it ended at Lenharré and Vitry-le-Francois, where the Fourth Army's sector began. He had a single cavalry division available to cover that stretch, and faced the very real prospect of his army being outflanked and attacked from behind. To add to his concerns, the Fourth Army had told him that he was on his own, as they were desperately trying to prevent their link with the Third Army to the east disintegrating completely at places like Vassincourt.

Foch tasked the Moroccan Division with preventing Bülow's Second Army from emerging out of the southern side of the Saint-Gond Marshes. With the 7th Tirailleurs, at dawn on 6 September, Senegalese volunteer Bakary Diallo sat on top of a ridge:

> Everywhere, especially in the east, the feeble light gets stronger and the darkness recedes from the hillsides… The sky grows lighter above us… The rifles, cannons, and other innocent tools that kill their masters aren't making any noise. The troops are eating breakfast and drinking coffee. Everything had been prepared during the night and we need to be nourished in order to have the strength to die.[14]

As soon as the battle began, the German artillery began pounding advanced groups of tirailleurs, forcing them back. Knowing how important it was to stop the enemy getting out of the marshes, the colonial troops launched three attacks, but each time they were pinned down by machine-guns and artillery. Back on the crest of the ridge they sat under a deluge of 'terrible violence'.[15] By lunchtime, Foch intervened. He ordered the men covering the marshes to find 'defensive positions of such indisputable strength' as to make it impossible for the Germans to dislodge them. To ram it home, he added: 'The location and distribution of troops… must be such as to obtain the above result without possibility of failure.'[16] They were to leave it all on the battlefield.

In the long stretch of plains manned by his cavalry, Foch's men had to cede ground, but despite being bludgeoned all day, the Ninth Army clung on. By nightfall, Bülow's men were emerging all along the southern edge of the marshes. French artillery was managing to keep them there, and in front, Foch's infantry, including the Moroccan Division, were dug in, waiting.

Lieutenant Becker was leading a company of IR 77 towards the French colonials in the village of Courjeonnet. As the leading platoon approached the first row of houses, they were met by heavy fire. 'All hell breaks loose. We're lying like snakes on the stubble field, no cover... A hail of bullets showers us and this damn machine-gun fire. You can hear every shell hitting the parched ground. Piu, piu, that's how it sounds left and right.' He stood up to watch. 'My forward platoon is in a terrible position. In the first few seconds everyone threw themselves down, nose in the dirt, but immediately the anger grew. We too can do what they're doing. Gun to the cheek and fire!' Becker realized that a frontal attack would be too costly. Instead, he ordered his men to find cover. 'The world speed skating champion could hardly have done it any faster! When the machine-gun company arrived and our artillery sent some kind greetings to the village, the Zouaves made sure they got away, and we followed suit with a *Hurrah*. But the harem-pants disappeared so quickly that we could no longer hold them.'[17]

The right flank of Foch's army began to fold, and with that came the terrifying prospect of the enemy coming around and ploughing into the back of his left, imperilling the likes of the Moroccan Division. On 8 September the German attacks became more violent, as both Bülow's Second and Hausen's Third Armies launched themselves at Foch's right. As his flank gave way, the centre of the Ninth Army's line began back-peddling too. Foch made a bold decision in keeping with his war philosophy. To defend their line, to prevent their flank being turned, his men would attack.

General Eydoux's corps was collapsing on his far right. Foch sent staff officer André Tardieu to find him and state the obvious:

'You cannot let them through.' Tardieu found Eydoux on top of a ridge to the south of Fère-Champenoise, having just given away his staff cars to transport the wounded. 'General Eydoux is seated, with his officers, among the dead, on the edge of a ditch.' All of them appeared to be in a complete stupor as he presented Foch's orders. They clearly thought the instructions were mad. 'Eydoux hands the paper over to his officers without saying a word. The orders are immediately transcribed and transmitted.' Tardieu was nearly in tears when he left:

The wounded were coming in... There's a lieutenant: between his jacket and his boots, only bloody mush. A German shell blew up a gun carriage, which broke his thighs. He dies twenty minutes later. 'Would you like, Tardieu,' said Eydoux to me softly, 'to go and inform General Foch that his orders have been transmitted and will be carried out? In what conditions? I dare not say. You have seen the state of my infantry.'[18]

Tardieu found Foch pacing in a garden at his headquarters. The winner, he reasoned, would be the side that cared the most. 'And he adds, pulling his moustache: "Go away! Leave immediately! Tell Eydoux that, more than ever, I maintain my order. Offensive! Offensive! Offensive!"'[19]

'The battle begins again', wrote Bakary Diallo, 'with the awful, sorrowful racket of cannon-fire, rifles, and machine-guns.' In front of the 7th Tirailleurs, the enemy was massing behind an embankment and preparing to attack. 'Our divisional artillery keeps watch and the 75s thunder non-stop.'[20] Overall, the colonial troops managed to hold their position, but in one spot, the Germans plunged into their lines and seized a château on the high ground at Mondement at 6.00 a.m. The Moroccan Division had no reserves to put into play, and so part of the 77th RI was summoned from 5 miles away to counter-attack.

The colonial troops fought on. Exhausted, they held on until the 77th arrived, then at mid-afternoon they lunged for

Mondement, straight into heavy machine-gun fire coming from the windows of the château. In the meantime, Foch had sent out a plea to his men. While it was true that his army was spent, news he received during the day confirmed that the opposition was in a similar state. They had to strike now:

> It is impossible to exaggerate the importance of taking advantage of this situation, and I ask each one of you to draw upon that last spark of energy which in its moments of supreme trial has never been denied our race. The disorder in the enemy's ranks is the herald of our victory. If you fight on with undiminished spirit, you will stop him today, and tomorrow we will begin to drive him out of our country. Remember that success will come to the side that holds out longest. The honour and safety of France are in the balance. One more effort and you are certain to win.[21]

Ridiculous, brave beyond reproach, or a combination of both, there was a reason that Foch was destined to become Supreme Commander of the Allied forces on the Western Front.

On the third attempt, the château at Mondement passed back into French hands. At 7.00 p.m. on 9 September, the commander of the 77th, Colonel Lestoquoi, 'sent the following laconic report: "I hold the village and Château de Mondement and am establishing myself there for the night."'[22] France owed much to his men, and to the Moroccan Division, which Foch wrote 'had been essential to the success of our armies... This ground in the hands of the enemy would have opened up to him that portion of the plain of Champagne to which the Ninth Army had been clinging for dear life for four long days.'[23]

*

In Vitry-le-François on the far left of the Fourth Army, as the Battle of the Marne began, Father Nottin and the other hostages were released on probation on the understanding that if a single civilian acted against a German soldier, they would be shot.

At this point, they had heard that threat so often that it barely alarmed them anymore. The local church was fated to become a field hospital. An imperious German officer announcing himself as chaplain of the divisional ambulance demanded the keys and bragged about the progress of the fighting in halting French. 'Now is the great battle. The Germans are victorious... always victorious... In two days it will be over... we will be in Paris... You? You will be Germans. Already now you are Germans... The town of Vitry belongs to us.'[24]

Lit by candles, the entire floor of the church was strewn with straw to soak up the blood. At barely 5.00 a.m. [on 6 September,] 'already, the aisles are filled with wounded. We begin to lay some on the straw beds of the great nave. Before noon, I will count 700 of them, including about thirty French.' As Hausen's Third Army tried to pry apart the tenuous link between Foch's force and Fourth Army, another field ambulance went into operation at a boarding school. Father Nottin began carrying out his Catholic rituals for the sick, and although the German officers looked at him oddly, nobody tried to stop him. 'Oh! the horrible spectacle of these men torn to pieces by our 75s,' he lamented. 'From all sides the cannonade rolled its thunder... We felt like we were locked in a ring of iron and fire... The wounded arrived in droves, brought on cars of all kinds: regimental ambulance cars, carts, harvest wagons and dump trucks.'[25]

In carrying out their work, the Germans he encountered were professional and well organized, but it was obvious that they were in no way prepared for the scale of this battle. The German sapper who wrote his anonymous memoirs arrived in Vitry with the remnants of his company. 'There was not a single house in the whole town that was not overcrowded with wounded men,' he wrote. They soon found Father Nottin's church.

We sat down and gazed at the misery around us... The dead were carried out to make room for others. The bodies were taken to one side where whole rows of them were lying already... Some of them were in uniforms that were still quite good, while [ours] were nothing but rags hanging from our backs… 'Let us take some infantry coats,' somebody ventured… 'A coat is a coat.' So we went and took the coats from several bodies and tried them on. Taking off their clothes was no easy job, for the corpses were already rigid like a piece of wood.[26]

Decent boots were harder to come by, and removing them was problematic when they did find a sturdy pair. 'Two were holding the leg of the dead man while the two others tugged at the boot. It was of no use; the leg and the foot were so rigid that it was impossible to get the boot off.' An infantryman watching them made a wry joke. 'Let them keep their old boots, they don't want to walk on their bare feet.' The sappers found this hilarious. They laughed. 'And why not? Here we were out of danger. What were the others to us? We were still alive and those lying there could hear no longer.'[27]

Outside, Father Nottin was mortified. 'Those who have not seen it with their own eyes will never be able to imagine exactly the state of dirt in which the Germans, in less than two days, had ruined our town.' As well as dead horses, empty cans and broken bottles, outside the buildings being used to house the wounded the sight was harrowing. 'Heaps of bandages smeared with blood and infected pus.' The occupying army refused to help clean up: 'The soldiers are for the war. This task is for the civilians.' Nottin grovelled to the remaining townspeople and they made him proud. 'We had at our disposal only two wagons, each harnessed to a single horse… So it was by harnessing themselves to handcarts that these men had to do much of the work.'[28]

*

By the morning of 8 September, the Germans had the remains of four exhausted cavalry divisions plugging the gap between the First and Second Armies, grateful that the British opposite them were not probing forward with any vigour. At this point, the Germans believed that they would continue their advance towards the Seine, but at 5.00 a.m. the horsemen got a nasty shock with the news that the infantry they were supporting were withdrawing. Now there was a new plan to cover them as they tried to disengage from the BEF and the French Fifth Army, a plan that was complicated by the roving presence of no small amount of cavalry belonging to both sides.

Twenty-five-year-old Second Lieutenant René Chambe was leading a portion of the 20e Régiment de Dragons. They had spent the previous day getting progressively more angry at the destruction levelled on their homeland as they followed the retiring German forces. '[We] are in the vanguard of the division,' he explained. 'My platoon is at the forefront. We are the first to discover everything, to see everything.' The enemy was mocking them on their way north. On one house was chalked: 'Thank you to the excellent French army for the good dinner they let us have!'[29]

Chambe could feel the rage simmering behind him as he led his men. 'Some, discovering each detail, each new horror, grit their teeth and murmur: "*The pigs! The bandits!*"' To some extent, this anger made them better soldiers. 'A few more shows like this and I won't be able to hold them anymore, they will become lions! I turn around in the saddle to see them behind me and I say to them: "You see what they came to do in France! *Never forget it!*"'[30]

Despite the filth and destruction they witnessed, it had not escaped the cavalrymen's notice that they were finally advancing. Morale was returning, but as they continued to ride forward, frustration mounted again. Bülow now had no choice but to pull back the flank of his army, and as he did so, he merely opened the way further for the Allies. They had a vulnerable enemy running away in front of them, and men like Chambe could not understand why they were not allowed to give chase. On the morning of 9 September, his regiment saddled up and moved off at 4.30 a.m. to ride into Château Thierry on the Marne. He peered down into the valley at the town, then with trepidation at the heights surrounding it. 'From the top of the ridges, I search using my binoculars.' As he observed, Chambe spotted a number of horsemen in grey uniforms on the heights above the other bank of the river.

His squadron was supporting a unit of artillery, and they promptly began loosing off relatively benign projectiles. 'The aim of this shot is to attract fire from enemy batteries which could be hidden in the surrounding area and would thus betray themselves.' In addition, the artillerymen hoped that it would also terrify any stragglers left behind by the Germans to slow their advance. By evening, the French cavalry was ready to exploit this preparation. Chambe watched as the first two squadrons of his regiment rode in to occupy Château Thierry at the main bridge over the Marne. It was taken at the point of the bayonet and the enemy guarding it were captured. 'Among them, nurses with Red Cross armbands. They risk being shot for taking up arms.' What to do with those women was significantly above Chambe's pay grade. 'It's not our business. We take them to the rear, someone else will decide.'[31]

As for his squadron, they were ordered to dismount and attack the town's railway station, and he described it as an 'easy and briskly handled affair'. His men found three 'shaggy and staggering Germans' in a first class carriage who were more than willing to become prisoners. 'They raise their hands, terrified. They are drunk and don't understand anything. But they are satisfied and laugh, reassured, when I shout to them: "*Gefangene* ['prisoners']!" They offer no resistance. On the contrary. They hurry to join us... It's done, Château Thierry is taken. No losses to my platoon.'

Throughout the town, hundreds of German troops began emerging with their hands up. These men had not wanted to die. 'They waited for the fight to end... There is everything, infantry, Uhlans, light horsemen, artillery. Others were found hidden even in wardrobes.' The men of the 20th Dragoons were intoxicated by the thought of what all of this meant. 'It's still broad daylight. We feel that there is nothing in front of us!... For the enemy to have let us cross the Marne so easily, he must not have had much to oppose us.'[32] They waited for the order to finally come, to mount their horses and run down the enemy in front of them.

1 (*above*). Crowds at Paris's Gare de l'Est clamour to watch men leaving for war. It would be weeks before their families would hear from them again.

2 (*left*). Summoned for war, a Frenchman bids goodbye to his loved ones at New York before sailing for Europe aboard *La France*.

3 (*right*). Smiling in their brand-new uniforms, a group of newly mobilised Hungarian soldiers rest in Budapest, July/August 1914.

4 (*right*). Muslims pray for victory for the Tsar's armies in a Petrograd mosque.

5 (*below*). Horses of a Russian cavalry regiment being loaded onto a train in Helsinki, 1914.

6 (*bottom*). A Belgian regiment leaves for the front, August 1914.

7 (*above*). German soldiers wounded in front of Liège receive treatment in the field.

8 (*left*). The image of French territorials as wizened old men was widely dispersed in wartime pictorial magazines. Their performance often exceeded expectation.

9 (*below*). Commander Hartigan of the NYPD investigates price gouging in 1914. Rising prices were rampant on every continent.

10. American women gather for a 'Peace Parade' in August 1914. New York also saw massive pro-war demonstrations.

11. Serbian infantry marching off to the front to the sound of drums and trumpets, 1914.

12 (*above*). Locals dispose of dead horses after the repeatedly disastrous German cavalry charges at Haelen in August 1914.

13 (*below*). An Austrian soldier lies unburied where he fell in the Balkans.

14 (*above*). The inhabitants of Brussels watch on miserably as German troops occupy their city. With no strategic value, it was left to the enemy to prevent bloodshed.

15 (*right*). A Serbian officer interrogates a group of Austro-Hungarian prisoners of war.

16 (*center*). An elderly Belgian woman attempts to harvest crops in the absence of able-bodied men. Across Europe, crops rotted in the fields.

17 (*below*). German women form long queues to obtain 'second grade' meat. Shortages were common as worldwide trade was disrupted and hoarding was common.

18. A rush on a Berlin bank on the outbreak of war. Similar scenes prevailed across the globe.

19. Despite the Spanish ban on discussing the war in print, crowds in Madrid gather at a 250ft display charting the progress of the war.

20 (*above*). French cavalry in dated uniforms occupy the trenches common in the opening weeks of war. They bear no resemblance to those seen later on.

21 (*right*). German infantry march through a battle-scarred village in East Prussia, September 1914.

22 (*below*). Polish refugees pictured fleeing their home during the opening weeks of war. Millions were displaced at the beginning of the conflict.

23 (*above*). Serbian refugees from Budapest rest by the roadside. Represented here are people from both the lower and middle classes.

24 (*left*). A French soldier attempts to help a wounded comrade on the battlefield.

25 (*right*). Civilians welcome members of the British Expeditionary Force to France. Kitchener issued strict instructions about the respectful behaviour he expected from troops.

26 (*right*). Members of 'the Black Squad'. Life below decks during the First World War was arduous and the rewards were pitiful.

27 (*center*). A Maurice Farman early in the war. The types of aircraft used in the opening weeks of the conflict were extremely flimsy.

28 (*below*). Battlefield clearance. With no infrastructure in place to dispose of the dead, Belgian civilians bury a German soldier.

29. A train full of Russian soldiers, captured by the Germans during the Battle of Tannenberg, make a short halt.

30. The destruction of Paris. Members of Gallieni's workforce dig trenches on the outskirts of the city as German armies approach.

31. A convoy of French Spahis from North Africa deployed on the Marne.

32. Senegalese soldiers care for their wounded in the opening weeks of the war. Thousands more would soon arrive in Europe.

33. An artist's rendering of the final moments of HMS *Aboukir*.

34. A commemorative German postcard celebrating the exploits of U-9 in sinking three British ships on one morning in September 1914.

35. A Japanese aviator on the outbreak of war. Launched from rudimentary aircraft carriers, they tormented the Germans at Tsingtao.

36. German officers with their indigenous troops in German New Guinea.

37. Russian cavalrymen commemorate their victory with a photograph in Galicia.

38. British soldiers pose with guns captured by the 1st Lincolns during the Battle of the Marne.

39. French colonial troops search through abandoned kit in the aftermath of the Miracle on the Marne. Their contribution was instrumental in the Allied victory.

40. Indian troops photographed next to their transport. It was always the plan to deploy them in the event of a world war, but not necessarily to Europe.

While René Chambe's cavalry regiment broke the line at Château Thierry late on 9 September, the BEF had beaten them across the Marne. Early in the day, the British had seized several bridges across the river starting from Château Thierry and moving west to La Ferté-sous-Jouarre, 17 miles away. Their efforts would have a knock-on effect up and down the Allied line.

Arthur Corbett-Smith described the fluid situation on the British front. 'You have the German rear-guards crossing the river and following the main bodies which are trekking off to the north as hard as they can move,' he recorded. 'The British are gradually gaining the southern ridges and then launching... in stern pursuit. But although it is definite pursuit, the fighting is deadly serious all through, and every point of vantage which can help the enemy is hotly contested by them.'[33]

It was a sensible observation. The Germans might have lost the river, but their withdrawal was still by no means a rout. A number of retiring troops had been fortifying the village of Orly, 8 miles from La Ferté-sous-Jouarre, when at 10.00 a.m. significant Allied forces were spotted. '[They] had made a lot of camouflaged positions which afterwards took the English in... for instance, to the right of the village a most conspicuous line of trenches was dug on the parapet of which were shakos and poles indicating the positions of the supposed defenders.' Instead, the defenders were actually in a well-shaded trench some distance away which largely escaped shell fire, 'while the dummy trench in front was almost wiped out by a tremendous rain of shells'. Hidden behind walls and hedges on the fringes of the village, the German sharpshooters waited to open fire. 'Everyone was in the best of spirits and awaited... the long desired attack of the enemy.' Lieutenant Nickisch von Rosenegk, commanding a pioneer section, described the wait:

I sat with the leader and an officer of the machine-gun company on a heap of straw and heard the first bullets from the enemy infantry whistling overhead. We crawled rapidly to our stations and started a return fire. The English shot at us in the craziest fashion. But luckily they fired too high, over our heads, at the high walls decorated with shakos and caps. I will never forget the whistling and singing of these bullets as long as I live. It was as if an immense swarm of bees was flying overhead.[34]

Determined as the defenders were, by the end of the day the BEF had a bridgehead some 5 miles on from the north bank of the Marne. At this point, German defeat here was assured. One of Bülow's staff officers wrote that 'the army received, absolutely unexpectedly... the order to withdraw from the Supreme Command... to fall back [north]. We... had to begin the retreat the same night... without any preparation having been made.'[35]

By the evening of 9 September, Joffre knew he had won the battle, on the left at least. Quietly, he informed the war minister that the British were over the Marne and that he anticipated the French would follow.

In Paris nothing had been left to chance. If the Germans tried to envelop the city again, Gallieni would be ready. After a night on high alert, at dawn on 10 September everybody was expected to man his posts to defend the city to the last, because if the enemy came, their chances of fending him off were slim. Gallieni was grateful to have got his hands on 300 wounded Germans. He wanted them put in hospitals throughout the city and treated like kings, because if their comrades arrived, it might lessen their wrath to see them well tended. With the greatest secrecy, he also had 100 taxis on standby to whisk away precious officers, allowed to take nothing but a satchel, so that they might remain free to lead the army in the event of disaster. None of them would be told of their escape until the last possible moment.

*

It was the men of the Sixth Army who were most surprised at events on 10 September. Paul Lintier was prepared to fight for his life. 'After yesterday... we had expected a furious cannonade to begin at dawn... The sun illuminated the plain and the slopes upon which we were waiting for the enemy in firing position. Not a single gun was fired, and we began to grow surprised and uneasy.' Eventually a passing infantry officer recognized Lintier's commander and stopped to talk: 'Then you don't know what's happened?' Clearly, the artillerymen did not. '"The Germans are retiring all along the line." The two officers looked at each other and smiled. "Then in that case..." "It's victory!" The news passed rapidly from gun to gun and nearly set the men dancing with joy. Victory, victory! And just when we were not expecting it!'[36]

*

Cavalryman Christian Mallet was entering his fifth day without food. He was exhausted, physically and emotionally. At a farm, 'for two hours we remained holed up, scanning the surrounding countryside to discover traces of life. Everything seems dead. Not a peasant, not a civilian, not even an animal.' At about 10.00 a.m. he saw a 'thin black [line] of soldiers' approaching:

My heart [feels] like it's beating out of my chest... If they are Germans, the game is lost... And I look, I look with bulging eyes. At times, because of the exaggerated tension, everything becomes blurred... then the next second I find the caterpillar growing, the details of which I begin to distinguish. They are squadrons of cavalry, but it is the colour that still escapes me, and my whole body goes from icy cold to burning heat... A patrol broke away at a trot and approached quickly, and this time I recognized French hussars.[37]

Any stoic resolve Christian Mallet had left evaporated. He collapsed on the grass and started screaming:

The fatigue of these five days without eating or drinking, almost without sleeping, living in a perpetual nightmare, gives me a brutal nervous attack, my whole body relaxes in spasms of madness; my comrades look at me with wide eyes, not having yet understood. With a gesture, I point out to them the column... and everyone then, as soon as they have seen it... some burst into sudden convulsive bursts and others dance, waving their arms like madmen, like poor beings who have spent days of suffering and anguish on a raft, in the open sea, and who suddenly see the liberating ship approaching them.[38]

*

At Vassincourt, no attack came overnight on 9 September as Georges Bertrand worked his way through his supply of sweets. His men were stunned as the enemy in front of them began packing up and leaving instead. At his headquarters the following morning, Crown Prince Wilhelm was shocked when the suggestion of a retreat came from German Supreme Command. '[It] came like a bolt from the blue,' he admitted. By lunchtime, he also had reports that all of the German armies to the west of him were already retreating. When the Germans departed Vassincourt on the night of 10 September, they left the village aflame. Georges Bertrand and his men, sitting on a bank and peering through smoke and fire, 'watched with satisfaction' as an endless line of Germans marched away. A few days later, the pitiful-looking remnants of the 6e Chasseurs Alpins passed again through Bar-le-Duc as victors, looking even worse than when they arrived, but having delivered the inhabitants from the enemy. 'I think that the population of Bar-le-Duc knew how to judge us that morning.'[39]

With the Ninth Army, Bakary Diallo and the 7th Tirailleurs reshuffled themselves into two or three weak companies with their remaining troops and began to move north. 'Along the roads, in the swamps, corpses everywhere. At the bottom of the slopes their accumulation reveals the... enormity of the massacre.'[40] Nearby, however, the men of the 20th Dragoons were bereft. There was to be no galloping pursuit of a vanquished enemy. It seemed as if the decisive moment had come, but the following day, with a huge gap between the two German armies in front of them, they saw nobody. 'Nothing. The void. Not a shot. Not a rider.'[41]

What Second Lieutenant Chambe did not know at the time was that the tide had well and truly turned. The key components of the German juggernaut that had ploughed through northern France on their way to victory were facing piecemeal actions as they now fled in the other direction. As 10 September dawned, their prospects were grim. In front of the BEF, cavalry officer Leutnant Graf von und zu Hoensbroech of Kürassier Regiment Nr.4 reported that 'everyone is retreating, terribly depressing. Nobody knows why... Columns pile up, everything is mixed together.'[42] Major von Westhoven concurred. 'A thousand serious thoughts are buzzing through your head. The mood that was just so victorious gives way to deep depression, and the enormous efforts of the last few weeks, which we are hardly aware of, weigh our limbs down as if lead. Silent and exhausted, as if in a dream, the column trudges on.'[43]

But even now, the Germans were not departing the battlefield in a panic. They were still a disciplined force, able to fight rear-guard actions. Seventeen miles north of La Ferté-sous-Jouarre, the 2nd Royal Sussex were marching towards the village of Priez in the rain. They arrived at the top of a hill looking down on the village at about 9.00 a.m. Planted on the road running north on top of another hill were German gunners, and they unleashed their weapons. Here, several British soldiers were killed by their own guns, too. Tragically, in the downpour some of the men had taken out their waterproof sheets and were wearing them as capes to keep the rain off. The colour was confusing, and they were mistaken for Germans. To add insult to injury, the enemy now targeted them with rifle fire. Isolated from their comrades behind them, the Sussex battalion fell back.

Coming up in support was reservist Frank Bolwell with the 1st Loyal North Lancashires. They had been marching since dawn. 'We must have done close on ten miles,' he recalled.[44] One subaltern had heard about the friendly-fire incident, and urged his platoon to take off their waterproof sheets and carry them.

Hardly any men listened, and more were then killed by their own countrymen.

*

Late on 10 September, Joffre finally informed the government that the Allies had claimed a significant victory. He knew, however, that the war was not yet won. The eastern flank of the German line was still actively attacking west of Verdun. His subsequent orders stated that 'to affirm and exploit the success, it is necessary to pursue energetically and leave the enemy no respite: victory depends on the legs of our infantry'.[45] What had passed, he referred to in his telegram to the war minister as the *Battle of the Marne*. The name hardly does the scale of the fight justice, but it was the name that Joffre chose. He thought it had gravitas, and as the man who orchestrated the 'miracle' and saved France from oblivion, it seems petty to deny him the honour.

Epilogue

For Britain, India, the jewel in the imperial crown, promised a bountiful reservoir of manpower. By the end of September, Indian blood had already been shed on Indian soil thanks to Admiral von Spee's squadron. Under cover of darkness, on the night of 22 September the *Emden* crept up to Madras and began firing at the shore. The first shells struck the small liner *Chupra*, but the bigger prizes were tanks belonging to the Burma Oil Company. With a capacity of 800,000 gallons each, they were conspicuous targets. Two caught light, and two more were damaged. The whole affair lasted fifteen minutes, but the attack made an impression. Locals flocked down to the beach in large numbers, in motor cars and rickshaws, 'as though it was a [firework] display, instead of a real bombardment'.[1]

The first victim was a child, struck by shrapnel that rebounded off a tram wire. One shell struck the bungalow belonging to the manager of the oil company. 'A shell dropped through a bedroom and drove through the floor.' One shot just missed his family as they ran away, but hit a servant, blowing him to pieces. 'Another hit a native policeman, whose body was picked up in the harbour', and a boy aboard a ship in the harbour also died.[2] In the town, a shell hit the surgical ward of a hospital. The nearby forts unleashed a bombardment in reply, but as soon as those shore batteries opened fire, the German ship extinguished her lights and slipped away to the south.

By the time the *Emden* attacked Madras, the first Indian contingent destined for Europe was four days away from Marseille. The Indian army was able to mobilize swiftly because deployment to Europe had long been part of the plan in the event of a major war. Said army existed primarily to maintain internal and border security, but by 1914 it was also considered an imperial reserve of troops ready to be sent anywhere in the world. Indian soldiers swore to fight anywhere when they enlisted, and they had done so in recent history. The Indian soldier of 1914 was not necessarily an insular peasant with no experience of life outside of his own region. Some 75,000 men since the turn of the century had explored the London Underground, trekked the jungles of Siam and carried out intelligence missions along the Yangtze River.

From the third week of August, trains puffed their way into Bombay and Karachi. There was still work to be done. Despite the intention to deploy the Indian army abroad, they were short of artillery, machine-guns and troopships. As the government scrambled to hire vessels, the men explored their new surroundings. Gurkhas clapped eyes on the ocean for the first time as they spilled out of trains. They could be seen wandering around the beaches at Bombay, baffled at the taste of seawater; mesmerized by ships, which they believed moved on underwater rails, just like trains.

The men of India's Force A set off into the unknown. On 30 August, they finally heard their destination via the wireless while at sea: Lord Kitchener had announced far away in London that two divisions of the Indian army were on their way to Europe. Cheers rang out on the deck. These men would fight shoulder to shoulder with their British counterparts. The colour bar principle that prevented them fighting white men had been abandoned.

Force A reached France on 26 September, having travelled 6,000 miles. First ashore were the 129th Baluchis, and the French turned out in droves to greet them. More men landed, wide-eyed. 'Many people were so excited they broke in among the marching Pashtun, Muslims and Sikhs, women running up to kiss them, pin roses to their tunics and hand them French flags.' 'The 101 new wonders of a European town', recalled one white officer, 'combined to complete the bewilderment of the

Gurkha ranks, whose feelings may well be compared to those of Alice in Wonderland.'[3] The French referred to them all as *Les Hindoues* whatever religion they adhered to. As they marched to their camp at a racecourse on the coast road, more crowds lined the route and cheered. 'The Indians replied with the only words they had learnt from their English officers: "*Hip, hip, hurrah!*"'[4]

*

Elsewhere in Europe, there was rather less enthusiasm among those that had already seen action. For the Central Powers, huge setbacks across Europe characterized the end of summer. In Belgium, King Albert sought to capitalize on Allied success after the Marne. During a four-day battle in front of Antwerp, his army provoked the wrath of mounting German reinforcements and heavy artillery, but in doing so prevented those German reinforcements from being deployed to France. Willy Breton's unit of chasseurs à pied was ordered to break off on 13 September, and his men did so in good spirits, despite scoring no precise victory. 'If they bore the traces of the fatigue and bruises of two months of campaigning', he wrote, 'they no less looked to the future with confidence. We knew that General Joffre had inflicted a resounding defeat on the Germans, and [was still] harassing them. A little more patience, and the Allies, without doubt, would drive away the Boche hiding in front of Antwerp.'[5]

*

In France, the British and the French were hard on the heels of the retiring Germans. It was the invaders' turn to find themselves falling back in moderate disarray. 'As a result of the movements and the five days of combat,' wrote Bülow's chief of staff, 'the army was completely disorganised... Anyone skilled in the art [of staff work] can imagine what the movements of columns and convoys were like. It was a tour de force to direct them, to avoid crossover, to prevent the congestion of the roads of retreat.'[6] The anonymous sapper described their lack of success:

Even the most stupid among us now began to fear that we had been humbugged. The streets became ever more densely crowded with retreating troops and trains... Munition wagons raced past us, singly, without any organization... Canteen and baggage wagons went past, and here already a wild confusion arose... One wagon would be overturned, another one would stick in the mud. No great trouble was taken to recover the vehicles, the horses were taken out and the wagon was left. The drivers took the horses and tried to get along; everyone was intent upon finding safety.[7]

He was growing increasingly bitter. 'Was that the terrible German war machine?' he wrote. 'Were those the cowardly degenerated Frenchmen whom we had driven before us for days? No; it was war, terrible, horrid war, in which fortune is fickle. To-day it smiles upon you; tomorrow the other fellow's turn comes.'[8]

The German armies that had been ravaged on the right flank during the Battle of the Marne came to a strategic halt on the north banks of the River Aisne. They immediately began fortifying the high ground. Despite his victory, Joffre knew quickly that the momentum had slipped away and as his men tried to break the deadlock, it became apparent that for now, the Allies lacked sufficient firepower to dislodge the enemy. The war would not be over by Christmas.

*

If the Germans managed to retain some semblance of dignity as they withdrew from the Marne, the same cannot be said of the Austro-Hungarian armies in Galicia. In early September, disaster struck. Russia stabilized her chaos-ridden Fourth Army with reinforcements and a change in command. In came General Aleksei Evert.

Meanwhile, morale had plummeted in the Austro-Hungarian ranks, as everyone was now painfully aware that the enormous bloodshed of the past three weeks had been in vain. 'Are we maybe going to give up our country too?' pondered a Hungarian cavalry officer.[9] For weeks his regiment had been waiting in reserve, and now, these proud cavalry units were being ordered to surrender many of their horses as draught animals for the retreating infantry. Life was about to take another turn for the worse.

In the last days of August, Stavka ordered the newly formed Russian Ninth Army, commanded by the capable General Platon Lechitsky, to take up position to the right of the Fourth Army. On this front, the beleaguered Austro-Hungarians were now outnumbered nearly two to one. When General Evert's force attacked, launching a powerful blow south from Lublin, the numerical superiority of the Russians quickly became overwhelming, and by 10 September, the Fourth Army had captured some 15,000 Austro-Hungarian soldiers. Troops fell back in chaos towards the border. Entire divisions were funnelled onto already wrecked, narrow tracks. University student Stanisław Kawczak, by now serving with the k.u.k. IR 20, gave a vivid account of the effect of Russian firepower on the retreat from Lublin:

Scenes from Dante's *Inferno* were happening on the road. Driven by instinct, both men and horses pressed forward, regardless of the corpses and wounded lying on the ground. Horses' hooves were treading over bellies and heads; intestines, guts, brains mixed with mud covered the road with a bloody mess... The screams of the wounded men and horses, together with the cracking rifles, grenade and shell explosions drove one to near insanity... Over there, a man strips naked and calls me: 'Come over, comrade!' with a blood-curdling laugh. In front of my very eyes, the captain of the 100th Regiment fires a revolver at his own head.[10]

With his First Army falling back in complete disarray before Evert and Lechitsky, Conrad finally ordered its commander, General Dankl, to break off. However, he maintained unrealistic hopes that the situation in East Galicia could yet be salvaged and that Lemberg could be recaptured. With his left flank wide open, General Auffenberg decided to deny Conrad this option and took matters into his own hands. His army was still heavily engaged in fierce fighting around Rawa Ruska, without available reserves to counter the new Russian threat. He ordered his troops to disengage and undertake an orderly retreat. Elsewhere along the Austro-Hungarian front, Böhm-Ermolli's Second Army was completely exhausted, and Conrad's orders to attack were largely ignored. Boroević's Third Army offensive had also begun to grind to a halt. His formations were too depleted and exhausted to achieve anything of note.

Conrad finally came to the realisation that the battle was lost. Lemberg could not be reached, and a general retreat to the River San was now the only way of avoiding a complete destruction of his forces. The order to retire some 100 miles was issued at 5.30 p.m. on 11 September, at almost the exact same time as the Germans began their withdrawal from the Marne. It got worse. On 18 September, General Ludendorff, fresh from victories in East Prussia, strongly advised him to withdraw a further 100 miles to a more defensible position in the Carpathian Mountains in order to rest and rebuild his battered armies. Conrad had little choice but to agree, and by the end of the month, the second flight had been completed.

Defeat at the hands of Serbia had been humiliating, but now roughly half of Galicia was now occupied by the Russians. This was a catastrophe. Of the 900,000 troops which had been committed to Conrad's offensive there since late August, only about half remained. In just over three weeks of fighting, the Austro-Hungarians had suffered more than 100,000 men killed, while around 220,000 had been wounded. Another 100,000 had been captured by the Russians, whose own casualties amounted to approximately a quarter of a million killed, wounded or missing.

Across the globe, conditions for troops worsened as summer receded and armies jostled for position ready for the inevitable fighting to come. Much of the Austro-Hungarian retreat in Galicia was conducted in pouring rain. 'All day, we kicked and kneaded the mud in the heavy and freezing rain,' wrote Pero

Blašković.[11] On 13 September, his regiment marched for eighteen hours without interruption, yet covered less than 4 miles.

The weather also got the better of French artilleryman Paul Lintier, who was sent to the rear 'partly on account of persistent diarrhoea, which was weakening me considerably'. With the BEF, Arthur Corbett-Smith was just as miserable. 'The roads became quagmires… The men left their bivouacs wet through; before half an hour had passed they had all got to that stage when nothing mattered… squelch, squelch through the mud. Teams strained at the guns, dragging them through the liquid glue away over fields of heavy soil wherein carriages sank well-nigh axle deep.' Men fashioned extra layers where they could:

One battalion found a few dozen oat sacks in a granary. Wrapped round the shoulders they were at least a reasonable substitute for greatcoats, and there was a mad rush for them. Another company appeared looking like a gang of Chinese coolies with bundles of straw tied together and hung over the shoulders by way of capes. Disconsolate-looking cavalry horses, heads and tails tucked down, plodded heavily past, carrying riders who sat grimly in pools of water. Squelch, squelch, and down came the rain. Oh for a glass of hot rum and water, and a pipe of tobacco![12]

If rain was a common thread in mid-September, other experiences differed massively. Joyfully following up the German retreat from the Marne, Marcel Dupont's cavalry regiment entered Montigny-lès-Condé 'at the moment when the last dragoons of the Prussian Guard were leaving it at full speed'. The inhabitants could not do enough for them:

What a dinner we had that evening!… On a chest placed near the door I can see still a big pile of ration loaves, thrown together anyhow; and leaning over the hearth of the large fireplace, lit up by the wood fire, was an unknown man who was stirring something in a pot. Round the large table a score of hungry and jaded but merry officers were fraternally sharing some pieces of meat.[13]

For the Germans in front of them, the contrast could not have been harsher. The anonymous sapper and his comrades found a previous German campsite:

The bread that had evidently been plentiful at that time now lay scattered in the field. Though [it] had been lying in the open for about a week and had been exposed to a rain lasting for days, we picked it up and swallowed it ravenously. As long as those pangs of hunger could be silenced, it mattered little what it was that one crammed into one's stomach.[14]

In Galicia, Austro-Hungarian supply trains and field kitchens were lost, and soldiers went days without receiving any rations. Even worse than the gnawing hunger was the insatiable thirst. Many had already not had anything to drink for several days by the time the retreat was ordered. The fleeing troops became desperate. 'The thirst drives us mad,' wrote Fritz Lederhaas. 'We secretly take water from puddles and swamps with our drinking cups and quench our thirst with the dirty yellow water.'[15] Diseases soon began to spread, including cholera, which appeared as an unwelcome guest in many regiments during the course of the retreat. 'Healthy people crumble in 24 hours,' wrote a Hungarian soldier, 'only to end up in a limestone pit a few days later.'[16] In one corps alone, 2,000 cases were reported in the second half of September, with around a third of the patients dying.

All of this took its toll on the minds of the men who had been pushed to the brink. Troops were already becoming desensitized to the horror of war. Georges Bertrand recalled entering Vassincourt:

A fetid odour emanated from the ruins and rubble. The wounded, Germans and French alike, had been burnt by the fire. The smoking inferno was like a mass grave. Yet – so great is the indifference one acquires in battle! Near the greenish and corrupted corpses, seated on a stone and behind a rickety wall, my comrade and I eat old cuts of cold meat for lunch. It is necessary that in the struggle the heart breaks or hardens.[17]

Psychological trauma was evident from the lowest rank to the very highest. In supreme command of the German armies, Moltke suffered a complete collapse and had to be replaced. Crown Prince Wilhelm observed a shadow of the man he knew when they met at his own Fifth Army headquarters at Varennes on 11 September:

General von Moltke had obviously gone to pieces under the weight of his great responsibilities, and all who saw him were deeply affected. Was this the man who had to direct the fate of the German army? In an incoherent way he tried to explain all the circumstances that had led to the [failure of the Schlieffen Plan]. In darkly pessimistic tones he spoke of the right wing of the army as beaten, and thought that it was even a matter of doubt when they would be able to make a stand… Apart from the alleged unsatisfactoriness of the strategic and tactical situation, he appeared to be greatly oppressed by the question of munitions supply: all avoidable consumption of munitions was to be strictly forbidden. When on these grounds, and contrary to the instructions received the day before, he [ordered] us… to shift our line back immediately, a stormy and painful discussion ensued between General von Moltke and myself, at this our first and last official encounter during the war.[18]

In liberated villages, jubilant refugees returned to their homes in the aftermath of the victory on the Marne. Some of those who had remained throughout the fighting, however, were broken vestiges of humanity. Belgian officer Willy Breton entered

Eppegem. 'Here and there, [we] saw terrified villagers appear on the thresholds of their houses. Haggard, dazed, they seemed to understand nothing of what was happening around them... In vain did our soldiers try to reassure them.' He could not get the image of one woman out of his head:

> Moaning heartbreakingly, shaking convulsively. In broken sentences, interspersed with sobs, she explained that the Germans, that very morning, had taken her husband and her son with other residents, screaming that they were going to shoot them all. On her knees, she asked for mercy for her family. With a kick, a filthy brute had thrown her to the ground... [Her] poor face tortured by anguish, the sad creature clung to the clothes of our soldiers and begged: 'Save me! If they come back, they will kill me! They are not men, but monsters!... Save me! Save me!'[19]

By no means was safety assured, even if the enemy had not arrived. Zeppelins roamed the skies above the Belgian army ensconced in Antwerp. Journalist Alexander Powell wrote of 'a woman [who] was decapitated by a piece of flying shrapnel when she leant out her window to see what was happening'. When he entered a collapsed house, he found the body of another woman that could 'only have been collected with a shovel. Ten were killed and forty wounded. Gloom descended on the city, and by eight in the evening every light had been turned off, every cafe closed, every window darkened.'[20]

Throughout the world, uncertainty reigned as the war continued its malevolent creep into every aspect of people's lives. Elsa Cahen and her family had been deprived of their home, their lives and their dignity by their own government and were stranded at a convent in the Pyrenees indefinitely. Other civilians were forced to get used to living under foreign occupation. In German Samoa, one resident was intensely bitter about his fate. He labelled the New Zealanders as completely inferior to German troops, referring to them as sheep farmers, rabbit catchers, and used-clothes salesmen.

He even described men arriving on the island as having 'woolly heads and protruding lips that gave away their Maori heritage'. The occupying troops were 'wild beasts', or evidently descended from the base criminals that Britain had originally deported to Australia. Even if, as he described, the New Zealanders 'clearly had no military discipline or sense of order', he could not escape the fact that they were the victors on this occasion.[21]

News that filtered back to the home fronts left its mark on those who had as yet seen nothing of the physical realities of war. At the end of September, the mood was subdued in Berlin. Sven Hedin, a Swede, had raced to Germany on the outbreak of war, devastated when his own country remained neutral:

'Why are the streets so silent?' I ask somebody. I understood that Berlin was in such high spirits. 'It is so long since we heard of any great victories,' is the answer. 'Patience,' I retort. 'You must not expect a Tannenberg every week.' As autumn took hold, it poured with rain, it was dark, windy, cold and raw. Shallow puddles covered the asphalt in *Unter den Linden.*[22]

Hedin surveyed empty streets from his balcony. One by one people withdrew from social life as bad news arrived from the fronts:

No calls are made, no visits paid, for the whole of the aristocracy is in mourning for lost relatives and everybody's thoughts are centred on the war. Nobody feels inclined for the futile pleasures of ordinary times when the newspapers speak of a father who has lost four sons at the front, or of a mother whose three sons have each died a hero's death for emperor and country.[23]

*

The scene in Petrograd was a stark contrast. In September, a gala was held to celebrate the capture of Lemberg by the Russians.

It was a welcome relief after the disappointment of Tannenberg. 'Inside the theatre the uniforms of the officers made a brilliant setting to the jewels and costly dresses of the women,' wrote a British observer, grimly mindful that things were not going well at all in France. Midway through the play, the curtain fell:

But the lights did not go up. In an instant the atmosphere became electrical. In the darkness rumour ran riot. Then the footlights went up again; the orchestra filed into their places, and a young girl of eighteen, the daughter of the President of the French Chamber of Commerce, came on to the stage. With her white dress, her face free of all make-up, and her glorious golden hair, she looked like the Angel Gabriel. In her trembling hands she held a slip of paper. The audience hushed itself in an expectant silence. Then, quivering with emotion and nervousness, the girl began to read: 'The following official telegram has just been received from French headquarters.' She stopped as if her tongue were chained. The tears streamed down her face.

In a shrill voice, she blurted out: *'Je suis heureux de vous annoncer victoire sur tout le front. Joffre.'* 'The lights blazed up. The girl ran wildly off the stage, and in a storm of cheering the orchestra struck up the *Marseillaise*. Bearded men kissed each other, women smiled and wept at the same time.'[24]

*

An arm and shoulder fly from the man just in front, exposing his throbbing heart... Another, dismembered, crawled along on all fours, his entrails trailing behind, and still another held up his tongue with his hand, a piece of shell having carried away his lower jaw.[25]

As yet, there was nothing unique about this war. It was not the dawn of a new, unexpected type of warfare. That dawn had occurred half a century before, on the other side of the Atlantic.

The scene described above is a snapshot of 1863, of the fighting at Chancellorsville during the American Civil War. Preliminary bombardments, such as the one at Fort Wagner the same year, saw massed artillery being used to attempt to pave the way for an infantry attack. In 1864, breaking into the enemy's trench system and struggling to hold on to gains, or trying to burst out the other side and rout the enemy, were the same challenges that would stump commanders five decades later during the First World War.

In 1914, nations clearly demonstrated that they had already begun addressing the conundrums thrown up by a modern, industrialized war. For all that the French were entranced by the idea of the offensive, as early as 15 August the commander of the Second Army, General Nöel de Castelnau, was preaching to Joffre ideas that were soon to be common sense: wait, bring up your artillery, prepare the way for your men. Russians demonstrated that they knew both how to dig in and defend themselves from a merciless bombardment, and how to use one on their own part to help their infantry advance. In the case of General Kamio, the Japanese also exercised repeated caution to protect men from wasting their lives on attacking intact entrenched positions. During the relief of Ladysmith in 1900, General Redvers Buller had made a rudimentary attempt to coordinate infantry with artillery: he actually ordered what would be recognizable by 1915 as the genesis of a curtain of protective shellfire for advancing troops. The Russo-Japanese War had provided yet another powerful lesson: the value of machine-guns. General Aleksey Kuropatkin, the commander of Russian land forces in Manchuria, noted after that war: 'The value of [them] is now so great that we cannot afford to be without them.'[26] In the years that followed, the number of machine-guns within the Imperial Russian Army was greatly increased, and efforts were made to include their recent combat experiences into established tactical doctrine.

*

So why did armies not implement what they were learning in time for 1914? Two reasons: In part, commanders can be accused of having been scared to let go of what they knew. In July 1914 it would still have been considered ridiculous to write off the cavalry as a thing of the past. This was an arm that had been decisive in warfare since the dawn of time. Also, armies were steeped in the spirit of the offensive, and were not yet ready to admit that recent advancements in technology such as repeating rifles, quick-firing artillery and machine-guns could shift wars from mobile clashes to that of entrenched, defensive positions. In Germany, General Alfred von Schlieffen viewed the defensive nature of the Russo-Japanese War as something that could be avoided next time: 'The attack must never come to a standstill as happened in the war in the Far East.'[27] French military thinkers concluded that if defences were stronger owing to modern weapons, then they should just attack harder.

However, it is also important to remember that delays in implementing change did not mean a lack of action. Change takes time to trickle down. You cannot simultaneously bring your army's strength up to millions and change the fundamental ethos of its operational doctrine overnight. To modernize, nations were going to have to go back to the theoretical drawing board, retrain everyone from the highest to the very lowest rank, then create and move millions of tons of equipment before it was even possible to try.

*

What *was* unprecedented in August and September 1914 was the sheer volume of bloodshed. By the end of the year, the French army alone counted approximately 350,000 killed in action. Neither did any nation anticipate the massive volume of material expenditure required to destroy their enemies. At the start of the war, the British had more shells available than were fired in the entire Boer War of 1899–1902. Prime Minister Herbert Asquith boasted of the surge in shell production in the first months of the war, and yet by the third week of October, field batteries would be rationing them. It took Bülow's army less than a fortnight to realize that they needed to scale those six heavy guns originally taken to Liège up to almost 100 in order to achieve the desired result.

Another significant change in 1914 was that as a result of the scale of it all, the overwhelming majority of men shedding all of this blood were not professional soldiers. They formed the largest citizen armies the world had seen. But how could they be employed? Without exception, every major combatant had tried to execute their pre-war plans in August 1914 and those plans had failed to produce a decisive victory. On all sides, nations now worked to further grow their armies, increase the availability of munitions; their capacity to inflict more misery on each other in order to tip the scale in their favour. The response, wrong in hindsight, was to attack bigger, *attack harder*. Across the world at the end of September 1914, the war that everyone had planned had already drawn to a close. What lay ahead now, and how to extricate themselves from it, not a soul knew.

Acknowledgements

A book of this size, covering such diverse material would not have been possible without the help of our wider military history community. It really did take a village. To that end, we thank Donald Winchester and the team at Watson Little for putting such faith in two newcomers writing about the war that gets so little attention compared to the sequel.

We owe special thanks to Frankie Lyell and everyone at Independent Talent, Charlie Sandhu and his print services, and Bart Parish, Sue Yoakum, Carolyn Day and Matt Cathey for providing writer's retreats at various points. Also Sam Daly, Steve Marsdin, Rok Stergar and Jim Smithson for lending their expertise and reading over the manuscript in part or in its entirety to catch any errors and ensure we remained true to our remit of producing a book that anybody might enjoy. We would also like to thank Trevor Torkington for his diligent transcribing of various naval diaries, and Philippe Maree at Visit Wallonia for his exhaustive efforts to help us explore the region as we wrote. We also owe a great deal to the people who have assisted with translations and sourcing materials in languages we are less familiar with, among them Marcin Parzyński, Jaka Marinšek, Maros, Vesper-Tink Lynd, Julián Péter, Adam Szedlak and Grant T. Harward.

We would also like to thank the family of George and Regie Fletcher for access to their private archive, as well as the Director and Staff of Churchill College Archives at the University of Cambridge in particular. Beginning this book in the aftermath of a pandemic as we did, they could not have offered more in time, resources and flexibility in getting us access to the material we needed. Finally, we would like to thank Dan Snow and everyone at History Hit for working with us to produce a documentary based on our work that we could be proud of, long in advance of having the benefit of seeing the finished manuscript.

Alex would also like to thank Peter Caddick-Adams, Matt Bone, Sam Daly, Gareth Davies, Jonny Dyer, Stephen Fisher, James Holland, Andrew Holmes, Andy Lock, Dan McAndrew, Doug McMillan, Owen Moody, Al Murray, Clive O'Connell, Josh Provan, Chris Sams, Jim Smithson, Guy Walters, Paul Woodadge and Zack White for providing a constant backbone of support in a man's world that makes it easier every day to approach working in military history. In this respect, most of all she owes thanks to Peter Hart, who though he is eminently annoying and supports a rubbish football team, has for some fifteen years now had her back at every turn; without being afraid to tell her off when she deserves it.

Nicolai in particular would like to thank his parents, Søren, who more than anyone is responsible for his interest in military history, and Jonna, who has always encouraged and supported him. However, the greatest thanks of all goes to his wonderful wife Linda and their two amazing kids, Deian and Theia. This book would not have been possible without their support and love, as well as their endurance when dad was busy writing or researching. Without them, there would be no reason.

In addition, we would also like to thank everyone at Fort Loncin for being so welcoming and letting us explore the site. Also: Tayo Agubiande, Philip Blood, Raph de Brant, Benoit Chenu, Jonathan Clements, Adam Cousins, Bart Debeer, William Donko, Beth Griffiths, Jean-François Husson, Lorraine Johnstone, Doug Macmillan, Wendy Maddocks, Alina Nowobilska, Chris Sams, Tamara Scheer, Wim van Schjindel, Wrong War Steve, Simon Verdegem, Merryn Walters, Vanda Wilcox, and Ben Wisdom.

Finally, we haven't met him, but we feel we need to make a nod to Jean Delhez. His tireless, monumental efforts to record the Battle of the Frontiers and compile French and German sources made it much, much easier to then bring this story into English as it deserved. We stood on his shoulders, and the meticulous nature of his work was a formidable basis on which to begin.

Bibliography

ARCHIVAL SOURCES

Balliol College, Oxford
    Papers of Sir Louis du Pan Mallet
The Caird Library, Greenwich
    BTY/3/1 Diary of Admiral Beatty, 1914
    JHS/3 Diary of Edward Jukes-Hughes, 1914
    HLD/1 - Diary of C. B. Heald, 1914
Churchill College, Cambridge University
    CLN/1/5 - Diary of Bernard Colson, 1914
    LASL 1/1/11 - Diary of Alan Lascelles, 1914
    RMSY 2/1 - Diary of Admiral Sir Bertram Home Ramsay, 1914
    SMVL 2/1 - Diary of Admiral Sir James Somerville, 1914
Copenhagen City Archive (KSA)
    Erindring: Agnes Bremer 1969/1816
Imperial War Museum, London (IWA)
    Sound Archive
    Alfred Fright
    Bessie Davies
    Raymond Mann
    Vera Waite
    Documents/Books
    10870 R. N. Clough
    8458 D. Harrop
    17495 Kendall
    LBY K. 43675 R.M.S. Carmania: Unsigned typescript letter giving an account of the fight between R.M.S. Carmania and the Cap Trafalgar
    LBY K. 1625 An account of the Carmania's victory over the German armed liner Cap Trafalgar
    LBY K. 50507 An account of the Carmania's victory over the German armed liner Cap Trafalgar
Hampshire Records Office
    9M68/1053-1125 Comtesse Francqueville
    128A08/1 Copeland
    9M75/F/C/21 Palmer
Leicestershire Records Office
    DE8535 - Day
    Private Papers of Walter George and Reginald William Fletcher

NEWSPAPERS

Allgemeiner Tiroler Anzeiger, 21 September 1914
Badener Zeitung, 3 October 1914
Daily Telegraph, 26 September 1914
Deutsches Nordmährerblatt, 27 August 1914
Grazer Tagblatt, 14 October 1914
Grazer Volksblatt, 25 September 1914
Grazer Volksblatt, 26 September 1914
Grazer Volksblatt, 30 September 1914
Flensborg Avis, 16 September 1986
Illustrierte Kronen Zeitung, 21 September 1914
Innsbrucker Nachrichten, 28 August 1924
Kolding Folkeblad, 1 August 1914, 2nd Edition
The Lagos Weekly Record, 9 & 16 April 1916
Le Siècle, 25 December 1914
Neue Freie Presse, 2 February 1915
Neues 8 Uhr Blatt, 26 September 1914
New York American, 8 August 1914
New York Times, 13 September 1914
The Nigerian Pioneer, 10 August 1917
Le Petit Journal. 5 August 1914
Slagelse-Posten, 19 August 1914
Sommerville, 6 August 1914
Sommerville, 8 August 1914
Tagblatt: Generalanzeiger für das Burgenland, 25 August 1929
Vorarlberger Volksfreund, 10 September 1914
Znaimer Tagblatt, 25 October 1914

PUBLISHED SOURCES

Abbenhuis, Maartje: *The Art of Staying Neutral: The Netherlands in the First World War* (Amsterdam, 2014)
Adams, Michael, *Living Hell: The Dark Side of the Civil War* (Baltimore, 2014)
Albert, Bill: *South America and the First World War: The Impact of the War on Brazil, Argentina, Peru and Chile* (Cambridge, 1988)
Airapetov, Oleg: *Участие Российской империи в Первой мировой войне (1914–1917)*, vol I. (Moscow, 2014)
Anonymous: *A German Deserter's War Experience* (London, 1917)
Antonelli, Quito: *Intimate History of the Great War: Letters, Diaries, and Memories from Soldiers on the Front* (New York, 2016)
Arcq, Alain & Van Yperzeele, Achille: *Leernes & Collarmont 1914* (Paris, 2008)
Ardaridi, K.: '27 пех. дивизия в боях 4 (17) Августа 1914 г. под Сталупененом и 7 (20) Августа под Гумбиненом' in *Военный сборник общества ревнителей военных знаний*, Book VIII (Belgrade, 1926)

Arlow, Viktor: *Kard És Fátyo: Lovag Arlow Viktor Ezredes, Przemyśl - Vlagyivosztok - Győr 1914–1920* (Budapest, 2015)

Astashov, Alexander: *Русский фронт в 1914 - начале 1917 года: военный опыт и современность* (Moscow, 2014)

Ba, Amadou Hampâté Amkoullell: *L'Enfant Peul* (Paris, 1991)

Barkhof, Sandra: 'My War Experiences in Samoa' Pro-colonialism in First World War Memoirs and Eyewitness Accounts' in Smith, Angela & Barkhof, Sandra (eds): *War, Experience and Memory in Global Cultures Since 1914* (London, 2020)

Basu, Shrabani: *For King and Another Country: Indian Soldiers on the Western Front, 1914–18* (London, 2015)

Batorović, Mato: 'Početak Prvoga svjetskog rata u Iloku u autobiografi ji franjevca o. Mladena Barbarića' in Stjepan Prutki and Krešimir Bušić (eds.): *Srijem u Prvom svjetskom ratu 1914–1918* (Vukovar, 2016)

Barnard, Charles: *Paris War Days: Diary of an American* (New York, 1914)

Baumann, Gabriele & Schmidl, Erwin A. (eds.): *Das Tagebuch eines Leutnants* (Vienna, 2019)

Beidler, Philip: *Beautiful War: Studies in a Dreadful Fascination* (Tuscaloosa, 2016)

Belova, Irina: 'Human Waves: Refugees in Russia, 1914–18' in Gatrell, Peter & Zhvanko, Liubov (eds.): *Europe on the Move: Refugees in the Era of the Great War* (Manchester, 2017)

Beloy, Alexander Sergeevich: *Галицийская битва* (Moscow, 1929)

Beloy, Alexander Sergeevich: *Выход из окружения 19-го армейского корпуса у Томашова в 1914 г.* (Moscow, 1937)

Benckendorff, Count Constantine: *Half a Life: Reminiscences of a Russian Gentleman* (London, 1954)

Benda, Vojtěch: *Halič 1914–1916: Vzpomínky z válečného tažení proti Rusku vojáka C.K.rakousko-uherské armády Wojtěcha Bendy* (year unknown) (Online: www.velkavalka.info/ osudy/Benda_Vojtech.pdf, accessed 10.12.2023)

Benkő, Levente: 'A vesztesek csak mi, a magyarok leszünk... (Szemelvények Tulics Kálmán csendőrőrmester galíciai naplójából)' in *Székelyföld*, 22/XI, 2018

Berndt, Otto Freiherr Josef von: *Die 5er Dragoner im Weltkrieg 1914–1918* (Vienna, 1940)

Bertrand, Georges: *Carnet de Route d'un Officier d'Alpins* (Paris, 1915)

Beşikçi, Mehmet: *The Ottoman Mobilization of Manpower in the First World War* (Leiden, 2012)

Bienaimé, Vice Amiral: *La Guerre Navale 1914–1915: Fautes et Responsabilités* (Paris, 1920)

Bisset, Sir James: *Tramps and Ladies* (London, 1989)

Blašković, Pero: *Sa Bošnjacima u Svjetskom ratu* (Belgrade, 2014)

Bolwell, Frank: *With a Reservist in France* (London, 1915)

Boubée, J.: *Parmi les Blesses Allemands, Aout–Decembre 1914* (Paris, 1916)

Boudon, Victor: *Avec Péguy de la Lorraine à la Marne, Aout–Septembre 1914* (Paris, 1916)

Bourachot, André: *Marshal Joffre: The Triumphs, Failures and Controversies of France' Commander-in-Chief in the Great War* (Barnsley, 2014)

Braun, Otto: *The Diary of Otto Braun* (New York, 1924)

Breton, Willy: *Un Régiment Belge en Campagne: Les Fastes de 2e Chasseurs à Pied, Août 1914–Janvier 1915* (Paris, 1917)

Brodersen, H. C.: *I Ildlinien* (Copenhagen, 2021)

Bruno, Wolfgang: *Przemysl 1914–1915* (Vienna, 1935)

Brusilov, A. A.: *Memories* (Moscow, 1963)

Buffin, Baron: *Recits de Combattants Recueillis* (Paris, 1916)

Bukvin, Ivica Ćosić: 'Rat viđen očima sudionika 1914–1918' in Prutki, Stjepan & Bušić, Krešimir (eds): *Srijem u Prvom svjetskom ratu 1914–1918* (Vukovar, 2016)

Burda, Matúš: *Vojnové nasadenie 'slovenských' pešich plukov rakús-ko-uhorskej armády na bojisku v Haliči v roku 1914* (Bachelor's Thesis, Univerzita sv. Cyrila a Metoda v Trnave, 2017)

Burdick, Charles: *The Japanese Siege of Tsingtau* (Hamden, 1976)

Burger, Josef: *Mit den Tiroler Landesschützen gegen Russland* (Innsbruck, 1917)

Burnell, Frederic: *Australia Versus Germany: The Story of the Taking of German New Guinea* (London, 1915)

Bülowius, Alfred & Hippler, Bruno: *Das Infanterie-Regiment von Boyen (5. Ostpreußisches) Nr. 41 im Weltkriege 1914–1918* (Berlin, 1929)

Carap, Albert: *Journal d'Un Parisien Pendant La Grande Guerre* (Paris, 2020)

Cavalié, Hélène & Longatte, Alexandrine: 'Petits Réfugiés De La Grande Guerre: Récits D'écoliers Des Frontières Évacués Dans Les Alpes-Maritimes', in *Recherches régionales. Alpes-Maritimes et contrées limitrophes,* number 211 (2016)

Clarke, M. E.: *Paris Waits* (London, 1915)

Clements, Jonathan: *Japan at War in the Pacific: The Rise and Fall of the Japanese Empire in Asia* (North Clarendon, 2022)

Chambe, René: *Adieu, Cavalerie! La Marne, Bataille Gagnée... Victoire Perdue* (Paris, 1979)

Chickering, Roger: *The Great War and Urban Life in Germany: Freiburg, 1914–1918* (Cambridge, 2007)

'Chr.': 'Med 84ernes 2. Bataillon i Verdenskrigen – En Nordslesvigers oplev-elser i den store Krig' in *Almanak For Nordslesvig* (Haderslev, 1935)

Churchill, Alexandra: *Over Land and Sea: Chelsea FC in the Great War* (Stroud, 2015)

Churchill, Sir Winston: *World in Crisis*, vol I (London, 1923)

Chwalba, Andrzej: *The People of Poland at War, 1914–1918* (Warsaw, 2018)

Clifton-Shelton, Captain A.: *On the Road from Mons with an Army Service Corps Train by Its Commander* (London, 1917)

Codera, Maximiliano Fuentes: *Spain and Argentina in the First World War* (London, 2021)

Corbett, Julian: *Official History of the War, Naval Operations: Vol. I* (London, 1920)

Corbett-Smith, Arthur: *The Retreat From Mons* (London, 1916)

Corbett-Smith, Arthur: *The Marne and After* (London, 1917)

Crown Prince William of Germany: *My War Experiences* (London, 1924)

Das, Santanu: *India, Empire, and First World War Culture: Writings, Images, and Songs* (Cambridge, 2018)

Dahlmann, Reinhold: *Das Reserve-Infanterie-Regiment Nr. 27 im Weltkriege 1914/1918* (Oldenburg i.O./Berlinn, 1934)

Deacu, Horațiu C.: *Ziarul unui erou: însemnări făcute pe câmpul de luptă din Galiția, între 12 August-21 Octomvrie 1914, ziua în care autorul a fost ucis de un glonte duşman* (Gherla, 1930)

Debaeke, Siegfried: *Vluchten Oor De Grote Oorlog: 1.5 miljoen Belgen op de vlucht* (Brugge, 2004)

Dehne, Phillip A.: *On the Far Western Front: Britain's First World War in South America* (Manchester, 2009)

de Jehay, Frédéric Steen: *L'Invasion du Grand-Duché de Luxembourg en Août 1914* (Paris, 1916)

Delécraz, Antoine: *Paris Pendant la Mobilisation: notes d'un immobilisé, des faits, des gestes, des mots 31 juillet–22 août* (Paris, 1914)

Delhez, Jean-Claude: *Assaut contre les Forts de Liege 1914* (Paris, 2018)

Delhez, Jean-Claude: *Le jour de deuil de l'armée française*, vol I (Privately published, 2011)

Delvert, Charles: *Carnets d'Un Fantassin* (Paris, 1935)

Denham, H. M.: *Dardanelles: A Midshipmans Diary, 1915–16* (London, 1981)

Diallo, Bakary & Lamine, Senghor: *White War, Black Soldiers: Two African Accounts of World War I* (London, 2021)

Dolgov, D.: 'Два лесных боя.13/26 и 15/28 августа 1914 г.' in *Военно-историческии Сборник*, vol III (Moscow, 1919)

Dorndorf, Georg: *Das Infanterie-Regiment Herzog Karl von Mecklenburg-Strelitz (6. Ostpreußisches) Nr. 43* (Oldenburg i.O./Berlin, 1923)

Doughty, Robert: *Pyrrhic Victory: French Strategy and Operations in the Great War* (Cambridge, 2008)

Driesmans, Marcel: *Le fort de Loncin - Le 15 août 1914* (Liège, 2018)

'DSK' (Dansksindede Sønderjydske Krigsdeltagere) Årbog (Aabenraa, various editions 1941–1972)

Dubravčić, Frane: *Živ sam i dobro mi je: uspomene iz Prvog svjetskog rata 1914–1918* (2002)

Dunn, Stephen: *Southern Thunder: The Royal Navy and the Scandinavian Trade in World War One* (Barnsley, 2020)

Dupont, Marcel: *En Campagne (1914–1915) Impressions D'Un Officier De Legere* (Paris, 1916)

Dupuy, Capitaine: *La Guerre dans les Vosges* (Paris, 2004)

Kerchnawe, Hugo: *Ehrenbuch unserer Artillerie*, vol I (Vienna, 1935)

Eisenhart-Rothe, Ernst von: *Ehemaliges 1. Ermländisches Infanterie-Regiment Nr. 150* (Berlin, 1938)

'En Grænsebo' (Anonymous): *Ved Grænsen: I Mindeåret og Mærkeåret 1914* (Kolding, 1914)

Estreikher-Egorov, R. A.: *Бой у Герритен в августе 1914 года* (Moscow, 1936)

Evseev, N.: *Августовское сражение 2-й русской армии в Восточной Пруссии (Танненберг) в 1914 г.* (Moscow, 1936)

Fabini, Ludwig von: 'Die Feuertaufe des Eisernen Korps: Der erste Tag der Schlacht von Zloczöw am 26 August 1914' in *Militärwissenschaftliche Mitteilungen,* vol 61 (1930)

Fahrner, Franz Leander & Trauner, Karl Reinhart (eds): *Kriegstagebücher: Wie Soldaten den Ersten Weltkrieg erlebten* (Vienna, 2020)

Fayolle, Maréchal: *Cahiers Secrets de la Grande Guerre* (Paris, 1964)

Fisher-Wood, Eric: *The Note Book of an Attaché: Seven Months in the War Zone* (New York, 1915)

Fleury-Lamure: *Charleroi, Notes et Impressions* (Paris, 1916)

Foch, Ferdinand: *The Memoirs of Marshal Foch* (East Grinstead, 2019)

Fogarty, Richard: *Race and War in France: Colonial Subjects in the French Army, 1914–1918* (Baltimore, 2012)

Formé, Abbé: *Souvenirs Personnels de la Bataille de la Marne* (Paris, 1916)

Frontali, Gino: *La Prima Estate di Guerra* (Bologna, 1998)

Fröhlich, Hermann: *Geschichte des steirischen k.u.k. Infanterie-Regimentes Nr. 27,* vol 1 (Graz, 1937)

Fulwider, Chad: *German Propaganda and U.S. Neutrality in World War I* (Columbia, 2016)

Gallieni, Joseph-Simon: *Mémoires de Général Galliéni: Defense de Paris, 25 Août–11 Septembre 1914* (Paris, 1916)

Gatrell, Peter: *The Making of the Modern Refugee* (Oxford, 2013)

Gerard, James: *My Four Years in Germany* (London, 1917)

Gippius, Zinaida Nikolayevna: *Синяя книга: петербургский дневник: 1914–1918* (Belgrade, 1929)

Glasmeier, Heinrich: *Geschichte des Kürassier-Regiment von Driesen (Westf.) Nr.4* (Oldenburg: 1932)

Golovin, Nikolai: *Из истории кампании 1914 г. Дни перелома Галицийской битвы (1-3 сентября нового стиля)* (Paris, 1940)

Golovin, Nikolai: *Из истории кампании 1914 г. на русском фронте. Начало войны и операции в Вост. Пруссии* (Prague, 1926)

Golovin, Nikolai: *The Russian Army in the World War* (New Haven, 1931)

Gottberg, Franz V.: *Das Grenadier-Regiment Kronprinz (1.Ostpreußisches) Nr.1 im Weltkrieg.* vol I (Oldenburg i.O./Berlin, 1927)

Gozdović, Pascha & Pariser, A.T.: *Österreichs Helden im Süden* (Kiepenheuer, 1915)

Gribble, Francis: *In Luxembourg in War Time* (London, 1916)

Guéno, Jean-Piérre (ed): *Paroles de Poilus 1914–1918* (Paris, 1998)

Guite, Jangkhomang: 'Response of Northeast India to The First World War' in Ashutosh, Kumar & Markovits, Claude: *Indian Soldiers in the First World War* (Abingdon, 2021)

Gumz, Jonathan E.: *The Resurrection and Collapse of Empire in Habsburg Serbia, 1914–1918* (Cambridge, 2009)

Gushchin, F. A.: *Жертвы стальных гроз: Пленные и погибшие генералы Российской императорской армии. 1914–1917* (Moscow, 2020)

Hadobás, Pál (ed.): *Bódva-völgyiek a Nagy Háborúban: Száz éve tört ki az I. világháború* (Edelény, 2014)

Hafkesbrink, Hanna: *Unknown Germany: An Inner Chronicle of the First World War Based on Letters and Diaries (*New Haven, 1948)

Hagen, Mark von: *War in a European Borderland: Occupations and Occupation Plans in Galicia and Ukraine, 1914–1918* (Washington, 2007)

Hall, Fock & Dahle: *Kriegsgeschichte des Königlich Preussischen Infanterie-Regiments von Borcke (4. Pommersches) Nr. 21; Nach amtlichen Unterlagen und Berichten der Mitkämpfer; Vorgeschichte, 1813–1918; Weltkrieg 1914–1918* (Zeulenroda, B. Sporn, 1931)

Hamelius, Paul: *The Siege of Liège* (London 1914)

Hamilton, Richard F. & Herwig, Holger H.: *Decisions for War, 1914–1917* (Cambridge, 2004)

Hart, Peter: *Fire and Movement: The British Expeditionary Force and the Campaign of 1914* (Oxford, 2014)

Hastings, Max: *Catastrophe 1914: Europe Goes to War* (New York, 2013)

Hazemali, David: 'The Battle of Galicia: The Disintegration of the Austro-Hungarian Land Forces on the Eastern Front in the First World War, With Special Emphasis on the Role of the Graz's III Corps and Slovenian Soldiers', *Studia Historica Slovenica* volume 17, number 1 (2017)

Hedin, Sven: *With the German Armies in the West* (London, 1917)

Heinz, Anton: *Das ehemalige Egerländer Feldjägerbataillon Nr. 22 im Weltkriege 1914–1918* (Reichenberg, 1935)

Hell, Stefan: *Siam and World War I: An International History* (Bangkok, 2017)

Hendrick, Burton: *The Life and Letters of Walter H. Page* (New York, 1922)

Hermann, Martina: 'Cities of Barracks: Refugees in the Austrian part of the Habsburg Empire during the First World War' in Gatrell, Peter & Zhvanko, Liubov (eds): *Europe on the Move: Refugees in the Era of the Great War* (Manchester, 2017)

Herwig, Holger H.: *The First World War: Germany and Austria–Hungary 1914–1918* (Bloomsbury, 2009)

Herwig, Holger H.: *The Marne, 1914: The Opening of World War I and the Battle That Changed the World* (Random House, 2011)

Hoen, Maxmilian Ritter von: *Geschichte des ehemaligen Egerländer Infanterie-Regiments Nr. 73* (Vienna, 1939)

Horne John & Kramer, Alan: *German Atrocities, 1914: A History of Denial* (Yale, 2002)

Houžvic, Juričič Bogdan M.: *Se Srby a komity: z deníku srbského dobrovolce* (Prague, 1928)

Hrušovský, Ján: *Zo svetovej vojny – Halič, Ruské Poľsko: 1914* (Turčiansky Svätý Martin, 1919)

Hülsemann: *Geschichte des Infanterie-Regiments von Manstein (Schleswigsches) Nr. 84 (1914–1918), in Einzeldarstellungen von Frontkämpfern. Erinnerungsblätter der ehemaligen Mansteiner* (Hamburg, 1929)

Huszár, János (ed): *Pápa város első világháborús emlékkönyve* (Pápa, 1998)

Iriye, Akira: *Global Community: The Role of International Organizations in the Making of the Contemporary World* (California, 2002)

Imrey, Ferenc: *Through Blood and Ice* (New York, 1929)

Imshenetsky, V. I.: *На восточно-прусском фронте* (Petrograd, 1914)

Ingpen, Roger: *The Pages of Glory, of the Belgian Army* (London, 1914)

IR 14 – ein Buch der Erinnerung an Große Zeiten: 1914–1918 (Linz, 1919)

Isheev, P. P.; *Осколки прошлого: Воспоминания, 1889–1959* (New York, 1959)

Izdebski, Edward: *Bitwa pod Zamościem 26–27 sierpnia 1914 r.* (Warsaw, 1929)

Jan, Peter: '«Нечисть царей, нечисть варваров». Русская оккупация осточной Пруссии 1914 г. в восприятии немецкой общественности.' in Eimermacher, Karl, Bordyuov, Gennady & Folpert, Astrid (eds): *Война как опыт, приобретенный на чужбине. Образ России в письмах с фронта Фридриха Грелле (1914–1915)* (Moscow, 2010)

Jarboe, Andrew: *Indian Soldiers in World War I: Race and Representation in an Imperial War* (Nebraska, 2021)

Jones, Jefferson: *The Fall of Tsingtau With a Study of Japan's Ambitions in China* (Boston, 1915)

Juzbašić, Vinko: 'Bošnjačani u Prvom svjetskom ratu' in Prutki, Stjepan & Bušić, Krešimir (eds): *Srijem u Prvom svjetskom ratu 1914–1918* (Vukovar, 2016)

Kaczmarek, Ryszard: *Poles in the Kaiser's Army On the Front in the First World War* (Kraków, 2014)

Katanić, Filip: 'Za Boga i cara: Bjelovarčani i stanovnici Bjelovarsko-križevačke županije u Varaždinskoj 16. pješačkoj pukovniji na Balkanskom bojištu 1914. Godine' in *Radovi Zavoda za znanstvenoistraživački i umjetnički rad u Bjelovaru br. 12* (2018)

Kawczak, Stanisław: *Dying Echoes: Memoirs of the War 1914–1920* (United Kingdom, 2019)

Kelemen, Pál: *Hussar's Picture Book: From the Diary of a Hungarian Cavalry Officer in World War I* (Bloomington, 1972)

Kenda, Daniel J.: *Lessons Learned From The Use Of The Machine Gun During The Russo-Japanese War And The Application Of Those Lessons By The Protagonists Of World War I* (Masters Thesis, Fort Leavenworth, 2005)

Kersnovsky, A. A.: *История русской армии. В 4 томах*, vol III (Moscow, 1994)

King Hall, Stephen: *A Naval Lieutenant 1914–1918* (London, 1919)

Kißling, Rudolf: 'Der Angriff im Waldkampf' in *Militärwissenschaftliche und technische Mitteilungen* (Vienna, 1928)

Klein, Felix: *The Diary of a French Army Chaplain* (London, 1915)

Klein-Pejšová, Rebekah; 'Between Refugees and the State: Hungarian Jewry and the Wartime Jewish Refugee Crisis in Austria-Hungary" in Gatrell, Peter & Zhvanko, Liubov (eds): *Europe on the Move: Refugees in the Era of the Great War* (Manchester, 2017)

Kosmač, Filip: *V spomin na mojo vojaško službo 1912–1918 in nekaj opisov o poteku vojne*, in the collection of Goriška library of France Bevka (Nova Gorica, 200?)

Kozelsky O.: *Записки батарейного командира: Составлено по письмам, заметкам и рассказам участника войны*, vol I (Petrograd, 1915)

Krafft von Dellmensingen, Konrad: *Schlachten des Weltkrieges: Das Marnedrama 1914 1. Teil* (Oldenburg, 1926)

Kreisler, Fritz: *Four Weeks in the Trenches* (Neptune City, 1981)

Kretinin, G. V.: *Война и мир: исследования по российской и всеобщей истории* (Kaliningrad, 2018)

Krulichová, Marie: *Zapomenuté hlasy: korespondence, deníkové záznamy a kresby z první světové války* (Hradec Králové, 1986)

Kuhl, Hermann: *Le Grand État-Major Allemand*, ed. *Général Douchy* (Paris, 1922)

Kuhr, Piete: *There We'll Meet Again: The First World War Diary of a Young German Girl* (United Kingdom, 1998)

Laeger, Alfred: *Das Feldartillerie-Regiment, Prinz August von Preußen (1. Litth.) Nr. 1 - 1772–1919* (Zeulenroda, 1939)

Laeger, Alfred: *Das 1. Westpreußische Fußartillerie-Regiment Nr.11 im Weltkrieg 1914/18* (Zeulenroda, 1939)

Lang, Otto-Peter & Arnold, Markus (eds): *Feldwebel Georg Pöllmann: Mein Tagebuch der großen Krieges* (Salzburg, 2020)

Lederhaas, Fritz: *Kriegstagebuch: Meine Erlebnisse im Krieg gegen Russland und Italien* (Nordersetedt, 2017)

Lehoczky, Tivadar: *Világháborúnk, I-II rész.* (Beregszász-Ungvár, 2016)

Leidinger, Hannes Moritz, Verena, Moser, Karin & Dornik, Wolfram: *Habsburgs schmutziger Krieg: Ermittlungen zur österreichisch-ungarischen Kriegsführung 1914–1918* (Vienna, 2014)

Lemke, M. K.: *250 дней в Царской Ставке* (Minks, 2003)

Lempicki, Michel: *Grand Problème International* (Lausanne, 1915)

Leppa, Konrad: *Die Schlacht bei Komarow* (Fischern-Karlsbad, 1932)

Letard Étienne: *Trois mois au premier corps de cavalerie; de Senlis à Liège, de Liège à Paris, de Paris à Ypres* (Paris, 1919)

Liedtke, Leo: *Das Füsilier-Regiment Graf Roon (Ostpreußisches) Nr. 33 im Weltkriege 1914/1918* (Oldenburg i.O./Berlin, 1935)

Lintier, Paul: *Avec une batterie de 75: Ma pièce, souvenirs d'un canonnier (1914)* (Paris, 1916)

Lohr, Tolz, Semyonov & Von Hagen (eds): *The Empire and Nationalism at War* (Bloomington, 2014)

Lyon, James: *Serbia and the Balkan Front, 1914: The Outbreak of the Great War* (Bloomsbury Academic, 2015)

Mácha, E.: *Vzpomínky českého zajatce z válečného tažení do Srbska* (Chicago, 1919)

Maksimova, A. (ed): *Царская армия в период мировой войны и февральской революции: (материалы к изучению истории империалистической и гражданской войны)* (Kazan, 1932)

Mallet, Christian: *Étapes et combats; Souvenirs* (Paris, 1916)

Mandl, Hildegard: 'Galizische Flüchtlinge in der Steiermark zu Beginn des ersten Weltkrieges' in *Zeitschrift des Historischen Vereines für Steiermark Jahrgang* 77 (1986)

Maraite, Louis: *Le Rôle des Cheminots dans la Bataille de Liège* (Liège, 2014)

Marks, Steven: 'The Russian Experience of Money, 1914–1924' in Frame, Murray, Marks, Steven, Stockdale, Melissa, Boi, Kolonitskii, Boris: *Cultural History of Russia in the Great War and Revolution 1914–22* (Bloomington, 2013)

Maricourt, André: *Le drame de Senlis: journal d'un témoin avant, pendant, après, août–décembre 1914* (Paris, 1916)

Martin, Abbé: *Fillières, la vie dans un village lorrain envahi et occupé: notes au jour le jour d'un rapatrié, témoin de la bataille de Fillières* (Paris, 1920)

Martini, Ferdinando: *Diario 1914–1918* (Milan, 1966)

Matičič, Ivan: *Na krvavih poljanah* (Ljubljana, 2006)

Mátyás, Alexander von: *Geschichte des k. und k. Infanterie-Regimentes Frhr. v. Gaudernak Nr. 85* (Budapest, 1916)

Maurice, Frederick: *Forty Days in 1914* (London, 1925)

McCudden, Major James V.C.: *Five Years in the Royal Flying Corps* (London, 1918)

McNair, Wilson: *Blood and Iron* (London, 1916)

Milkic, Miljan: 'The Serbian Army in 1914: Tradition, Religion and Moral', in *Hadtörténelmi Közlemények*, volume 130, issue 2 (Budapest, 2017)

Mitrovic, Andrej: *Serbia's Great War 1914–1918* (West Lafayett, 2007)

Molostvova E. V.: *Солдатские письма* (Kazan, 1917)

Moore, Colleen: 'Urban and Rural Responses to War in Russia in 1914' in Lohr, Tolz, Semyonov & Von Hagen (eds): *The Empire and Nationalism at War* (Bloomington, 2014)

Moreau, Jean Victor Marie: *Rossignol 22 Aout 1914 Journal du commandant Jean Moreau* (Paris, 2002)

Morton-Jack, George: *The Indian Empire at War* (London, 2018)

Mott, T. Bentley: *Myron T. Herrick: Friend of France: An Autobiographical Biography* (London, 1930)

Moszeik, Pfarrer: *Stallupönen: Geschichtliches bis zum Russeneinfall 1914* (Leipzig-Stötteritz, 1915)

Mrvka, Viktor: *Jak jsem se měl v ruském zajetí* (České Budějovice, 1916)

Mwalilino, Walusako A.: 'The Battle of Karonga Revisited: Janet Nyaunthali Remembers', in *The Society of Malawi Journal*, volume 58, number 2 (2005)

Nadezhny, Dmitry Nikolaevich: *Бой у Лащева 27/14 и 28/15 августа 1914 г.* (Moscow, 1926)

На передовых позициях: из рассказов и писем участников сражений (Moscow, 1914)

Nelipovich, Sergei: *Первый блин комом: Восточно-Прусская операция 1914 года* (Saarbrücken, 2012)

Nemes-Tóthi Nemestóthy-Szabó, Béla: *Naplóm 1914–1918: A császári és királyi 12-ik huszárezredben* (Budapest, 2015)

Nielsen, Harald (ed): *Russiske Soldaterbreve* (Copenhagen, 1917)

Nottin, Léopold: *Vitry-le-François pendant la bataille de la Marne: Occupation de la ville par les Allemands, 5–11 Septembre 1914* (Paris, 1917)

Novotný, Josef: *Deník z války - můj příběh* (2015) (Online: www.doubravnik. cz/ view.php?cisloclanku=2015080201, accessed 21/12/2023)

Oeltjen, Jan: *'Ich bin kein Krieger und will keiner werden: Bilder und Tagebücher aus dem I. Weltkrieg* (Jaderberg, 2005)

Ohnet, Georges: *Journal d'un Bourgeois de Paris pendant la Guerre de 1914* (Paris, 1914)

Olip, Boštjan: *Dnevnik 1914–1918* (Radovljica, 2018)

Orga, Irfan: *Portrait of a Turkish Family* (London, 2002)

O'Shaughnessy, Edith: *Marie Adelaide, Grand Duchess of Luxemborg, Duchess of Nassau* (London, 1932)

Oskin, M. V.: 'Российские Дезертиры Первой Мировой Войны', *St Tikhons University Review*, volume 60, number 5 (2014)

Oskin, M. V.: 'Снабжение Северо-Западного фронта в Период первой мировой войны (1914–1915)' in *Via in* История. Политология. (2018. No. 3)

Österreich-Ungarns letzter Krieg 1914–1918, vol I (Vienna, 1931)

Page, Melvin: *The Chiwaya War: Malawians In The First World War* (London, 2002)

Page Melvin: *Chiwaya War Voices: Malawian Oral Histories of the Great War in Africa*, vols I and II (Great War in Africa Association Private Publication)

Pakhalyuk, Konstantin: '27-я дивизия в сражениях в Восточной Пруссии (1914–15 гг.) in *Рейтар 2012, No.1* (Online: www.grwar.ru/library/ Pakhaluk27InfDivision/PK_01.html, accessed 23/12/2023)

Pakhalyuk, Konstantin: 'Русский оккупационный режим в Восточной Пруссии в 1914–15 гг' in *Military Historical Archive* 153/9 (2012) (2012)

Pastre, Gaston: *Trois ans de front: Belgique, Aisne et Champagne, Verdun, Argonne, Lorraine: notes et impressions d'un artilleur* (Paris, 1939)

Pati, Budheswar: *India and the First World War* (New Delhi, 1996)

Payen, Joseph-Eugène: *L'âme du poilu: Journal de route d'un aumônier militaire du 7e corps, pendant la Grande-Guerre, 1914–1918* (Paris, 1924)

Pellegrinetti, Jean-Paul: *Une île dans la Guerre: La Corse 1914–1918* (Paris, 2020)

Pennell, Catriona: *A Kingdom United: Popular Responses to the Outbreak of the First World War in Britain and Ireland* (Oxford, 2012)

Petersen, Hans: *Er Aar i Krig* (Odense, 1920)

Pitreich, Max von Freiherr: *Lemberg 1914* (Holzhausen, 1929)

Popper, Kurt: *Quer durch den Krieg (Aufzeichnungen eines Sechserjägers): 1914–1918* (Prague, 1937)

Pourcher, Yves: *Les jours de guerre: La vie des français au jour le jour 1914–1918* (Paris, 2008)

Prašnički, Martin: *Vojni luzerji: 1914–1918; spominsko-dokumentarna zgodba o slovenskih vojakih 87. pešpolka - IR. 87* (Ljubljana, 2014)

Први Светски Рат У Белешкама Савремених Људи in *Istorijska Sveska*, number 8 (August, 2014)

Prodanović, Mileta M.: *Ратни дневник 1914–1918* (Dečje Novine, 1994)

Rauchensteiner, Manfried: *The First World War and the End of the Habsburg Monarchy, 1914–1918* (Vienna/Cologne/Weimar, 2014)

Rausch, Jane M.: *Colombia and World War I: The Experience of a Neutral Latin American Nation during the Great War and Its Aftermath, 1914–1921* (Lanham, 2014)

Reiss, Rudolphe Archibald: *How Austria-Hungary Waged War in Serbia: Personal Investigations of a Neutral* (Paris, 1915)

Reiss, Rudolphe Archibald: *Report Upon the Atrocities Committed by the Austro-Hungarian Army During the First Invasion of Serbia* (London, 1916)

Renner, Gusztáv: *A Polychnai ütközet 1914. augusztus 23-án* (Sopron, 1931)

Reserve-Infanterie Regiment Nr. 3 (Oldenburg, 1926)

Ribblesdale, Lord: *Charles Lister: Letters and Recollections* (London, 1917)

Richert, Dominik: *The Kaiser's Reluctant Conscript* (Barnsley, 2012)

Richthofen, Baroness von: *Mother of Eagles: The War Diary of Baroness Von Richthofen* (Atglen, 2004)

Riess, Werner N. & Riess, Warren C. (eds): *On the Eastern Front 1914 - Meine Kriegserinnerungen* (Bristol, 2020)

Riótor, Léon: *Journal de marche d'un bourgeois de Paris, 1914–1919* (Paris, 1934)

Robinson, Joe, Robinson, Janet & Hendricks, Francis: *The Last Great Cavalry Charge: The Battle for the Silver Helmets, 12 August 1914* (Stroud, 2015)

Rogan, Eugene: 'No Stake in Victory: North African Soldiers of the Great War in Studies', *Ethnicity and Nationalism*, volume 14, number 2 (2014)

Röhl, John: *Wilhelm II: Into the Abyss of War and Exile, 1900–1941* (Cambridge, 2014)

Rose, Kenneth: *The Great War and Americans in Europe, 1914–1917* (Abingdon, 2017)

Rosenhainer, Ernst: *Forward, March! Memoirs of a German Officer* (Shippensburg, 2000)

Rossfeld, Roman, Buomberger, Thomas & Kury, Patrick: *14/18 La Suisse et la Grande Guerre* (Neuchâtel, 2019)

Rozenshild-Paulin A.: '29-я пех. дивизия в первый поход в Восточной Пруссии' in Военный сборник общества ревнителей военных знаний. Book VIII (Belgrade 1926)

Ruebesamen, Friedrich Wilhelm & Bartelsi, Willi: *Feldartillerie-Regiment Prinzregent Luitpold von Bayern (Magdeburgisches) Nr. 4* (Magdeburg, 1927)

Sanborn, Joshua A.: *Imperial Apocalypse: The Great War and the Destruction of the Russian Empire* (Oxford, 2015)

Sayansky, L. V.: *Три месяца в бою : дневник казачьего офицера* (Moscow, 1915)

Sayn-Wittgenstein, E. N.: *Дневник, 1914–1918* (Paris, 1986)

Scheer, Reinhard: *Germany's High Sea Fleet in the World War* (New York, 1934)

Schillmann, Fritz: *Grenadier-Regiment König Friedrich Wilhelm I. (2. Ostpreußisches) Nr. 3 im Weltkriege 1914–1918* (Oldenburg i.O./Berlin, 1924)

Schindler, John R.: 'Disaster on the Drina: The Austro-Hungarian Army in Serbia, 1914', *War in History*, volume 9, issue 2 (April, 2002)

Schindler, John R.: *Fall of the Double Eagle: The Battle for Galicia and the Demise of Austria–Hungary* (Potomac Books, 2015)

Schneider, Constantin: *Die Kriegserinnerungen 1914–1919* (Vienna, 2002)

Schneider, Henriette: *Ein Ostpreußisches Tagebuch: Tagebuchaufzeichnungen 1913–1947 der Henriette Schneider (1872–1947)* (Online, available at www.ostpreussen-tagebuch.de/, accessed on 27/12/2023)

Schoß, Alfred Michael: *Verklungene Tage: Kriegserinnerungen eines Artilleristen* (Vienna/Leipzig, 1933)

Schulte-Umberg, Thomas: 'Serbien 1914, Karpaten - San - Błożewkasumpf 1915 - Ein Weltkriegstagebuch des österreichisch-ungarischen Soldaten Richard Riedl', *Mitteilungen des Instituts für Österreichische Geschichtsforschung 127* (2019)

Schwarzleitner-Domonkus, Chlodwig: 'Die Grazer 6. Infanterie-Division in den Schlachten um Lemberg. (26. bis 30. August und 8. bis 11. September 1914.)' in *Hugo Kerchnawe: Im Felde unbesiegt: Der Weltkrieg in 24 Einzeldarstellungen*, vol III (Munich, 1923)

Šehić, Zijad: *U smrt za cara i domovinu* (Sarajevo, 2007)

Selyavkin, A. I.: В трех войнах на броневиках и танках *(*Prapor, 1981)

Sergeevsky B.N.: *Пережитое. 1914* (Belgrade, 1933)

Sharov, Laila Andreevna: *Life in Sibereia and Manchuria, 1898–1922, A Memoir* (University of California, 1986)

Shcherbachev D. G.: 'Львов — Рава Русская — Перемышль. 9-й Корпус и 3-я армия в Галиции в 1914 г.' in *Военный сборник, Book 10* (Belgrade, 1929)

Showalter, Dennis E.: *Tannenberg: Clash of Empires* (Hamden, 1991)

Siebert, Heinrich: *Geschichte des Infanterie-Regiments Generalfeldmarschall von Hindenburg (2. Masurisches) Nr. 147 im Weltkriege* (Oldenburg i.O./Berlin, 1927)

Skar, Marius C. (udg.): *To Faldne Brødre. Breve fra Jeppe og Peter Østergård hjem til Nordslesvig* (Kolding, 1931)

Skoko, Savo & Opacic, Petar: *Duke Stepa Stepanovic in the Wars of Serbia 1876–1918* (Belgrade, 1981)

Smith, Stephen: *The Samoa (N.Z.) Expeditionary Force, 1914–1915: An Account Based on Official Records of the Seizure and Occupation by New Zealand of the German Islands of Western Samoa* (Wellington, 1924)

Spears, Edward: *Liaison 1914: A Narrative of the Great Retreat* (London, 2000)

Stevens, Stevan Idjidovic: *The Snows of Serbia: A Child-soldier in the Great War* (2012)

Stewart-Gordon, George: *Mons and The Retreat* (London, 1919)

Stewart, Herbert: *From Mons to Loos: Being the Diary of a Supply Officer* (London, 1916)

Stoff, Laurie: *They Fought for the Motherland: Russia's Women Soldiers in World War I and the Revolution* (Lawrence, 2015)

Stone, David R.: *The Kaiser's Arm: The German Army in World War One* (Bloomsbury, 2015)

Stone, David R.: *The Russian Army in the Great War: The Eastern Front, 1914–1917* (Lawrence, 2015)

Ströer, Hans: *Von Schabatz bis Schabatz: Lose Blätter aus meinem Kriegstagebuche* (Prague, 1916)

Szenti, Tibor: *Vér és pezsgő: Harctéri naplók, visszaemlékezések, frontversek, tábori és családi levelek az első világháborúból (*Budapest, 1988)

Szuścik, Jan: *Pamiętnik z wojny i niewoli: 1914–1918* (Cieszyn, 1925)

Szűcs, Mihály: *Huszárként a világháborúban 1914–1918* (Hódmezővásárhely, 2018)

Tanty, Etienne: *Les violettes des tranchées: Lettres d'un poilu qui n'aimait pas la Guerre* (Paris, 2002)

Tardieu, André: *Avec Foch (Août–Novembre 1914)* (Paris, 1939)

Tăslăuanu, Octavian Codru: *With the Austrian Army in Galicia* (London, 1920)

Tharann, Willy: *Aus dem Kriegstagebuch eines Gefallenen* (Leipzig, 1918)

Thomas, Rudolf: *Infanterie-Regiment 94 im Weltkriege*, Supp. Vol. (Reichenberg, 1933)

Thomazi, Auguste: *La Guerre Navale dans la Mediterranée* (Paris, 1929)

Toller, Ernst: *I Was A German* (New York, 1934)

Tonda, Fric: *Zápisky z války se Srbskem 1914 - ?* (Online: www.svetmysli.net/img/Denik.pdf, accessed 10/12/2024)

Tsikhovich Ya.K.: *Стратегический очерк войны 1914–1918 гг. Ч. 1. Период от объявления войны до начала сентября 1914 г. Первое вторжение русских армий в Вост. Пруссию и Галицийская битва* (Moscow, 1922)

Turczynowicz, Laura de Gozdawa: *When the Prussians Came to Poland. The Experiences of an American Woman During the German Invasion* (Toronto, 1916)

Uspensky, A. A.: *На войне* (Kaunas, 1932)

Utkin A. I.: *Первая Мировая война* (Moscow, 2002)

Van der Essen, Leon: *The Invasion and the War in Belgium* (London, 1917)

Van Dijk, Kees: *The Netherlands Indies and the Great War 1914–1918* (Leiden, 2007)

Van Overstaeten, General: *The War Diaries of Albert I, King of the Belgians* (London, 1954)

Verhey, Jeffrey: *The Spirit of 1914: Militarism, Myth, and Mobilization in Germany* (Cambridge, 2000)

Verkhovsky, A. I.: *Россия на Голгофе: (из походного дневника 1914–1918 гг.* (Moscow, 2014)

Vermaut, Claudia (ed): *Het Oostendse oorlogsdagboek van Charles Castelein, 1914–1918* (Oostende, 1998)

Viereck, Helmut: *Königlich Preußisches 2. Hannoversches Infanterie-Regiment Nr. 77 im Weltkriege 1914–1918. Das Heideregiment* (Celle, 1934)

Virc, Zlatko: 'Vinkovački kraj u Velikom ratu' in Prutki, Stjepan & Busic, Kresimir (eds): *Srijem u Prvom svjetskom ratu 1914–1918* (Vukovar, 2016)

Vogt, Armand-Paul: *Nancy pendant la Guerre 1914–1918* (Nancy, 1920)

Voitolovsky, Lev Naumovich: *Всходил кровавый Марс: по следам войны* (Moscow, 1928)

В огне. Боевые впечатления участников войны (Petrograd, 1914)

Von Kluck, Alexander: *The March on Paris: The Memoirs of Alexander von Kluck, 1914–1918* (Barnsley, 2012)

Von Lettow-Vorbeck, Paul: *My Reminiscences of East Africa* (London, 1920)

Vošta, Jan: *Pětasedmdesátníci vzpomínají z pamětí účastníků světové války* (Tábor, 1936)

Wagner, Karl: *S českým plukem na ruské frontě* (Prague, 1936)

Watson, Alexander: *Ring of Steel: Germany and Austria–Hungary at War, 1914–1918* (United Kingdom, 2015)

Watson, Alexander: 'Unheard-of Brutality': Russian Atrocities against Civilians in East Prussia, 1914–1915', *The Journal of Modern History*, volume 86, number 4 (2014)

Wawro, Geoffrey: *A Mad Catastrophe: The Outbreak of World War I and the Collapse of the Habsburg Empire* (Basic Books, 2014)

Weiland, Hans & Kern, Leopold (eds): *In Feindeshand* (Vienna, 1931)

Whitlock, Brand: *The Letters and Journal of Brand Whitlock* (New York, 1936)

Wilcox, Vanda: *The Italian Empire and the Great War* (Oxford, 2021)

Winegard, Timothy: *Indigenous Peoples of the British Dominions and the First World War* (Cambridge, 2011)

Wißhaupt, Ernst: *Die Tiroler Kaiserjäger im Weltkriege 1914–1918*, vol I (Vienna, 1935)

Wolf, Hubert (ed.): *93 im Weltkrieg 1914–1918*, vol I (Mähr.-Trübau, 1931)

Young, Kenneth (ed): *The Diaries of Sir Robert Bruce Lockhart: 1915–1938* (London, 1975)

Young, T. Cullen: 'The Battle of Karonga', *The Nyasaland Journal*, volume 8, number 2 (July, 1955)

Yurlova, Marina: *Cossack Girl* (London, 1934)

Zhelondkovsky V. E.: 'Воспоминания полковника Желондковского об участии в действиях XV корпуса во время операции армии ген. Самсонова' in *Military Collection*, Book VII (Belgrade, 1925)

Ziemann, Benjamin: *Violence and the German Soldier in the Great War: Killing, Dying, Surviving* (Bloomsbury, 2017)

Žipek, Alois: *Domov za války*, vol I (Prague, 1929)

Zoerner, Georg: *Das 10. lothringische Infanterie-Regiment 174 im Weltkriege 1914–1918* (Zeulenroda, B. Sporn, 1930)

Zombory-Moldován, Béla: *The Burning of the World: A Memoir of 1914* (New York, 2014)

Zündel, Ernst: *Journal de la Grande Guerre à Mulhouse* (Embermévil, 2005)

Notes

Introduction

1. GBR/0014/LASL
2. Ramsay 2/1 29 July 1914
3. King Hall (1919) p.25
4. Ibid.
5. Ibid. p.25
6. Barnard (1914) pp.27-28
7. Pellegrinetti (2020) p.38
8. Verhey (2000) p.33
9. Moore (2014) p.562
10. Ibid. p.555
11. Pastre (1939) p.4
12. Braun (1924) p.123
13. Mann, IWM Sound 34244
14. Lemke (2003) pp.21-22
15. Verkhovsky (2014) p.31
16. Sharov (1986) pp.ii-33
17. Page (2020) Vol.II p.462
18. Ibid. Vol.I p.462
19. Ibid. Vol.II p.477
20. Rogan (2014) p.323
21. Diallo & Lamine (2021) p.105
22. Codera (2021) p.28
23. Guite (2021) p.127
24. Hafkesbrink (1948) p.31
25. Kawczak (2019) pp.12-13
26. Pennell (2012) p.36
27. Page (2002) p.14
28. Ba (1991) p.390
29. Brusilov (1963) p.81
30. Davies, IWM Sound 828
31. Ba (1991) p.375
32. GBR/0014/LASL
33. Röhl (2014) p.1107
34. Klein (1915) p.80
35. Selyavkin (1981) pp.5-10
36. Žipek (1929) Vol.I pp.198-199
37. GBR/0014/SMVL 2/1
38. Fayolle (1964) p.14
39. Richert (2012) p.1
40. De Maricourt (1916) p.34
41. Abbenhuis (2014) p.67
42. Page (2020) Vol.II p.399
43. Ibid. p.525
44. Ibid. p.729
45. Page (2002) p.15
46. Toller (1934) p.43
47. Fisher-Wood (1915) p.16
48. Martini (1916) p.14
49. Turczynowicz (1916) pp.15-16
50. Gippius (1929) p.7
51. Wise (1938) p.139

Chapter One

1. Payen (1924) p.5
2. Rogan (2014) pp.324-325
3. Richthofen (2004) p.13
4. *See* Stoff (2015)
5. Lister (1917) p.119
6. Fulwider (2016) p.17
7. 'Anonimo' (Online: www. idiariraccontano.org/autore/ anonimo/, accessed 9/12/2024)
8. Corbett-Smith (1916) p.5
9. Benckendorff (1954), p.155
10. Diallo & Lamine (2021) p.107
11. Spears (1914) p.18
12. Petersen (1920) p.6 - MIB
13. Delécraz (1914) p.30
14. Pellegrinetti (2020) p.45
15. Van der Essen (1917) p.47
16. Ibid.

17. Boudon (1916) p.5
18. Guéno (1998) p.44
19. Yurlova (1934) p.20
20. Ibid. p.21
21. KSA: Agnes Bremer 1969/1816
22. Flensborg Avis,
    16 September 1986
23. Žipek (1929) Vol.I pp.198-199
24. Ibid. pp.89-90
25. Hastings (2013) p.105
26. Corbett-Smith (1916) p.18
27. Churchill (1923) p.139
28. Stewart (1916) p.3
29. Private Papers
30. Grant (2014) p.3
31. Denham (2021) pp.1-5
32. Scheer (1934) p.19
33. Delécraz (1914) p.43
34. Fisher-Wood (1915) p.4
35. Gerard (1917) p.100
36. Dabaeke (2004) p.17
37. Gerard (1917) p.106
38. Le Petit Journal. 5 August 1914
39. Slagelse-Posten, 19 August 1914
40. Ibid.
41. New York Times,
    13 September 1914
42. Ibid.
43. Ibid.
44. Ibid.
45. Ibid.
46. Hampshire Records Office:
    54M76/F218
47. Ibid.
48. Ibid.
49. Ibid.
50. Ibid.
51. Ibid.

7. Neues 8 Uhr Blatt,
   26 September 1914
8. 'Chr.' (1935) p.65
9. Whitlock (1936) p.87
10. Maraite (2014) p.45
11. Anonymous (1917) p.5
12. Buffin (1916) p.7
13. Ibid.
14. Ibid.
15. Anonymous (1917) p.8
16. Ibid. p.10
17. Ibid. p.10
18. Trauwitz-Hellwig (1931)
    pp.17-18 - MIB
19. Ibid. p.18
20. Anonymous (1917) p.7
21. Delhez (2018) p.41
22. Van der Essen (1917) p.55
23. Hamelius (1914) p.43
24. Ibid. p.46
25. Ibid. (1914) p.64
26. Delhez (2018) p.96
27. Van der Essen (1917) p.58
28. Ibid. p.69
29. Delhez (2018) p.13
30. Rübesamen (1927)
    pp.35-36 - MIB
31. Ibid.
32. Robinson, Robinson &
    Hendricks (2017) pp.97-98
33. Ibid. p.83
34. Buffin (1916) p.70
35. Robinson, Robinson &
    Hendricks (2017) p.94
36. The Pages of Glory, of the
    Belgian Army: First Series, From
    The Gette To The Yser p.83
37. Buffin (1916) p.73

Chapter Two

1. Gribble (1916) p.19
2. de Jehay (1916) p.11
3. O'Shaughnessy (1932) p.126
4. Gribble (1916) p.26
5. Ibid. p.50
6. Ibid.

Chapter Three

1. Winegard (2011) p.69
2. Pati (1996) p.11
3. Jarboe (2021) p.60
4. Hampshire Records Office:
   19M75/F/C/21 25 November
   1914

5. Das (2018) p.81
6. Morton-Jack (2018) p.112
7. Das (2018) p.106
8. Diallo & Lamine (2021) p.65
9. Wilcox (2021) p.155
10. Morton-Jack (2018) p.111
11. Letard (1919) pp.72-73
12. Winegard (2011) p.63
13. Van Dijk (2007) p.144
14. The Lagos Weekly Record,
    9 & 16 April 1916
15. Winegard (2011) p.90
16. Ibid. p.87
17. The Nigerian Pioneer,
    10 August 1917
18. Fogarty (2008) p.78
19. Fogarty (2008) p.79
20. Fogarty (2008) p.85
21. Page (2020) Vol.II, p.462
22. Ba (1991) p.387
23. Ibid. p.388
24. Ibid. p.389
25. Ibid. pp.389-390
26. Ibid. p.390
27. Page (2020) Vol.II p.700
28. Ibid. p.646
29. Ibid. p.439
30. Ibid. p.646
31. Ibid. p.450
32. Ibid. p.530
33. Ibid. p.641
34. Ibid. p.407
35. Ibid. p.646
36. Lempicki (1915) p.46
37. Ibid. p.103

Chapter Four

1. Von Lettow-Vorbeck (1920) p.33
2. Mwalilino (2005) pp.13-21
3. Cullen Young (1955) pp.27-30

Chapter Five

1. GBR/0014/SMVL 2/1
2. Ibid.
3. Caird: CLN/1/5 21 August 1914

4. GBR/0014/SMVL 2/1
5. Thomazi (1929) p.14
6. Le Siècle, 25 Décembre 1914
7. Ibid.
8. 'SMS ZENTA Geschichte
   eines kleinen tapferen Schiffes'
   (Online: https://forum-
   marinearchiv.de/smf/index.
   php/topic,4058.msg55011.
   html#msg55011, accessed
   09/12/2024)
9. Thomazi (1929) p.14
10. Barnard (1914) p.32
11. Kolding Folkeblad, 1 August
    1914, 2nd Edition
12. Vogt (1920) p.83
13. Delécraz (1914) pp.43-44
14. McNair (1916) p.34
15. Vogt (1920) p.87
16. McNair (1916) p.34
17. Delécraz (1914) p.74
18. Chickering (2007) p.66
19. Mikkelsen (1917) pp.5-6 - MIB

Chapter Six

1. 'A halálmars krónikása, Szakraida
   István naplója' (Online: https://
   nagyhaboru.blog.hu/2020/06/08/_
   nagyon_kivancsi_vagyok_hogy_
   nez_ki_egy_kis_osszeutkozes
   accessed 10/12/2024)
2. Houžvic (1928) p.37
3. 'A halálmars krónikása,
   Szakraida István naplója'
   (Online: https://nagyhaboru.
   blog.hu/2020/06/08/_nagyon_
   kivancsi_vagyok_hogy_nez_ki_
   egy_kis_osszeutkozes accessed
   10/12/2024)
4. Hoen (1939) p.12
5. Ibid. p.13
6. Krulichová (1986) p.43
7. Ibid.
8. Mácha (1919) p.26
9. Ibid. pp.29-30
10. Ströer (1916) pp.14-15

11. Dubravčić (2002) p.20
12. 'Jaroslav Michal' (Online: www.kk8lir.com/fotogalerie/dobove-fotografie/denicky-vojaku-lir-nr-8/jaroslav-michal/, accessed 26/09/2016)
13. Kisch (1930) p.29

Chapter Seven

1. Buffin (1916) p.51
2. 'Le bombardement de LIEGE en août 1914.' (Online: http://awans-memoire-et-vigilance.over-blog.com/2018/06/le-bombardement-de-liege-en-aout-1914.html, accessed 09/12/2024)
3. Ibid.
4. Van der Essen (1917) p.81
5. Buffin (1916) p.55
6. Ibid. pp.57-58
7. Driesmans (2018) p.232
8. Ibid. p.257
9. Ibid. p.243
10. Ibid. p.244
11. Ibid. p.253
12. Ibid. p.250
13. Ibid. p.251
14. Ibid.
15. Ibid. p.245
16. Ibid. p.271
17. Ibid. p.279
18. Ibid. p.260
19. Ibid. p.289
20. Van der Essen (1917) p.125
21. Ibid. p.126
22. Ibid. p.139

Chapter Eight

1. Skoko & Opacic (1981) p.322
2. Mácha (1919) p.44
3. Ibid.
4. Skoko & Opacic (1981) p.322
5. 'Jaroslav Míchal' (Online: www.kk8lir.com/fotogalerie/dobove-fotografie/denicky-vojaku-lir-nr-8/jaroslav-michal/, accessed 26/09/2016)
6. Prodanović (1994) p.19
7. Krulichová (1986) p.49
8. 'Jaroslav Michal' (Online: www.kk8lir.com/fotogalerie/dobove-fotografie/denicky-vojaku-lir-nr-8/jaroslav-michal/, accessed 26/09/2016)
9. Krulichová (1986) p.49
10. Ristanović (1989) - MIB
11. 'Jaroslav Míchal' (Online: www.kk8lir.com/fotogalerie/dobove-fotografie/denicky-vojaku-lir-nr-8/jaroslav-michal/, accessed 26/09/2016)
12. Fahrner & Trauner (2020) p.149
13. Mácha (1919) p.46
14. 'Deník mého pradědečka-legionáře ze Světové války, doby před ní a těžkých dob vzniku Československé republiky' (Online: http://legionaruv.blog.cz/0905/16-17-srpna-1914-zbesily-ustup, accessed 22/08/2020)
15. 'A halálmars krónikása, Szakraida István naplója' (Online: https://nagyhaboru.blog.hu/2020/06/08/_nagyon_kivancsi_vagyok_hogy_nez_ki_egy_kis_osszeutkozes, accessed 10/12/2024)
16. Ristanović (1989)
17. Houžvic (1928) p.42
18. Blašković (2014) p.87
19. Krulichová (1986) pp.51-52
20. Ibid. pp.52-53
21. Kisch (1930) p.61
22. Krulichová (1986) p.53
23. Prodanović (1994) pp.22-24
24. Dubravčić (2002) p.25
25. Ibid.
26. Stevens (2012) pp.30-31
27. Ristanović (1989)
28. Ibid.
29. Ibid.
30. Ibid.

Chapter Nine

1. Jones (1915) p.17
2. 'En Grænsebo' (1914) p.25
3. New York American, 8 August 1914
4. Orga (2002) p.54
5. Ibid. p.56
6. Frontali (1998) p.4
7. United States Congress, Proceedings Published in 1939, p.1322
8. United States Congress, Senate Special committee on investigation of the munitions industry (1939) p.75
9. Fuldwider (2017) p.94
10. Rossfeld, Boumberger & Kury (2019) p.62
11. Abbenhuis (2006) p.175
12. Mott & Herrick (1930) p.144
13. Dunn (2019) p.24
14. Churchill (1923) p.277
15. Beşikçi (2012) p.50
16. Balliol College: Sir Louis Mallet: IV
17. Lister (1917) p.121
18. Balliol College: Sir Louis Mallet: IV
19. Fisher-Wood (1915) p.6
20. Martini (1966) p.64

Chapter Ten

1. Guéno (1998) p.42
2. Payen (1924) p.10
3. Dupuy (2004) p.10
4. Riótor (1934) p.23
5. Zündel (2005) p.7
6. Carap (2020) p.16
7. Richert (2012) p.3
8. Ibid.
9. Dupuy (2004) p.14
10. Richert (2012) p.4
11. Ibid. p.5
12. Bertrand (1915) p.17
13. Ibid. pp.19-21

14. Zoerner (1930) pp.25-26
15. Bertrand (1915) p.22-23
16. Ibid. p.23
17. Ibid. p.25
18. Ibid. p.27
19. Ibid. p.28
20. Zoerner (1930) pp.26-27
21. Bertrand (1915) p.30

Chapter Eleven

1. Gottberg (1927) Vol.I p.26
2. Moszeik (1915) p.20
3. Dorndorf (1923) p.14
4. Adaridi (1926) p.168
5. Uspensky (1932) pp.33-34
6. Ibid. pp.33-34
7. Quoted in *На передовых позициях...* (1914) p.15
8. Pakhalyuk (2012) '27-я дивизия...'
9. Gottberg (1927) Vol.I p.35
10. Ibid. pp.35-37
11. DSK (1945) p.72
12. *В огне...* (1914) p. 28
13. Hall, Fock & Dahle (1931) p.50
14. Pakhalyuk (2012) "27-я дивизия..."
15. Hall, Fock & Dahle (1931) p.51
16. Skar (1931) pp.21-22
17. Ibid. p.22
18. Hall, Fock & Dahle (1931) p.52
19. Liedtke (1935) p.49
20. 'DSK' (1967) pp.41-42
21. Uspensky (1936) pp.34-35
22. Utkin (2002) p.132
23. Adaridi (1929) p.181
24. Uspensky (1936) pp.34-35
25. Tharann (1918) p.10

Chapter Twelve

1. Ristanović (1989)
2. 'Мајор Јоксим: Дозволите да покажемо непријатељу како се Срби предају' (Online: www.in4s.net/major-joksim-

dozvolite-da-pokazemo-neprijatelju-kako-se-srbi-predaju/, accessed 10/12/2024)
3. '*Први Светски Рат…*' (2014) pp.47-48
4. Kuhr (1998) p.25
5. Bruno (1935) p.53
6. Voitolovky (1928) p.8
7. Vermaut (1998) p.8
8. Gatrell (2013) p.17
9. Cavalié & Longatte (2016) p.47
10. Lehoczky (2016) p.97
11. Huszár (1998) p.18
12. Martin (1920) p.34
13. Horne & Kramer (2002) p.98
14. Ibid. p.95
15. 'DSK' (1959) p.10
16. Horne & Kramer (2002) p.121
17. Deutsches Nordmährerblatt, 27 August 1914
18. Brodersen (2021) p.29
19. 'DSK' (1962) p.74
20. 'Kalisz – 1914: Progrom Miasta' (Online: http://info.kalisz.pl/kal1914/, accessed 03/04/2016)
21. Ibid.
22. Ibid.
23. Ibid.
24. Allgemeiner Tiroler Anzeiger, 21 September 1914
25. 'DSK' (1968) pp.40-42
26. Watson (2015) pp.176-177
27. Horne & Kramer (2002) p.100
28. Szűc (2018) p.20
29. Olip (2018) p.33 & Arlow (2015) p.47
30. Chwalba (2018) p.108
31. Antonelli (2016) p.85
32. Watson (2015) p.102
33. 'Deník Františka Vančury' (Online: https://signumbelli1914.cz/osudy/Vancura_Frantisek-denik.pdf, accessed 10/12/2024)
34. Schulte-Umberg (2019) p.97
35. Gozdović & Pariser (1915) p.71
36. Schulte-Umberg (2019) p.100
37. Tonda (Online) pp.5-6
38. Reiss (1915) p.23
39. Ibid. p.45
40. Szenti (1988) p.111

Chapter Thirteen

1. Delvert (1935) p.30
2. Ibid. p.31
3. Delhez (2011) p.281
4. Ibid.
5. Ibid. p.282
6. Martin (1920) p.27
7. Ibid. p.30
8. Anonymous (1917) p.22
9. Delhez (2011) p.194
10. Ibid. pp.155-156
11. Martin (1920) p.35
12. Delhez (2011) p.231
13. Ibid. p.383
14. Kaczmarek (2014) p.70
15. Delhez (2011) p.385
16. Kaczmarek (2014) p.72
17. Moreau (2002) p.70
18. Ibid.
19. Ibid. p.73
20. Ibid. p.132
21. Ibid. p.133
22. Kaczmarek (2014) p.71
23. Moreau (2002) p.74
24. Delhez (2011) p.410
25. Moreau (2002) p.134

Chapter Fourteen

1. Maurice (1925) p.58
2. Rogan (2014) p.325
3. Ibid.
4. Arcq (2008) p.54
5. Rogan (2014) p.326
6. Maurice (1925) p.58
7. Cobbett-Smith (1918) p.81
8. Bolwell (1915) p.18
9. 'DSK' (1963) pp.97-98
10. Hart (2015) p.90
11. 'DSK' (1950) pp.12-13
12. 'DSK' (1958) pp.80-81

13. 'DSK' (1963) pp.98-99
14. Hülsemann (1929) p.55
15. 'DSK' (1963) pp.98-99
16. 'DSK' (1963) pp.98-99
17. Hart (2015) p.99
18. Lipkes (2007) p.344
19. Boubée (1916) p.13
20. Young (1914) p.67
21. Van der Essen (1917) p.150
22. Buffin (1916) p.101
23. Van der Essen (1917) p.150
24. Anonymous (1917) p.16
25. Van der Essen (1917) p.152
26. Fleury-Lamure (1916) p.87
27. Ibid. p.92
28. Arcq (2008) p.84

Chapter Fifteen

1. Churchill College: Lascelles, 16 August 1914
2. Ibid.
3. Ibid.
4. Ibid.
5. Bisset (1962) p.25
6. Ibid. p.26
7. Ibid. p.27
8. IWM: LBY K. 1625
9. Bisset (1962) p.31
10. Ibid. p.32
11. Ibid. p.33
12. IWM: LBY K. 1625
13. Ibid.
14. Ibid.
15. Ibid.
16. Ibid.
17. Ibid.
18. Ibid.
19. IWM: LBY K. 43675
20. IWM: LBY K. 1625
21. Ibid.
22. Ibid.
23. Ibid.
24. IWM Sound: Waite, 10114
25. Hell (2017) p.17
26. Albert (2002) p.40
27. Ibid. p.51

28. Ibid. p.49
29. Juzbašić (2016) p.274
30. Marks (2014) p.124
31. Van Dijk (2007) p.143
32. Martini (1916) p.48
33. Codera (2021) p.32
34. Penneli (2012) p.49
35. Leicestershire Records Office DE8535
36. Pourcher (2008) p.62
37. Ba (1991) p.392
38. Ibid. pp.392-393

Chapter Sixteen

1. Kaczmarek (2014) p.74
2. Boubée (1916) p.87
3. 'DSK' (1958) pp.80-81
4. Kaczmarek (2014) p.75
5. Hart (2014) p.76
6. Arcq (2008) p.103
7. Moreau (2002) p.79
8. Kaczmarek (2014) p.74
9. Martin (1920) p.34
10. Boubée (1916) p.57
11. Arcq (2008) p.105
12. Corbett-Smith (1917) p.183
13. Lintier (1916) p.91
14. Corbett-Smith (1917) p.109
15. Ibid.
16. Ibid. p.139
17. Ruebesamen & Bartels (1927) p.61
18. Gordon (1918) p.46
19. IWM Documents: 8458
20. Bolwell (1915) p.24
21. Viereck (1934) pp.61-62
22. Lintier (1916) p.162
23. Churchill (2015) p.34
24. Ibid. p.35
25. Corbett-Smith (1917) p.198
26. Lintier (1916) p.195
27. Corbett-Smith (1917) p.224
28. Letard (1919) p.70
29. Ibid. p.71
30. Lintier (1916) p.196
31. Corbett-Smith (1917) p.184

32. Private Papers
33. Ibid.
34. Ibid.
35. Private Papers
36. McNair (1916) p.89
37. Ibid.

Chapter Seventeen

1. Tharann (1918) p.11
2. Maksimova (1932) p.18
3. Sayn-Wittgenstein (1986) p.17
4. Golovin (1931) p.143
5. Stone (2015) p.73
6. Airapetov (2014) p.188
7. Ibid.
8. Zhelondkovsky (1925) pp.283-284
9. Ibid. pp.284-285
10. Laeger (1934) pp.41-42
11. Airapetov (2014) p.198
12. 'DSK' (1968) p.83
13. Airapetov (2014) p.198
14. Ibid. p.200
15. Ibid. p.202
16. Zhelondkovsky (1925) pp.294-295
17. Airapetov (2014) pp.205-206
18. Bülowius & Hippler (1929) p.23
19. Schillmann (1924) p.31
20. Zhelondkovsky (1925) pp.295-296
21. Airapetov (2014) p.206
22. Ibid. p.207
23. Eisenhart-Rothe (1938) pp.29-30
24. Tharann (1918) p.14
25. Airapetov (2014) p. 207
26. Vorarlberger Volksfreund, 10 September 1914

Chapter Eighteen

1. Burger (1917) p.21
2. Zombrony-Moldován (2014) pp.31-36
3. Popper (1937) p.13
4. Wolf (1931) p.11
5. Ibid. p.12
6. Renner (1931) pp.23-24
7. Neue Freie Presse, 2 February 1915
8. Tagblatt: Generalanzeiger für das Burgenland, 25 August 1929
9. Renner (1931) p. 29
10. Tagblatt: Generalanzeiger für das Burgenland, 25 August 1929
11. Burda (2017) p.50
12. Badener Zeitung, 3 October 1914
13. Tagblatt: Generalanzeiger für das Burgenland, 25 August 1929
14. Renner (1931) pp.42-43
15. Grazer Volksblatt, 26 September 1914
16. Schoß (1933) pp.23-24
17. В огне... (1914) p.11
18. 'Horváth Lajos naplói és fényképalbuma, 1914-1918' (Online: https://nagyhaboru. blog.hu/2020/02/12/ horvath_lajos_naploi_es_ fenykepalbuma_1914-1918, accessed 10/12/2024)
19. Airapetov (2014) p.193
20. Znaimer Tagblatt, 25 October 1914
21. Dolgov (1919) p.12
22. Ibid. p.14
23. Nadezhny (1926) p.19
24. Illustrierte Kronen Zeitung, 21 September 1914
25. Nadezhny (1926) p.22
26. Vošta (1936) pp.77-80
27. Ibid.
28. Wißhaupt (1935) p.55
29. Dolgov (1919) pp.22-26
30. Innsbrucker Nachrichten, 28 August 1924
31. Dolgov (1919) p.26
32. Hrušovský (1919) pp.175-183
33. Ibid.
34. Ibid.
35. Ibid.

Chapter Nineteen

1. Klein (1915) p.63
2. Gallieni (1916) p.39
3. Ibid. p.38
4. Ibid. p.123
5. Ibid. p.37
6. Clarke (1915) p.42
7. Ibid. p.43
8. Ibid. p.48
9. Ibid. p.284
10. Ibid. p.54
11. Ohnet (1914) p.14
12. Gallieni (1916) p.59
13. Ibid. p.65
14. Corbett-Smith (1917) p.210
15. Ibid. p.184
16. Letard (1919) pp.61-62
17. Lintier (1916) p.92
18. Letard (1919) p.64
19. 'DSK' (1950) pp.12-13
20. Anonymous (1917) p.40
21. Ibid. p.25
22. Brodersen (2021) p.42
23. Petersen (1920) p.39
24. Anonymous (1917) p.52 - MIB
25. Ibid. p.53
26. Ibid. p.59
27. Von Kluck (2012) pp.7-8
28. Ibid. p.7
29. Clifton-Shelton (1917) p.76
30. McCudden (1919) p.42
31. Ibid.
32. Formé (1916) p.3
33. Doughty (2008) p.85
34. Terraine (2000) p.198
35. Klein (1915) p.75
36. Von Kluck (2012) p.100

Chapter Twenty

1. IWM Sound: Fright, 22248
2. Churchill College: Sommerville, 6 August 1914
3. Churchill College: Sommerville, 8 August 1914

4. Caird: HLD/1 – Charles Heald, 1 September 1914
5. Spiess (2020) p.29
6. Ibid. pp.30-31
7. Ibid. p.31
8. Ibid. p.32
9. Ibid. p.33
10. Ibid.
11. Official History, Naval Operations: Vol. I, p.178
12. Churchill College: Colson, 26 September 1914
13. Bienaimé (1920) p.130

Chapter Twenty-One

1. Lederhaas (2017) p.24
2. Kreisler (1981) pp.17-18
3. *В огне…* (1914) p.7
4. Ibid. p.21
5. Lederhaas (2017) p.25
6. Grazer Tagblatt, 14 October 1914
7. Kosmač (200?) p.9
8. Weiland & Kern (1931) p.59
9. Prašnički (2014) p.46
10. Grazer Volksblatt, 30 September 1914
11. *В огне…* (1914) p.60
12. Shcherbachev (1930) p.122
13. Prašnički (2014) p.48
14. Kosmač (200?) pp.10-11
15. Lederhaas (2017) p.26
16. Kosmač (200?) pp.11-12
17. Matičič (2006) p.17
18. Kosmač (200?) pp.12-13
19. Lederhaas (2017) p.27
20. Kosmač (200?) pp.12-13
21. Baumann & Schmidl (2019) p.30
22. Weiland & Kern (1931) pp.59-60
23. Ibid.
24. Benkõ (2018) pp.13-14
25. Nielsen (1917) p.36
26. Tăslăuanu (1920) p.59
27. Nielsen (1917) p.33
28. Berndt (1940) p.60
29. 'Részletek Dr. Szojka Kornél emlékirataiból' (Online: https://

nagyhaboru.blog.hu/2015/12/28/
reszletek_dr_szojka_kornel_
emlekirataibol, accessed
10/12/2024)
30. Golovin (1940) p.132
31. Nielsen (1917) p.36
32. Golovin (1940) pp.71-72
33. Imrey (1929) p.59

Chapter Twenty-Two

1. Wilcox (2021) p.25
2. Martini (1916) pp.51-2
3. Atwell 'The Zandfontein Disaster 1914' (Online: www.kaiserscross.com/40117/47501.html, accessed 09/12/2024)
4. Ibid.
5. Godley (1939) p.156
6. Burnell (1915) p.33
7. Smith (1924) p.33
8. Ibid. p.30
9. Burnell (1915) p.40
10. Smith (1924) p.33
11. Ibid. p.10
12. Ibid. p.53
13. Ibid. p.60
14. Caird: Jukes-Hughes JHS/3, 12 August 1914
15. Burnell (1915) p.59
16. Ibid. p.87
17. Ibid. p.108
18. Ibid. p.111
19. Ibid. p.99
20. Stephenson (2017) p.87
21. Burnell (1915) p.116
22. Ibid. p.124
23. Ibid. p.118
24. Ibid. p.123
25. Clements (2022) p.68
26. Iriye (2002) p.282
27. Burdick (1976) p.75
28. Ibid. p.76
29. Ibid. p.86
30. Ibid. p.90
31. Beidler (2016) p.62
32. Burdick (1976) p.114

33. Ibid. p.121
34. Ibid. p.122
35. Ibid. p.126

Chapter Twenty-Three

1. Nottin (1917) p.6
2. Tardieu (1939) p.46
3. Dupont (1916) p.80
4. Ibid. p.86
5. Ibid. p.92
6. Ibid. pp.96-97
7. Ibid. pp.97-98
8. Corbett-Smith (1917) p.17
9. Boudon (1916) pp.122-123
10. Gallieni (1916) p.160
11. Dahlmann (1934) p.64
12. Ibid.
13. Boudon (1916) p.137
14. Ibid. p.142
15. Dahlmann (1934) p.68
16. Bourachot (2014) p.121
17. Brodersen (2021) pp.44-47
18. Ibid.
19. Petersen (1920) p.47
20. 'DSK' (1950) pp.13-14
21. Petersen (1920) p.48
22. Krafft von Dellmensingen (1929) p.100
23. Ibid.
24. Lintier (1916) p.145
25. Ibid. p.210
26. Ibid. p.211
27. 'Taxis de la Marne - Souvenir d'un chauffeur en 1964' (Online: www.facebook.com/watch/?v=274168060953881, accessed 09/12/2024)
28. Reproduced in Jean-Bertrand (1916) *Histoire Generale et Anecdotique de la Guerre de 1914*. Tome 2, Numero 9-18

Chapter Twenty-Four

1. Kozelsky (1915) p.3
2. Voitolovky (1928) p.23

3. Oeltjen (2005) p.18
4. Ibid.
5. Arlow (2015) p.44
6. Hadobás (2014) p.101
7. 'Horváth Lajos naplói és fényképalbuma, 1914-1918' (Online: https://nagyhaboru. blog.hu/2020/02/12/ horvath_lajos_naploi_es_ fenykepalbuma_1914-1918, accessed 10/12/2024)
8. Imrey (1929) pp.59-60
9. Zombory-Moldován (2014) pp.31-36
10. Ibid. p.54
11. Ibid.
12. Antonelli (2016) p.80
13. Wißhaupt (1935) p.103
14. Antonelli (2016) pp.80-81
15. Grazer Volksblatt, 25 September 1914
16. Antonelli (2016) pp.83-84
17. 'Részletek Dr. Szojka Kornél emlékirataiból' (Online: https:// nagyhaboru.blog.hu/2015/12/28/ reszletek_dr_szojka_kornel_ emlekirataibol, accessed 10/12/2024)
18. Antonelli (2016) p.84
19. Ibid.
20. Olip (2018) pp.34-35
21. Ibid.

Chapter Twenty-Five

1. Lintier (1916) p.226
2. Ibid. p.228
3. Delvert (1935) p.69
4. Bertrand (1915) pp.63-64
5. Ibid. p.72
6. 'Hugo Birkner Tagebuch' (Online: www.lagis-hessen.de/de/subjects/ browse/sourceId/12/page/5/sn/ qhg, accessed 09/12/2024)
7. Bertrand (1915) pp.73-74
8. Ibid. pp.75-76
9. Ibid. p.77
10. Ibid. p.79
11. 'Hugo Birkner Tagebuch' (Online: www.lagis-hessen.de/ de/subjects/browse/sourceId/12/ page/5/sn/qhg, accessed 09/12/2024)
12. Bertrand (1915) p.79
13. Ibid. p.81
14. Diallo & Lamine (2021) p.113
15. Ibid. p.115
16. Foch (2019) p.69
17. Krafft von Dellmensingen (1926) pp.184-185
18. Tardieu (1939) p.53
19. Ibid. p.55
20. Diallo & Lamine (2021) p.114
21. Foch (2019) p.92
22. Ibid. p.89
23. Ibid.
24. Nottin (1917) p.59
25. Ibid.
26. Anonymous (1917) p.108
27. Ibid. p.109
28. Nottin (1917) p.76
29. Chambe (1979) p.86
30. Ibid.
31. Ibid. p.96
32. Ibid. p.97
33. Corbett-Smith (1917) p.55
34. Krafft von Dellmensingen (1929) p.100
35. Douchy (1922) p.141
36. Lintier (1916) p.230
37. Mallet (1916) pp.95-96 - MIB
38. Ibid. p.97
39. Bertrand (1915) p.64
40. Diallo & Lamine (2021) p.115
41. Douchy (1922) p.143
42. Glasmeier (1932) p.87
43. Ibid.
44. Bolwell (1915) p.37
45. Doughty (2008) p.97

Epilogue

1. Daily Telegraph, 26 September 1914

2. Ibid.
3. Morton-Jack (2018) p.113
4. Basu (2015) p.20
5. Breton (1917) p.59
6. Douchy (1922) p.143
7. Anonymous (1917) p.113
8. Ibid. p.97
9. Nemes-Tóthi Nemestóthy-Szabó (2015) p.42
10. Kawczak (2019) p.41
11. Blašković (2014) 110
12. Corbett-Smith (1917) p.105
13. Dupont (1916) p.102
14. Anonymous (1917) p.119
15. Lederhaas (2017) pp.41-2
16. 'Részletek Dr. Szojka Kornél emlékirataiból' (Online: https://nagyhaboru.blog.hu/2015/12/28/reszletek_dr_szojka_kornel_emlekirataibol, accessed 10/12/2024)
17. Bertrand (2015) p.86
18. Crown Prince Wilhelm (1924) p.89
19. Breton (1917) p.43
20. Rose (2017) p.34
21. Barkhof (2020) p.224
22. Hedin (2014) p.7
23. Ibid. p.8
24. Lockhart (2011) p.99
25. Adams (2014) p.71
26. Kenda (2005) p.14
27. Ibid. pp.60-6

Image Credits

1. Photo by: Photo 12/Universal Images Group via Getty Images
2. Library of Congress, Prints & Photographs Division, [LC-B2-3173-3 [P&P]]
3. Library of Congress, Prints & Photographs Division, [LC-DIG-ggbain-24232]
4. Bibliothèque nationale de France
5. Photographer: Ivan Timiriasew / Helsinki City Museum
6. Library of Congress, Prints & Photographs Division, [LC-DIG-ggbain-17463]
7. Chronicle / Alamy Stock Photo
8. EMU history / Alamy Stock Photo
9. Library of Congress, Prints & Photographs Division, [LC-DIG-ggbain-16943]
10. Library of Congress, Prints & Photographs Division, [LC-B2-3207-12 [P&P]]
11. Sueddeutsche Zeitung Photo / Alamy Stock Photo
12. Library of Congress, Prints & Photographs Division, [LC-B2-3249-11 [P&P]]
13. Print Collector / Getty Images
14. Bibliothèque nationale de France
15. The Print Collector / Alamy Stock Photo
16. Library of Congress, Prints & Photographs Division, [LC-B2-3249-11 [P&P]]
17. Library of Congress, Prints & Photographs Division, [LC-B2-3219-9 [P&P]]
18. Library of Congress, Prints & Photographs Division, [LC-B2-3189-14 [P&P]]
19. Bibliothèque nationale de France
20. Library of Congress, Prints & Photographs Division, [LC-B2-3212-6 [P&P]]
21. Sueddeutsche Zeitung Photo / Alamy Stock Photo
22. Library of Congress, Prints & Photographs Division, [LC-B2-3459-7 [P&P]]
23. Bibliothèque nationale de France
24. Bibliothèque nationale de France
25. Public domain
26. Imperial War Museum
27. Bibliothèque nationale de France

28. Bibliothèque nationale de France

29. Library of Congress, Prints & Photographs Division, [LC-B2-3285-14 [P&P]]

30. Library of Congress, Prints & Photographs Division, [LC-B2-3248-8 [P&P]]

31. Library of Congress, Prints & Photographs Division, [LC-B2-3272-5 [P&P]]

32. Bibliothèque nationale de France

33. Norman Wilkinson / Wikimedia Commons

34. Unknown author / Wikimedia Commons

35. The Protected Art Archive / Alamy Stock Photo

36. Chronicle / Alamy Stock Photo

37. PA Images / Alamy Stock Photo

38. PA Images / Alamy Stock Photo

39. Library of Congress, Prints & Photographs Division, [LC-B2-3255-4 [P&P]]

40. Bibliothèque nationale de France

Index